128.2 MOD

WESTMINSTER

D0756669

erdue bool

Note on the Editor   vii
Note on the Texts   viii
Chronology of Modern Philosophy of Mind   x
Introduction   xlv


MODERN PHILOSOPHY OF MIND

William James, 'The Stream of Consciousness'   3
John B. Watson, 'Psychology as the Behaviorist Views It'   24
Rudolf Carnap, 'Psychology in the Language of Physics'   43
Ludwig Wittgenstein, 'On Believing'   80
Gilbert Ryle, 'A Puzzling Element in the Notion
of Thinking'   89
U. T. Place, 'Is Consciousness a Brain Process?'   106
J. J. C. Smart, 'Sensations and Brain Processes'   117
Hilary Putnam, 'Philosophy and Our Mental Life'   133
Donald Davidson, 'Psychology as Philosophy'   148
Thomas Nagel, 'What is it Like to Be a Bat?'   159
David Armstrong, 'The Causal Theory of the Mind'   175
Daniel Dennett, 'Intentional Systems'   191
Paul Churchland, 'Eliminative Materialism and the
Propositional Attitudes'   214
Jerry Fodor 'The Persistence of the Attitudes'   240
Colin McGinn, 'Can We Solve the Mind-Body Problem?'   272

Suggestions for Further Reading   296
Acknowledgements   304
Index   307

26 0065988 3

# NOTE ON THE EDITOR

WILLIAM LYONS is Professor of Philosophy in the School of
Mental and Moral Science at Trinity College, Dublin, a Fellow
of Trinity College, and a Member of the Royal Irish Academy.
He was born in Melbourne, Australia, and has studied or taught
at universities in Australia, New Zealand, Canada, Italy, Scot-
land and Ireland. His main interests are in philosophy of mind
and philosophical psychology. As well as numerous articles in
journals, he has published *Gilbert Ryle: An Introduction to his
Philosophy* ( Harvester and Humanities Presses, 1980), *Emotion*
(Cambridge University Press, 1980), *The Disappearance of
Introspection* (Bradford Books-The MIT Press, 1986), and
*Approaches to Intentionality* (Oxford, at the Clarendon Press,
1995). His latest book, *Matters of the Mind*, is due out in 2000.

# NOTE ON THE TEXTS

*These essays first appeared in the following publications:*

'The Stream of Consciousness', from William James, *Psychology: Briefer Course*, 1892, Chapter XI.

'Psychology as the Behaviorist Views It', from *Psychological Review*, Volume 20, 1913.

'Psychology in the Language of Physics', from *Erkenntnis*, Volume 2, 1931; this text is a new translation from the German by Niamh Ní Bhleithín, Fionnula Meehan and Daniel Steur.

'On Believing', extracts from *The Blue and Brown Book* (1958), edited by R. Rhees, Part II, sections 7–9, and from the *Philosophical Investigations* (1953), translated by G. E. M. Anscombe, Part II, section X.

'A Puzzling Element in the Notion of Thinking', from *Proceedings of the British Academy*, Volume 44, 1958.

'Is Consciousness a Brain Process?', from *British Journal of Psychology*, Volume 47, 1956.

'Sensations and Brain Processes', from *The Philosophical Review*, Volume 68, 1959.

'Philosophy and Our Mental Life', (1973), Paper 14 in Hilary Putnam, *Mind, Language and Reality: Philosophical Papers*, Volume 2, 1975.

'Psychology as Philosophy', (1971), in *Philosophy of Psychology*, edited by S. C. Brown, 1974.

'What is it Like to Be a Bat?' from *The Philosophical Review*, Volume 83, 1974.

'The Causal Theory of Mind', from *Neue hefte für Philosophie*, Volume 11, 1977; reprinted as Chapter 2 in David Armstrong, *The Nature of Mind and Other Essays*, 1980.

'Intentional Systems', from *The Journal of Philosophy*, Volume 68, 1971; reprinted in Daniel Dennett, *Brainstorms: Philosophical Essays on Mind and Psychology*, Part I, Chapter 1.

'Eliminative Materialism and the Propositional Attitudes', *The Journal of Philosophy*, Volume 78, 1981.

'The Persistence of the Attitudes', from 'Introduction: The Persistence of the Attitudes', in Jerry Fodor, *Psychosemantics: The Problem of Meaning in the Philosophy of Mind*, 1987, Chapter 1.

'Can We Solve the Mind-Body Problem?' from *Mind*, Volume 98, 1989.

# CHRONOLOGY OF MODERN PHILOSOPHY
# OF MIND

| Year | Events in the History of Modern Philosophy of Mind and Related Fields |
|------|------------------------------------------------------------------------|
| 1890 | William James, *Principles of Psychology*; C. Lloyd Morgan, *Animal Life and Intelligence*; Christian von Ehrenfels, publishes 'On Gestalt Qualities' and begins Gestalt psychology |
| 1892 | William James, *Psychology: Briefer Course* |
| 1894 | C. Lloyd Morgan, *An Introduction to Comparative Psychology*; this book, together with his previous one, introduces the idea of 'trial and error learning' in animals, which influences Behaviourism |
| 1895 | Freud and Breuer publish the first work on psychoanalysis, *Studies on Hysteria* |
| 1896 | Henri Bergson, *Matter and Memory*; Franz Muller-Lyer, 'Concerning the Theory of Optical Illusions: On Contrast and Confluxion' |
| 1897 | First volume of Havelock Ellis, *Studies in the Psychology of Sex* |
| 1898 | Psychologist Edward Lee Thorndike, using mazes and his 'problem box', performs some of the first controlled experiments on animal learning and publishes his results in *Animal Intelligence* |
| 1900 | Freud, *The Interpretation of Dreams*; Wilhelm Wundt, *Comparative Psychology* |

# CHRONOLOGY OF THE TIMES

| Year | Historical & Literary Events | Scientific Events |
|------|------------------------------|-------------------|
| 1890 | Chancellor Bismarck dismissed by the Kaiser | Discovery of tetanus and diptheria viruses |
| 1892 | In the USA the first automatic telephone exchange is opened | |
| 1893 | In New Zealand women gain the right to vote<br>Last volume of Karl Marx's *Das Kapital* appears | Gottlob Frege publishes the first volume of *The Basic Laws of Arithmetic* |
| 1894 | Beginning of Dreyfus affair in France | Ernst Mach, *Popular Scientific Lectures* |
| 1895 | Wells, *The Time Machine* | Roentgen discovers X-rays |
| 1896 | Ethiopians defeat Italians at Adowa | |
| 1897 | | Pierre and Marie Curie discover radium |
| 1898 | Battle of Omdurman: British general Kitchener defeats the Sudan rebels<br>USA and Spain at war over Cuba<br>USA takes over Hawaii; Spain hands over Puerto Rico, Guam and the Philippines to the USA | |
| 1899 | Anglo-Boer War begins<br>First Hague Peace Conference<br>Ernest Haeckel, *The Riddle of the Universe* | |
| 1900 | Boxer Rebellion in China | Rediscovery of Gregor Mendel's work on heredity |

*Year    Events in the History of Modern Philosophy of Mind and Related Fields*

1901    Freud, *The Psychology of Everyday Life*

1904    James Angell, *Psychology: An Introductory Study of the Structure and
        Function of Human Consciousness*, an important text of the early, pre-
        behaviourist 'psychology as the study of mind as related to behavioural
        functions' school

1905    In answer to a request from the French Ministry of Education,
        psychologist Alfred Binet, in collaboration with Theodore Simon,
        devises the first standardized intelligence test to discover 'defective'
        primary school children

1906    Ivan Pavlov publishes the results of his work on conditional reflexes.
        Physiologist Charles (later Sir Charles) Sherrington publishes an account
        of his work on spinal reflexes, the control of muscles and the
        relationship between the voluntary and involuntary nervous system, in
        *The Integrative Action of the Nervous System*

1907    Pierre Janet delivers a series of lectures at Harvard University, published
        under the title *The Major Symptoms of Hysteria*

1908    William McDougall, *An Introduction to Social Psychology*, one of the
        seminal works in social psychology. Kurt Goldstein gives one of the
        earliest careful clinical descriptions of the startling behavioural effects of
        cerebral hemispheric disconnection caused by damage to the corpus
        callosum

| Year | Historical & Literary Events | Scientific Events |
|------|------------------------------|-------------------|
| 1901 | Commonwealth of Australia established; Edmund Barton is first Prime Minister<br>Max Weber, *The Protestant Ethic and the Birth of Capitalism* | Adrenalin is successfully synthesized<br>Max Planck, *Laws of Radiation* |
| 1902 | Trotsky and Lenin meet for the first time in exile<br>William James, *The Varieties of Religious Experience* | |
| 1903 | Emmeline Pankhurst founds the Women's Social and Political Union in Britain<br>G. E. Moore, *Principia Ethica* | First successful flight in a petrol-fuelled aeroplane by the Wright brothers in America |
| 1904 | Outbreak of Russo-Japanese War<br>'Entente Cordiale' settles Anglo-French colonial differences | Pavlov wins the Nobel Prize for his research into digestion. Elster invents photoelectric cell |
| 1905 | End of union between Norway and Sweden<br>Sinn Fein party founded in Dublin<br>Wilhelm Dilthey, *Experience and Poetry*; George Santayana, *Life of Reason*; Freud, *Three Treatises on the Theory of Sex*<br>Bertrand Russell puts forward his 'theory of descriptions' in his paper 'On denoting' in *Mind* | Einstein proposes Special Theory of Relativity |
| 1906 | San Francisco earthquake<br>Alfred Dreyfus is rehabilitated<br>Suffragette campaign begins in Britain | |
| 1907 | Cubist exhibition in Paris<br>Pius X condemns modernism in encyclical 'Pascendi Gregis'<br>Henri Bergson, *Creative Evolution*<br>William James, *Pragmatism* | |
| 1908 | Bosnian crisis: Austria annexes Bosnia and Herzegovina (from Turkey)<br>Henry Ford produces first 'T Model' Ford car | |

Year    *Events in the History of Modern Philosophy of Mind and Related Fields*

1909    E. B. Titchener, *Lectures on the Experimental Psychology of the Thought Processes*

1910    Wilhelm Wundt publishes the first of the ten-volume *Folk Psychology*

1911    William McDougall, *Body and Mind*

1912    With the publication of 'The Experimental Study of the Perception of Motion', Max Wertheimer puts Gestalt psychology on a firm foundation

1913    Edmund Husserl, *Ideas – General Introduction to Pure Phenomenology*; John B. Watson, seminal behaviourist paper 'Psychology as the Behaviorist Views it'. The term 'neuropsychology' is first used in an address by Sir William Osler

1914    E. B. Holt, *The Concept of Consciousness*

| Year | Historical & Literary Events | Scientific Events |
|------|------------------------------|-------------------|
| 1909 | Robert Edwin Peary reaches North Pole; Louis Bleriot crosses English Channel by monoplane<br>Lenin, *Materialism and Empiric Criticism*<br>William James, *A Pluralistic Universe* | |
| 1910 | Revolution in Portugal; republic declared | Mount Wilson 100-inch telescope completed<br>Manufacture of first roller bearings<br>Marie Curie, *Treatise on Radiography*. First volume of Russell and Whitehead's *Principia Mathematica* |
| 1911 | Sun Yat-Sen forms first Chinese republic<br>Norwegian Roald Amundsen reaches the South Pole | Ernest Rutherford discovers the proton |
| 1912 | First Balkan War<br>Robert Falcon Scott reaches the South Pole<br>The *Titanic* sinks: 1,513 die | Casimir Funck introduces word 'vitamine' |
| 1913 | Freud, *Totem and Taboo* | The 'orbiting electron atomic theory' proposed by Niels Bohr<br>Russell and Whitehead publish the third and final volume of *Principia Mathematica* |
| 1914 | Archduke Francis Ferdinand of Austria and his wife assassinated at Sarajevo: ourbreak of First World War<br>Irish Home Rule Act passed<br>Bertrand Russell, *Our Knowledge of the External World as a Field for Scientific Method in Philosophy* | |
| 1915 | Hugo Junkers develops first fighter aeroplane<br>Ferdinand de Saussure, *Course in General Linguistics* | Einstein publishes his General Theory of Relativity |

Year    *Events in the History of Modern Philosophy of Mind and Related Fields*

1917   Wolfgang Kohler publishes the results of his celebrated studies of the
       behaviour of anthropoid apes on the island of Tenerife in *The Mentality
       of Apes*

1919   Henri Bergson, *Spiritual Energy* (its English translation in the following
       year is entitled *Mind-Energy*)

1920   Carl Jung, *Psychological Types*; J. B. Watson, 'Is Thinking Merely the
       Action of Language Mechanisms?'

1921   Bertrand Russell publishes one of the important early texts in modern
       philosophy of mind, *The Analysis of Mind*; Russell jettisons his previous
       dualism in favour of a 'neutral monism'

1922   Psychiatrist Hermann Rorschach develops 'ink blot tests' as a diagnostic
       device for distinguishing personality types and personality disabilities.
       Psychologist Edward Chace Tolman, in 'A New Formula for
       Behaviorism', attempts to include cognitive states and purposiveness
       into a 'non-physiological behaviourism'

| Year | Historical & Literary Events | Scientific Events |
|------|------------------------------|-------------------|
| 1916 | Easter Rising in Dublin by Sinn Fein suppressed<br>Vilfredo Pareto, *Treatise of General Sociology*<br>Joyce, *Portrait of the Artist as a Young Man* | |
| 1917 | Russian Revolution; Nicholas II abdicates | |
| 1918 | First World War ends when Germany signs armistice<br>Influenza epidemic kills 20 million<br>Nicholas II and his family executed. Women (over thirty) permitted to vote in Britain. First volume of Oswald Spengler's *The Decline of the West*<br>Russell, 'The philosophy of logical atomism' | |
| 1919 | Peace Conference at Versailles opens, adopts principle of a League of Nations. Formation of National Socialist German Workers' Party<br>J. M. Keynes, *The Economic Consequences of the Peace*; Havelock Ellis, *The Philosophy of Conflict* | J. W. Alcock and A. W. Brown fly across the Atlantic in sixteen and a half hours |
| 1920 | Palestine established as a Jewish state under British control<br>Wells, *Outline of History* | |
| 1921 | Irish Free State established<br>Ludwig Wittgenstein, *Tractatus Logico-Philosophicus* | |
| 1922 | Mussolini marches on Rome; is asked by King Victor Emmanuel to form a government<br>Herbert Hoover, *American Individualism*; Eliot, *The Waste Land*; Joyce, *Ulysses* | |

Year    *Events in the History of Modern Philosophy of Mind and Related Fields*

1923    Karl Lashley, 'The Behavioristic Interpretation of Consciousness'.
        Psychologist Jean Piaget publishes *The Language and Thought of the
        Child* and in effect begins developmental psychology

1924    First edition of J. B. Watson's *Behaviorism*

1925    John Laird, *Our Minds and Their Bodies*; C. D. Broad, *The Mind and
        its Place in Nature*

1929    Psychiatrist Hans Berger invents the electroencephalogram. Karl
        Lashley, *Brain Mechanisms and Intelligence*; E. G. Boring publishes the
        first edition of his *History of Experimental Psychology*

| Year | Historical & Literary Events | Scientific Events |
|------|------------------------------|-------------------|
| 1923 | German bank rate raised to 90 per cent, Hitler's Munich *coup* fails<br>The first collection of C. S. Pierce's papers appears, *Chance, Love and Logic* | |
| 1924 | First Labour Government in Britain<br>Stalin assumes control in Russia on death of Lenin<br>Thomas Mann, *The Magic Mountain* | |
| 1925 | Hindenburg elected President of Germany<br>Hitler, *Mein Kampf* (first volume); Fitzgerald, *The Great Gatsby*; Virginia Woolf, *Mrs Dalloway* | Birdseye extends deep-freezing process to pre-cooked foods<br>A. N. Whitehead's *Science and the Modern World* |
| 1926 | General Strike in Britain; Civil War in China<br>R. H. Tawney, *Religion and the Rise of Capitalism*; T. E. Lawrence, *Seven Pillars of Wisdom*; Franz Kafka, *The Castle* (posthumously) | |
| 1927 | Chian Kai-shek purges communism in China. Trotsky expelled by Stalin from Soviet Communist Party<br>Freud, *The Future of an Illusion*; Heidegger, *Being and Time*; Russell, *Analysis of Matter* | Heisenberg propounds his 'Uncertainty Principle' in quantum physics |
| 1928 | Japan occupies Shantung in China<br>Huxley, *Point Counter Point*; Lawrence, *Lady Chatterley's Lover*; Rudolf Carnap, *The Logical Structure of the World* | Alexander Fleming discovers penicillin<br>Geiger and Muller construct Geiger Counter |
| 1929 | Wall Street stock market collapse. The term 'apartheid' first used in South Africa<br>Hemingway, *A Farewell to Arms*; Remarque, *All Quiet on the Western Front*; Heidegger, *What is Philosophy?*; John Dewey, *The Quest for Certainty* | |

*Year    Events in the History of Modern Philosophy of Mind and Related Fields*

1930    Karl Lashley, 'Basic Neural Mechanisms in Behavior'

1931    Edmund Husserl, *Cartesian Meditations*; Rudolf Carnap, 'Psychology in the Language of Physics'; G. F. Stout, *Mind and Matter*. John Anderson reads his paper 'Mind as Feeling'

1932    Frederick Bartlett, *Remembering: A Study in Experimental and Social Psychology*. Receiving the Nobel Prize for physiology and medicine, Lord Adrian publishes an account of his work in *The Mechanism of Nervous Action: Electrical Studies of the Neurone*

1933    Edwin G. Boring, *The Physical Dimensions of Consciousness*; Wittgenstein dictates *The Blue Book* to his students

| Year | Historical & Literary Events | Scientific Events |
|---|---|---|
| 1930 | Ras Tafari crowned as Emperor Haile Selassie I in Ethiopia Mahatma Ghandi opens campaign of civil disobedience in India Auden, *Poems*; Freud, *Civilization and its Discontents*; F. R. Leavis, *Mass Civilization and Minority Culture* | |
| 1931 | 'Commonwealth of Nations' replaces British Empire. Japan occupies parts of Manchuria Otto Neurath, *Empirical Sociology*; John Dewey, *Philosophy and Civilization*; first volume of C. S. Pierce's *Collected Papers*; Moritz Schlick, 'The Turning Point in Philosophy' | Ernest O. Lawrence constructs first cyclotron for the production of artificial radioactivity |
| 1932 | Nazis become the largest party in Germany in July Reichstag elections. Japanese occupy Shanghai Karl Jaspers, *Philosophy*; John Strachey, *The Coming Struggle for Power*; Hemingway, *Death in the Afternoon*; Huxley, *Brave New World* Rudolf Carnap, 'The Elimination of Metaphysics Through the Logical Analysis of Language' | British physicist James Chadwick discovers the neutron. American radio engineer Karl Janksky pioneers radio-astronomy Kurt Gödel produces his 'incompleteness theorems' |
| 1933 | Hitler appointed Chancellor; the Bauhaus school is closed by the Nazis Gertrude Stein, *The Autobiography of Alice B. Toklas*; Malraux, *The Human Condition* | |

*Year    Events in the History of Modern Philosophy of Mind and Related Fields*

1934    Wittgenstein dictates *The Brown Book* to two of his pupils – three
        typed copies are made. John Wisdom, *Problems of Mind and Matter*; G.
        H. Mead, *Mind, Self and Society: From the Standpoint of a Social
        Behaviorist*

1935    Carl Hempel, 'The Logical Analysis of Psychology'

| Year | Historical & Literary Events | Scientific Events |
|---|---|---|
| 1934 | Germany signs non-aggression pact with Poland; Austrian Chancellor Dollfuss is murdered in attempted Nazi coup; Hitler is made Führer of Germany with sole executive power<br>Stalin purges the Communist party in the U.S.S.R.<br>President Franklin Delano Roosevelt launches New Deal<br>Mao Tse-tung and the Chinese Communist forces begin the 'Long March'<br>Publication of first volume of Arnold Toynbee's *A Study of History* and Karl Popper's *The Logic of Scientific Discovery* | |
| 1935 | Hitler repudiates disarmament clauses of the treaty of Versailles; Italian forces invade Ethiopia<br>Sidney James Webb and Martha Beatrice Webb, *Soviet Communism: A New Civilization*; Margaret Mead, *Growing up in New Guinea*; J. B. S. Haldane, *Philosophy of a Biologist*; Christopher Isherwood, *Mr Norris Changes Trains* | The 35mm Kodachrome film is produced |
| 1936 | Germany reoccupies the Rhineland. Spanish Civil War begins. Chian Kai-shek is forced to declare war on Japan<br>J. M. Keynes, *General Theory of Employment, Interest and Money*; A. J. Ayer, *Language, Truth and Logic* | |

Year    *Events in the History of Modern Philosophy of Mind and Related Fields*

1937    Lev Vygotsky's *Thought and Language* is published posthumously (in Russian)

1938    B. F. Skinner, *The Behavior of Organisms*, describes his early work on 'operant conditioning' (or 'behaviour operating on the environment' conditioning)

1941    C. I. Lewis's paper 'Some Logical Considerations Concerning the Mental', appears in *The Journal of Philosophy*

| Year | Historical & Literary Events | Scientific Events |
|------|------------------------------|-------------------|
| 1937 | Japanese invade China and capture Shanghai and Peking German aeroplanes support Franco's offensive in Spanish Civil War and bomb Guernica Pope Pius XII issues encyclical on atheistic Communism Orwell, *The Road to Wigan Pier*; Martin Buber, *I and Thou* | In Germany von Braun develops the V–2 rocket |
| 1938 | Germany invades and annexes Austria. Britain, France, Germany and Italy agree to the transfer of the Sudetenland (in Czechoslovakia) to Germany Kristallnacht pogrom against the Jews in Germany and Austria Cyril Connolly, *Enemies of Promise*; Christopher Isherwood, *Goodbye to Berlin* | |
| 1939 | Franco becomes dictator of Spain; Germany annexes the whole of Czechoslovakia and invades Poland. Britain and France declare war on Germany: Second World War begins Joyce, *Finnegan's Wake*; Steinbeck, *The Grapes of Wrath* | The first jet fighter plane, a Messerschmidt, flies successfully. Paul Muller produces the insecticide DDT |
| 1940 | Churchill becomes Prime Minister in Britain Prehistoric cave paintings are discovered at Lascaux, France A. J. Ayer, *The Foundations of Empirical Knowledge*; Carl Jung, *The Interpretation of Personality* | Howard Florey develops penicillin as an antibiotic |
| 1941 | U.S. joins war Benedetto Croce, *History as the Story of Liberty*; Rudolf Bultmann, *New Testament and Mythology*; Fitzgerald, *The Last Tycoon* | 'Manhattan Project' of atomic research begun at Chicago and Los Angeles |

*Year   Events in the History of Modern Philosophy of Mind and Related Fields*

1943   Kenneth Craik, *The Nature of Explanation*, which postulates that the
       brain may make use of models that provide humans with their forward-
       planning capacities
1944   With the help of the International Business Machines Corporation
       (IBM), Howard Aiken of Harvard University develops the first fully
       automated calculating machine (called the 'Automatic Sequence
       Controlled Calculator')

1946   The first electronic computer (the Electronic Numerical Integrator and
       Calculator, or ENIAC) is built by a team directed by John Von
       Neumann at the Electrical Engineering School of the University of
       Pennsylvania

| Year | Historical & Literary Events | Scientific Events |
|---|---|---|
| 1942 | Allied forces defeat Germans at El Alamein<br>Eric Fromm, *The Fear of Freedom*; Albert Camus, *The Outsider* | Enrico Fermi produces the first controlled nuclear reaction<br>Germans successfully launch the V–2 rocket<br>Ball-point pen patented by Hungarian, Biro |
| 1943 | Mussolini falls from power in Italy<br>Sartre, *Being and Nothingness* | |
| 1944 | Allies liberate Paris; bomb plot to assassinate Hitler fails<br>John Von Neumann publishes first edition of *The Theory of Games and Economic Behavior*; Alfred Tarski, 'The Semantic Conception of Truth and the Foundation of Semantics' | |
| 1945 | Conference in Yalta; Hitler commits suicide; U.S. drops atomic bomb on Hiroshima; Germany surrenders to Allied forces; Japan surrenders; end of the Second World War<br>Karl Popper, *The Open Society and its Enemies*; Sartre, *The Age of Reason*; Orwell, *Animal Farm*; Maurice Merleau-Ponty, *The Phenomenology of Perception* | |
| 1946 | Nuremberg War Crimes trials begin; first meeting of the United Nations General Assembly<br>Russell, *The History of Western Philosophy*; Sartre, *Existentialism and Humanism* | |
| 1947 | India and Pakistan gain their independence. Partition of Palestine into Arab and Jewish states<br>Camus, *The Plague* | First supersonic air flight |

Year    Events in the History of Modern Philosophy of Mind and Related Fields

1948    Mathematician Norbert Wiener invents the term 'cybernetics' in *Cybernetics, or Control and Communication in the Animal and the Machine*

1949    Donald Hebb, *The Organization of Behavior: A Neuropsychological Theory*; Gilbert Ryle, *The Concept of Mind*

1950    Alan Turing, 'Computing Machinery and Intelligence'; James Gibson, *The Perception of the Visual World*; Lashley, 'In Search of the Engram'

1951    George Humphrey, *Thinking: An Introduction to its Experimental Psychology*; Nikolaas Tinbergen, *The Study on Instinct*. Publication of Jean-Paul Sartre's *The Psychology of Imagination* and of Ryle's essay 'Feelings'

1952    Nobel Laureate neurophysiologist Roger Sperry publishes his classic paper 'Neurology and the Mind-Brain Problem', arguing that much of human behaviour can be explained in terms of the coordination of innate patterns of neural connections.

1953    B. F. Skinner, *Science and Human Behavior*. Posthumous publication of Wittgenstein's *Philosophical Investigations*

1954    Piaget, *The Construction of Reality in the Child*; Gilbert Ryle, *Dilemmas* (his Tarner Lectures at Cambridge in 1953)

| Year | Historical & Literary Events | Scientific Events |
|------|------------------------------|-------------------|
| 1948 | Communist takeover in Czechoslovakia; U.S.S.R. blockades Berlin: Allies airlift supplies Publication of A. C. Kinsey's *Sexual Behaviour in the Human Male*; Norman Mailer, *The Naked and the Dead* | Transistor invented by Bell Telephone Company scientists |
| 1949 | Formation of NATO. The Communist People's Republic of China proclaimed South Africa formally adopts policy of apartheid Simon de Beauvoir, *The Second Sex*; Orwell, *Nineteen Eighty-four* | First atomic bomb tests in U.S.S.R. |
| 1950 | Korean War begins Margaret Mead, *Social Anthropology*; Malraux, *Psychology of Art*; W. V. O. Quine, *Methods of Logic* | |
| 1951 | Quine attacks distinction between analytic and synthetic propositions in 'Two Dogmas of Empiricism' | Electric power is produced from atomic energy in America |
| 1952 | Linguist Michael Ventris deciphers the 'Linear B' tablets | First contraceptive pill is produced. U. S. explodes first hydrogen bomb. Archeologists use radioactive carbon tests for dating artifacts |
| 1953 | Death of Stalin. Treaty of Panmunjon ends Korean War Edmund Hillary and Sherpa Tenzing reach the top of Mt Everest | Francis Crick, James Watson and Maurice Wilkins discover the structure of DNA (deoxyribonucleic acid) |
| 1954 | Vietnam War begins Algerian War begins Kingsley Amis, *Lucky Jim*; William Golding, *Lord of the Flies* | U.S. launches its first nuclear submarine |
| 1955 | Formation of the Warsaw Pact Herbert Marcuse, *Eros and Civilization* | |

Year    *Events in the History of Modern Philosophy of Mind and Related Fields*

1956    U. T. Place publishes 'Is Consciousness a Brain Process?', a key paper in the development of the mind-brain identity theory

1957    The neurophysiologist Wilder Penfield gives an account of his work in eliciting memories and sensations by the implantation of electrodes into the human brain, later published as 'The Excitable Cortex in Conscious Man'. Noam Chomsky, *Syntactic Structures*; Peter Geach, *Mental Acts*; Elizabeth Anscombe, *Intention*

1958    Hubel and Wiesel begin their pioneering work on the visual cortex of the brain. Posthumous publication of Wittgenstein's *The Blue Book* and *The Brown Book*. Herbert Simon and colleagues, *Elements of a Theory of Problem Solving*; R. S. Peters, *The Concept of Motivation*; Ryle's lecture 'A Puzzling Element in the Notion of Thinking' is published

1959    Marvin Minsky and John McCarthy set up the M.I.T. Artificial Intelligence Project. Norman Malcolm publishes *Dreaming*. Noam Chomsky's review of B. F. Skinner's *Verbal Behavior* appears. Peter Strawson publishes *Individuals*, which puts forward a 'double aspect' theory of mind. J. J. C. Smart, 'Sensations and Brain Processes'

1960    Hilary Putnam publishes his seminal 'Functionalist' paper, 'Minds and Machines'

1961    Donald Broadbent, *Behaviour*

| Year | Historical & Literary Events | Scientific Events |
|------|------------------------------|-------------------|
| 1956 | Suez crisis – President Nasser of Egypt nationalizes the Suez Canal Hungarian uprising crushed by Soviet troops Gilbert Ryle edits the published lectures on analytic philosophy from BBC radio broadcast, *The Revolution in Philosophy* | |
| 1957 | Treaty of Rome establishes the European Economic Community | Soviet Union launches the space satellite Sputnik I into orbit around the earth |
| 1958 | Foreign troops withdrawn from Korea J. K. Galbraith, *The Affluent Society*; Boris Pasternak, *Dr Zhivago* | U.S. launches the space satellite Explorer I |
| 1959 | Castro becomes President of Cuba Pierre Teilhard de Chardin, *The Phenomenon of Man*; C. P. Snow, *The Two Cultures and the Sciences* | U. S. launches first atomic-powered submarine |
| 1960 | 'Sharpville Shootings' in South Africa; the 'Congo Crisis' John F. Kennedy elected President of the U.S. Peter Geach and Max Black publish *Translations from the Philosophical Writings of Gottlob Frege*; Quine, *Word and Object* | |
| 1961 | The East German communist government builds the Berlin Wall Bay of Pigs raid on Cuba Michel Foucault, *History of Madness* | Soviet Cosmonaut Yuri Gagarin becomes the first man in space |

Year    Events in the History of Modern Philosophy of Mind and Related Fields

1962    David Armstrong, *Bodily Sensations*

1963    The journal *Neuropsychologia* is founded. Anthony Kenny, *Action, Emotion and Will*; Sydney Shoemaker, *Self-Knowledge and Self-Identity*; J. J. C. Smart, *Philosophy and Scientific Realism*. Donald Davidson presents his paper 'Actions, Reasons, and Causes' at a meeting of the American Philosophical Association. Paul Feyerabend produces probably the earliest statement of 'eliminative materialism' in 'Materialism and the mind-body problem'

1964    Roger Sperry publishes a popular account of the theoretical significance of his 'split-brain experiments' with regard to lower vertebrates in 'The great Cerebral Commissure'

1966    Alexander Luria's work on the psychological effects of brain traumas becomes widely known and influential with the English publication of *The Higher Cortical Functions in Man*. Warren McCulloch produces *Embodiments of Mind*, a central work in 'artificial intelligence'

1967    Neurophysiologist Michael Gazzaniga publishes an overview of the 'split-brain experiments' with epileptic humans, in 'The Split Brain in Man'. Putnam, 'The Mental Life of Some Machines'

| Year | Historical & Literary Events | Scientific Events |
|---|---|---|
| 1962 | Cuban Missile Crisis. Algeria becomes independent of France Publication of Henry Miller's *Tropic of Capricorn*; J. L. Austin, *Sense and Sensibilia* and *How to Do Things with Words* (posthumously); Thomas Kuhn, *The Structure of Scientific Revolutions*; Claude Lévi-Strauss, *The Savage Mind* | |
| 1963 | South Vietnamese government overthrown by military coup Assassination of President Kennedy in Dallas, Texas Publication of Bishop John Robinson's *Honest to God*; Mary McCarthy, *The Group*; Gunter Grass, *The Tin Drum* | |
| 1964 | Saul Bellow, *Herzog*; Philip Larkin, *The Whitsun Weddings* | China explodes an atomic bomb |
| 1965 | Ian Smith and white minority government in Rhodesia declare independence from Britain | |
| 1966 | Konrad Lorenz, *On Aggression*; Jacques Lacan, *Writings*; Theodor Adorno, *Negative Dialectics* | |
| 1967 | Civil War in Nigeria. American casualties mount in Vietnam War Six-day Arab-Israeli War Desmond Morris, *The Naked Ape*; Jacques Derrida, *Speech and Writing*. *The Encyclopedia of Philosophy*, with Paul Edwards as editor, is published | In South Africa Dr Christian Barnard performs first heart transplant |

| Year | Events in the History of Modern Philosophy of Mind and Related Fields |
|------|----------------------------------------------------------------------|
| 1968 | Chomsky, *Language and Mind* (an extended version of his Beckman Lectures); Armstrong, *A Materialist Theory of the Mind*. Davidson delivers his paper 'Mental Events' |
| 1969 | D. O. Hebb, 'The Mind's Eye'; Daniel Dennett, *Content and Consciousness* |
| 1971 | In his commentary on the Lighthill Report, Christopher Longuet-Higgins introduces the term 'cognitive science'. Davidson reads his papers 'Psychology as Philosophy' and 'The Material Mind'. Dennett's paper 'Intentional Systems' is published |
| 1972 | David and Ann Premack publish a brief account of their work with chimpanzees in 'Teaching Language to an Ape'. Armstrong, 'Materialism, Properties and Predicates' |

| Year | Historical & Literary Events | Scientific Events |
|------|------------------------------|-------------------|
| 1968 | Dubcek's 'Prague Spring' liberal reforms stopped by invasion of Soviet troops. Student riots in Paris. Assassination in U.S. of Martin Luther King and of presidential candidate Robert Kennedy. Race riots in the U.S. Eldridge Cleaver, *Soul on Ice*; Carlos Castañeda, *The Teachings of Don Juan* | |
| 1969 | Vietnam War peace talks begin in Paris. Britain sends troops to Northern Ireland<br>Philip Roth, *Portnoy's Complaint* | Oil discovered in the North Sea American astronaut Neil Armstrong walks on the moon First supersonic airline flight is made by the Concorde |
| 1970 | Nigerian civil war ends. Colonel Qadhafi seizes power in Libya Theodore Rozak, *The Making of a Counter Culture*; Charles Reik, *The Greening of America*; Kate Millett, *Sexual Politics* | |
| 1971 | East Pakistan breaks from West Pakistan to form Bangladesh Communist China joins the United Nations; Taiwan expelled from the U.N. Major General Idi Amin seizes power in Uganda | |
| 1972 | U.S. airplanes bomb Haiphong and Hanoi in North Vietnam Ceylon becomes republic of Sri Lanka. Britain imposes direct rule over Northern Ireland. Beginning of the 'Watergate' scandal | |

*Year   Events in the History of Modern Philosophy of Mind and Related Fields*

1973   Bernard Williams, *Problems of the Self* (a collection of essays). Putnam reads his paper 'Philosophy and our Mental Life'

1974   Thomas Nagel, 'What is it Like to Be a Bat?'

1975   Shoemaker, 'Functionalism and Qualia'. Putnam, *Mind, Language and Reality* (collected essays); Jerry Fodor, *The Language of Thought*

1977   Armstrong, 'The Causal Theory of the Mind'

1978   Dennett, *Brainstorms: Philosophical Essays on Mind and Psychology*, (collection of essays)

| Year | Historical & Literary Events | Scientific Events |
|------|------------------------------|-------------------|
| 1973 | Military Coup in Chile overthrows Marxist President Salvador Allende, who is later killed. Peace settlement signed in Vietnam – U.S. troops withdraw. 'Yom Kippur' War between Arab states and the Israelis ends in Israeli victory. Oil-producing Arab states cut production and quadruple the price of oil, sparking off world-wide economic crisis<br>Armstrong publishes *Belief, Truth and Knowledge* | |
| 1974 | Greek-Turkish conflict in Cyprus. President Nixon forced to resign over the 'Watergate' affair<br>Alexander Solzhenitsyn expelled from the U.S.S.R. after publication of *The Gulag Archipelago*; Patrick White, *The Eye of the Storm* | |
| 1975 | Spanish dictator General Franco dies; Juan Carlos becomes king<br>South Vietnam surrenders to North Vietnam | |
| 1976 | Riots in the black township of Soweto in South Africa | U.S. spacecraft Viking II orbits Mars |
| 1977 | Death of Steve Biko in South Africa | |
| 1978 | U.S. establishes diplomatic relations with Communist China. U.S. President Carter arranges the Camp David summit meeting between President Sadat of Egypt and Prime Minister Begin of Israel<br>A Pole, Karol Wojtyla, is elected Pope | The world's first test-tube baby is born in England |

*Year*  *Events in the History of Modern Philosophy of Mind and Related Fields*

1979  A collection of papers written by Ryle in the first half of the 1970s is posthumously published as *On Thinking*. Nagel, *Mortal Questions*; Paul Churchland, *Scientific Realism and the Plasticity of Mind*

1980  Davidson, *Essays on Actions and Events*

1981  Paul Churchland, 'Eliminative Materialism and the Propositional Attitudes'; Fodor, *RePresentations*

1982  The collection *Neuropsychology after Lashley*, edited by J. Orbach, is published. Posthumous publication of David Marr's *Vision: A Computational Investigation into the Human Representation and Processing of Visual Information*; Colin McGinn, *The Character of Mind*

1983  Philip Johnson-Laird, *Mental Models: Towards a Cognitive Science of Language, Inference and Consciousness*; John Searle, *Intentionality: An Essay in the Philosophy of Mind*; Stephen Stich, *From Folk Psychology to Cognitive Science: The Case Against Belief*; Fodor, *The Modularity of Mind: An Essay on Faculty Psychology*; McGinn, *The Subjective View: Secondary Qualities and Indexical Thoughts*

1984  John Searle delivers the BBC Reith Lectures published in the following year as *Minds, Brains and Science*

1985  Oliver Sacks publishes a series of essays arising out of his case work entitled *The Man Who Mistook His Wife for a Hat*

| Year | Historical & Literary Events | Scientific Events |
|------|------------------------------|-------------------|
| 1979 | The Shah of Persia and his family are forced to flee. The religious leader Ayatollah Khomeini returns from exile in France, assumes leadership in Persia and proclaims the Islamic Republic of Iran. Idi Amin overthrown in Uganda. Independence of Zimbabwe Britain elects first female prime minister, Margaret Thatcher | |
| 1980 | Beginning of the Iran-Iraq War Formation of non-Communist Solidarity trade union in Poland Richard Rorty, *Philosophy and the Mirror of Nature* | U.S. spacecraft Voyager I flies past Saturn |
| 1981 | President Sadat of Egypt assassinated. Riots in Northern Ireland after the death in prison of the IRA hunger-striker Bobby Sands | |
| 1982 | Argentina invades the Falkland Islands but is forced to surrender when Britain sends forces After four and a half centuries Britain establishes full diplomatic relations with the Vatican | |
| 1983 | Terrorists explode car bomb in precincts of U.S. Embassy in Beirut: 241 people killed. U.S. troops invade Grenada after Marxist coup on the island | The virus responsible for AIDS is identified |
| 1984 | Indian Prime Minister Indira Ghandi is assassinated by her Sikh bodyguard Davidson publishes essays, *Inquiries into Truth and Interpretation* | |
| 1985 | | Large hole discovered in the ozone layer above the South Pole. British geneticist Alec Jeffreys devises 'genetic fingerprinting' |

Year   Events in the History of Modern Philosophy of Mind and Related Fields

1986   The 'connectionist bible', Parallel Distributed Processing, edited by J. L.
       McClelland, D. E. Rumelhart and the PDP Research Group, appears.
       Nagel, The View From Nowhere; Patricia Churchland,
       Neurophilosophy: Toward a Unified Science of the Mind/Brain

1987   Dennett, The Intentional Stance; Fodor, Psychosemantics: The Problem
       of Meaning in Philosophy of Mind

1988   Putnam, Representation and Reality

1989   Jerry Fodor delivers the Donnellan Lectures, 'Problems of Content in
       Philosophy of Mind'; McGinn, 'Can we solve the Mind/Body Problem?'
       and Mental Content

| Year | Historical & Literary Events | Scientific Events |
|------|------------------------------|-------------------|
| 1986 | President Marcos of the Philippines is forced to resign | Explosion at the Chernobyl nuclear plant near Kiev in the Soviet Union |
| 1987 | U.S. and U.S.S.R. sign treaty to reduce the number of ground-based missiles in both territories World-wide stock exchange crash on 'Black Monday' Putnam publishes *The Many Faces of Realism: The Paul Carus Lectures* | |
| 1988 | Benazir Bhutto becomes Prime Minister of Pakistan, the first female leader of an Islamic state | Soviet cosmonauts spend a record year in space The Human Genome Project is established in Washington Astronomers detect the most distant star ever recorded: a supernova some 5 billion light years away |
| 1989 | The Communist government in East Germany collapses after mass protest rallies; the Berlin Wall is torn down. In Poland 'Solidarity' is declared legal and its supporters have a resounding victory in elections. The entire Czechoslovakian politburo resigns. The Hungarian Communist Party dissolves itself. In Bulgaria the Communist leader Zhivkov resigns. In Romania the Communist regime under President Ceausescu is overthrown by a military coup and he is executed The Islamic world claims that Salman Rushdie's novel *Satanic Verses* is blasphemous and condemns the author to death | |

Year    *Events in the History of Modern Philosophy of Mind and Related Fields*

1991    Dennett, *Consciousness Explained*; McGinn, *The Problem of Consciousness*

1992    Searle, *The Rediscovery of the Mind*; Fodor, *A Theory of Content and Other Essays*; Putnam, *Renewing Philosophy*

| Year | Historical & Literary Events | Scientific Events |
|------|------------------------------|-------------------|
| 1990 | President Sadam Hussein orders Iraqi invasion of Kuwait. East Germany is reunited with West Germany. Release of ANC leader Nelson Mandela from prison in South Africa begins the dismantling of apartheid | |
| 1991 | The Warsaw Pact and COMECON (the pact and economic union between the Soviet Union and other eastern European communist countries) are disbanded. Allied forces defeat Iraqi forces on the ground in six days of Operation Desert Storm, and Kuwait is liberated. Civil war in Yugoslavia begins | Body of man 5,300 years old found preserved in Italian Alps |

# INTRODUCTION

Philosophy of mind over the last hundred years has been a scene of intense, almost frenetic, activity. There have been more theoretical changes, confrontations, coups and revolutions than in the previous two thousand years. These have not merely been exciting years in philosophy of mind, however, they have been years of genuine progress. Theories have been replaced by new ones, and, generally speaking, the changes have been improvements.

Paradoxically the seventeenth-century philosopher-scientist Descartes has hovered over and sometimes landed among this activity. Certainly it was as a reaction against his account of mind that caused the first major theoretical change during the last century, and it is arguably one aspect of his viewpoint bedevilling the shiny new functionalist accounts of mind that stormed to the front row in the 1970s and 1980s. On the other hand, with the exception of the early part of this century, debates in philosophy of mind (in the analytic tradition) have been neither couched in Cartesian terms nor based on explicit discussions of Cartesian texts. Cartesianism has exercised its influence in a much more oblique way.

## Cartesian Origins

Let us return to the beginning of the period in question. It was Cartesianism rather than pure Descartes that survived into the late nineteenth century in both philosophy of mind and its young offspring, psychology. In the seventeenth century Descartes argued that mind and body must be separate 'stuffs', or substances, for we know with the privileged certainty of a subject's own self-consciousness and introspection that the essence of mind is consciousness. Descartes maintained that we can also come to know, though with less immediacy and certainty, that the essence of body is extension. Just as it probably did in Plato's time, such a view seemed no more than common sense with a little bit of theoretical elaboration. Thoughts and the other inhabitants of mind are items in our stream of consciousness, which is what having a mind means from the 'inside out', or subjective, point of view. What is more, his theory seemed to make good theological sense. When the body gets old, decays and breaks down, the mind cannot function properly and so leaves behind the bodily wreck, and this is death. The mind, having no extension, and so no parts, cannot be broken up into bits. It cannot decay. It is immortal and enduring, a soul. Certainly it becomes rather mysterious in this view as to how there can be a causal interface between matter and 'soul stuff', which is everything that matter isn't. But who cares about a mystery or two at the foundations if the superstructure looks fine?

The late-nineteenth-century philosopher Franz Brentano was arguably the most sophisticated of all the Cartesians, perhaps even the apotheosis of Cartesianism, though the phenomonologist Edmund Husserl would have claimed that title for himself. Brentano believed that a scientific philosophy of mind – or psychology, as he preferred to call it – was still the science of the soul. As he explained in his masterpiece *Psychology from an Empirical Standpoint*, however, this science should proceed in a genuinely empirical fashion, that is, by studying the mental events of our own streams of consciousness by means of careful inner perception of those events in self-conscious reflection. After all, these inner perceptions are the only first-hand, eye-witness experiences of the mind at work we can have. How else could a truly *empirical* psychology proceed?

In somewhat the same way as Descartes used the 'clear and distinct idea' as a prophylactic against doubt and error, so Brentano employed his 'intuitions of reason about what is evident or manifest' as his insurance policy that empirical investigations employing inner perception and producing phenomenological descriptions would deliver what is essential about the nature of mind. Brentano did not advocate that we should record our daydreams. Rather, he believed that the production of a scientific psychology required a mechanism for sifting what was essential to the very nature of all true mental events from the quotidian mental events in our own streams of consciousness. In one direction this Brentanian account of scientific method in psychology led to the ever-increasing subtleties and complexities, if not obscurities, of Husserl's attempts to make this phenomenology more pure and transcendental. In another direction it led to the Gestalt psychology of Christian von Ehrenfels and his followers. In yet another direction it led to modern experimental psychology.

The birth of psychology as a separate discipline began with the formation of the Cartesian laboratories, or perhaps – though strictly speaking it is a distortion of what he was about – the Brentanian laboratories of the philosopher-psychologists Wilhelm Wundt at Leipzig, and his former pupil, E. B. Titchener, at Cornell University. Although he was much less experimentally minded, William James also set up a laboratory at Harvard. The object of study of this new experimental discipline was the mind. The essence of mind was consciousness, and the only way to gain immediate experiential knowledge was by employing introspection in careful controlled laboratory conditions.[1] These early German experimentalists and their pupils had become as William James put it, 'prism, pendulum and chronograph-philosophers [who meant] business, not chivalry'[2], and their rigorous pedantic, Cartesian experiments produced some of the most tedious descriptive literature that had ever been written.

By the turn of the century some form of Cartesianism, reconstructed or otherwise, was still the dominant view of mind in both philosophy and psychology. In psychology, while sheer boredom was possibly a contributory factor, it was the lack of discernible results that caused the downfall of introspectionism. Introspection experiments came to be seen as too subjective and too unscientific and as producing no agreed data. Furthermore, the achievements of the experimenters in animal behaviour – such as the Russians Pavlov and Bekhterev, the Englishmen Spalding, Lubbock and Lloyd Morgan, and the Americans Thorndike and Loeb – suggested a new method for psychology, namely the scientific study of the behaviour of the human animal. It is no accident or coincidence that the founder of psychological behaviourism, J. B. Watson, began his academic career with experiments in animal behaviour.

## Wittgenstein

One of those who helped modern philosophy rid itself of Cartesian prejudices was undoubtedly the Austrian Ludwig

Wittgenstein, who was able to do this because he had once been in the grip of the Cartesian view of the nature of mind. The *Tractatus Logico-Philosophicus*, usually known as the *Tractatus*, was published in 1921; the first English edition appeared the following year. In it Wittgenstein wrestled with, among other ideas, the topic of thinking and its correlative, thought. He envisaged thoughts as 'psychical constituents' in a sort of psychological 'gaseous medium' (to use Anthony Kenny's phrase)[3] in terms of which something not too distant from a Cartesian ego did its thinking.

By the time Wittgenstein's *Philosophical Investigations* was published in 1953, however, it was clear that Wittgenstein had engaged in a long and arduous march away from Cartesianism and its psychological close relative, Introspectionism, to a position that had elements of behaviourism as well as contemporary functionalism. In various ways and at different times Wittgenstein floated ideas in philosophical psychology that have only been explored in detail in recent decades. He had ideas, for example, about the conventional or 'folk' nature of our psychological vocabulary and talk, and about the source of our psychological vocabulary and talk lying not in investigations focused on any sort of inner arena, mental or physical, but in our observation of human behaviour, gesture and expression while wearing our cultural spectacles.

In a real sense Wittgenstein's approach to philosophy of mind was through his philosophy of language. His later views on language, as embodied in his *Philosophical Investigations*, included the notion that the meaning of a sentence did not attach to the words in it but was a function of the use of words in a particular context, which in turn was rich in 'surroundings'. All words gained their meaning in this way, as part of a practice or 'language game' in which words were instruments for doing various tasks. Our vocabulary of mental or psychological terms is no exception. When we speak of someone deciding or believing or intending, then we must be attributing these terms on the basis of observing their public performance or practice, not on the basis of some privileged access to intrinsically private objects or acts in their stream of consciousness. Unfortunately, because the *Investigations* was published posthumously in 1953 and because the thinking that led up to it was known mainly only to a privileged few and took a long time to surface,

Wittgenstein's influence on the philosophy of mind took some time to take hold. Before its publication, therefore, the philosophy of mind took a different direction, in that it went the long way round, via a thorough immersion in behaviourism, for example, before facing and moving in the direction Wittgenstein was pointing.

## Logical Positivism

In the 1920s and 1930s less secretive philosophers began openly to adopt behaviouristic analyses of mental terms, but for reasons quite different from those held by psychologists. If psychology had become behaviourist for methodological purposes, then philosophy became so for logico-linguistic reasons. Through the work of many hands, Positivism had gradually evolved in the nineteenth century into the fairly stable doctrine that the only genuine knowledge was positive or scientific knowledge, that the only real method for gaining knowledge – including knowledge about all aspects of human life – was the scientific method of producing and testing causal hypotheses by reference to observation and experiment. The whole of science could in principle, therefore, be reduced to one fundamental science in which the basic observed elements were faithfully described and tabulated. As a consequence the bases of all our knowledge were the sense experiences resulting from those observations. This latter-day neo-Positivism was born when Moritz Schlick was appointed to the Chair of Inductive Philosophy at the University of Vienna in 1922, succeeding the physicist-philosopher Ernst Mach, who could reasonably be described as the last of the nineteenth-century positivists. Schlick gathered around him a marvellous and clever assortment of philosophers, scientists, social scientists and mathematicians who eventually became known as the Vienna Circle.

What these neo-Positivists added to nineteenth-century Positivism were the achievements and spirit of the analytical cum logical work of Frege, Russell and Wittgenstein. Schlick greatly admired Wittgenstein's *Tractatus*, particularly its more positivistic doctrines. Thus, in typical fashion, the neo-Positivists sometimes expressed their pro-scientific and anti-metaphysical stance in terms of an uncompromisingly clear and austere logico-linguistic principle, called the 'Verification Principle'. A simple version of a verification principle claims that a statement (or sentence) is literally meaningful (or significant) if and only if it is either empirically verifiable (or falsifiable) or it can be seen, or shown, to be true (or self-contradictory) simply by analyzing the conventional meanings of the signs or symbols used in the statement. The meaning of all terms or phrases or sentences is therefore anchored to checkable facts about either language or the world. The particular statements and general laws of mainstream natural sciences were grouped under the 'empirically verifiable' label, and the indispensable statements of logic and mathematics fell under the 'verifiable by the analysis of their conventional meanings' label. So all that was worth preserving was shown to be meaningful; the rest could be consigned to the bonfire of the inanities.

In regard to its account of mind Logical Positivism was drawn inexorably, though by a circuitous logico-linguistic route, to behaviourism. One of the principal Logical Positivists was Rudolph Carnap, and one of his most famous papers was 'Psychology in the Language of Physics' (1931). Background doctrines of that paper, held by Carnap as well as many other Logical Positivists, included the claim that any true science must ultimately be expressible in physical language, for only a language made up of terms for observable objects, properties and events will be truly universal and objective, hence truly scientific. Further, strictly speaking there are only physical events, so only statements about physical events could be literally true statements about the world. In the context of psychology this means, so Carnap argued, that in the absence of a mature neurophysiology, we must fall back on a behaviouristic physical language for psychology:

> All sentences of psychology are about physical processes, namely about the physical behaviour of humans and other animals.[4]

These 'sentences' are not the sentences psychologists themselves may employ, for they may be unredeemed Cartesian Introspectionists or Associationists or whatever. They are the sentences into which, Carnap believed, any meaningful sentences employed by psychologists could and should be translated. In due course these sentences describing the physical behaviour of humans would be retranslated into statements in the language of physics, the fundamental science. Thus, said Carnap:

Now psychology, which has hitherto enjoyed a certain elevated position as the theory of psychic or mental processes, is to be degraded into a part of physics.[5]

When he came to the task of delineating the details, Carnap admitted that at present one could not go much further than a translation of, say, 'He is excited' into something like 'His body is characterized by a high pulse rate, and respiration rate, by the occurrence of agitated movements, by vehement and factually unsatisfactory answers to questions, etc.'[6] Carnap was under no illusion about what sort of 'translation' work was possible. In regard to psychology, he realized that his 'translations' had advanced no farther than those of the psychological behaviourists. What he believed was important in his way of getting to this point was in seeing the task as one of *translating* one language (more accurately, one vocabulary) into another. The task of philosophy of mind, or philosophical psychology, was to give a correct account of the signs occurring in the language of psychology. This in turn would eventually enable the translation of our psychological vocabulary into the language of physics. In short, the task of a scientific philosophy of mind is the task of decoding the signs in our psychological vocabulary.

## Logical Behaviourism

Carnap was not particularly interested in philosophy of mind and so did not fill in the details of his research programme for this area. Indeed behaviourism never really gained in philosophy the commanding position it attained in psychology, and what gains it did make in philosophy were made much more slowly than in psychology. Thus when Gilbert Ryle published his swingeing anti-Cartesian and pro-behaviourist masterpiece *The Concept of Mind* in 1949, it seemed to many philosophers strangely new and shocking, although this may only be an indication that far too few philosophers had read either Carnap or the work of the psychological behaviourists. More likely it was the first time philosophical behaviourism had been presented in great detail and with consummate style by a master of the philosophical arts.

It can still be maintained, without too much difficulty, that in certain areas of theoretical explanation, behaviourist accounts work well and are probably more or less the right way to look at matters. For example, when we refer to someone as vain or an extrovert, we are probably not saying, nor entitled to say, any more than that they are prone to exhibit certain sorts of behaviour in certain specifiable circumstances. To say someone is vain should be analyzed as saying that he or she is liable to spend a lot of time in front of a mirror in a state of absorbed self-regard, or is always making his or her own achievements, such as they are, the subject of conversation, and so on. It all depends on what the person concerned is vain about. In similar fashion, saying that someone is an extrovert should be analyzed as saying that he or she is more likely than a non-extrovert to introduce himself or herself at a party or to answer the host's request for someone to start the karaoke. Such analyses might well be correctly applied to our talk about knowledge, belief, understanding, remembering, as well as wanting, willing, and desiring, though admittedly, such dispositional analyses are more controversial. There have also been indubitable successes for behaviourism in clinical psychology. Despite theoretical misgivings in some quarters, behavioural therapy has met with some success when what is required is no more than the modification of phobic behaviour.

On the other hand, being basically an unusually honest lot, the central figures in behaviourism in both psychology and philosophy have been all too aware of its shortcomings. They have realized, and admitted, that behaviourism copes very badly when it is forced to produce explanations or accounts of those very cases of mental events which an ordinary person would consider to be the central and paradigm cases of mental 'goings on', namely, such cases as consciously thinking to oneself or imagining what it would be like to be very rich or going over a tune in one's head or reading silently to oneself. For in such cases of pure cognitive events no outward behaviour is taking place, and the person is probably taking no notice of what is going on around him. In such cases behaviourist explanations have nothing to take hold of. The usual behaviourist explanation is to say that an alleged mental event is just a disposition to exhibit ordinary observable behaviour, or some readily observable physiological reaction, in some ordinary and readily describable context, where the former is the response to the latter. But here we have a 'true-blue' mental event, such as thinking to oneself, where there is no behaviour going on and the context plays no part. The psychological behaviourist, B. F. Skinner, called this worrying problem 'The Problem of Privacy',[7] for he realized that thinking to oneself seems to be a real cognitive activity, yet one that is wholly private to the subject of that activity. More memorably, as we shall see, Ryle called it 'the Problem of what *Le Penseur* is doing',[8] for such private cognitive activity seems to be what Rodin's sculpted figure is engaged in.

The psychological behaviourists tried to solve this problem in various ways. Most famously, or notoriously, by suggesting that thinking to oneself is really a sort of behaviour, namely truncated or stopped-short movements in the muscles of speech. It is talking in such a way that no utterance takes place, a talking silently to ourselves. This view was taken seriously enough in its day to prompt the authorities in some World War II veterans' hospitals in the U.S. to make the lives of those suffering from throat wounds even more tedious by forbidding them to read in bed.

Ryle admitted that he was unable to solve the problem of what *Le Penseur* was doing because he was not prepared to refer to any sort of inner activity, truncated or not, as the basis of an account of what thinking to oneself was. For to refer to an inner activity landed one back *either* into talk about truncated movements in the muscles we would normally employ for speech, which had been shown to be factually incorrect by psychologists themselves, *or* into talk about Cartesian entities, which was the very thing behaviourism was invented to avoid. In fact Ryle did try out some 'adverbial manoevres', which amounted to saying that we could avoid referring to any inner activities if we denied that thinking was an activity, suggesting instead that it was nothing more than the adverbial modification of an ordinary uncontroversial outer activity: to think was to do something, such as play chess or tennis, thinkingly. However, Ryle was too clever not to realize that such manoevring could not really avoid giving an answer to the persistent question 'What is *Le Penseur* doing?' when *no* outward behaviour, such as chess or tennis, is taking place. Ryle was forced to admit that in cases of circumstance-disengaged and behaviour-free thought he could find no activity peg upon which to hang an adverbial hat.

## The Identity Theory

In his 1956 paper 'Is consciousness a brain process?' the philosopher-psychologist U. T. Place suggested that there was a clear solution to the problem of privacy if we were brave enough to face its consequences, for the solution involves saying unequivocally, loudly and unshrinkingly that the mind is nothing but the brain:

> In the case of cognitive concepts like 'knowing', 'believing', 'understanding', 'remembering', and volitional concepts like 'wanting' and 'intending', there can be little doubt, I think, that an analysis in terms of dispositions to behave is fundamentally sound. [Here Place refers the reader to Wittgenstein's *Philosophical Investigations* and Ryle's *The Concept of Mind*.] On the other hand, there would seem to be an intractable residue of concepts clustering around the notions of consciousness, experience, sensation, and mental imagery, where some sort of inner process story is unavoidable. It is possible, of course, that a satisfactory behaviouristic account of this conceptual residuum will ultimately be found. For our present purposes, however, I shall assume that this cannot be done and that statements about pains and twinges, about how things look, sound, and feel, about things dreamed of or pictures in the mind's eye, are statements referring to events and processes which are in some sense private or internal to the individual of whom they are predicated ... I shall argue that an acceptance of inner processes does not entail dualism and that the thesis that consciousness is a process in the brain cannot be dismissed on logical grounds.[9]

Thus began what came to be called the Mind-Brain Identity Theory. From it derives Central State Materialism in which the theory is extended so as to include the 'cognitive and volitional concepts' which Place specifically excludes from its scope in the passage quoted above. Such theories are someties called 'Nothing buttery' theories because of their bald claim that mental things are nothing but brain things. In a sense the Identity Theory was carrying the Logical Positivists' programme for philosophy of mind and psychology one step further: it advocated the reduction not merely of mental talk but of some behaviourist talk to talk about brain states and processes. For the Identity Theory saw the task of a scientific psychology as ultimately that of discovering the brain states or processes that are the real referents of our mental terms. This was in effect William James without the dualism. James had seen the task of a scientific psychology as that of finding correlations, of a one-to-one sort, between introspectively identified mental events and brain processes discovered by the neurophysiologists. The Identity Theorists said that they were not in the business of finding *correlations* but of fashioning *reductions*, for mental events are an illusion created by our misunderstanding of the proper analysis of our mental talk.

It is informative to see this standpoint from another angle. Just as it was a discovery in the history of astronomy that the Evening Star (a star seen in the western hemisphere of an evening) is the same star as the Morning Star (a star seen in the eastern hemisphere in the morning), so, said the Identity Theorists, it will be a discovery of the twentieth or twenty-first century that my thought that Lake Louise is beautiful is the same thing as such-and-such brain state on a completed chart of brain states and processes. At a stroke the problem of privacy and the problem of how to make psychology scientific were solved. The drawback to the solution was that some psychologists – and virtually all psychoanalysts – would be out of a job. Psychology would become part of neurophysiology, or at least cognitive psychology would.

The Identity Theory of mind also seemed to be in tune with the scientific materialism of the twentieth century because it was a harmonic of the general theme that all there is in the universe is matter and energy and motion and that humans are a product of the evolution of species just as much as buffalos and beavers are. Evolution is a seamless garment with no holes wherein souls might be inserted from above. The mind is not a soul: it is nothing but the evolved human brain and its complex electrochemical functioning. This theory found ready acceptance among Australian philosophers, most notably J. J. C. Smart, who elaborated this view in his *magnum opus*, *Philosophy and Scientific Realism* (1963). Indeed the Identity Theory was sometimes dubbed 'the Australian Heresy', though this term was mainly employed by those whose cricketers had once again been soundly thrashed by the notably unspiritual Australian test team.

## Eliminative Materialism

If the Identity Theorists were uncompromising, the Eliminative Materialists – a breakaway group from among the Identity Theorists – are the hard men and women of twentieth-century philosophy of mind. For Eliminative Materialism advocates the elimination of our mental vocabulary on the grounds that it is irredeemably unscientific and misleading. It might remain as a 'folk psychology' for ordinary people, in the way that 'folk medicine' does, but it should play no part in a scientific psychology or a self-respecting, rigorous philosophy of mind. In the not too distant future a philosopher or psychologist who propounds his explanations and theories in terms of beliefs, desires, hopes, wants, imaginings, and so on, will be on a par with a scientist who talks seriously about phlogiston or the ether. In their view our everyday mental vocabulary is the detritus of an obsolete folk psychology full of occult Cartesian entities, faculties and activities. Thus, *pace* the Identity Theorists, the way to make psychology scientific is not to look for brain states and activities as the true referents of our ordinary mental terms but to *eliminate* such terms altogether because they are hopelessly inadequate and misleading. Indeed, say the Eliminative Materialists, it is hard now to imagine how the Identity Theorists thought that it was the task of a scientific psychology to find the brain states and processes that were the referents of our ordinary folk psychological terms – 'belief', 'desire', 'hope', etc. The terms 'belief', 'desire' and 'hope' no more pick out or are to be identified with real psychological realities in the brain than the terms 'ether' and 'phlogiston' are to be identified with real physical entities or events.

Eliminative Materialism has flourished chiefly on the American contintent, and its most vociferous proponents are the Canadian husband-and-wife team Paul and Patricia Churchland. However, it is probably true to say that Eliminative Materialism has been more attractive to scientists with strong philosophical interests and to philosophers with strong scientific interests than to philosophers of mind *en masse*. This is especially true, I think, of Patricia Churchland's large and formidable work *Neurophilosophy*, which is subtitled 'Toward a Unified Science of the Mind-Brain', and carries a recommendation from the Nobel Prize-winning molecular biologist Francis Crick. The subtitle is also unmistakably redolent of that most important phase in twentieth-century philosophy, Logical Positivism. Carnap, and for that matter his one-time student and great admirer, Quine, would surely approve of the aims and ethos of the Eliminative Materialists, if not necessarily of all their conclusions, for it is arguable that Eliminative Materialism marks the high water mark of Logical Positivism in philosophy of mind and that subsequent theorizing indicates the turning of the tide.

Doubts about and theoretical quarrelling with the Eliminativists is only one of the sources, and one that has come rather late
in the day, of what is the latest phase in philosophy of mind.
For this latest phase began to emerge long before the Eliminativists were leaving the Identity Theorists in their tracks.

## Davidson

Donald Davidson was certainly one of those who took a very
different direction from that of the Eliminativists and Identity
Theorists in particular, and from the Positivists in general.
Equally certainly he could be said to have anticipated some of
the views that have been canvassed openly only in very recent
philosophy of mind. On the other hand, because of his somewhat elusive writing style and because he has not produced a
monograph in philosophy of mind that systematically unites his
scattered thoughts in this area, and finally because he is more
interested in philosophy of language than in philosophy of mind,
his views in philosophy of mind have so far not had as marked
or direct an influence on recent theory as they deserve to. His
work in philosophy of mind could be described as both highly
original and maverick, in somewhat the same way as Wittgenstein's was during his time.

Put in very general terms, Davidson offers an account of mind
called 'anomalous monism'.[10] It is 'anomalous', he argues,
because there can be no general psychophysical laws that
correlate in a regular or law-like way our talk about mental
events, such as a person believing or hoping or desiring something or other, to our talk about physical states and processes in
that person's brain. It is 'monistic' because if one is talking
about states and processes that can take their place in scientific
laws or predictions, then there are only brain states and processes. There are no mental states and processes of that sort.
Thus when I say today that 'I believe it is not now raining,' and
my utterance is true, then some brain process has taken place,
but if I have the same belief tomorrow, it may be instantiated in
the brain as a different neurophysiological state. Thus, somewhat paradoxically, the conditions that must be satisfied before
someone can say that my utterance, 'I believe it is not now
raining,' is true, have nothing to do with my brain states or

processes. The truth conditions for talk about beliefs and desires are, more or less, the truth conditions for utterances in general, and so are such conditions as sincerity of utterance, correct use of terms, the rationality of the utterance in the context, the coherency of the utterance in relation to other utterances in the context, what is happening in the immediate context, and so on.

Davidson does, however, maintain that there are mental events. For while events such as mental acts are realities or real parts of nature, they are so at a different level from brain states and processes; they are genuine realities because they can have real causes and real effects. Reasons are the usual causes of human beliefs and desires, and behaviour the usual effects of beliefs and desires. Davidson also maintains that while we can talk of the causal connections between reasons and beliefs and behaviour, we cannot produce detailed causal laws linking them because mental-action talk or mental-event talk is not the right level or context to look for scientifically detailed causal laws or fool-proof predictions in regard to human behaviour. There are no such strict laws in psychology. The right level for strict causal laws is the micro-level of physics and so of physical events.

## Functionalism

What has undeniably had a profound effect on recent work in philosophy of mind is the computer, which has been one of the inspirations for almost all of the modern materialist accounts of mind. But this is especially true of the theory of the mind called 'Functionalism', which, though already dividing itself up into various subspecies, has been something approaching an ortho-doxy over the last ten years. Here the catch cry is not 'the mind is nothing but the brain' but 'the mind is to the brain as a computer's software is to its hardware'. In short, the mind is the brain's program. If the mind is seen in this way, it is argued, then we will no longer have any temptation whatever to look for either correlations or identifications between mind and brain, and *a fortiori* any temptation to eliminate our mental vocabu-lary. For just as it makes no sense to correlate or identify a computer's software with its hardware, so it makes no real sense to correlate or identify mental descriptions with neurophysiol-ogical descriptions. Our mental talk is program or functional talk about the brain, and so different from talk about the brain's neurophysiological construction and electrochemical reactions; mind talk and brain talk are two equally legitimate but different ways of talking about the human brain and central nervous system. Seeing our mental talk in this way shows how nonsensical is any suggestion that we could or should eliminate it. Just as a computer scientist could not get by without ever mentioning computer programs and programming, so a philosopher of mind or cognitive psychologist could not get by without talking about a human's mental life. It is another matter, of course, and a subject of keen debate, as to whether or not we could get by without our ordinary 'folk' version of our mental cum functional talk about the brain (expressed in terms of 'belief', 'desire', 'want', 'wish', 'intend', and so on).

The name most associated with the early days of Functionalism, sometimes called Computer Functionalism, is that of the Harvard philosopher Hilary Putnam. The baldest statement of his early views appears in the introduction to volume two of his collected philosophical papers, *Mind, Language and Reality*:

> The theory for which I argue is a form of functionalism – not functionalism as a doctrine about the meanings of psychological words, but functionalism as a synthetic hypothesis about the nature of mental states.
>
> According to functionalism, the behaviour of, say, a computing machine is not explained by the physics and chemistry of the computing machine. It is explained by the machine's *program*. Of course, that program is realized in a particular physics and chemistry, and could, perhaps, be deduced from that physics and chemistry. But that does not make the program a physical or chemical property of the machine: it is an abstract property of the machine. Similarly, I believe that the psychological properties of human beings are not physical and chemical properties of human beings, although they may be realized by physical and chemical properties of human beings.[11]

A bonus resulting from this way of explaining the human mind is that it returns to psychology the status of being an autonomous science by blocking the gradual reduction of psychology to neurophysiology and eventually physics. Just as it makes no sense to eliminate mention of software[12] for computers and to deal entirely in terms of their electronic hardware, it equally makes no sense to eliminate discussion of the brain's functions and to investigate only its electrochemistry. Psychology cannot be reduced to physics or even to physiology, said the Function-alists, and in so saying brought about much of the current rapprochement between philosophy of mind and cognitive psychology. It also helped produce in psychology such eminent adherents of Functionalism as Ulric Neisser and Philip Johnson-Laird.

One way of summing up Functionalism is to say that it has produced an exceedingly attractive and plausible answer to Ryle's question 'What is *Le Penseur* doing?' For the answer given by the Functionalists is that, quite simply, *Le Penseur* is thinking or ruminating or deciding or believing – or some combination of these things – for our vocabulary of 'belief', 'desire', 'thought' applies literally to human brains. It does so because it is a literal account of their functioning, not of their micro electrochemical functioning but of the macro or 'writ-large' tasks they perform in relation to perceptual input and behavioural output and other internal functional states. On the other hand, I should not hide the fact that within Functionalism there has been, and continues to be, a hard-fought debate about the status of our talk about beliefs, desires, thoughts, wants and their ilk. Sometimes this has been described as a debate about the nature of 'the propositional attitudes', for typically the full expression of a person's particular belief or desire would take the form, grammatically speaking, of a mental verb operating over (or attitudinizing over) a content expressed in propositional or 'that-clause' form. Thus, typically, we might say, 'she *believes that* it will be a mild winter' or 'he *hopes that* the train will not be late'.

The result of the debate has been a bifurcation of Functionalism into what might be called a Centralist group and a Periph-eralist group. The Centralist group, led by Jerry Fodor, would say that our ordinary belief-desire vocabulary does not merely apply literally to humans at the macro level but that it also applies literally to humans at if not a micro level then at least at a sub-macro level. For true descriptions of human cognitive functioning, in terms of our belief-desire (or propositional attitude) vocabulary, are true descriptions of the way human brains actually operate. Human brains are like digital computers in so far as they are 'semantic engines'. That is, human brains operate by representing incoming perceptual information in a language of the brain ('the language of thought') in propositional form and then operating over it in much the way that our propositional attitude vocabulary says it does. As Fodor said in a fit of combative hyperbole, any attempt on the part of psychology or philosophy of mind to give up the firm basis of psychological explanation in our common-sense belief-desire accounts would be 'beyond comparison, the greatest intellectual catastrophe in the history of our species'.[13] The Peripheralist group, led by Daniel Dennett, would say that our ordinary belief-desire vocabulary does not produce a vehicle for literal description of how the human brain functions. It does not carve nature at its neurophysiological joints. How could it, since it was generated aeons ago by our ancestors who wore woad or nothing at all. When they viewed humans from the outside or periphery, our ancestors concocted a Functionalist story about what goes on inside human heads. This way of talking may now be indispensable in our quotidian commerce, but it cannot be literally true of how human brains function, for neither our ancestors nor most of us have any knowledge of neurophysiology. Indeed, on bad days neurophysiologists are prone to muttering that they have no knowledge of how the human brain really works. Talk about beliefs and desires, and how desires might stem from beliefs or vice versa, and our talk about propositional attitudes in general, have much the same status as our talk about the equator and lines of longitude and latitude: namely, we have found it useful to have invented them and we may now have to admit that they have become indispensable. If I were asked to predict which of these two competing sorts is likely to gain the ascendancy in the future of Functionalism, I would say the Peripheralists, but I could easily be wrong because the Centralists are the darlings of cognitive science and on more than nodding terms with workers in the field of artificial intelligence. The Centralists make a lot of people feel good; the Peripheralists make a lot of people feel uncomfortable.

If I were also asked to make a more general prediction about whether Functionalism would still be the orthodoxy of the next decade in philosophy of mind and cognitive psychology, I would be inclined to say no. If it does last, it will be, I suggest, because it has managed to transform itself in the light of its difficulties – possibly by espousing some position between the Centralists and Peripheralists, one that suggests that our belief-desire descriptions are not literally true of brain functioning yet that there must be more to it than being just a useful confabulation.

## Connectionism

Connectionism[14] is a theory of how the brain operates and its application in terms of computer models of brain functioning and in artificial-intelligence machines. The theory is radically different from the theory of brain functioning that underlies the Functionalism of Fodor. Fodorian Functionalism is based on an information-processing view of the brain, on the premises that there is a language or representational system in the brain and that the brain operates in terms of a program in much the same way a digital computer does. Fodor has admitted that 'it may, after all, turn out that the whole information-processing approach to psychology is somehow a bad idea. If it is, then such theories of mind as it suggests are hardly likely to be true.'

Recently a growing number of philosophers of mind (some non-Fodorian Functionalists and some Eliminative Materialists, for example) as well as psychologists, neurophysiologists and computer scientists have suggested that the whole information-processing approach is indeed a bad idea and that a Connectionist account of brain functioning is a more plausible theory. In brief, Connectionism suggests that the brain operates in a non-representational way. There is no program and so no central-processing unit of an executive kind that oversees and administers the program. Since there is no executive commander, there are no executive commands and therefore no rules or rule-following. Rather, our neurophysiological system is driven on a more ad hoc basis, by trial and error, though the 'learning period' for producing success from this process is that of evolution combined with individual development. The human brain, at least when healthy and mature, is a system of neuronal networks that are both interconnected among themselves (hence the name 'Connectionism') and conjoined to the sensory input systems and the behavioural cum reactive output systems. Thus the brain is just a very complex nodal-and-network system intermediate between input and output. Input is registered in an analogue way not in a representational way. For example, if a boxer punches my nose with a right jab at ten miles per hour, then let us say that my nose is flattened to a depth of ten millimetres before recovering its usual shape; if the same boxer delivers a right jab to my nose at twenty miles per hour, then let us say that my nose is flattened to a depth of twenty millimetres before recovering its usual shape, and so on for punches delivered at thirty and forty miles per hour. At least fleetingly, in terms of the different depths to which my nose has been flattened, my nose has registered one aspect of the boxer's punch in an analogue way, namely its speed. But there is no language of my nose and no representational system. On the other hand, the input (the punch) and my analogue registering of it (on my nose) could be linked to an appropriate response (expressions of pain). In seeing the brain in this analogue, non-representational way (though the story is complicated by feedback mechanisms, thresholds of response, and many other bits and pieces) Connectionism is an increasingly sophisticated response to any quasi-linguistic view of the mind. From our panoramic point of view of philosophy of mind, it is important to note the increasing influence of such areas as neurophysiology, psychology, computing and artificial intelligence. Nowadays it is more or less impossible to do work in philosophy of mind without crossing discipline boundaries. This is something that someone from a previous era, such as Ryle or Wittgenstein, would have been uneasy about.

## Current Developments

As we near the end of the twentieth century it could be said that views closer to Cartesianism than to any of the moves that form the long march away from Cartesianism are gaining influence. At the centre of Cartesianism are the subjective experiences that we call consciousness, and the opponents of any form of Functionalism (such as Tom Nagel)[15] are fond of causing embarrassment by pointing out that you cannot give a functional account of consciousness. A human may function in a certain way *and* be conscious of it, but this consciousness is not a further or second-level function attached to, or symbiotic with, the first-level functioning; it is a subjective reactive experience, not an objective task performed. Further, many states of consciousness, such as of pain, do not have *propositional* content and so do not easily take their place as program material for a computational semantic engine such as the human brain, at least

as described by some Functionalists. Some version of Functionalism, Descartes might say, may well make sense of our ordinary
belief-desire vocabulary, but it has too little in its descriptive-
explanatory storehouse for it to be able to make sense of our
subjective world of conscious experience. Ryle, if he were alive
today, might say, 'I can't help saying, I told you so, for I did
emphasize that philosophy of mind has to take seriously, indeed
as of the utmost importance, the attempt to answer the question,
"What is *Le Penseur* doing?" as he sits on his rock, consciously
ruminating but immobile and impervious to what is going on
around about.' More than most philosophers of mind in this
century, Ryle realized that while we have advanced considerably
our understanding of the criteria for the attribution of the
propositional attitudes to ourselves and others, we have passed
over a central problem. Although we have produced convincing
accounts of the status of our common-sense explanations of our
actions in terms of beliefs, desires, intentions and so on, we have
failed even to acknowledge that we do not yet know how to
knit this understanding to our subjective knowledge by
acquaintance of our own conscious states. Indeed Ryle would
probably say that we are still not even clear about what our
direct knowledge by acquaintance of our own conscious states
amounts to because in terms of self-consciousness and introspection we are still wedded to a Cartesian account.

In the last few years philosophy of mind has begun to take
subjective conscious states in earnest. In his most recent book,
*The Rediscovery of the Mind* (1992), John Searle argues that
the essence of mind is consciousness and that all current
materialist theories have been unable to cope with this fact. In
consequence such theories have been put forward either as if
consciousness did not exist or as if it should be identified with
brain states or processes or as if the term 'consciousness' itself
was a misnomer that should be discarded. Searle, however,
insists that our conscious states have quite specific, subjective,
phenomenological and thus irreducible properties. This, he says,
does not amount to a denial that consciousness is just a
biological feature of humans that has evolved over time like any
other biological feature. Rather, such a biological feature is a
physical feature but it is not reducible to *other* physical features.

More radically, and far less optimistically, Colin McGinn has
suggested in his paper, 'Can we solve the mind-body problem?'

(*Mind*, 1989) that it is the case that no theory, now or in the future, will ever be able to make sense of the fact that our brain gives rise to conscious states. While he believes that consciousness is a material property that has resulted from the long evolution of animal brains, McGinn believes that humans are probably incapable of *ever* conceptualizing the psychophysical means by which conscious states are caused by brain processes. This is not merely a failure in understanding, such as a child might experience when confronted with the theory of relativity, but a fundamental failure of resources. It is more than likely that we do not even possess the requisite cognitive powers to develop a theory of the genesis of consciousness from the brain. What investigative powers we do have are either perceptual, which will reveal to us (at least when instrument aided) truths about the brain, or introspective, which will reveal to us truths about consciousness. But we do not have an additional 'bridging' cognitive power that could supply us with the concepts adequate for explaining the genesis of consciousness from the brain.

We are, then, victims of 'cognitive closure' in regard to the causal link between consciousness and brains. We should not doubt that there is some property that would make sense of this link, but we will never be able to grasp it because we can neither experience it nor conceptualise it in the way that a blind person cannot have the experience of seeing red. It may be possible for a more evolved human, some thousands of years hence, to form an adequate theory of the causal nexus between brain and consciousness, but we humans of this century and the next millennium are condemned to outer darkness on this matter.

Ryle would have said (and Wittgenstein would have agreed) that if we can talk sensibly and informatively about our subjective conscious states, then there must be a way in to the understanding of them, namely through language. In gaining an understanding of the truth conditions (or some relevant philosophical cousin of these) for describing our subjective conscious states we will gain what understanding it is possible to have. Ryle, like Searle, would reject any move to eliminate, reduce or simply neglect our talk about the subjective inner life of our conscious states.

Yet I do not want to give the impression that there has been no progress in philosophy of mind in this century. Immense gains have been made in understanding the descriptions and explanations of ourselves and others in terms of the propositional attitudes and in our understanding of the relation between these descriptions and a physiologist's descriptions of our brain states and processes. And philosophy of mind has finally found acceptable (if still provisional) reconciliations between, on the one hand, the seemingly ineliminable dualism of our indispensable everyday talk about mental events and our scientifically authorized talk about our physiology and, on the other hand, the pressure from evolutionary theory to accept that we humans are entirely material beings. Furthermore, these developments have been coherent. There is a reasonably clear line of first-stage dialectical development in psychology in the twentieth century from Introspectionism to psychological or methodological behaviourism. Interconnecting with that line is another in philosophy of mind from Logical Positivism plus psychological behaviourism, with some push from Linguistic Analysis, to logical or philosophical behaviourism. Alongside that latter move forward is the influence of Wittgenstein on the logical behaviourist Ryle and on other participants in those developments. The dissatisfaction with behaviourism was one of the main sources of the move forward to the Identity Theory, which in turn led some philosophers on to the Eliminative Materialism. Next to this was another line of development through Carnap, Quine, Davidson and Putnam to Fodor and Dennett. Finally, the most recent developments might be characterized as refinements to, or second thoughts about, certain aspects of these penultimate developments.

What is certain is that philosophy of mind has moved ineluctably away from any concept of the mind as a separate non-physical substance. In addition, philosophy of mind has moved inexorably in the direction of fitting our mental powers into that pigeonhole marked 'evolved human capacities'. To its credit, while moving in these directions it has refused to settle upon the easy solutions. While philosophy of mind has flirted with behaviourism and mind-to-brain reductionism, it has moved on in the certainty that these are crude explanations. In so progressing it has found it difficult to resist some form of non-Cartesian dualism, toying with dualisms of function versus structure, two distinct levels of description, subjective versus objective, and pragmatic stances of various kinds. My belief is that philosophy of mind is on the verge of producing something approaching a definitive account, but it will be a complex and sophisticated account. In our ordinary discourse we will probably still speak as if minds were ghostly drivers of our bodily machines.

WILLIAM LYONS

## References

1. The subject who is engaged in an introspection experiment might be seated in front of a screen upon which objects or events are depicted for short, carefully timed periods. The subject might then be asked to express a choice or to make a decision in connection with the depicted objects or events. The reaction time between the request and its being carried out would be measured. This time would be taken as the duration of the mental events of choosing or deliberating or deciding. In another kind of experiment the subject might be asked to report on features of the image that remained in his or her stream of consciousness after the depiction of the object or event had been removed from the screen. Such features might be the intensity or duration of this after-image. It was hoped that, at least eventually, the basic elements of our mental life and the laws governing their interplay would be revealed by such experiments.

2. James (1950), vol. 1, p. 193.

3. Kenny (1984), p. 9. See also Norman Malcolm (1967), p. 331.

4. Carnap (1995), p. 43.

5. Ibid. p. 46.

6. An adaptation of material in Carnap (1995), pp. 51ff.

7. Skinner (1965), ch. 17 especially pp. 280–282.

8. Ryle (1979), especially paper 2, pp. 33ff.

9. Place (1962), pp. 101–102. See also Smart (1963), pp. 88–92.

10. Davidson (1980), especially pp. 214–225.

11. Putnam (1975), p. xiii.

12. 'Software' is, strictly speaking, a misleading term in this context. For a computer scientist 'software' means much more than just a description of the tasks performed by a computer, while this is all that a Functionalist seems to mean by the term. For a computer scientist the term 'software' means the activity of programming the computer to incorporate operating instructions, which are themselves incarnated

into the machine, and only then, if at all, the tasks performed in accordance with these operating instructions.

13. Fodor (1987), Preface, p. xii.

14. The best short introduction to Connectionism is probably Tienson (1987) or Bechtel (1987).

15. See both Nagel (1974) and Nagel (1986) especially pp. 7ff.

# MODERN PHILOSOPHY
# OF MIND

# The Stream of Consciousness

The order of our study must be analytic. We are now prepared to begin the introspective study of the adult consciousness itself. Most books adopt the so-called synthetic method. Starting with 'simple ideas of sensation', and regarding these as so many atoms, they proceed to build up the higher states of mind out of their 'association', 'integration', or 'fusion', as houses are built by the agglutination of bricks. This has the didactic advantages which the synthetic method usually has. But it commits one beforehand to the very questionable theory that our higher states of consciousness are compounds of units; and instead of starting with what the reader directly knows, namely his total concrete states of mind, it starts with a set of supposed 'simple ideas' with which he has no immediate acquaintance at all, and concerning whose alleged interactions he is much at the mercy of any plausible phrase. On every ground, then, the method of advancing from the simple to the compound exposes us to illusion. All pedants and abstractionists will naturally hate to abandon it. But a student who loves the fulness of human nature will prefer to follow the 'analytic' method, and to begin with the most concrete facts, those with which he has a daily acquaintance in his own inner life. The analytic method will discover in due time the elementary parts, if such exist, without danger of precipitate assumption. The reader will bear in mind that our own chapters on sensation have dealt mainly with the physiological conditions thereof. They were put first as a mere matter of convenience, because incoming currents come first. *Psychologically* they might better have come last. Pure sensations were described [...] as processes which in adult life are well-nigh unknown, and nothing was said which could for a moment lead the reader to suppose that they were the *elements of composition* of the higher states of mind.

**The Fundamental Fact.** The first and foremost concrete fact which every one will affirm to belong to his inner experience is

the fact that *consciousness of some sort goes on. 'States of mind'
succeed each other in him.* If we could say in English 'it thinks',
as we say 'it rains' or 'it blows', we should be stating the fact
most simply and with the minimum of assumption. As we
cannot, we must simply say that *thought goes on.*

**Four Characters in Consciousness.** How does it go on? We
notice immediately four important characters in the process, of
which it shall be the duty of the present chapter to treat in a
general way:

1) Every 'state' tends to be part of a personal consciousness.

2) Within each personal consciousness states are always
changing.

3) Each personal consciousness is sensibly continuous.

4) It is interested in some parts of its object to the exclusion
of others, and welcomes or rejects – *chooses* from among them,
in a word – all the while.

In considering these four points successively, we shall have to
plunge *in medias res* as regards our nomenclature and use
psychological terms which can only be adequately defined in
later chapters of the book. But every one knows what the terms
mean in a rough way; and it is only in a rough way that we are
now to take them. This chapter is like a painter's first charcoal
sketch upon his canvas, in which no niceties appear.

When I say *every 'state' or 'thought' is part of a personal
consciousness,* 'personal consciousness' is one of the terms in
question. Its meaning we know so long as no one asks us to
define it, but to give an accurate account of it is the most
difficult of philosophic tasks. This task we must confront [later];
here a preliminary word will suffice.

In this room – this lecture-room, say – there are a multitude
of thoughts, yours and mine, some of which cohere mutually,
and some not. They are as little each-for-itself and reciprocally
independent as they are all-belonging-together. They are neither:
no one of them is separate, but each belongs with certain others
and with none beside. My thought belongs with *my* other
thoughts, and your thought with *your* other thoughts. Whether
anywhere in the room there be a *mere* thought, which is
nobody's thought, we have no means of ascertaining, for we
have no experience of its like. The only states of consciousness
that we naturally deal with are found in personal consciousnesses, minds, selves, concrete particular I's and you's.

Each of these minds keeps its own thoughts to itself. There is no giving or bartering between them. No thought even comes into direct *sight* of a thought in another personal consciousness than its own. Absolute insulation, irreducible pluralism, is the law. It seems as if the elementary psychic fact were not *thought* or *this thought* or *that thought*, but *my thought*, every thought being *owned*. Neither contemporaneity, nor proximity in space, nor similarity of quality and content are able to fuse thoughts together which are sundered by this barrier of belonging to different personal minds. The breaches between such thoughts are the most absolute breaches in nature. Every one will reconize this to be true, so long as the existence of *something* corresponding to the term 'personal mind' is all that is insisted on, without any particular view of its nature being implied. On these terms the personal self rather than the thought might be treated as the immediate datum in psychology. The universal conscious fact is not 'feelings and thoughts exist', but 'I think' and 'I feel'. No psychology, at any rate, can question the *existence* of personal selves. Thoughts connected as we feel them to be connected are *what we mean* by personal selves. The worst a psychology can do is to interpret the nature of these selves as to rob them of their *worth*.

Consciousness is in constant change. I do not mean by this to say that no one state of mind has any duration – even if true, that would be hard to establish. What I wish to lay stress on is this, that *no state once gone can recur and be identical with what it was before*. Now we are seeing, now hearing; now reasoning, now willing; now recollecting, now expecting; now loving, now hating; and in a hundred other ways we know our minds to be alternately engaged. But all these are complex states, it may be said, produced by combination of simpler ones; – do not the simpler ones follow a different law? Are not the *sensations* which we get from the same object, for example, always the same? Does not the same piano-key, struck with the same force, make us hear in the same way? Does not the same grass give us the same feeling of green, the same sky the same feeling of blue, and do we not get the same olfactory sensation no matter how many times we put our nose to the same flask of cologne? It seems a piece of metaphysical sophistry to suggest that we do not; and yet a close attention to the matter shows that *there is no proof that an incoming current ever gives us just the same bodily sensation twice*.

*What is got twice is the same* OBJECT. We hear the same *note* over and over again; we see the same *quality* of green, or smell the same objective perfume, or experience the same *species* of pain. The realities, concrete and abstract, physical and ideal, whose permanent existence we believe in, seem to be constantly coming up again before our thought, and lead us, in our carelessness, to suppose that our 'ideas' of them are the same ideas. When we come, some time later, to [a subsequent chapter on] Perception, we shall see how inveterate is our habit of simply using our sensible impressions as stepping-stones to pass over to the recognition of the realities whose presence they reveal. The grass out of the window now looks to me of the same green in the sun as in the shade, and yet a painter would have to paint one part of it dark brown, another part bright yellow, to give its real sensational effect. We take no heed, as a rule, of the different way in which the same things look and sound and smell at different distances and under different circumstances. The sameness of the *things* is what we are concerned to ascertain; and any sensations that assure us of that will probably be considered in a rough way to be the same with each other. This is what makes off-hand testimony about the subjective identity of different sensations well-nigh worthless as a proof of the fact. The entire history of what is called Sensation is a commentary on our inability to tell whether two sensible qualities received apart are exactly alike. What appeals to our attention far more than the absolute quality of an impression is its *ratio* to whatever other impressions we may have at the same time. When everything is dark a somewhat less dark sensation makes us see an object white. Helmholtz calculates that the white marble painted in a picture representing an architectural view by moonlight is, when seen by daylight, from ten to twenty thousand times brighter than the real moonlit marble would be.

Such a difference as this could never have been *sensibly* learned; it had to be inferred from a series of indirect consider-ations. These make us believe that our sensibility is altering all the time, so that the same object cannot easily give us the same sensation over again. We feel things differently accordingly as we are sleepy or awake, hungry or full, fresh or tired; differently at night and in the morning, differently in summer and in winter; and above all, differently in childhood, manhood, and old age. And yet we never doubt that our feelings reveal the same world, with the same sensible qualities and the same sensible things occupying it. The difference of the sensibility is shown best by the difference of our emotion about the things from one age to another, or when we are in different organic moods. What was bright and exciting becomes weary, flat, and unprofitable. The bird's song is tedious, the breeze is mournful, the sky is sad.

To these indirect presumptions that our sensations, following the mutations of our capacity for feeling, are always undergoing an essential change, must be added another presumption, based on what must happen in the brain. Every sensation corresponds to some cerebral action. For an identical sensation to recur it would have to occur the second time *in an unmodified brain*. But as this, strictly speaking, is a physiological impossibility, so is an unmodified feeling an impossibility; for to every brain-modification, however small, we suppose that there must correspond a change of equal amount in the consciousness which the brain subserves.

But if the assumption of 'simple sensations' recurring in immutable shape is so easily shown to be baseless, how much more baseless is the assumption of immutability in the larger masses of our thought!

For there it is obvious and palpable that our state of mind is never precisely the same. Every thought we have of a given fact is, strictly speaking, unique, and only bears a resemblance of kind with our other thoughts of the same fact. When the identical fact recurs, we *must* think of it in a fresh manner, see it under a somewhat different angle, apprehend it in different relations from those in which it last appeared. And the thought by which we cognize it is the thought of it-in-those-relations, a thought suffused with the consciousness of all that dim context. Often we are ourselves struck at the strange differences in our successive views of the same thing. We wonder how we ever could have opined as we did last month about a certain matter. We have outgrown the possibility of that state of mind, we know not how. From one year to another we see things in new lights. What was unreal has grown real, and what was exciting is insipid. The friends we used to care the world for are shrunken to shadows; the women once so divine, the stars, the woods,

and the waters, how now so dull and common! – the young girls
that brought an aura of infinity, at present hardly distinguishable
existences; the pictures so empty; and as for the books, what
*was* there to find so mysteriously significant in Goethe, or in
John Mill so full of weight? Instead of all this, more zestful than
ever is the work, the work; and fuller and deeper the import of
common duties and of common goods.

I am sure that this concrete and total manner of regarding the
mind's changes is the only true manner, difficult as it may be to
carry it out in detail. If anything seems obscure about it, it will
grow clearer as we advance. Meanwhile, if it be true, it is
certainly also true that no two 'ideas' are ever exactly the same,
which is the proposition we started to prove. The proposition is
more important theoretically than it at first sight seems. For it
makes it already impossible for us to follow obediently in the
footprints of either the Lockian or the Herbartian school,
schools which have had almost unlimited influence in Germany
and among ourselves. No doubt it is often *convenient* to
formulate the mental facts in an atomistic sort of way, and to
treat the higher states of consciousness as if they were all built
out of unchanging simple ideas which 'pass and turn again'. It is
convenient often to treat curves as if they were composed of
small straight lines, and electricity and nerve-force as if they
were fluids. But in the one case as in the other we must never
forget that we are talking symbolically, and that there is nothing
in nature to answer to our words. *A permanently existing 'Idea'
which makes its appearance before the footlights of consciousness at periodical intervals is as mythological an entity as the
Jack of Spades.*

**Within each personal consciousness, thought is sensibly con-
tinuous.** I can only define 'continuous' as that which is without
breach, crack, or division. The only breaches that can well be
conceived to occur within the limits of a single mind would
either be *interruptions, time*-gaps during which the consciousness went out; or they would be breaks in the content of the
thought, so abrupt that what followed had no connection
whatever with what went before. The proposition that consciousness feels continuous, means two things:

*a.* That even where there is a time-gap the consciousness after
it feels as if it belonged together with the consciousness before
it, as another part of the same self;

*b*. That the changes from one moment to another in the quality of the consciousness are never absolutely abrupt.

The case of the time-gaps, as the simplest, shall be taken first.

*a*. When Paul and Peter wake up in the same bed, and recognize that they have been asleep, each one of them mentally reaches back and makes connection with but *one* of the two streams of thought which were broken by the sleeping hours. As the current of an electrode buried in the ground unerringly finds its way to its own similarly buried mate, across no matter how much intervening earth; so Peter's present instantly finds out Peter's past, and never by mistake knits itself on to that of Paul. Paul's thought in turn is as little liable to go astray. The past thought of Peter is appropriated by the present Peter alone. He may have a *knowledge*, and a correct one too, of what Paul's last drowsy states of mind were as he sank into sleep, but it is an entirely different sort of knowledge from that which he has of his own last states. He *remembers* his own states, while he only *conceives* Paul's. Remembrance is like direct feeling; its object is suffused with a warmth and intimacy to which no object of mere conception ever attains. This quality of warmth and intimacy and immediacy is what Peter's *present* thought also possesses for itself. So sure as this present is me, is mine, it says, so sure is anything else that comes with the same warmth and intimacy and immediacy, me and mine. What the qualities called warmth and intimacy may in themselves be will have to be matter for future consideration. But whatever past states appear with those qualities must be admitted to receive the greeting of the present mental state, to be owned by it, and accepted as belonging together with it in a common self. This community of self is what the time-gap cannot break in twain, and is why a present thought, although not ignorant of the time-gap, can still regard itself as continuous with certain chosen portions of the past.

Consciousness, then, does not appear to itself chopped up in bits. Such words as 'chain' or 'train' do not describe it fitly as it presents itself in the first instance. It is nothing jointed; it flows. A 'river' or a 'stream' are the metaphors by which it is most naturally described. *In talking of it hereafter, let us call it the stream of thought, of consciousness, or of subjective life.*

*b*. But now there appears, even within the limits of the same self, and between thoughts all of which alike have this same sense of belonging together, a kind of jointing and separateness among the parts, of which this statement seems to take no account. I refer to the breaks that are produced by sudden *contrasts in the quality* of the successive segments of the stream of thought. If the words 'chain' and 'train' had no natural fitness in them, how came such words to be used at all? Does not a loud explosion rend the consciousness upon which it abruptly breaks, in twain? No; for even into our awareness of the thunder the awareness of the previous silence creeps and continues; for what we hear when the thunder crashes is not thunder *pure*, but thunder-breaking-upon-silence-and-contrasting-with-it.    Our feeling of the same objective thunder, coming in this way, is quite different from what it would be were the thunder a continuation of previous thunder. The thunder itself we believe to abolish and exclude the silence; but the *feeling* of the thunder is also a feeling of the silence as just gone; and it would be difficult to find in the actual concrete consciousness of man a feeling so limited to the present as not to have an inkling of anything that went before.

**'Substantive' and 'Transitive' States of Mind.** When we take a general view of the wonderful stream of our consciousness, what strikes us first is the different pace of its parts. Like a bird's life, it seems to be an alternation of flights and perchings. The rhythm of language expresses this, where every thought is expressed in a sentence, and every sentence closed by a period. The resting-places are usually occupied by sensorial imaginations of some sort, whose peculiarity is that they can be held before the mind for an indefinite time, and contemplated without changing; the places of flight are filled with thoughts of relations, static or dynamic, that for the most part obtain between the matters contemplated in the periods of comparative rest.

*Let us call the resting-places the 'substantive parts', and the places of flight the 'transitive parts', of the stream of thought.* It then appears that our thinking tends at all times towards some other substantive part than the one from which it has just been dislodged. And we may say that the main use of the transitive parts is to lead us from one substantive conclusion to another.

Now it is very difficult, introspectively, to see the transitive parts for what they really are. If they are but flights to a conclusion, stopping them to look at them before the conclusion is reached is really annihilating them. Whilst if we wait till the conclusion *be* reached, it so exceeds them in vigor and stability that it quite eclipses and swallows them up in its glare. Let anyone try to cut a thought across in the middle and get a look at its section, and he will see how difficult the introspective observation of the transitive tracts is. The rush of the thought is so headlong that it almost always brings us up at the conclusion before we can arrest it. Or if our purpose is nimble enough and we do arrest it, it ceases forthwith to be itself. As a snowflake crystal caught in the warm hand is no longer a crystal but a drop, so, instead of catching the feeling of relation moving to its term, we find we have caught some substantive thing, usually the last word we were pronouncing, statically taken, and with its function, tendency, and particular meaning in the sentence quite evaporated. The attempt at introspective analysis in these cases is in fact like seizing a spinning top to catch its motion, or trying to turn up the gas quickly enough to see how the darkness looks. And the challenge to *produce* these transitive states of consciousness, which is sure to be thrown by doubting psychologists at anyone who contends for their existence, is as unfair as Zeno's treatment of the advocates of motion, when, asking them to point out in what place an arrow *is* when it moves, he argues the falsity of their thesis from their inability to make to so preposterous a question an immediate reply.

The results of this introspective difficulty are baleful. If to hold fast and observe the transitive parts of thought's stream be so hard, then the great blunder to which all schools are liable must be the failure to register them, and the undue emphasizing of the more substantive parts of the stream. Now the blunder has historically worked in two ways. One set of thinkers have been led by it to *Sensationalism*. Unable to lay their hands on any substantive feelings corresponding to the innumerable relations and forms of connection between the sensible things of the world, finding no *named* mental states mirroring such relations, they have for the most part denied that any such states exist; and many of them, like Hume, have gone on to deny the reality of most relations *out* of the mind as well as in it. Simple substantive 'ideas', sensations and their copies, juxtaposed like dominoes in a game, but really separate, everything else verbal illusion, – such is the upshot of this view. The *Intellectualists*, on the other hand, unable to give up the reality of relations *extra mentem*, but equally unable to point to any distinct substantive feelings in which they were known, have made the same admission that such feelings do not exist. But they have drawn an opposite conclusion. The relations must be known, they say, in something that is no feeling, no mental 'state', continuous and consubstantial with the subjective tissue out of which sensations and other substantive conditions of consciousness are made. They must be known by something that lies on an entirely different plane, by an *actus purus* of Thought, Intellect, or Reason, all written with capitals and considered to mean something unutterably superior to any passing perishing fact of sensibility whatever.

But from our point of view both Intellectualists and Sensationalists are wrong. If there be such things as feelings at all, *then so surely as relations between objects exist* in rerum naturâ, *so surely, and more surely, do feelings exist to which these relations are known*. There is not a conjunction or a preposition, and hardly an adverbial phrase, syntactic form, or inflection of voice, in human speech, that does not express some shading or other of relation which we at some moment actually feel to exist between the larger objects of our thought. If we speak objectively, it is the real relations that appear revealed; if we speak subjectively, it is the stream of consciousness that matches each of them by an inward coloring of its own. In either case the relations are numberless, and no existing language is capable of doing justice to all their shades.

We ought to say a feeling of *and*, a feeling of *if*, a feeling of *but*, and a feeling of *by*, quite as readily as we say a feeling of *blue* or a feeling of *cold*. Yet we do not: so inveterate has our habit become of recognizing the existence of the substantive parts alone, that language almost refuses to lend itself to any other use. Consider once again the analogy of the brain. We believe the brain to be an organ whose internal equilibrium is always in a state of change – the change affecting every part. The pulses of change are doubtless more violent in one place than in another, their rhythm more rapid at this time than at that. As in a kaleidoscope revolving at a uniform rate, although the figures are always rearranging themselves, there are instants during which the transformation seems minute and interstitial and almost absent, followed by others when it shoots with magical rapidity, relatively stable forms thus alternating with forms we should not distinguish if seen again; so in the brain the perpetual rearrangement must result in some forms of tension lingering relatively long, whilst others simply come and pass. But if consciousness corresponds to the fact of rearrangement itself, why, if the rearrangement stop not, should the consciousness ever cease? And if a lingering rearrangement brings with it one kind of consciousness, why should not a swift rearrangement bring another kind of consciousness as peculiar as the rearrangement itself?

**The object before the mind always has a 'Fringe'.** There are other unnamed modifications of consciousness just as important as the transitive states, and just as cognitive as they. Examples will show what I mean.

Suppose three successive persons say to us: 'Wait!' 'Hark!' 'Look!' Our consciousness is thrown into three quite different attitudes of expectancy, although no definite object is before it in any one of the three cases. Probably no one will deny here the existence of a real conscious affection, a sense of the direction from which an impression is about to come, although no positive impression is yet there. Meanwhile we have no names for the psychoses in question but the names hark, look, and wait.

Suppose we try to recall a forgotten name. The state of our consciousness is peculiar. There is a gap therein; but no mere gap. It is a gap that is intensely active. A sort of wraith of the name is in it, beckoning us in a given direction, making us at moments tingle with the sense of our closeness, and then letting us sink back without the longed-for term. If wrong names are proposed to us, this singularly definite gap acts immediately so as to negate them. They do not fit into its mould. And the gap of one word does not feel like the gap of another, all empty of content as both might seem necessarily to be when described as gaps. When I vainly try to recall the name of Spalding, my consciousness is far removed from what it is when I vainly try to recall the name of Bowles. There are innumerable consciousnesses of *want*, no one of which taken in itself has a name, but all different from each other. Such a feeling of want is *toto cœlo* other than a want of feeling: it is an intense feeling. The rhythm of a lost word may be there without a sound to clothe it; or the evanescent sense of something which is the initial vowel or consonant may mock us fitfully, without growing more distinct. Every one must know the tantalizing effect of the blank rhythm

of some forgotten verse, restlessly dancing in one's mind, striving
to be filled out with words.

What is that first instantaneous glimpse of some one's meaning which we have, when in vulgar phrase we say we 'twig' it?
Surely an altogether specific affection of our mind. And has the
reader never asked himself what kind of a mental fact is his
*intention of saying a thing* before he has said it? It is an entirely
definite intention, distinct from all other intentions, an absolutely distinct state of consciousness, therefore; and yet how
much of it consists of definite sensorial images, either of words
or of things? Hardly anything! Linger, and the words and things
come into the mind; the anticipatory intention, the divination is
there no more. But as the words that replace it arrive, it
welcomes them successively and calls them right if they agree
with it, it rejects them and calls them wrong if they do not. The
intention *to-say-so-and-so* is the only name it can receive. One
may admit that a good third of our psychic life consists in these
rapid premonitory perspective views of schemes of thought not
yet articulate. How comes it about that a man reading something
aloud for the first time is able immediately to emphasize all his
words aright, unless from the very first he have a sense of at
least the form of the sentence yet to come, which sense is fused
with his consciousness of the present word, and modifies its
emphasis in his mind so as to make him give it the proper accent
as he utters it? Emphasis of this kind almost altogether depends
on grammatical construction. If we read 'no more', we expect
presently a 'than'; if we read 'however', it is a 'yet', a 'still', or a
'nevertheless', that we expect. And this foreboding of the coming
verbal and grammatical scheme is so practically accurate that a
reader incapable of understanding four ideas of the book he is
reading aloud can nevertheless read it with the most delicately
modulated expression of intelligence.

It is, the reader will see, the reinstatement of the vague and
inarticulate to its proper place in our mental life which I am so
anxious to press on the attention. Mr Galton and Prof Huxley
have, as we shall see in the chapter on Imagination, made one
step in advance in exploding the ridiculous theory of Hume and
Berkeley that we can have no images but of perfectly definite
things. Another is made if we overthrow the equally ridiculous
notion that, whilst simple objective qualities are revealed to our
knowledge in 'states of consciousness', relations are not. But

these reforms are not half sweeping and radical enough. What must be admitted is that the definite images of traditional psychology form but the very smallest part of our minds as they actually live. The traditional psychology talks like one who should say a river consists of nothing but pailsful, spoonsful, quartpotsful, barrelsful, and other moulded forms of water. Even were the pails and the pots all actually standing in the stream, still between them the free water would continue to flow. It is just this free water of consciousness that psychologists resolutely over-look. Every definite image in the mind is steeped and dyed in the free water that flows round it. With it goes the sense of its relations, near and remote, the dying echo of whence it came to us, the dawning sense of whither it is to lead. The significance, the value, of the image is all in this halo or penumbra that surrounds and escorts it – or rather that is fused into one with it and has become bone of its bone and flesh of its flesh; leaving it, it is true, an image of the same *thing* it was before, but making it an image of that thing newly taken and freshly understood.

*Let us call the consciousness of this halo of relations around the image by the name of 'psychic overtone' or 'fringe'.*

**Cerebral Conditions of the 'Fringe'.** Nothing is easier than to symbolize these facts in terms of brain-action. Just as the echo of the *whence*, the sense of the starting point of our thought, is probably due to the dying excitement of processes but a moment since vividly aroused; so the sense of the whither, the foretaste of the terminus, must be due to the waxing excitement of tracts or processes whose psychical correlative will a moment hence be the vividly present feature of our thought. Represented by a curve, the neurosis underlying consciousness must at any moment be like this:

Let the horizontal in Fig. 52 be the line of time, and let the three curves beginning at *a, b,* and *c* respectively stand for the neural processes correlated with the thoughts of those three letters. Each process occupies a certain time during which its intensity waxes, culminates, and wanes. The process for *a* has not yet died out, the process for *c* has already begun, when that for *b* is culminating. At the time-instant represented by the vertical line all three processes are *present*, in the intensities shown by the curve. Those before *c*'s apex *were* more intense a moment ago; those after it *will be* more intense a moment hence.

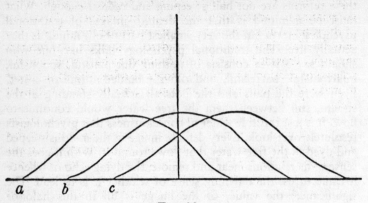

FIG. 52.

If I recite *a*, *b*, *c*, then, at the moment of uttering *b*, neither *a* nor *c* is out of my consciousness altogether, but both, after their respective fashions, 'mix their dim lights' with the stronger *b*, because their processes are both awake in some degree.

It is just like 'overtones' in music: they are not separately heard by the ear; they blend with the fundamental note, and suffuse it, and alter it; and even so do the waxing and waning brain-processes at every moment blend with and suffuse and alter the psychic effect of the processes which are at their culminating point.

**The 'Topic' of the Thought.** If we then consider the *cognitive function* of different states of mind, we may feel assured that the difference between those that are mere 'acquaintance' and those that are 'knowledges-*about*' is reducible almost entirely to the absence or presence of psychic fringes or overtones. Knowledge *about* a thing is knowledge of its relations. Acquaintance with it is limitation to the bare impression which it makes. Of most of its relations we are only aware in the penumbral nascent way of a 'fringe' of unarticulated affinities about it. And, before passing to the next topic in order, I must say a little of this sense of affinity, as itself one of the most interesting features of the subjective stream.

**Thought may be equally rational in any sort of terms.** *In all our voluntary thinking there is some* TOPIC *or* SUBJECT *about* which all the members of the thought revolve. Relation to this topic or interest is constantly felt in the fringe, and particularly the relation of harmony and discord, of furtherance or hindrance of the topic. Any thought the quality of whose fringe lets us feel ourselves 'all right', may be considered a thought that furthers the topic. Provided we only feel its object to have a place in the scheme of relations in which the topic also lies, that is sufficient to make of it a relevant and appropriate portion of our train of ideas.

Now we may think about our topic mainly in words, or we may think about it mainly in visual or other images, but this need make no difference as regards the furtherance of our knowledge of the topic. If we only feel in the terms, whatever they be, a fringe of affinity with each other and with the topic, and if we are conscious of approaching a conclusion, we feel that our thought is rational and right. The words in every language have contracted by long association fringes of mutual repugnance or affinity with each other and with the conclusion, which run exactly parallel with like fringes in the visual, tactile, and other ideas. The most important element of these fringes is, I repeat, the mere feeling of harmony or discord, of a right or wrong direction in the thought.

If we know English and French and begin a sentence in French, all the later words that come are French; we hardly ever drop into English. And this affinity of the French words for each other is not something merely operating mechanically as a brain-law, it is something we feel at the time. Our understanding of a French sentence heard never falls to so low an ebb that we are not aware that the words linguistically belong together. Our attention can hardly so wander that if an English word be suddenly introduced we shall not start at the change. Such a vague sense as this of the words belonging together is the very minimum of fringe that can accompany them, if 'thought' at all. Usually the vague perception that all the words we hear belong to the same language and to the same special vocabulary in that language, and that the grammatical sequence is familiar, is practically equivalent to an admission that what we hear is sense. But if an unusual foreign word be introduced, if the grammar trip, or if a term from an incongruous vocabulary suddenly appear, such as 'rat-trap or 'plumber's bill' in a philosophical discourse, the sentence detonates as it were, we receive a shock from the incongruity, and the drowsy assent is gone. The feeling of rationality in these cases seems rather a negative than a positive thing, being the mere absence of shock, or sense of discord, between the terms of thought.

Conversely, if words do belong to the same vocabulary, and if the grammatical structure is correct, sentences with absolutely no meaning may be uttered in good faith and pass unchallenged. Discourses at prayer-meetings, reshuffling the same collection of cant phrases, and the whole genus of penny-a-line-isms and newspaper-reporter's flourishes give illustrations of this. 'The birds filled the tree-tops with their morning song, making the air moist, cool, and pleasant', is a sentence I remember reading once in a report of some athletic exercises in Jerome Park. It was probably written unconsciously by the hurried reporter, and read uncritically by many readers.

We see, then, that it makes little or no difference in what sort of mind-stuff, in what quality of imagery, our thinking goes on. The only images *intrinsically* important are the halting-places, the substantive conclusions, provisional or final, of the thought. Throughout all the rest of the stream, the feelings of relation are everything, and the terms related almost naught. These feelings of relation, these psychic overtones, halos, suffusions, or fringes about the terms, may be the same in very different systems of imagery. A diagram may help to accentuate this indifference of the mental means where the end is the same. Let $A$ be some experience from which a number of thinkers start. Let $Z$ be the

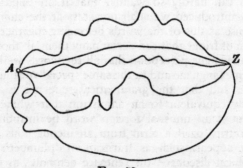

FIG. 53.

practical conclusion rationally inferrible from it. One gets to this conclusion by one line, another by another; one follows a course of English, another of German, verbal imagery. With one, visual images predominate; with another, tactile. Some trains are tinged with emotions, others not; some are very abridged, synthetic and rapid; others, hesitating and broken into many steps. But when the penultimate terms of all the trains, however differing *inter se*, finally shoot into the same conclusion, we say, and rightly say, that all the thinkers have had substantially the same thought. It would probably astound each of them beyond measure to be let into his neighbor's mind and to find how different the scenery there was from that in his own.

The last peculiarity to which attention is to be drawn in this first rough description of thought's stream is that —

**Consciousness is always interested more in one part of its object than in another, and welcomes and rejects, or chooses, all the while it thinks.**

The phenomena of selective attention and of deliberative will are of course patent examples of this choosing activity. But few of us are aware how incessantly it is at work in operations not ordinarily called by these names. Accentuation and Emphasis are present in every perception we have. We find it quite impossible to disperse our attention impartially over a number of impressions. A monotonous succession of sonorous strokes is broken up into rhythms, now of one sort, now of another, by the different accent which we place on different strokes. The simplest of these rhythms is the double one, tick-tóck, tick-tóck, tick-tóck. Dots dispersed on a surface are perceived in rows and groups. Lines separate into diverse figures. The ubiquity of the distinctions, *this* and *that, here* and *there, now* and *then*, in our minds is the result of our laying the same selective emphasis on parts of place and time.

But we do far more than emphasize things, and unite some, and keep others apart. We actually *ignore* most of the things before us. Let me briefly show how this goes on.

To begin at the bottom, what are our very senses themselves [. . .] but organs of selection? Out of the infinite chaos of movements, of which physics teaches us that the outer world consists, each sense-organ picks out those which fall within certain limits of velocity. To these it responds, but ignores the rest as completely as if they did not exist. Out of what is in itself an undistinguishable, swarming *continuum*, devoid of distinction or emphasis, our senses make for us, by attending to this motion and ignoring that, a world full of contrasts, of sharp accents, of abrupt changes, of picturesque light and shade.

If the sensations we receive from a given organ have their causes thus picked out for us by conformation of the organ's termination, Attention, on the other hand, out of all the sensations yielded, picks out certain ones as worthy of its notice and suppresses all the rest. We notice only those sensations which are signs to us of *things* which happen practically or æsthetically to interest us, to which we therefore give substantive names, and which we exalt to this exclusive status of independence and dignity. But in itself, apart from my interest, a particular dust-wreath on a windy day is just as much of an individual *thing*, and just as much or as little deserves an individual name, as my own body does.

And then, among the sensations we get from each separate thing, what happens? The mind selects again. It chooses certain of the sensations to represent the thing most *truly*, and considers the rest as its appearances, modified by the conditions of the moment. Thus my table-top is named *square*, after but one of an infinite number of retinal sensations which it yields, the rest of them being sensations of two acute and two obtuse angles; but I call the latter *perspective* views, and the four right angles the *true* form of the table, and erect the attribute squareness into the table's essence, for æsthetic reasons of my own. In like manner, the real form of the circle is deemed to be the sensation it gives when the line of vision is perpendicular to its centre – all its other sensations are *signs* of this sensation. The real sound of the cannon is the sensation it makes when the ear is close by. The real color of the brick is the sensation it gives when the eye looks squarely at it from a near point, out of the sunshine and yet not in the gloom; under other circumstances it gives us other color-sensations which are but signs of this – we then see it looks pinker or bluer than it really is. The reader knows no object which he does not represent to himself by preference as in some typical attitude, of some normal size, at some characteristic distance, of some standard tint, etc., etc. But all these essential characteristics, which together form for us the genuine objectivity of the thing and are contrasted with what we call the subjective sensations it may yield us at a given moment, are mere sensations like the latter. The mind chooses to suit itself, and decides what particular sensation shall be held more real and valid than all the rest.

Next, in a world of objects thus individualized by our mind's selective industry, what is called our 'experience' is almost entirely determined by our habits of attention. A thing may be present to a man a hundred times, but if he persistently fails to notice it, it cannot be said to enter into his experience. We are all seeing flies, moths, and beetles by the thousand, but to whom, save an entomologist, do they say anything distinct? On the other hand, a thing met only once in a lifetime may leave an indelible experience in the memory. Let four men make a tour in Europe. One will bring home only picturesque impressions – costumes and colors, parks and views and works of architecture, pictures and statues. To another all this will be non-existent; and distances and prices, populations and drainage-arrangements, door- and window-fastenings, and other useful statistics will take their place. A third will give a rich account of the theatres, restaurants, and public halls, and naught beside; whilst the fourth will perhaps have been so wrapped in his own subjective broodings as to be able to tell little more than a few names of places through which he passed. Each has selected, out of the same mass of presented objects, those which suited his private interest and has made his experience thereby.

If now, leaving the empirical combination of objects, we ask how the mind proceeds *rationally* to connect them, we find selection again to be omnipotent. In a future chapter we shall see that all Reasoning depends on the ability of the mind to break up the totality of the phenomenon reasoned about, into parts, and to pick out from among these the particular one which, in the given emergency, may lead to the proper conclusion. The man of genius is he who will always stick in his bill at the right point, and bring it out with the right element – 'reason' if the emergency be theoretical, 'means' if it be practical – transfixed upon it.

If now we pass to the æsthetic department, our law is still more obvious. The artist notoriously selects his items, rejecting all tones, colors, shapes, which do not harmonize with each other and with the main purpose of his work. That unity, harmony, 'convergence of characters', as M. Taine calls it, which gives to works of art their superiority over works of nature, is wholly due to *elmination*. Any natural subject will do, if the artist has wit enough to pounce upon some one feature of it as characteristic, and suppress all merely accidental items which do not harmonize with this.

Ascending still higher, we reach the plane of Ethics, where choice reigns notoriously supreme. An act has no ethical quality whatever unless it be chosen out of several all equally possible. To sustain the arguments for the good course and keep them ever before us, to stifle our longing for more flowery ways, to keep the foot unflinchingly on the arduous path, these are characteristic ethical energies. But more than these; for these but deal with the means of compassing interests already felt by the man to be supreme. The ethical energy *par excellence* has to go farther and choose which *interest* out of several, equally coercive, shall become supreme. The issue here is of the utmost pregnancy, for it decides a man's entire career. When he debates, Shall I commit this crime? choose that profession? accept that office, or marry this fortune? – his choice really lies between one of several equally possible future Characters. What he shall *become* is fixed by the conduct of this moment. Schopenhauer, who enforces his determinism by the argument that with a given fixed character only one reaction is possible under given circumstances, forgets that, in these critical ethical moments, what consciously *seems* to be in question is the complexion of the character itself. The problem with the man is less what act he shall now resolve to do than what being he shall now choose to become.

Taking human experience in a general way, the choosings of different men are to a great extent the same. The race as a whole largely agrees as to what it shall notice and name; and among the noticed parts we select in much the same way for accentuation and preference, or subordination and dislike. There is, however, one entirely extraordinary case in which no two men ever are known to choose alike. One great splitting of the whole universe into two halves is made by each of us; and for each of us almost all the interest attaches to one of the halves; but we all draw the line of division between them in a different place. When I say that we all call the two halves by the same names, and that those names are '*me*' and *not-me*' respectively, it will at once be seen what I mean. The altogether unique kind of interest which each human mind feels in those parts of creation which it can call *me* or *mine* may be a moral riddle, but it is a fundamental psychological fact. No mind can take the same interest in his neighbor's *me* as in his own. The neighbor's me falls together with all the rest of things in one foreign mass against which his own *me* stands out in startling relief. Even the trodden worm, as Lotze somewhere says, contrasts his own suffering self with the whole remaining universe, though he have no clear conception either of himself or of what the universe may be. He is for me a mere part of the world; for him it is I who am the mere part. Each of us dichotomizes the Kosmos in a different place.

JOHN B. WATSON

# Psychology as the Behaviorist Views it

Psychology as the behaviorist views it is a purely objective experimental branch of natural science. Its theoretical goal is the prediction and control of behavior. Introspection forms no essential part of its methods, nor is the scientific value of its data dependent upon the readiness with which they lend themselves to interpretation in terms of consciousness. The behaviorist, in his efforts to get a unitary scheme of animal response, recognizes no dividing line between man and brute. The behavior of man, with all of its refinement and complexity, forms only a part of the behaviorist's total scheme of investigation.

It has been maintained by its followers generally that psychology is a study of the science of the phenomena of consciousness. It has taken as its problem, on the one hand, the analysis of complex mental states (or processes) into simple elementary constituents, and on the other the construction of complex states when the elementary constituents are given. The world of physical objects (stimuli, including here anything which may excite activity in a receptor), which forms the total phenomena of the natural scientist, is looked upon merely as means to an end. That end is the production of mental states that may be 'inspected' or 'observed'. The psychological object of observation in the case of an emotion, for example, is the mental state itself. The problem in emotion is the determination of the number and kind of elementary constituents present, their loci, intensity, order of appearance, etc. It is agreed that introspection is the method *par excellence* by means of which mental states may be manipulated for purposes of psychology. On this assumption, behavior data (including under this term everything which goes under the name of comparative psychology) have no value *per se*. They possess significance only in so far as they may throw light upon conscious states.[1] Such data must have at least an analogical or indirect reference to belong to the realm of psychology.

Indeed, at times, one finds psychologists who are sceptical of even this analogical reference. Such scepticism is often shown by the question which is put to the student of behavior, 'what is the bearing of animal work upon human psychology?' I used to have to study over this question. Indeed it always embarrassed me somewhat. I was interested in my own work and felt that it was important, and yet I could not trace any close connection between it and psychology as my questioner understood psychology. I hope that such a confession will clear the atmosphere to such an extent that we will no longer have to work under false pretences. We must frankly admit that the facts so important to us which we have been able to glean from extended work upon the senses of animals by the behavior method have contributed only in a fragmentary way to the general theory of human sense organ processes, nor have they suggested new points of experimental attack. The enormous number of experiments which we have carried out upon learning have likewise contributed little to human psychology. It seems reasonably clear that some kind of compromise must be affected: either psychology must change its viewpoint so as to take in facts of behavior, whether or not they have bearings upon the problems of 'consciousness'; or else behavior must stand alone as a wholly separate and independent science. Should human psychologists fail to look with favor upon our overtures and refuse to modify their position, the behaviorists will be driven to using human beings as subjects and to employ methods of investigation which are exactly comparable to those now employed in the animal work.

Any other hypothesis than that which admits the independent value of behavior material, regardless of any bearing such material may have upon consciousness, will inevitably force us to the absurd position of attempting to *construct* the conscious content of the animal whose behavior we have been studying. On this view, after having determined our animal's ability to learn, the simplicity or complexity of its methods of learning, the effect of past habit upon present response, the range of stimuli to which it ordinarily responds, the widened range to which it can respond under experimental conditions – in more general terms, its various problems and its various ways of solving them – we should still feel that the task is unfinished and that the results are worthless, until we can interpret them by analogy in the light of consciousness. Although we have solved our problem we feel uneasy and unrestful because of our definition of psychology: we feel forced to say something about the possible mental processes of our animal. We say that, having no eyes, its stream of consciousness cannot contain brightness and color sensations as we know them – having no taste buds this stream can contain no sensations of sweet, sour, salt and bitter. But on the other hand, since it does respond to thermal, tactual and organic stimuli, its conscious content must be made up largely of these sensations; and we usually add, to protect ourselves against the reproach of being anthropomorphic, 'if it has any consciousness'. Surely this doctrine which calls for an anological interpretation of all behavior data may be shown to be false: the position that the standing of an observation upon behavior is determined by its fruitfulness in yielding results which are interpretable only in the narrow realm of (really human) consciousness.

This emphasis upon analogy in psychology has led the behaviorist somewhat afield. Not being willing to throw off the yoke of consciousness he feels impelled to make a place in the scheme of behavior where the rise of consciousness can be determined. This point has been a shifting one. A few years ago certain animals were supposed to possess 'associative memory', while certain others were supposed to lack it. One meets this search for the origin of consciousness under a good many disguises. Some of our texts state that consciousness arises at the moment when reflex and instinctive activities fail properly to conserve the organism. A perfectly adjusted organism would be lacking in consciousness. On the other hand whenever we find the presence of diffuse activity which results in habit formation, we are justified in assuming consciousness. I must confess that these arguments had weight with me when I began the study of behavior. I fear that a good many of us are still viewing behavior problems with something like this in mind. More than one student in behavior has attempted to frame criteria of the psychic – to devise a set of objective, structural and functional criteria which, when applied in the particular instance, will enable us to decide whether such and such responses are positively conscious, merely indicative of consciousness, or whether they are purely 'physiological'. Such problems as these can no longer satisfy behavior men. It would be better to give

up the province altogether and admit frankly that the study of
the behavior of animals has no justification, than to admit that
our search is of such a 'will o' the wisp' character. One can
assume either the presence or the absence of consciousness
anywhere in the phylogenetic scale without affecting the problems of behavior by one jot or one tittle; and without influencing
in any way the mode of experimental attack upon them. On the
other hand, I cannot for one moment assume that the parame-
cium responds to light; that the rat learns a problem more
quickly by working at the task five times a day than once a day,
or that the human child exhibits plateaux in his learning curves.
These are questions which vitally concern behavior and which
must be decided by direct observation under experimental
conditions.

This attempt to reason by analogy from human conscious
processes to the conscious processes in animals, and *vice versa*:
to make consciousness, as the human being knows it, the center
of reference of all behavior, forces us into a situation similar to
that which existed in biology in Darwin's time. The whole
Darwinian movement was judged by the bearing it had upon
the origin and development of the human race. Expeditions
were undertaken to collect material which would establish the
position that the rise of the human race was a perfectly natural
phenomenon and not an act of special creation. Variations were
carefully sought along with the evidence for the heaping up
effect and the weeding out effect of selection; for in these and
the other Darwinian mechanisms were to be found factors
sufficiently complex to account for the origin and race differentiation of man. The wealth of material collected at this time was
considered valuable largely in so far as it tended to develop the
concept of evolution in man. It is strange that this situation
should have remained the dominant one in biology for so many
years. The moment zoology undertook the experimental study
of evolution and descent, the situation immediately changed.
Man ceased to be the center of reference. I doubt if any
experimental biologist today, unless actually engaged in the
problem of race differentiation in man, tries to interpret his
findings in terms of human evolution, or ever refers to it in his
thinking. He gathers his data from the study of many species of
plants and animals and tries to work out the laws of inheritance
in the particular type upon which he is conducting experiments.

Naturally, he follows the progress of the work upon race differentiation in man and in the descent of man, but he looks upon these as special topics, equal in importance with his own yet ones in which his interests will never be vitally engaged. It is not fair to say that all of his work is directed toward human evolution or that it must be interpreted in terms of human evolution. He does not have to dismiss certain of his facts on the inheritance of coat color in mice because, forsooth, they have little bearing upon the differentiation of the *genus homo* into separate races, or upon the descent of the *genus homo* from some more primitive stock.

In psychology we are still in that stage of development where we feel that we must select our material. We have a general place of discard for processes, which we anathematize so far as their value for psychology is concerned by saying, 'this is a reflex'; 'that is a purely physiological fact which has nothing to do with psychology'. We are not interested (as psychologists) in getting all of the processes of adjustment which the animal as a whole employs, and in finding how these various responses are associated, and how they fall apart, thus working out a systematic scheme for the prediction and control of response in general. Unless our observed facts are indicative of consciousness, we have no use for them, and unless our apparatus and method are designed to throw such facts into relief, they are thought of in just as disparaging a way. I shall always remember the remark one distinguished psychologist made as he looked over the color apparatus designed for testing the responses of animals to monochromatic light in the attic at Johns Hopkins. It was this: 'And they call this psychology!'

I do not wish unduly to criticize psychology. It has failed signally, I believe, during the fifty-odd years of its existence as an experimental discipline to make its place in the world as an undisputed natural science. Psychology, as it is generally thought of, has something esoteric in its methods. If you fail to reproduce my findings, it is not due to some fault in your apparatus or in the control of your stimulus, but it is due to the fact that your introspection is untrained.[2] The attack is made upon the observer and not upon the experimental setting. In physics and in chemistry the attack is made upon the experimental conditions. The apparatus was not sensitive enough, impure chemicals were used, etc. In these sciences a better technique will give reproducible results. Psychology is otherwise. If you can't observe 3–9 states of clearness in attention, your introspection is poor. If, on the other hand, a feeling seems reasonably clear to you, your introspection is again faulty. You are seeing too much. Feelings are never clear.

The time seems to have come when psychology must discard all reference to consciousness; when it need no longer delude itself into thinking that it is making mental states the object of observation. We have become so enmeshed in speculative questions concerning the elements of mind, the nature of conscious content (for example, imageless thought, attitudes, and Bewusseinslage, etc.) that I, as an experimental student, feel that something is wrong with our premises and the types of problems which develop from them. There is no longer any guarantee that we all mean the same thing when we use the terms now current in psychology. Take the case of sensation. A sensation is defined in terms of its attributes. One psychologist will state with readiness that the attributes of a visual sensation are *quality, extension, duration*, and *intensity*. Another will add *clearness*. Still another that of *order*. I doubt if any one psychologist can draw up a set of statements describing what he means by sensation which will be agreed to by three other psychologists of different training. Turn for a moment to the question of the number of isolable sensations. Is there an extremely large number of color sensations – or only four, red, green, yellow and blue? Again, yellow, while psychologically simple, can be obtained by superimposing red and green spectral rays upon the same diffusing surface! If, on the other hand, we say that every just noticeable difference in the spectrum is a simple sensation, and that every just noticeable increase in the white value of a given colour gives simple sensations, we are forced to admit that the number is so large and the conditions for obtaining them so complex that the concept of sensation is unusable, either for the purpose of analysis or that of synthesis. Titchener, who has fought the most valiant fight in this country for a psychology based upon introspection, feels that these differences of opinion as to the number of sensations and their attributes; as to whether there are relations (in the sense of elements) and on the many others which seem to be fundamental in every attempt at analysis, are perfectly natural in the present undeveloped state of psychology. While it is admitted that every growing science is full of unanswered questions, surely only those who are wedded to the system as we now have it, who have fought and suffered for it, can confidently believe that there will ever be any greater uniformity than there is now in the answers we have to such questions. I firmly believe that two hundred years from now, unless the introspective method is discarded, psychology will still be divided on the question as to whether auditory sensations have the quality of 'extension', whether intensity is an attribute which can be applied to color, whether there is a difference in 'texture' between image and sensation and upon many hundreds of others of like character.

The condition in regard to other mental processes is just as chaotic. Can image type be experimentally tested and verified? Are recondite thought processes dependent mechanically upon imagery at all? Are psychologists agreed upon what feeling is? One states that feelings are attitudes. Another finds them to be groups of organic sensations possessing a certain solidarity. Still another and larger group finds them to be new elements correlative with and ranking equally with sensations.

My psychological quarrel is not with the systematic and structural psychologist alone. The last fifteen years have seen the growth of what is called functional psychology. This type of psychology decries the use of elements in the static sense of the structuralists. It throws emphasis upon the biological significance of conscious processes instead of upon the analysis of conscious states into introspectively isolable elements. I have done my best to understand the difference between functional psychology and structural psychology. Instead of clarity, confusion grows upon me. The terms sensation, perception, affection, emotion, volition are used as much by the functionalist as by the structuralist. The addition of the word 'process' ('mental act as a whole', and like terms are frequently met) after each serves in some way to remove the corpse of 'content' and to leave 'function' in its stead. Surely if these concepts are elusive when looked at from a content standpoint, they are still more deceptive when viewed from the angle of function, and especially so when function is obtained by the introspection method. It is rather interesting that no functional psychologist has carefully distinguished between 'perception' (and this is true of the other psychological terms as well) as employed by the systematist, and 'perceptual process' as used in functional psychology. It seems illogical and hardly fair to criticize the psychology which the systematist gives us, and then to utilize his terms without carefully showing the changes in meaning which are to be attached to them. I was greatly surprised some time ago when I opened Pillsbury's book and saw psychology defined as the 'science of behavior'. A still more recent text states that psychology is the 'science of mental behavior'. When I saw these promising statements I thought, now surely we will have texts based upon different lines. After a few pages the science of behavior is dropped and one finds the conventional treatment of sensation, perception, imagery, etc., along with certain shifts in emphasis and additional facts which serve to give the author's personal imprint.

One of the difficulties in the way of a consistent functional psychology is the parallelistic hypothesis. If the functionalist attempts to express his formulations in terms which make mental states really appear to function, to play some active role in the world of adjustment, he almost inevitably lapses into terms which are connotative of interaction. When taxed with this he replies that it is more convenient to do so and that he does it to avoid the circumlocution and clumsiness which are inherent in any thoroughgoing parallelism.[3] As a matter of fact I believe the functionalist actually thinks in terms of interaction and resorts to parallelism only when forced to give expression to his views. I feel that *behaviorism* is the only consistent and logical functionalism. In it one avoids both the Scylla of parallelism and the Charybdis of interaction. Those time-honored relics of philosophical speculation need trouble the student of behavior as little as they trouble the student of physics. The consideration of the mind-body problem affects neither the type of problem selected nor the formulation of the solution of that problem. I can state my position here no better than by saying that I should like to bring my students up in the same ignorance of such hypotheses as one finds among the students of other branches of science.

This leads me to the point where I should like to make the argument constructive. I believe we can write a psychology, define it as Pillsbury, and never go back upon our definition: never use the terms consciousness, mental states, mind, content, introspectively verifiable, imagery, and the like. I believe that we can do it in a few years without running into the absurd terminology of Beer, Bethe, Von Uexküll, Nuel, and that of the so-called objective schools generally. It can be done in terms of stimulus and response, in terms of habit formation, habit integrations and the like. Furthermore, I believe that it is really worth while to make this attempt now.

The psychology which I should attempt to build up would take as a starting point, first, the observable fact that organisms, man and animal alike, do adjust themselves to their environment by means of hereditary and habit equipments. These adjustments may be very adequate or they may be so inadequate that the organism barely maintains its existence; secondly, that certain stimuli lead the organisms to make the responses. In a system of psychology completely worked out, given the response the stimuli can be predicted; given the stimuli the response can be predicted. Such a set of statements is crass and raw in the extreme, as all such generalizations must be. Yet they are hardly more raw and less realizable than the ones which appear in the psychology texts of the day. I possibly might illustrate my point better by choosing an everyday problem which anyone is likely to meet in the course of his work. Some time ago I was called upon to make a study of certain species of birds. Until I went to Tortugas I had never seen these birds alive. When I reached there I found the animals doing certain things: some of the acts seemed to work peculiarly well in such an environment, while others seemed to be unsuited to their type of life. I first studied the responses of the group as a whole and later those of individuals. In order to understand more thoroughly the relation between what was habit and what was hereditary in these responses, I took the young birds and reared them. In this way I was able to study the order of appearance of hereditary adjustments and their complexity, and later the beginnings of habit formation. My efforts in determining the stimuli which called forth such adjustments were crude indeed. Consequently my attempts to control behavior and to produce responses at will did not meet with much success. Their food and water, sex and other social relations, light and temperature conditions were all beyond control in a field study. I did find it possible to control their reactions in a measure by using the nest and egg (or young) as stimuli. It is not necessary in this paper to develop further how such a study should be carried out and how work of this kind must be supplemented by carefully controlled laboratory experiments. Had I been called upon to examine the natives of some of the Australian tribes, I should have gone about my task in the same way. I should have found the problem more difficult: the types of responses called forth by physical stimuli would have been more varied, and the number of effective stimuli larger. I should have had to determine the social setting of their lives in a far more careful way. These savages would be more influenced by the responses of each other than was the case with the birds. Furthermore, habits would have been more complex and the influences of past habits upon the present responses would have appeared more clearly. Finally, if I had been called upon to work out the psychology of the educated European, my problem would have required several lifetimes. But in the one I have at my disposal I should have followed the same general line of attack. In the main, my desire in all such work is to gain an accurate knowledge of adjustments and the stimuli calling them forth. My final reason for this is to learn general and particular methods by which I may control behavior. My goal is not 'the description and explanation of states of consciousness as such', nor that of obtaining such proficiency in mental gymnastics that I can immediately lay hold of a state of consciousness and say, 'this, as a whole, consists of gray sensation number 350, of such and such extent, occurring in conjunction with the sensation of cold of a certain intensity; one of pressure of a certain intensity and extent,' and so on *ad infinitum*. If psychology would follow the plan I suggest, the educator, the physician, the jurist and the business man could utilize our data in a practical way, as soon as we are able, experimentally, to obtain them. Those who have occasion to apply psychological principles practically would find no need to complain as they do at the present time. Ask any physician or jurist today whether scientific psychology plays a practical part in his daily routine and you will hear him deny that the psychology of the laboratories finds a place in his scheme of work. I think the criticism is extremely just. One of the earliest conditions which made me dissatisfied with psychology was the feeling that there was no realm of application for the principles which were being worked out in content terms.

What gives me hope that the behaviorist's position is a defensible one is the fact that those branches of psychology which have already partially withdrawn from the parent, experimental psychology, and which are consequently less dependent upon introspection are today in a most flourishing condition. Experimental pedagogy, the psychology of drugs, the psychology of advertising, legal psychology, the psychology of tests, and psychopathology are all vigorous growths. These are sometimes wrongly called 'practical' or 'applied' psychology. Surely there was never a worse misnomer. In the future there may grow up vocational bureaus which really apply psychology. At present these fields are truly scientific and are in search of broad generalizations which will lead to the control of human behavior. For example, we find out by experimentation whether a series of stanzas may be acquired more readily if the whole is learned at once, or whether it is more advantageous to learn each stanza separately and then pass to the succeeding. We do not attempt to apply our findings. The application of this principle is purely voluntary on the part of the teacher. In the psychology of drugs we may show the effect upon behavior of certain doses of caffeine. We may reach the conclusion that caffeine has a good effect upon the speed and accuracy of work. But these are general principles. We leave it to the individual as to whether the results of our tests shall be applied or not. Again, in legal testimony, we test the effects of recency upon the reliability of a witness's report. We test the accuracy of the report with respect to moving objects, stationary objects, color, etc. It depends upon the judicial machinery of the country to decide whether these facts are ever to be applied. For a 'pure' psychologist to say that he is not interested in the questions raised in these divisions of the science because they relate indirectly to the application of psychology shows, in the first place, that he fails to understand the scientific aim in such problems, and secondly, that he is not interested in a psychology which concerns itself with human life. The only fault I have to find with these disciplines is that much of their material is stated in terms of introspection, whereas a statement in terms of objective results would be far more valuable. There is no reason why appeal should ever be made to consciousness in any of them. Or why introspective data should ever be sought during the experimentation, or published in the results. In experimental pedagogy especially one can see the desirability of keeping all of the results on a purely objective plane. If this is done, work there on the human being will be comparable directly with the work upon animals. For example, at Hopkins, Mr Ulrich has obtained certain results upon the distribution of effort in learning – using rats as subjects. He is prepared to give comparative results upon the effect of having an animal work at the problem once per day, three times per day, and five times per day. Whether it is advisable to have the animal learn only one problem at a time or to learn three abreast. We need to have similar experiments made upon man, but we care as little about his 'conscious processes' during the conduct of the experiment as we care about such processes in the rats.

I am more interested at the present moment in trying to show the necessity for maintaining uniformity in experimental procedure and in the method of stating results in both human and animal work, than in developing any ideas I may have upon the changes which are certain to come in the scope of human psychology. Let us consider for a moment the subject of the range of stimuli to which animals respond. I shall speak first of the work upon vision in animals. We put our animal in a situation where he will respond (or learn to respond) to one of two monochromatic lights. We feed him at the one (positive) and punish him at the other (negative). In a short time the animal learns to go to the light at which he is fed. At this point questions arise which I may phrase in two ways: I may choose the psychological way and say 'does the animal see these two lights as I do, *i.e.*, as two distinct colors, or does he see them as two grays differing in brightness, as does the totally color blind?' Phrased by the behaviorist, it would read as follows: 'Is my animal responding upon the basis of the difference in intensity between the two stimuli, or upon the difference in wavelengths?' He nowhere thinks of the animal's response in terms of his own experiences of colors and grays. He wishes to establish the fact whether wave-length is a factor in that animal's adjustment.[4] If so, what wave-lengths are effective and what differences in wave-length must be maintained in the different regions to afford bases for differential responses? If wave-length is not a factor in adjustment he wishes to know what difference in intensity will serve as a basis for response, and whether that same difference will suffice throughout the spectrum. Furthermore, he wishes to test whether the animal can respond to wave-lengths which do not affect the human eye. He is as much interested in comparing the rat's spectrum with that of the chick as in comparing it with man's. The point of view when the various sets of comparisons are made does not change in the slightest.

However we phrase the question to ourselves, we take our animal after the association has been formed and then introduce certain control experiments which enable us to return answers to the questions just raised. But there is just as keen a desire on our part to test man under the same conditions, and to state the results in both cases in common terms.

The man and the animal should be placed as nearly as possible under the same experimental conditions. Instead of feeding or punishing the human subject, we should ask him to respond by setting a second apparatus until standard and control offered no basis for a differential response. Do I lay myself open to the charge here that I am using introspection? My reply is not at all; that while I might very well feed my human subject for a right choice and punish him for a wrong one and thus produce the response if the subject could give it, there is no need of going to extremes even on the platform I suggest. But be it understood that I am merely using this second method as an abridged behavior method.[5] We can go just as far and reach just as dependable results by the longer method as by the abridged. In many cases the direct and typically human method cannot be safely used. Suppose, for example, that I doubt the accuracy of the setting of the control instrument, in the above experiment, as I am very likely to do if I suspect a defect in vision? It is hopeless for me to get his introspective report. He will say: 'There is no difference in sensation, both are reds, identical in quality.' But suppose I confront him with the standard and the control and so arrange conditions that he is punished if he responds to the 'control' but not with the standard. I interchange the positions of the standard and the control at will and force him to attempt to differentiate the one from the other. If he can learn to make the adjustment even after a large number of trials it is evident that the two stimuli do afford the basis for a differential response. Such a method may sound nonsensical, but I firmly believe we will have to resort increasingly to just such method where we have reason to distrust the language method.

There is hardly a problem in human vision which is not also a problem in animal vision: I mention the limits of the spectrum, threshold values, absolute and relative, flicker, Talbot's law, Weber's law, field of vision, the Purkinje phenomenon, etc. Every one is capable of being worked out by behavior methods. Many of them are being worked out at the present time.

I feel that all the work upon the senses can be consistently carried forward along the lines I have suggested here for vision. Our results will, in the end, give an excellent picture of what each organ stands for in the way of function. The anatomist and the physiologist may take our data and show, on the one hand, the structures which are responsible for these responses, and, on the other, the physico-chemical relations which are necessarily involved (physiological chemistry of nerve and muscle) in these and other reactions.

The situation in regard to the study of memory is hardly different. Nearly all of the memory methods in actual use in the laboratory today yield the type of results I am arguing for. A certain series of nonsense syllables or other material is presented to the human subject. What should receive the emphasis are the rapidity of the habit formation, the errors, peculiarities in the form of the curve, the persistence of the habit so formed, the relation of such habits to those formed when more complex material is used, etc. Now such results are taken down with the subject's introspection. The experiments are made for the purpose of discussing the mental machinery[6] involved in learning, in recall, recollection and forgetting, and not for the purpose of seeking the human being's way of shaping his responses to meet the problems in the terribly complex environment into which he is thrown, nor for that of showing the similarities and differences between man's methods and those of other animals.

The situation is somewhat different when we come to a study of the more complex forms of behavior, such as imagination, judgment, reasoning, and conception. At present the only statements we have of them are in content terms.[7] Our minds have been so warped by the fifty-odd years which have been devoted to the study of states of consciousness that we can envisage these problems only in one way. We should meet the situation squarely and say that we are not able to carry forward investigations along all of these lines by the behavior methods which are in use at the present time. In extenuation I should like to call attention to the paragraph above where I made the point that the introspective method itself has reached a *cul-de-sac* with respect to them. The topics have become so threadbare from much handling that they may well be put away for a time. As our methods become better developed it will be possible to undertake investigations of more and more complex forms of behavior. Problems which are now laid aside will again become imperative, but they can be viewed as they arise from a new angle and in more concrete settings.

Will there be left over in psychology a world of pure psychics, to use Yerkes' term? I confess I do not know. The plans which I most favor for psychology lead practically to the ignoring of consciousness in the sense that that term is used by psychologists today. I have virtually denied that this realm of psychics is open to experimental investigation. I don't wish to go further into the problem at present because it leads inevitably over into metaphysics. If you will grant the behaviorist the right to use consciousness in the same way that other natural scientists employ it – that is, without making consciousness a special object of observation – you have granted all that my thesis requires.

In concluding, I suppose I must confess to a deep bias on these questions. I have devoted nearly twelve years to experimentation on animals. It is natural that such a one should drift into a theoretical position which is in harmony with his experimental work. Possibly I have put up a straw man and have been fighting that. There may be no absolute lack of harmony between the position outlined here and that of functional psychology. I am inclined to think, however, that the two positions cannot be easily harmonized. Certainly the position I advocate is weak enough at present and can be attacked from many standpoints. Yet when all this is admitted I still feel that the considerations which I have urged should have a wide influence upon the type of psychology which is to be developed in the future. What we need to do is to start work upon psychology, making *behavior*, not *consciousness*, the objective point of our attack. Certainly there are enough problems in the control of behavior to keep us all working many lifetimes without ever allowing us time to think of consciousness *an sich*. Once launched in the undertaking, we will find ourselves in a short time as far divorced from an introspective psychology as the psychology of the present time is divorced from faculty psychology.

## Summary

1. Human psychology has failed to make good its claim as a natural science. Due to a mistaken notion that its fields of facts are conscious phenomena and that introspection is the only direct method of ascertaining these facts, it has enmeshed itself in a series of speculative questions which, while fundamental to its present tenets, are not open to experimental treatment. In the pursuit of answers to these questions, it has become further and further divorced from contact with problems which vitally concern human interest.

2. Psychology, as the behaviorist views it, is a purely objective, experimental branch of natural science which needs introspection as little as do the sciences of chemistry and physics. It is granted that the behavior of animals can be investigated without appeal to consciousness. Heretofore the viewpoint has been that such data have value only in so far as they can be interpreted by analogy in terms of consciousness. The position is taken here that the behavior of man and the behavior of animals must be considered on the same plane; as being equally essential to a general understanding of behavior. It can dispense with consciousness in a psychological sense. The separate observation of 'states of consciousness', is, on this assumption, no more a part of the task of the psychologist than of the physicist. We might call this the return to a non-reflective and naïve use of consciousness. In this sense consciousness may be said to be the instrument or tool with which all scientists work. Whether or not the tool is properly used at present by scientists is a problem for philosophy and not for psychology.

3. From the viewpoint here suggested the facts on the behavior of amœbæ have value in and for themselves without reference to the behavior of man. In biology studies on race differentiation and inheritance in amœbæ form a separate division of study which must be evaluated in terms of the laws found there. The conclusions so reached may not hold in any other form. Regardless of the possible lack of generality, such studies must be made if evolution as a whole is ever to be regulated and controlled. Similarly the laws of behavior in amœbæ, the range of responses, and the determination of effective stimuli, of habit formation, persistency of habits, interference and reinforcement of habits, must be determined and evaluated in and for themselves,

regardless of their generality, or of their bearing upon such laws in other forms, if the phenomena of behavior are ever to be brought within the sphere of scientific control.

4. This suggested elimination of states of consciousness as proper objects of investigation in themselves will remove the barrier from psychology which exists between it and the other sciences. The findings of psychology become the functional correlates of structure and lend themselves to explanation in physico-chemical terms.

5. Psychology as behavior will, after all, have to neglect but few of the really essential problems with which psychology as an introspective science now concerns itself. In all probability even this residue of problems may be phrased in such a way that refined methods in behavior (which certainly must come) will lead to their solution.

## References

1 That is, either directly upon the conscious state of the observer or indirectly upon the conscious state of the experimenter.

2 In this connection I call attention to the controversy now on between the adherents and the opposers of imageless thought. The 'types of reactors' (sensory and motor) were also matters of bitter dispute. The complication experiment was the source of another war of words concerning the accuracy of the opponents' introspection.

3 My colleague, Professor H. C. Warren, by whose advice this article was offered to the *Review*, believes that the parallelist can avoid the interaction terminology completely by exercising a little care.

4 He would have exactly the same attitude as if he were conducting an experiment to show whether an ant would crawl over a pencil laid across the trail or go round it.

5 I should prefer to look upon this abbreviated method, where the human subject is told in words, for example, to equate two stimuli; or to state in words whether a given stimulus is present or absent, etc., as the *language method* in behavior. It in no way changes the status of experimentation. The method becomes possible merely by virtue of the fact that in the particular case the experimenter and his animal have systems of abbreviations or shorthand behavior signs (language), any one of which may stand for a habit belonging to the repertoire both of the experimenter and his subject. To make the data obtained by the language method virtually the whole of behavior – or to attempt to

mould all of the data obtained by other methods in terms of the one which has by all odds the most limited range – is putting the cart before the horse with a vengeance.

6 They are often undertaken apparently for the purpose of making crude pictures of what must or must not go on in the nervous system.

7 There is need of questioning more and more the existence of what psychology calls imagery. Until a few years ago I thought that centrally aroused visual sensations were as clear as those peripherally aroused. I had never accredited myself with any other kind. However, closer examination leads me to deny in my own case the presence of imagery in the Galtonian sense. The whole doctrine of the centrally aroused image is, I believe, at present, on a very insecure foundation. Angell as well as Fernald reach the conclusion that an objective determination of image type is impossible. It would be an interesting confirmation of their experimental work if we should find by degrees that we have been mistaken in building up this enormous structure of the centrally aroused sensation (or image).

The hypothesis that all of the so-called 'higher thought' processes go on in terms of faint reinstatements of the original muscular act (including speech here) and that these are integrated into systems which respond in serial order (associative mechanisms) is, I believe, a tenable one. It makes reflective processes as mechanical as habit. The scheme of habit which James long ago described – where each return or afferent current releases the next appropriate motor discharge – is as true for 'thought processes' as for overt muscular acts. Paucity of 'imagery' would be the rule. In other words, wherever there are thought processes there are faint contractions of the systems of musculature involved in the overt exercise of the customary act, and especially in the still finer systems of musculature involved in speech. If this is true, and I do not see how it can be gainsaid, imagery becomes a mental luxury (even if it really exists) without any functional significance whatever. If experimental procedure justifies this hypothesis, we shall have at hand tangible phenomena which may be studied as behavior material. I should say that the day when we can study reflective processes by such methods is about as far off as the day when we can tell by physicochemical methods the difference in the structure and arrangement of molecules between living protoplasm and inorganic substances. The solutions of both problems await the advent of methods and apparatus.

[After writing this paper I heard the addresses of Professors Thorndike and Angell, at the Cleveland meeting of the American Psychological Association. I hope to have the opportunity to discuss them at another time. I must even here attempt to answer one question raised by Thorndike.

Thorndike [ . . . ] casts suspicions upon ideo-motor action. If by ideo-motor action he means just that and would not include sensori-motor action in his general denunciation, I heartily agree with him. I should throw out imagery altogether and attempt to show that practically all natural thought goes on in terms of sensori-motor processes in the larynx (but not in terms of 'imageless thought') which rarely come to consciousness in any person who has not groped for imagery in the psychological laboratory. This easily explains why so many of the well-educated laity know nothing of imagery. I doubt if Thorndike conceives of the matter in this way. He and Woodworth seem to have neglected the speech mechanisms.

It has been shown that improvement in habit comes unconsciously. The first we know of it is when it is achieved – when it becomes an object. I believe that 'consciousness' has just as little to do with *improvement* in thought processes. Since, according to my view, thought processes are really motor habits in the larynx, improvements, short cuts, changes, etc., in these habits are brought about in the same way that such changes are produced in other motor habits. This view carries with it the implication that there are no reflective processes (centrally initiated processes): The individual is always *examining objects*, in the one case objects in the now accepted sense, in the other their substitutes, viz., the movements in the speech musculature. From this it follows that there is no theoretical limitation of the behavior method. There remains, to be sure, the practical difficulty, which may never be overcome, of examining speech movements in the way that general bodily behavior may be examined.]

# RUDOLF CARNAP

Translated by NIAMH NÍ BHLEITHÍN,
FIONNULA MEEHAN AND DANIEL STEUER

# Psychology in the Language of Physics

## Introduction: The Language of Physics and Protocol Language

The following sets out to explain and establish the thesis that
every sentence of psychology can be formulated in the language
of physics. In the material mode of speech, the thesis is that all
sentences of psychology are about physical processes, namely
about the physical behavior of humans and other animals. This
is a sub-thesis of the general thesis of physicalism, according to
which the language of physics is a universal language, i.e. a
language into which every sentence can be translated. This more
general thesis has been discussed in a previous article[1] the
exposition of which provides a starting point for the present
work. First, let us briefly repeat some of the results of these
previous reflections.

In talking about a language we distinguish between the
customary 'material mode of speech' (e.g. 'The sentences of this
language are about such and such an object') and the more
correct 'formal mode of speech' (e.g. 'The sentences of this
language contain such and such words and are constructed in
such and such a way'). The use of the material mode of speech
creates a danger of confusion and pseudo-problems. When it is
used now and again in the following, because it is easier to
understand, this is only by way of paraphrasing the formal
mode of speech.

In discussing epistemological issues, what is important above
all is the protocol language in which the ordinary protocol
sentences of a particular subject are formulated (in the material
mode of speech: sentences about the given) and the system
language in which the sentences of the scientific system are
formulated. The testing (verification) of system sentences, by a
subject S, takes place when S derives sentences in the protocol

language from these system sentences and then compares these derived protocol sentences with the sentences of his own protocol. It is the possibility of this kind of derivation of sentences of the protocol language from system sentences that determines whether or not a system sentence has content. If a system sentence does not permit any such derivations, it has no content; it is meaningless. If two system sentences allow the same protocol sentences to be derived from them, then they have the same content. They say the same thing and are inter-translatable.

Every sentence of the system language is inter-translatable with a sentence of the language of physics. That this is so for the sentences of psychology will be shown in what follows. Furthermore, every sentence of the protocol language of any particular subject is inter-translatable with a sentence of the language of physics, namely a sentence about the physical state of the subject in question. Thus the various protocol languages become sub-languages of the language of physics. The language of physics is universal and inter-subjective. This is the thesis of physicalism.

Once the language of physics, due to its nature as universal language, has become the system language of science, all science will become physics. Metaphysics will be eliminated as meaningless. The various spheres of science will become branches of unified science. In the material mode of speech: there is, fundamentally, only one type of object, namely physical processes. They are wholly governed by laws.

Let us make clear that physicalism does not want to dictate that psychology should confine itself to physically expressible states of affairs. Our claim is rather that, whatever psychology chooses to deal with and however it chooses to formulate its sentences, these sentences will be translatable into the language of physics.

We say of a sentence P that it is translatable into (more precisely, inter-translatable with) a sentence Q, if there are general (i.e. spatio-temporally independent) rules according to which Q may be inferred from P, and P from Q. In the material mode of speech: P and Q are about the same state of affairs. Epistemologically speaking: every protocol sentence that confirms P also confirms Q, and vice versa. The definition of an expression *a* with the help of the expressions *b, c* . . . constitutes a rule of translation by means of which any sentence in which *a* appears is inter-translatable with a sentence in which *a* no longer appears but rather *b, c,* . . . The translatability of all sentences of a language, L₁, into a wholly or partly different language, L₂, is secured when, for every expression of L₁, a definition exists which leads directly, or indirectly (i.e. with the help of further definitions), back to expressions of L₂. Our thesis is, then, that for every psychological concept (i.e. expression) a definition can be established through which the psychological concept can be led back, directly or indirectly, to physical concepts. The psychologist is not required to formulate all of his sentences in the terminology of physics. Psychology may continue to use its own terminology for its own purpose. All that is required is the establishing of definitions by means of which the language of psychology may be incorporated into the language of physics. We maintain that such definitions can be established, as they already implicitly form the basis of the procedures of psychology.

If our thesis is correct, even the general sentences of psychology, i.e., the psychological laws, can be translated into the language of physics. They are, therefore, physical laws. This says nothing, however, about whether or not these physical laws can be derived from the physical laws that obtain in the field of anorganic physics. The question of the derivation of the laws is entirely independent from the question of the derivation of the concepts. This has earlier been considered in our discussions of biology.[2] However, as soon as one recognizes that the sentences of psychology belong to the language of physics, and especially as soon as one succeeds in overcoming the emotional resistance which this demonstrable thesis encounters, one will be inclined towards the as yet undemonstrable supposition that the laws of psychology are special cases of the physical laws which also obtain in the anorganic sphere. But this supposition does not concern us at present.

A brief remark on the emotional resistance to the thesis of physicalism may be permitted, though it lies outside our present concerns. Such resistance is always encountered against a thesis that dethrones an idol, a thesis that asks us to give up an idea connected with feelings of dignity and grandeur. Through Copernicus man was cast out of his lofty position at the centre of the universe; through Darwin he was robbed of the dignity of his position as a special being superior to animals; through Marx the factors by means of which the course of history can be causally explained were demoted from the realm of ideas to the sphere of material occurrences; through Nietzsche the aura was stripped from the origins of morals; through Freud the factors by means of which the ideas and actions of men can be causally explained were banished to 'nether' regions, to the darkest depths. It is well known to what extent emotional resistance has disturbed the sober and objective examination of these theories. Now psychology, which has hitherto enjoyed a certain elevated position as the theory of psychic or mental processes, is to be degraded into a part of physics. There will certainly be those who find this thesis vilely presumptuous. We may therefore be permitted to ask the reader to take special care here to retain the objectivity and impartiality which is always indispensable in the examination of any scientific thesis.

## The Forms of Psychological Sentences

The distinction between singular and general sentences is important for psychology, as it is elsewhere. A singular psychological sentence, e.g. 'Mr A was angry at midday yesterday' (analogous to the sentence of physics, 'The air-temperature in Vienna at midday yesterday was 28 Celsius'), refers to a particular person at a particular time. General psychological sentences take various forms, of which the following two are perhaps the most important. A sentence can indicate a specific constitution of a specific type of occurrence, e.g. 'An experience of an unexpected nature always (or: always in the case of Mr A; or: always in the case of persons of such and such a group) has such and such a structure.' The physical analogy: 'Chalk (or: chalk of such and such a type) is always white.' The second important form is that of a general conditional sentence about consecutive occurrences, that is to say, the form of a causal law. Example: 'When ideas of such and such a sort arise under such and such conditions, then an emotion of such and such a type always (or: often; or: sometimes) arises in all persons (or: Mr A; or: persons of such and such a group).' The physical analogy: 'When a body is heated, it usually expands.'

Research strives above all to produce general sentences. These cannot, however, be directly established, but can only be established on the basis of previously established singular sentences through the process of so-called induction, i.e. through the construction of hypotheses.

Phenomenology claims to be able to formulate generally valid synthetic sentences about psychic qualities, which are supposedly not established by induction. They are supposedly known either *a priori* or on the basis of a single exemplary case. In our view the possibility of such knowledge does not exist. However, we do not need to pursue this question further here, as these sentences, according to the opinion of the phenomenologists themselves, do not belong to the realm of psychology.

It happens in physics that a universal law is established seemingly on the basis of one single case. For example, a physicist may establish a constant of a specific material, for instance the thermal conductivity of a specific pure metal, by one single experiment. He is then convinced that not only will the result hold good for the same body at other times but also that all other bodies of the same material will, very probably, exhibit the same material constant at all times. But here too the method of induction is used. On the basis of many previous observations the physicist possesses a general sentence of a higher order which enables him to use such an abbreviated method here. This sentence reads roughly as follows; 'All (or such and such) material constants of pure metals vary only slightly with time and from body to body.'

Certain results in psychology are analogous to this. When a psychologist establishes in one single experiment that two notes sounded together are experienced as dissonant by an experimental subject A, he infers (under favourable conditions) the general sentence, that the same experiment would produce the same result for A at other times. He even ventures – and rightly so – to extend the result with some probability to combinations of notes of the same acoustic interval that do not lie too far from those of the first experiment. Here too it only appears that a universal sentence is derived from a single singular sentence. In reality a sentence obtained through the method of induction from many observations is made use of, e.g. 'The reaction of a certain person concerning the dissonance or consonance of a chord changes very little over time and also relatively little when the chord is transposed over not too large a distance.' Thus we may still maintain that every universal sentence is established through induction on the basis of singular sentences, indeed of several singular sentences.

Finally, we have to consider sentences about psychophysical correlations, e.g. sentences about the relation between physical stimulus and perception. They are likewise gained by induction, in part from physical, in part from psychological singular sentences. The most important sentences of Gestalt psychology also belong to this category.

Universal (general) sentences have the character of hypotheses in relation to (with respect to) concrete sentences; that is to say, a universal sentence is verified by verifying the concrete sentences derivable from it. A universal sentence has content to the extent that, and only to the extent that, the concrete sentences derivable from it have content. For this reason, logical analysis must direct itself in the first place towards these latter sentences.

When A utters a singular psychological sentence, e.g. 'B was happy yesterday morning', the epistemological situation is different depending on whether A and B are different people or the same person. For this reason we distinguish between psychological sentences about other minds (psyches) and psychological sentences about matters internal to the psyche. This distinction has no relevance in the case of the sentences of intersubjective science, as we shall see later. By contrast, the above distinction is indispensable for the epistemological examination of the initially subjective singular sentences.

## Sentences about matters pertaining to another psyche

The epistemological character of singular sentences about matters pertaining to another psyche will first be made clear by analogy with a sentence about a physical property defined as a disposition to exhibit a certain behavior ('reaction') under certain circumstances ('stimuli'). Example: A body is called 'plastic' if under the influence of deforming forces of a certain type and magnitude it suffers permanent changes to its shape without breaking.

We will carry out the analogy by contrasting two examples. What matters to us here is the epistemological situation in the psychological example; the parallel example of the physical property is only meant to make it easier to understand the psychological example and is not meant to serve as an inference by analogy. (Where the same text would appear both left and right it will be written only once for the sake of brevity.)

| *Sentence about a physical property of a material.* | *Sentence about the condition (state) of some other psyche.* |
|---|---|
| Example: I assert the sentence P1: 'This wooden beam has a high solidity.' | Example: I assert the sentence P1: 'Mr A is now excited.' |

There are two different ways by which it is possible to arrive at the sentence P1; we may call them the 'rational' and the 'intuitive' procedure. According to the rational procedure, P1 is inferred from a protocol sentence p1 (or from several protocol sentences), more specifically from a perception sentence

| about the shape and colour of the wooden beam | about A's expressive movements, e.g. facial expressions, gestures and such like, or about physical effects of such movements, e.g. characteristics of his handwriting |
|---|---|

This conclusion requires another superordinate sentence, O, namely the general sentence which states that:

| when I perceive this colour and shape in a wooden beam, it (usually) proves to be firm. (A sentence about the perceptual signs of firmness) | when I perceive these facial expressions or these handwriting characteristics in a person, such a person usually proves to be excited. (Sentence about the expressive or graphological signs of excitedness) |
|---|---|

It is easy to see that the content of P1 does not coincide with but exceeds that of p1; for O is required for the derivation of P1 from p1. That this is how p1 and P1 are related is also shown by the fact that the inference from p1 to P1 may in certain circumstances be mistaken. It may happen that although p1 appears in the protocol, I must, because of the further protocol, withdraw the proposed system sentence $P_1$. I would then say, 'I was mistaken; re-examination has shown

| that the beam was not firm, although it had such and such a shape and colour' | that A was not excited, although he had such and such a facial expression' |

In practical life the intuitive method is used more frequently than the rational method, which presupposes theoretical knowledge and requires reflection. Here the sentence $P_1$ is obtained directly from the protocol sentence of the same wording, $p_2$:

| 'The beam is firm.' | 'A is excited.' |

Hence one also speaks in this case of 'immediate perception'

| of the material properties e.g. the firmness of the beam | of other psyches (minds), e.g. the excitedness of A |

In this case, too, the protocol sentence $p_2$ and the system sentence $P_1$ are not identical in content. The difference is usually not taken into account because in their usual formulation both sentences sound the same. Here, too, we can best make the difference clear by considering the possibility of error. It can happen that although $p_2$ appears in my protocol I must, because of the further protocol, withdraw the proposed system sentence $P_1$. I would then say 'I was mistaken, further examination has shown

| that the beam was not firm, although I had the intuitive impression that it was firm' | that A was not excited, although I had the intuitive impression that he was excited' |

[The difference between $p_2$ and $P_1$ is the same as that between the identically worded sentences $p$ and $P_1$: 'On this table there is a red marble' of our earlier example.[3] Our considerations there showed that, when carried out rigorously, the inference from $p_2$ to $P_1$, also requires a general (universal) superordinate sentence and is far from straightforward. In practice, however, the inference is simplified to the point of triviality in that common linguistic usage, for convenience sake, assigns to both sentences the same wording.]

Our next problem is now: what meaning does the sentence

P1 have? This question can only be answered by providing another sentence (or several others), which (or which together) have the same content as P1. The view I want to put forward is that P1 is identical in content to a sentence P2 asserting the existence of a physical structure characterized by the disposition to react in a certain way to certain physical stimuli. In our example, P2 asserts the existence of the physical structure (microstructure)

| | |
|---|---|
| of the wooden beam, characterized by the fact that the beam will not suffer any noticeable change in shape when subjected to slight pressure and will bend to such and such an extent when subjected to greater pressure, but will not yet break | of the body of Mr A, in particular of his central nervous system, characterized by increased frequency of breathing and pulse (which may in turn rise further in response to certain stimuli), by the emphatic and usually vehement and factually unsatisfactory answering of questions, by the occurrence of excited movements in response to certain stimuli, and so forth |

In our view, a perfect analogy exists, in this case too, between the example from physics and the psychological example. However, were we to consult the experts in these fields about the two examples, we would at present receive entirely non-analogous answers from the majority. For the claim that P1 and P2 are identical in content is

| | |
|---|---|
| held to be self-evident by all physicists, with regard to the physical sentence P1 | rejected by almost all psychologists (with the exception of the radical behaviourists), with regard to the psychological sentence P1 |

The opposing view, that is most often advocated by the psychologists, holds that: 'A sentence of the form P1 asserts the presence of a state which is not identical with the corresponding physical structure but is merely accompanied and given external expression by it.' In our example,

P1 says that not only does the beam have the physical structure described in P2, it also has a certain force, namely its firmness.

P1 says that Mr A not only has a body with the physical structure described in P2 (at the time in question), but that, since he is a 'psycho-physical being', he also has a consciousness, a certain force or entity, in which the excitedness was to be found.

This firmness is not identical with the physical structure but stands in parallel relation to it such that it is always present when and only when a physical structure of the type characterized is present.

The excitedness cannot, therefore, be identical with the physical structure of the body, but stands in parallel relation (or interactive relation) to the body such that it is always present when and only when (or at least often when) a physical structure of the body of the type characterized is present.

As a result of this parallelism the described behavioral reaction of the beam to certain stimuli, which is a physical causal effect of that structure, may be taken as an 'expression' of the firmness. The firmness itself is thus a *qualitas occulta*, a hidden force standing behind and manifesting itself in the physical structure, but not itself identifiable.

As a result of this parallelism the described behavioural reaction to certain stimuli may be taken as the 'expression' of the excitement. The excitement itself or the consciousness whose attribute or affective expression it is, is, therefore, a *qualitas occulta*, a hidden force standing behind and manifesting itself in the physical structure, but not itself identifiable.

This view commits the mistake of hypostatizing and thus giving rise to a peculiar doubling: beside or behind a state whose presence can be empirically verified, a 'parallel' entity is assumed, whose presence is not verifiable. (Please note that we are still speaking of sentences about matters pertaining to another psyche.) But, one might object, the possibility of a verification may exist after all, namely through the protocol sentence p2 about the intuitive impression of

the firmness of the beam          the excitement of A

According to the objection, this sentence also appears in the protocol next to the perception sentence p1. Why, then, cannot a further system sentence whose content exceeds that of P2 be based on it? To this we may reply as follows. A sentence says no more than what is verifiable about it. Now if the verification of P1 consisted in the derivation of the protocol sentence p2, then these sentences would be identical in content; but we have already seen that this cannot possibly be the case.

There is no other way of verifying P1 except through protocol sentences of the type of p1 and p2. Now if the content of P1 is to go beyond that of P2, then those components that go beyond are not verifiable, hence they are senseless. So if one refuses to interpret P1 through P2, P1 becomes a metaphysical pseudo-sentence.

The various sciences are currently at very different stages with regard to their decontamination from metaphysical admixtures. Physics is, largely through the efforts of Mach, Poincaré and Einstein, practically free of metaphysics. By contrast, psychology has hardly begun the effort of becoming a science free of metaphysics. The difference is especially apparent in the assessment that the opinion which we previously rejected as metaphysical and senseless would receive from the experts. With regard to the example from physics, the opinion would be rejected by most physicists as anthropomorphism, mythology, and metaphysics. Here the anti-metaphysical attitude of physicists is evident, an attitude which is in accord with our own. By contrast, the opinion in the psychological example (though perhaps not in our crude formulation) appears self-evident on intuitive grounds to most contemporary psychologists. Here we see the metaphysical attitude of psychologists, which is opposed to our attitude.

## Response to Four Typical Objections

If we generalize the result of the considerations carried out on the basis of our example, we arrive at the thesis that a singular sentence about matters pertaining to another psyche is identical in content to a physical sentence. In the material mode of speech: a sentence about matters pertaining to another psyche says that a physical process of a certain type takes place in or on the body of the person concerned. We will now discuss some objections to this thesis of physicalism.

A. *Objection on the ground of our lack of knowledge of physiology*: 'Our present knowledge of physiology, in particular the physiology of the central nervous system, has not progressed far enough for us to know which class of physical conditions corresponds e.g. to 'excitedness'. Therefore, when today we utter the sentence 'A is excited', we cannot mean the corresponding physical condition.'

Rebuttal: It is true that today the sentence P1 'A is excited' cannot be translated into a physical sentence P3 of the form 'In the body of A such and such a chemical-physical process in taking place' (expressed through the distribution of the physical variables and through chemical formulae). Our current state of physiological knowledge is not sufficient for this. However, even today P1 can be translated into a different sentence about the physical condition of the body of A, namely into the previously mentioned sentence P2 of the form 'The body of A is now in a state characterized by the fact that when I perceive the body of A the protocol sentence p1 (perception of changes of expression) and (or) p2 (intuitive impression of the excitedness of A) or other corresponding protocol sentences of such and such a type occur to me.' Just as in the example from physics the sentence P1 'The wooden beam is firm' refers to the physical structure of the wooden beam even though the person who utters the sentence may not be in a position to describe this structure by stating the distribution of the physical variables, so equally the psychological sentence P1 'A is excited' refers to the physical structure of the body of A even though we cannot describe this structure by providing the measurements of the state, but can describe it only in terms of possible perceptions, impressions, dispositions to react in a certain way, and suchlike. Our lack of knowledge of physiology can therefore influence only the type of description of the physical state; it cannot affect the point of principle that the sentence P1 refers to a physical state.

B. *Objection on the ground of the inference by analogy*: 'In my own case, when I am angry I also experience, in addition to the angry behaviour, the feeling of anger. When I observe angry behaviour in another person I may, therefore, if not with certainty then at least with probability, make the analogical inference that he too has a feeling of anger (which does not mean a physical condition), in addition to the angry behaviour.

Rebuttal: While it is true that analogical inferences do not provide certainty, they are no doubt permissible as inferences conferring probability. Let us consider an example of an ordinary inference by analogy. I see a box of a certain shape, size and colour. I establish that it contains steel nibs. I discover another box of the same appearance. I infer by analogy that it probably also contains steel nibs. Now the objection maintains that the proposed analogical inference about matters pertaining to another psyche is of the same logical form. If this were the case, the inference would be legitimate. But it is not the case. The concluding sentence is meaningless, a mere pseudo-sentence. For, since it is a sentence about matters pertaining to another psyche, which is not supposed to be interpreted physically, it is in principle unverifiable. This was the result of our previous consideration and objection D will provide a further opportunity to discuss the point. The difference to our present example lies precisely in the fact that the concluding sentence is unverifiable. It can in principle be verified that the second box also contains steel nibs, and confirmed, say, through the observational sentences of the protocol. The two analogous sentences 'There are steel nibs in the first box' and 'There are steel nibs in the second box' are logically and epistemologically of the same type. Therefore, the analogical inference is legitimate here. But this is not the case with regard to the two sentences 'I am angry' and 'The other person is angry'. We consider that the first sentence makes sense while the second sentence (when the physical interpretation is ruled out) makes no sense. The objection, which maintains that the second sentence makes sense too, will maintain that the second sentence must be verified by the speaker in a completely different way from the first. Thus either way we arrive at the same result, namely that the second sentence is epistemologically of a different type to the first. Using the same form of language is not logically legitimate. It makes the two sentences seem similar and thus makes the analogical inference seem legitimate.

If we acknowledge that the concluding sentence makes no sense, we still need to explain how this pseudo-sentence came about. Logical analysis of the formation of concepts and sentences in science, and especially in philosophy, very often leads us to pseudo-sentences. However, apart from this, a pseudo-sentence very rarely occurs as a concluding sentence of an analogical inference with meaningful premises. It is easy to explain why this is so. An analogical inference has (in simple cases) the following form. Premises: If A has the property E then A invariably also has the property F; A1 is similar to A in many respects; A1 has the property E. We infer that A1 probably also has the property F. Now semantics (the logical syntax of language) teaches the following. If 'A' and 'B' are names of an object, and if 'E' and 'F' are names of a property, and if 'E(A)' means that A has the property E, then it follows that (a) when 'E(A)' and 'E(B)' make sense (regardless of whether they are true or false), then 'A' and 'B' belong to the same semantic genus; and (b) if two names 'A' and 'B' belong to the same semantic genus, and if 'F(A)' makes sense, then 'F(B)' makes sense too. In our case, 'E(A)' and 'E(A1)' make sense. Therefore, according to (a), 'A' and 'A1' belong to the same genus. According to the first premise, 'F(A)' makes sense. Therefore, according to (b), the concluding sentence 'F(A1)' of the analogical inference makes sense too. That the premises of an analogical inference should make sense and that, despite this, the concluding sentence should make no sense, can thus occur only when the linguistic expression is open to objection on logical grounds. And this is precisely the case in the analogical inference proposed by the objection. The predicative form of speech 'I am angry' does not adequately convey the intended state of affairs. It states that a certain object has a certain property. But all that we are presented with is an experienced feeling of anger. This would have to be linguistically formulated e.g. as 'Now anger is present'. This correct formulation, however, precludes the possibility of the analogical inference. For now the premises read: When I, that is my body, exhibits angry behaviour, anger is present; the body of the other person is similar to my body in many respects; the body of the other person exhibits angry behaviour. But the concluding sentence can no longer be formed. For the sentence 'Now (or: then) anger is present' lacks an 'I' which can be replaced by 'the other person'. Should one wish to form the concluding sentence without making any replacement but by simply retaining the form of the premise, this would result in the more meaningful but obviously false concluding sentence – 'So now anger is present' – which of course means, in ordinary language, 'I am now angry'.

C. *Objection on the ground of telepathy*: Telepathic transference of contents of consciousness (ideas, feelings, thoughts) occurs without (ascertainable) physical mediation. Here we have a case of knowing about matters pertaining to another psyche without perceiving the body of the other person. For example, I wake up suddenly at night, experiencing a clear feeling of fear while also knowing that my friend is simultaneously experiencing the fear. It is later confirmed that my friend's life was in danger at that moment. Here my knowledge of the fear of the friend cannot mean the knowledge of the physical condition of his body, as I know nothing about this. My knowledge refers directly to the feeling of fear experienced by the friend.

Rebuttal: At present psychologists are not in agreement about the extent to which the existence of telepathic occurrences may be considered as proven. This is an empirical question which we do not have to decide here. We shall accommodate the objection and assume the occurrence of telepathic transference to be empirically confirmed. We shall demonstrate that our considerations are not thereby affected. The question now reads: What meaning does the sentence P1 'My friend is now experiencing fear' have, by which I express telepathically gained knowledge? We maintain that the meaning is exactly the same as if I express the sentence P1 on the basis of knowledge gained in the normal (be it rational or intuitive) way. The occurrence of telepathy makes no difference to the interpretation of P1.

Let us consider an exactly analogous situation with reference to physical knowledge. Let us assume that it suddenly occurs to me that a picture has fallen from the wall at home, while neither I nor anybody else is in a position to perceive this in the normal way. It is later confirmed that the picture did fall. I go on to express my clairvoyantly gained knowledge in the sentence Q, 'Now the picture has fallen from the wall'. What meaning does the sentence have? The meaning of Q here is obviously the same as if I were to utter it on the basis of knowledge gained in the normal way (by which we mean direct perception). For in both cases it refers to a physical event, namely a particular movement of a particular body.

The same is true of telepathic knowledge. We have already

considered the case where a matter pertaining to another psyche is apprehended intuitively, although by perceiving the body of that person. If telepathic knowledge of the psychological state of another person exists, it too relies on an intuitive impression, but without the accompanying perception. In both cases, however, what is known is the same. We have earlier seen that P1 is not identical in content with the protocol sentence p2 about the normal-intuitive impression and that a sentence about something outside or behind the physical state of the body of the other person cannot rely on p2. Our considerations are valid in exactly the same way for telepathic-intuitive impressions.

D. *Objection on the ground of the statements of the other person.* 'First of all we agree that A is in a physical state of a certain kind expressing itself in reactive behaviour of a certain kind and producing in me, in addition to sensory perceptions, the intuitive impression of anger in A. That, in addition to this, A is also actually experiencing a feeling of anger is something that I can establish simply by asking him. He will then testify that he experienced a feeling of anger. Having known him as a credible person and a good observer, why should I not consider his statement as true, or at least probably true?'

Rebuttal: Before I can decide whether I should accept A's statement as true, false or probably true, indeed before I can even consider this question, I must first understand the statement; it must have a meaning for me. And it only makes sense if I can verify it, that is to say if sentences of my protocol language can be derived from it. If the statement is physically interpreted, it is verifiable through my protocol sentences of the type p1 and p2, and others, that is to say sentences about particular perceptions and intuitive impressions. But since the objection rejects the physical interpretation of the statement, there is, in principle, no possibility of my verifying it. Consequently, it is meaningless for me. The question whether I should accept it as true or false or probably true cannot even arise.

If strange shining patterns were to appear in the sky, science would have to register, describe and explain these patterns first of all as physical facts (that is to say, subscribe them under general conditional sentences), even if they assumed the form of letters forming a sentence. The question of whether such a complex of signs constitutes a meaningful sentence must be decided without considering whether the complex appears in the sky. If the complex of signs is not a meaningful sentence beforehand, it cannot become so, however brightly it appears in the sky. This is because it depends on the contingent content of experience whether a particular sentence is true or not, but not whether it is meaningful. This is determined by the syntax of language.

The case of acoustic phenomena emitted from the mouth of certain vertebrates is the same as that of shining patterns in the sky. They are above all facts, physical occurrences, namely sound waves of a particular kind. In addition I may interpret them linguistically as signs. Whether this complex of signs is meaningful or not cannot depend on its occurrence as an acoustic phenomenon. If the sentence 'A was angry yesterday at midday' has no meaning for me, because it cannot be verified by me (since it is, according to the objection, denied a physical sense), it will not become meaningful by virtue of the fact that an acoustic phenomenon with the form of this sentence is emitted from the mouth of A.

But, it will be said, do we not need the statements of our fellow men in order to construct intersubjective science? How poor would physics, geography and history become if I had to restrict myself to the events that I had directly observed myself! This is true. But there is a fundamental difference between a statement of A about the geographical condition of China, or about an historical event of the past, and a statement of A about his anger yesterday. I can in principle verify statements of the first type through perception sentences of my protocol, e.g. sentences about perceptions of China itself, or of a map, or of historical documents. But I cannot even in principle verify the statement about the anger if, in accordance with the objection, the physical interpretation is ruled out. If I have repeatedly had the experience that, for instance, the geographical or historical reports of A have been confirmed by me, then I will make use of his further utterances, provided that they are meaningful to me, to extend my scientific knowledge on the basis of probabilistic inductive inferences. Intersubjective science arises in this way. But a sentence that is not verifiable and therefore meaningless without the utterance of A, cannot become meaningful through such an utterance. If, on the other hand, I interpret A's statement about his anger yesterday as a statement about the physical condition of A's body yesterday, as I must on our view, then this statement will also be used for the construction of intersubjective science. For on the basis of this statement and according to the 'credibility' of A established so far, a corresponding physical structure is assigned to the corresponding space-time coordinate of our physical world. The conclusions we draw from this assignment are not different then in the case of other physical statements. We base our expectation of future perceptions on them, in this case about A's behaviour and in general about the behaviour of other physical systems.

It is true that the speech of our fellow men contributes considerably to the extension of the scope of our knowledge. But it cannot deliver us anything fundamentally new, that is to say anything that we could not in principle acquire in a different way. For the statements of our fellow men are not of a fundamentally different type from any other physical occurrences. It is true that physical occurrences differ in that they can be used as indications of further physical occurrences to varying degrees. For those physical occurrences which we call 'statements of fellow men', this degree is especially high. Therefore, science rightly treats them as especially important. But, in principle, there exists at most a difference in degree between what the statement of a fellow human being contributes to our scientific knowledge and what a barometer contributes.

## Behaviourism and 'Interpretive' Psychology

The view put forward here corresponds in its main points to the movement in psychology called 'behaviourism' or 'behavioural psychology', provided that we consider the basic epistemological thesis of this movement rather than its special method or empirical results. We have not based our own presentation on that of behaviourism because we are only interested in fundamental epistemological positions, while behaviourism is primarily interested in particular methods of inquiry and particular ways of forming concepts. So far behaviourism, developed in America, has not received the attention in Germany that it deserves, above all for its epistemological principle. But with the recent publication of a German translation of a synoptic work by the most radical champion of the movement, it will perhaps exert a stronger influence.[4]

The representatives of behaviourism were led to their view

through their study of animal psychology. It is in this area, where no verbal statements but only wordless behaviour can be observed, that the correct basic attitude is most easily acquired. From this basic attitude one can reach a correct interpretation of the statements of experimental subjects, by interpreting these statements as acts of 'verbal' behaviour that are not in principle different from other types of behaviour.

In America radical behaviourism is opposed by some currents of opinion which also consider themselves behaviourist, in that they recognize as the object of psychology only the behaviour of living things. But they are of the opinion that psychology is only concerned with a particular type of behaviour, namely 'meaningful behaviour', which, they claim, cannot be characterized in physical concepts. Although this approach is close to behaviourism with regard to practical method, in its epistemological foundation it is related more closely to so-called 'interpretive' psychology, which is widespread in Germany. This movement believes that the behaviour of subjects, although it is not, strictly speaking, the object of psychology, does constitute a fundamental point of reference for psychological knowledge. It is likewise emphasized that it is 'meaningful behaviour', not behaviour in its physical form that is in question. According to this theory, grasp of meaningful behaviour requires a particular method, 'understanding' [*verstehen*] or 'understanding of meaning'. The method, it is claimed, is foreign to physics, and meaningful behaviour either taken as a whole or in its individual types as examined by psychology, cannot in principle be characterized in physical concepts.

In interpretive psychology this view is usually associated with the view that, in addition to behaviour, psychological processes exist which are the real object of psychology and which we come to know through 'understanding'. We do not want to pursue this idea any further, as it has already been discussed in detail earlier.

But even if we leave this idea aside, from the point of view of interpretive psychology, and equally from that of moderate (we would prefer to call it 'inauthentic') behaviourism, the following objection to physicalism remains.

*Objection on the ground of 'meaningful behaviour'*: 'When psychology considers the behaviour of livings things (for the moment we leave the question open whether psychology is

concerned with behaviour only) it comprehends it in its character as "meaningful behaviour". But this character cannot be
comprehended in physical concepts, it can be grasped only
through the intuitive method of "understanding". For this
reason psychological sentences cannot be translated into the
language of physics.'

Rebuttal: Let us recall an example, discussed earlier,[5] of the
physicalization of an intuitive impression, i.e. of a qualitative
characterization of the protocol language. We realized that it
was possible with the help of a thorough inspection of the
system of optical variables to establish and formulate as a law
the entirety of those physical conditions that correspond to the
qualitative characterization 'Green of such and such a kind'.
The same is possible here. It depends only on the physical nature
of an action, for instance of an arm movement, whether I
intuitively consider it as understandable, e.g. as an act of waving.
[We prefer 'understandable' to 'meaningful' as a psychological
term because we commonly use 'meaningful' as a logical-
semantical concept (= 'in accordance with syntax').] Consequently, physicalization is possible in this case also. The class of
arm movements, to which the protocol-characterization 'to
wave' corresponds, can be established and described in physical
concepts. But perhaps there may be some doubt as to whether
the division of arm movements into understandable and not
understandable, and the further division of understandable arm
movements into waving movements and others, is really only
dependent on the physical characteristics of the arm, the entire
body and the environment. Such doubts can be easily removed
if we think of, say, a sound-film. We understand the 'meaning'
of an action of a person in a sound-film. Doubtless, our
understanding would be exactly the same if, instead of the
original one, another film was shown which physically corre-
sponded to the first film down to the last detail. It follows that
our understanding of meaning, both with respect to its existence
or non-existence and with respect to the individual form it takes,
is functionally completely determined by the physical nature of
the physical (i.e. in this instance optical and acoustic) stimuli
which reach our sensory organs.

The problem of physicalization in this area, that is to say the
problem of describing the class of 'understandable' behaviour
and the subclasses of individual kinds of such behaviour in

systematic, physical concepts, has not yet been solved. Does not then our fundamental thesis hang in the air? It says that all psychological sentences are capable of being translated into the language of physics. Now one will ask to what extent such a translation is feasible at our present stage of knowledge? Already today every psychological sentence can be translated into a sentence about the physical behaviour of living things. It is true that in the course of characterization of this physical behaviour concepts arise which are not yet physicalized, i.e. can not be reduced to concepts of the scientific-physical system. But, these concepts, too, are physical concepts, even if at a primitive level – just as the concepts 'warm' and 'green' (referring to bodies) were physical concepts even at the stage when they could not be expressed through physical variables (temperature and electromagnetic field).

Let us once again clarify the situation with a physical example. Let us suppose that we have found a body that noticeably increases its electrical conductivity when acted upon by some types of light. We do not, however, know the inner composition of the body and, consequently, cannot explain its behaviour. We may call such a body a detector for these types of light. Suppose that we have not already established systematically which types of light the detector reacts to. But we find that the types of light that the detector reacts to have a certain other property in common, e.g. the property of accelerating a particular chemical reaction. If this photo-chemical effect of the types of light is in question, and if establishing this effect for a particular type of light is difficult and time-consuming, but establishing the reaction of the detector to this type of light is easy and quick, it will be useful for us to adopt the detector as a test-instrument. By using it we can establish whether the desired photo-chemical effect is to be expected in the context of a given type of light. This practical usage is not hindered by the fact that we do not know the detailed physical composition of the detector, nor by the fact that we cannot explain its reaction physically. Certainly, despite this lack of knowledge, we can say that the detector selects for us a certain class of light-types which is physically defined. It would be a mistake to object that this class of light-types is not a physical class because we have characterized it not on the basis of the physical specification of the optical variables of the light-types but only by way of the behaviour of the detector. For we know that we could specify this class of rays, to which the detector reacts, through an exact and thoroughly empirical investigation of the physical system of the light-types. On the basis of this specification we could then physicalize the detector-related characterization of the light-types, namely replace it with a characterization established in terms of systematic, physical concepts. But even that physical characterization of the class of light-types in terms of detector reaction, which is already possible today, is a physical characterization, even if an indirect one. It differs from the sought-after direct characterization only in being more circuitous. The difference is only one of degree, not one of principle, but it is still substantial enough to make us search for the direct physical characterization by means of empirical investigation.

Whether the detector is of an organic or anorganic nature is of no importance for the epistemological issue. The function of the detector is fundamentally the same whether we are dealing with a physical detector for a particular sort of light, with a tree-frog as a detector for particular meteorological conditions, or (if one is to believe the newspaper report) with a sniffing dog as a detector for particular human sicknesses. If one has a practical interest in meteorological prognosis, one may use a frog as long as there is no barometer. We must recognize, however, that by this method we are not establishing the state of the tree-frog's soul, but a physically specified weather condition, even if one could not specify this condition in terms of systematic-physical concepts. If one has a practical interest in medical diagnosis, one may use the fine sense of smell of a dog, if the directly ascertainable symptoms are not sufficient. It is at the same time clear to the doctor that he is not establishing the state of the dog's soul, but a physically specified condition of the patient's body. Perhaps, given the present state of physiological knowledge, the doctor is not in a position to characterize the condition of sickness in question in terms of systematic-physical concepts. In spite of this, the doctor knows that through his diagnosis, whether it is based on directly observed symptoms of the patient or on the reaction of the diagnostic dog, nothing other than a determination of the physical condition of the patient is established and can be established. And, over and above this, the physiologist recognizes the demand to physicalize. This would consist in expressing the characteristic specifications of that bodily condition, that is to say, in giving the definition of the illness in question, in purely physiological concepts, while eliminating the reaction of the dog. Furthermore, the physiological concepts would have to be reduced to chemical ones, and these in turn to physical ones.

The situation of the 'interpretive' psychologist is exactly analogous to this. Only here epistemological analysis is made more complicated (even though psychological practice is made simpler) by the fact that the 'interpretive' psychologist is both observer and detector when examining an experimental subject. The doctor is his own diagnostic dog (which is also generally the case in medical diagnosis, namely in regard to the intuitive components of diagnosing). The psychologist calls the behaviour of the experimental subject 'understandable', or in a particular case, e.g. 'nod of approval', to which his detector reacts: that is, where the sentence 'A nods approvingly' occurs in his protocol. Science is not a system of 'experiences', but of sentences. It is not the 'interpretive experience' of the psychologist that is part of science, but his protocol sentence. The utterance of the psychologist's protocol sentence is a reaction whose epistemological function is analogous to the climbing of the tree-frog or the barking of the diagnostic dog. However, the psychologist far surpasses the reactive animals by the multiplicity of his reactions. In this way he certainly becomes very valuable for the enterprise of science. But this constitutes only a difference in degree, not one of principle.

There are thus two demands to be made of the psychologist. First, he must, just as the doctor had to, realize that despite this complicated diagnostic reaction, he is ascertaining nothing other than the existence of a particular physical condition of the experimental subject, although this condition is, for the time being, only indirectly characterized through that diagnostic reaction. Secondly, he must, just as the physiologist had to, recognize the physicalization of this indirect characterization as a task of scientific inquiry. It must be established which physical conditions correspond to every one of his intuitive detector reactions. If this is carried out for every such reaction, that is for every type of result of 'understanding', psychological conceptualization can be physicalized. Here the indirect definitions based on the detector reactions are replaced by direct definitions with the aid of systematic-physical concepts. Psychology, too, must and will reach the point where the tree-frog is replaced with a barometer. But even at the tree-frog stage psychology speaks the language of physics, even if in a primitive form.

## Physicalization in Graphology

The considerations of this section are not supposed to serve as a justification for the physicalist thesis, but are meant only to show what forms the practical implementation of the physicalization of psychological concepts takes. For this purpose we want to consider an area of psychology, in which the task of physicalization has already begun with considerable success. In this way the misgivings occasionally expressed, that the completion of this task, if it is at all possible, will in any case be uninspiring and unproductive, will perhaps be allayed. One could, for example, it is said, perhaps establish the class of those arm-movements which (given further conditions that remain to be specified concerning the cultural horizon, the situation of the persons involved, and the like) would be understood as waving, in such a way that it could be characterized in cinematic (spatio-temporal) concepts. But such a conclusion, so it is believed, would not provide any interesting insights, least of all into any connections with other processes.

Strangely enough, physicalization has proven remarkably successful in graphology, an area of psychology which up to relatively recently was pursued with purely intuitive (or at best pseudo-rational) methods on the basis of altogether inadequate empirical evidence and which could thus make no claim to be scientific. Theoretical graphology, which is all that we will be dealing with, investigates the lawlike correlations between properties relating to the form of a person's handwriting and his psychological properties usually called 'character traits (properties)'.

First of all, we need to explain in which sense we may speak of 'character traits (properties)' in the context of a physical psychology. Every psychological property is defined as a disposition towards behaviour of a particular type. An 'actual property' we take to be a property whose definition indicates characteristics which can be directly observed. A 'disposition' (or a 'dispositional concept') we take to be a property which is defined by an implication (conditional relationship, if-sentence).

Examples of known physical dispositional concepts may serve as illustration. In this way we can also illustrate a different distinction which is important for psychology, that between momentary and permanent properties. An example of a physical 'momentary property' is a particular temperature. Its definition is 'A body B has the temperature T' means 'If a sufficiently small amount of mercury is brought into contact with B, then . . .'. With this form of definition the concept of temperature is a dispositional concept. After physics has discovered the microstructure of matter, and has established the laws of molecular movement, a different definition for temperature is put forward. Temperature is the average kinetic energy of the molecules. Here temperature is no longer a dispositional concept but an actual property. The psychological momentary-properties are, in their conceptual form, analogous to the familar physical concepts of disposition. Indeed they are, in our view, nothing but physical concepts. Example: 'Person X is excited' means 'If stimuli of such and such a kind are now used, X reacts in such and such a way' (where stimuli as well as reactions are both physical processes). Here, too, scientific inquiry aims at replacing the previous form of definition with a different form of definition on the basis of more precise knowledge of the micro-structure of the body, i.e. at replacing the dispositional concept with an actual property. We shall not regard these efforts as utopian once we realize that even at present a number of actual characteristics of psychological momentary states are known, due to a more detailed knowledge of the physiological macro-processes (e.g. for feelings of different types: frequency and strength of pulse and breathing, glandular secretion, innervation of intestinal muscles and the like). With regard to determining non-emotional states, this transformation of definitions is, however, considerably more difficult, because it presupposes a knowledge of the micro-processes within the central nervous system which very considerably exceeds the present level of knowledge.

Examples of physical 'permanent-properties' are, for instance, material constants, such as thermal conductivity, refraction index and the like. These, too, were originally defined as dispositional concepts. For example 'A body has the refractory index $n$' means 'If a ray of light enters the body, then . . .' Here, too, the transformation of the definition has already been carried out for some concepts and it is desired for the remaining concepts. An actual determination of the construction of the body in question out of protons and electrons replaces the disposition. The psychological permanent-properties or 'character traits' (the word 'character' is used here in a very broad and neutral sense, not merely for properties of the will or attitudes) can at present be defined only in terms of dispositional concepts. Example: 'X is more receptive than Y' means 'If an impression is experienced, stronger feelings will occur in X than in Y, under otherwise similar conditions'. Thus names for psychological momentary-properties, for which the task of physicalization is not yet completed, will appear in both the characterization of the stimuli (situation) and in the characterization of the reactions. The physicalization of permanent-properties can be carried out only after the physicalization of momentary-properties. As long as the latter has not been carried out, the former, and with it characterology as a whole, must remain in a scientifically incomplete state, no matter how rich the intuitive results may be.

There is no clear borderline between momentary-properties and permanent-properties. At the same time, the difference in degree is substantial enough to make separate names and separate treatment appropriate, and, therefore, also the distinction between characterology and psychology as a whole (as a theory of behaviour). Graphology sets itself the task of using handwriting to gather evidence about character traits and to a lesser degree also about momentary properties. For the practicing graphologist the rational method is not meant to replace intuition, but only to support and correct it. It has, however, been shown that it is useful even for this purpose to undertake the task of physicalization. In this context graphology has recently achieved remarkable results.

Because the task of graphology consists in establishing relations between properties of handwriting and character traits, we may analyze the task of physicalization into three parts. The physicalization of the properties of handwriting forms the first sub-task. I get from a particular script, for example, the intuitive impression of 'fullness, juicyness'. So far, what is meant is a property of the handwriting, not of the character of the writer. The task now consists in replacing such intuitively characterized properties of the handwriting with purely figural ones, that is with properties defined in terms of geometrical concepts alone. It is clear that this problem is solvable. One only needs systematically to scan the system of possible forms of letters, words and lines, in order to establish which of these forms makes on us the intuitive impression in question. So we find, for example, that a script appears 'full' or 'dimensioned' (opposite: 'thin', 'linear') if rounded connections ('curves') predominate over pointed ones ('angles'); further, if in relation to a normal script the loops are enlarged, the strokes are broader, and so on. In many cases this task of the physicalization of the properties of handwriting has already to a large degree been completed by graphologists.[6] There is no objection against retaining the descriptions taken from the intuitive impression (e.g. 'full', 'thin', 'slim', 'powerful', and the like). Our demand is met as soon as a definition in purely figural characterizations is put forward for such a description. The task is, as we can see, exactly analogous to the task, already mentioned several times, of stating in quantitative terms the class of physical processes which correspond to a qualitative characterization in protocol language, such as 'green of such and such a kind'.

The second task consists in the physicalization of the character traits which occur in the statements of graphology. The traditional concepts of characterology, whose meaning is mostly not given by clear definitions but often only arises out of everyday language usage or through the interpretation of the metaphorical usage of language, must be systematized and must receive a physicalistic (behaviourist) definition. We saw earlier that such a definition refers to a disposition towards a particular reactive behaviour, and that to formulate such definitions is difficult and presupposes the physicalization of the psychological momentary-properties.

We see that with regard to the first two tasks, we are concerned with replacing primitive-intuitive conceptualizations by systematic ones, as if we were replacing an observer equipped with a tree-frog by an observer equipped with a barometer (in graphology both sorts of observer are united in the same person, as in the case of the intuitively diagnosing doctor).

To these tasks of rendering the concepts more precise is now added the third task, the actual empirical task of graphology. It consists in ascertaining the correlations between properties of handwriting and character traits. Here too a rationalization takes place, but in a somewhat different form. The knowledge of the correspondence between a particular property of handwriting and a particular character trait is, in many cases, intuitively gained at first, e.g. by thinking one's way into the movements involved in writing. Here then, the task of rationalization consists in determining the degree of correlation of the two features through statistical comparison on the basis of a variety of empirical material.

Our view, then, is that the further development and expression of concepts in a more precise way should be carried out for the entirety of psychology along the lines which we have indicated with the example of graphology, that is to say, in the direction of physicalization. But psychology, as has already frequently been emphasized, is a physical science even before this introduction of conceptual precision. Its task is systematically to describe the (physical) behaviour of living things, in particular that of humans, and to subsume it under laws. These laws are of very different types, e.g. a hand movement can be interpreted from different perspectives. Firstly, it can be interpreted semiotically, as a more or less conventional sign for a signified state of affairs. Secondly, it can be interpreted mimetically, as an expression for the current psychological state, i.e. of the 'momentary-properties' of the person in question. Thirdly, it can be interpreted physiognomically, as an expression of the 'permanent-properties', i.e. of the 'character' of the person in question. For example, in order to examine mimetically and physiognomically the hand movements of people (of particular groups), one could record them cinematographically in order to obtain cinematic diagrams for the movements, like those drawn up by a technician for the movement of parts of a machine. In this way, the customary cinematic (i.e. movement-related, purely spatio-temporal) traits of those hand movements, upon whose perception a particular intuitive protocol characterization usually appears (e.g. 'this hand movement appears hurried', '. . . generous . . .', and the like), would have to be established. This explains why graphology in particular, that is to say, the characterological examination of very particular sorts of hand movements, characterized by their particular purpose, that is, of writing movements, has been the only examination of its kind which up to now has proved successful. The reason lies in the fact that writing movements already deliver something similar to a cinematic diagram, namely penstrokes on paper. Here, we ought to note, it is only the track of the movements that is recorded. The temporal processes [involving hand movements] are not recorded, but can only be inferred retrospectively, though not completely, by the graphologist on the basis of indirect characteristics. More exact results would ensue if we had the complete three-dimensional spatio-temporal diagram at our disposal, not merely its projection onto the writing surface. But even the results of graphology currently available allay the misgivings that investigations aiming at the physicalization of psychological concepts are bound to lack interest. Perhaps the supposition is not too bold that interesting parallels are to be found between the results of a characterological examination of the movements of the parts of the body, including both spontaneous movements and purposeful actions, and the results of graphology already available. If, on the one hand, particular character traits express themselves in particular forms of handwriting properties and, on the other hand, they express themselves in particular forms of movement of the arms, legs and of particular features of the face, might it not be the case that similarities exist between the former and the latter? Perhaps graphology itself, having first given us useful suggestions for the investigation of other sorts of movements, may be stimulated into an awareness of handwriting characteristics which it previously did not take into account. All these are, however, mere suppositions. Whether they turn out to be true or not does not matter for our thesis, which maintains the possibility of translating all psychological sentences into the language of physics. This translatability holds in every case, whether or not the concepts of psychology are in fact physicalized. Physicalization simply means a higher and more strictly systematized scientific form of conceptualization. Its implementation is a practical task which is no longer up to the epistemologist but up to the psychologist.

## Sentences about matters pertaining to one's own psyche; 'Introspective' Psychology

The considerations so far have shown that a sentence about matters pertaining to another psyche is about physical processes in the body of that person. If one wants to interpret it in a different way, the sentence becomes in principle unverifiable, hence meaningless. The same is true of sentences about matters pertaining to one's own psyche. But here the emotional resistance to the physical interpretation is considerably greater. The close relationship between a sentence about matters pertaining to another psyche and a sentence about matters pertaining to one's own psyche is most easily seen if we consider a sentence about matters pertaining to one's own psyche in the past, e.g. P1: 'Yesterday I was excited'. Here verification takes place either by rational inference from protocol sentences of the type p1 that are perceived now but that refer to my handwriting yesterday, or to pictures or films of me yesterday. Or else verification takes place in the intuitive way, e.g. on the basis of a protocol sentence p2 'I remember having been excited yesterday'. The content of the sentence P1 exceeds the content of both the individual protocol sentence p1 as well as that of p2, as can be seen most clearly from the possibility of error and repudiation. P1 simply receives a progressively higher degree of confirmation by being verified by a series of protocol sentences of the types p1 and p2. The same protocol sentences also serve as confirmation of the physical sentence P2 'Yesterday my body was in the physical state usually called "excitedness".' It follows that P1 has the same content as P2.

In the case of a sentence about matters pertaining to one's own psyche now, e.g. P1 'I am now excited', a clear distinction needs to be made between the system sentence P1 and the protocol sentence p2 which may also read 'I am now excited'. The difference lies in the fact that the system sentence P1 may be withdrawn, whereas the protocol sentence, being the point of departure, will remain. The protocol sentences p1, which rationally support P1, take the following form: 'I feel my hands shaking', 'I see my hands shaking', 'I hear my voice trembling', etc. Here too the content of P1 exceeds that of p1 and p2 in that it encompasses all possible sentences of this type. P1 has the same content as the physical sentence P2 'My body is now in the physical condition which exhibits such and such signs of excitedness when tested by me or by others'. These are the signs that occur in my protocol sentences of the types p1 and p2 as well as in the protocol sentences of other subjects (as discussed earlier when we considered sentences about matters pertaining to another psyche).

# PHYSICALISTIC INTERPRETATION OF PSYCHOLOGICAL SENTENCES

| | 1 Sentence about wooden beam (serving as an analogy) | 2 Sentence about matters pertaining to another psyche | 3 Sentence about matters pertaining to one's own psyche in the past | 4 Sentence about matters pertaining to one's own psyche in the present |
|---|---|---|---|---|
| *System sentence* P1 | 'The beam is firm' | 'A is excited' | 'I was excited yesterday' | 'I am excited now' |
| a) *rationally* inferred from protocol sentence P1 | 'The beam is of such colour and shape' | 'A exhibits such and such facial expressions' | 'These handwriting characteristics (of mine, yesterday) are of such and such a form' | 'My hands here are trembling' |
| or b) *intuitively* inferred from protocol sentence P2 | 'The beam looks firm' | 'A is excited' ('A looks excited') | 'Now, memory of excitedness' | 'Now excited' |
| P1 has the same content as the *physical sentence* P2 | 'The beam is physically firm' | 'The body of A is physically excited' | 'My body was physically excited yesterday' | 'My body is now physically excited' |
| The physical concept | 'Physically firm' | 'physically-excited' | | |
| is defined as the disposition to react in such and such a way under such and such conditions | 'Given such and such strain, such and such bending will occur; given such and such strain, collapse will occur' | 'Under such and such conditions, such and such movements, facial expressions, actions, words will occur' | | |

The table on the [previous] page indicates the parallelism between, on the one hand, sentences about matters pertaining to another psyche, about matters pertaining to one's own psyche in the past, and about matters pertaining to one's own psyche in the present, and, on the other hand, a physical sentence about a wooden beam. In this way it provides a clear illustration of the analogy in the use of the thesis of physicalism in the three cases.

*Objection on the part of introspective psychology.* 'If the psychologist does not examine someone else as the experimental subject, but engages in self-observation or "introspection", he will gain an immediate grasp of something that is not physical. This is the real object of psychology.'

Rebuttal: We need to distinguish between the question of the legitimacy of an established practical method of inquiry and the question of the legitimacy of some established interpretation of the results of that inquiry. *Any* method of inquiry is legitimate. All we can argue about here is the effectiveness and fruitfulness of a method, but this does not form part of our present concerns. We are free to employ any method we please; but we are not free to interpret as we please the sentences thereby obtained. The meaning of a sentence [expressing the results], no matter how the sentence was derived, results unambiguously from the logical analysis of the method whereby we derive and verify the sentence. We cannot object to a psychologist who employs the method of so-called introspection; i.e. to one who includes, in his experimental protocol, sentences of the form: 'I experienced such and such processes of consciousness'. Such a psychologist, by appealing to inductive generalizations, by forming hypotheses, and finally by comparing his own experiences with those of other persons, will then use such disparate material to propose general sentences of psychology. But, here too, epistemological and logical analysis leads us once again to the result that both the singular and general sentences are to be interpreted physicalistically. Let the psychologist A write in his protocol the sentence p2: '(I am) now excited'. Previous reflection[7] showed us that the view that protocol sentences are not to be interpreted physicalistically, but are to be taken as speaking of something non-physical ('psychical', 'contents of experience', 'data of consciousness' and the like), has the consequence that each protocol sentence would be meaningful only for the subject itself. The protocol sentence p2 of A, if not interpreted physically, could not be verified by another subject B, and therefore would be meaningless for B. Furthermore, we showed on that occasion that non-physical interpretation leads one into insoluble contradictions. Finally, we found that each protocol sentence corresponds in content to a physical sentence[8] and that this physicalistic translation is possible at present and without presupposing any exact knowledge of the physiology of the central nervous system. It follows that sentences about matters pertaining to one's own psyche are in any case translatable into sentences of the language of physics, whether we take them to be intersubjective system sentences or so-called introspective protocol sentences of the individual subject.

Perhaps one will object to our view that surely there is a difference between experiencing and expressing what is experienced. After all, not everything experienced needs to find expression in a protocol sentence. The difference does indeed exist, though it is formulated differently by us. The sentences P1 'A is now seeing red' and P2 'A now says: "I see red"' are not of the same content. Nor does P2 follow from P1; all that follows is a conditional clause 'If such and such, then P2'. For P1 states a physical condition of A, which is such that the process of expression indicated by P2 follows under certain conditions.

If we look at the method by which the results of so-called introspection are usually incorporated into science, we notice that they are as a matter of fact evaluated physicalistically. Only, the physicalism which is in fact practised is not usually acknowledged in theory. The psychologist, A, publishes his investigations. The reader, B, reads the sentence 'A was excited' (for the sake of clarity we write 'A' instead of the word 'I', which B when reading has to replace by 'A'). For B, this sentence is a sentence about matters pertaining to another psyche. All that B can verify here is that A's body was in a certain physical state (this is also what we found when analyzing a sentence, P1, about matters pertaining to another psyche). B, it is true, was not in a position to observe this state himself, but he can now infer it in an indirect way. For he sees the sentence in a book on the front page of which A is mentioned as the author. On the basis of a general sentence, gained from previous induction, B infers (with probability) that A wrote the sentences printed in the book. Further, on the basis of a sentence which implies the credibility of A, and which has also been gained by induction, he infers that, if he had observed A's body at the time, he (probably) would have confirmed the existence of this condition of (physical) excitedness. Since this confirmation can only refer to a physical condition of the body of A, the sentence read in the book can also only have a physical meaning for the reader, B.

Generally speaking, protocol sentences that are spoken, written or printed by a psychologist on the basis of so-called introspection are to be understood by the reader (and thereby by intersubjective science in general) in the first instance not as scientific sentences but as scientific facts. The confused state of the epistemological situation that psychology finds itself in at present is to a large extent due to the confusion of facts which assume the form of sentences with these sentences as elements of the system of science. We may recall the example of the celestial patterns. The introspective statements of the psychologist are in principle not to be understood in any other way than the statements of his experimental subjects which he records. At best, one may be inclined to accept the former as statements made by an experimental subject of special credibility and experience. Furthermore, in principle the statements of an experimental subject are not to be understood as being any different from the rest of his voluntary and involuntary movements. At best, it may be possible to use his movements of speech as particularly informative movements. And the movements of the speech organs and other parts of the body of an experimental subject are, in principle, not to be understood in a different way from the movements of animals, though the former may, at best, be more valuable for the task of establishing general sentences. The movements of an animal are, in principle, not to be understood in a different way from the movements of a voltmeter, though the movements of an animal may, at best, be evaluated in a greater variety of ways than those of the voltmeter. The movements of the voltmeter are in principle not to be understood in a different way from the movements of a raindrop, though the former may open up more possibilities for making inferences about other processes. All the cases mentioned share the same fundamental feature: from a certain physical sentence further sentences are inferred by causal inference, i.e. with help from general physical formulae, the so-called natural laws. The only difference among the various examples is the degree to which their premises are fruitful. It may be possible to infer more sentences of scientific relevance from the movements of a voltmeter than from the movement of a particular drop of rain; or from the movements of speech rather than from other human movements. Now, in the case with which we are here concerned, the inference leading from the sign to the indicated state of affairs takes a particularly noteworthy form. When evaluating a statement about matters pertaining to one's own psyche, gained by introspection (e.g. A states: 'A is excited'), this statement, when taken as an acoustic event, is the sign. And the indicated state of affairs here is such that it is to be described by a sentence which possesses just the same form as its sign, the acoustic event ('A is excited'), given favorable conditions which often occur within the scientific enterprise. [These conditions consist in the subject in question being considered credible and acquainted with psychological reporting, and in the language used by the subject being the same as the one in which the scientific system is being written.] This identity of form, between acoustical fact and the scientific sentence to be derived from it, explains why confusion between the two arises so easily and persists so stubbornly. The fateful confusion resolves itself as soon as we realize that this is a case of inference from sign to the indicated state of affairs, which is no different from the other cases that we considered.

The inadmissibility of the non-physical interpretation of so-called introspective statements becomes particularly clear when we consider how speaking on the basis of so-called introspection is learned [how these introspective statements become part of speech]. A tired child says 'I am happy to be in bed now'. If we examine how the child learned to use such sentences about matters pertaining to its own psyche, it emerges that on similar occasions the mother told the child 'You are happy to be in bed now'. So we see that A learns how to utter the protocol sentence p2 from B, who by means of the same words refers to the system sentence, P1, which is, for B, a sentence about matters pertaining to another psyche. To learn to speak thus consists in B teaching A a certain habit, namely the habit of 'verbalizing', as the behaviourists say, in a certain way in certain situations. And this habit is usually guided in such a way that the words produced by the speech movements of the child, A, correspond with the sentence of the intersubjective physical language which expresses the condition in question of A. But, and this is the crucial point, what is expressed is the condition of A as perceived by B, that is, the physical condition of the body of A. The example of the child shows this with particular clarity. The sentence 'You are happy', spoken by the mother, is a sentence about matters pertaining to another psyche, hence, according to our previous considerations, it can only refer to a physical state. It follows that the child is taught the habit of uttering under certain conditions a sentence expressing the physical state in himself as observed (or inferred from signs observed) by another person. Hence if the child produces the same sounds again, no more may be inferred from this than that the body of the child is in the same physical state.

## Summary

So-called psychological sentences are always translatable into the language of physics, be they specific sentences about matters pertaining to another psyche, about matters pertaining to one's own psyche in the past, about matters pertaining to one's own psyche in the present, or general sentences. Every psychological sentence refers to physical processes of the body of the subject(s) in question. Therefore, psychology is a part of unified science based on physics. By 'physics' we mean not the system of physical laws known today, but science characterized by the following kind of concept formation: each concept is derived from the 'variables', i.e. from the assignation of numbers to spatio-temporal points according to defined procedures. Thus we can put our thesis, which is a sub-thesis of physicalism, as follows: psychology is a branch of physics.

## References

1 Carnap, 'Die physikalische Sprache als Universalsprache der Wissenschaft' (The Language of Physics as the Universal Language of Science), *Erkenntnis* II, 1931, pp. 432-465.

2 *Ibid.* pp. 449 ff.

3 *Ibid.* p. 460.

4 John B. Watson, *Der Behaviourismus* (Behaviourism), Stuttgart, 1930.

5 Carnap, R. 'Die physikalische Sprache als Universalsprache der Wissenschaft' ('The Language of Physics as the Universal Language of Science'), *Erkenntnis* II, 1931, pp. 444 ff.

6 Cf. e.g. L. Klages, *Handschrift und Charakter* (Handwriting and Character), Leipzig, 1920. Several examples are either taken from this book or based on it.

7 *Erkenntnis*, II, 1931, p. 454.

8 *Ibid.* pp. 457ff.

LUDWIG WITTGENSTEIN

## 'On Believing'

# Extract from *The Brown Book*

Let us then consider the proposition 'Believing something cannot merely consist in saying that you believe it, you must say it with a particular facial expression, gesture, and tone of voice'. Now it cannot be doubted that we regard certain facial expressions, gestures, etc. as characteristic for the expression of belief. We speak of a 'tone of conviction'. And yet it is clear that this tone of conviction isn't always present whenever we rightly speak of conviction. 'Just so', you might say, 'this shows that there is something else, something behind these gestures, etc. which is the real belief as opposed to mere expressions of belief'. – 'Not at all', I should say, 'many different criteria distinguish, under different circumstances, cases of believing what you say from those of not believing what you say'. There may be cases where the presence of a sensation other than those bound up with gestures, tone of voice, etc. distinguishes meaning what you say from not meaning it. But sometimes what distinguishes these two is nothing that happens while we speak, but a variety of actions and experiences of different kinds before and after.

To understand this family of cases it will again be helpful to consider an analogous case drawn from facial expressions. There is a family of friendly facial expressions. Suppose we had asked 'What feature is it that characterizes a friendly face?' At first one might think that there are certain traits which one might call friendly traits, each of which makes the face look friendly to a certain degree, and which when present in a large number constitute the friendly expression. This idea would seem to be borne out by our common speech, talking of 'friendly eyes', 'friendly mouth', etc. But it is easy to see that the same eyes of which we say they make a face look friendly do not look friendly, or even look unfriendly, with certain other wrinkles of the forehead, lines round the mouth, etc. Why then do we ever say that it is these eyes which look friendly? Isn't it wrong to say that they characterize the face as friendly, for if we say they do so 'under certain circumstances' (these circumstances being the other features of the face) why did we single out the one feature from amongst the others? The answer is that in the wide family of friendly faces there is what one might call a main branch characterized by a certain kind of eyes, another by a certain kind of mouth, etc.; although in the large family of unfriendly faces we meet these same eyes when they don't mitigate the unfriendliness of the expression. There is further the fact that when we notice the friendly expression of a face, our attention, our gaze, is drawn to a particular feature in the face, the 'friendly eyes', or the 'friendly mouth', etc., and that it does not rest on other features although these too are responsible for the friendly expression.

'But is there no difference between saying something and meaning it, and saying it without meaning it?' There needn't be a difference while he says it, and if there is, this difference may be of all sorts of different kinds according to the surrounding circumstances. It does not follow from the fact that there is what we call a friendly and an unfriendly expression of the eye that there must be a difference between the eye of a friendly and the eye of an unfriendly face.

One might be tempted to say 'This trait can't be said to make the face look friendly, as it may be belied by another trait'. And this is like saying 'Saying something with the tone of conviction can't be the characteristic of conviction, as it may be belied by experiences going along with it'. But neither of these sentences is correct. It is true that other traits in this face could take away the friendly character of this eye, and yet in this face it is the eye which is the outstanding friendly feature.

It is such phrases as 'He said it and meant it' which are most liable to mislead us. Compare meaning 'I shall be delighted to see you' with meaning 'The train leaves at 3.30'. Suppose you had said the first sentence to someone and were asked afterwards 'Did you mean it?', you would then probably think of the feelings, the experiences, which you had while you said it. And accordingly you would in this case be inclined to say 'Didn't you see that I meant it?' Suppose that on the other hand, after having given someone the information 'The train leaves at 3.30', he asked you 'Did you mean it?', you might be inclined to answer 'Certainly. Why shouldn't I have meant it?'

In the first case we shall be inclined to speak about a feeling characteristic of meaning what we said, but not in the second. Compare also lying in both these cases. In the first case we should be inclined to say that lying consisted in saying what we did but without the appropriate feelings or even with the opposite feelings. If we lied in giving the information about the train, we would be likely to have different experiences while we gave it than those which we have in giving truthful information, but the difference here would not consist in the absence of a characteristic feeling, but perhaps just in the presence of a feeling of discomfort.

It is even possible while lying to have quite strong experience of what might be called the characteristic for meaning what one says – and yet under certain circumstances, and perhaps under the ordinary circumstances, one refers to just this experience in saying, 'I meant what I said', because the cases in which something might give the lie to these experiences do not come into the question. In many cases therefore we are inclined to say: 'Meaning what I say' means having such and such experiences while I say it.

If by 'believing' we mean an activity, a process, taking place while we say that we believe, we may say that believing is something similar to or the same as expressing a belief.

It is interesting to consider an objection to this: What if I said 'I believe it will rain' (meaning what I say) and someone wanted to explain to a Frenchman who doesn't understand English what it was I believed. Then, you might say, if all that happened when I believed what I did was that I said the sentence, the Frenchman ought to know what I believe if you tell him the exact words I used, or say 'Il croit "It will rain"'. Now it is clear that this will not tell him what I believe and consequently, you might say, we failed to convey just that to him which was essential, my real mental act of believing. – But the answer is that even if my words had been accompanied by all sorts of experiences, and if we could have transmitted these experiences to the Frenchman, he would still not have known what I believed. For 'knowing what I believe' just doesn't mean: feeling what I do while I say it; just as knowing what I intend with this move in our game of chess doesn't mean knowing my exact state of mind while I'm making the move. Though, at the same time, in certain cases, knowing this state of mind might furnish you with very exact information about my intention.

We should say that we had told the Frenchman what I believed if we translated my words for him into French. And it *might* be that thereby we told him nothing – even indirectly – about what happened 'in me' when I uttered my belief. Rather, we pointed out to him a sentence which in his language holds a similar position to my sentence in the English language. – Again one might say that, at least in certain cases, we could have told him much more exactly what I believed if he had been at home in the English language, because then, he would have known exactly what happened within me when I spoke.

We use the words 'meaning', 'believing', 'intending' in such a way that they refer to certain acts, states of mind given certain circumstances; as by the expression 'checkmating somebody' we refer to the act of taking his king. If on the other hand, someone, say a child, playing about with chessmen, placed a few of them on a chess board and went through the motions of taking a king, we should not say the child had checkmated anyone. – And here, too, one might think that what distinguished this case from real checkmating was what happened in the child's mind.

Suppose I had made a move in chess and someone asked me 'Did you intend to mate him?', I answer 'I did', and he now asks me 'How could you know you did, as all you *knew* was what happened within you when you made the move?', I might answer 'Under *these* circumstances this was intending to mate him'.

What holds for 'meaning' holds for 'thinking'. – We very often find it imposssible to think without speaking to ourselves half aloud, – and nobody asked to describe what happened in this case would ever say that something – the thinking – accompanied the speaking, were he not led into doing so by the pair of verbs 'speaking'/'thinking', and by many of our common phrases in which their uses run parallel. Consider these examples: 'Think before you speak!' 'He speaks without thinking', 'What I said didn't quite express my thought', 'He says one thing and thinks just the opposite', 'I didn't mean a word of what I said', 'The French language uses its words in that order in which we think them'.

If anything in such a case can be said to go with the speaking, it would be something like the modulation of voice, the changes in timbre, accentuation, and the like, all of which one might call means of expressiveness. Some of these, like the tone of voice and the accent, nobody for obvious reasons would call the accompaniments of the speech; and such means of expressiveness as the play of facial expression or gestures which can be said to accompany speech, nobody would dream of calling thinking.

## Extract from the *Philosophical Investigations*

How did we ever come to use such an expression as 'I believe
...'? Did we at some time become aware of a phenomenon (of
belief)? Did we observe ourselves and other people and so
discover belief?

Moore's paradox can be put like this: the expression 'I believe
that this is the case' is used like the assertion 'This is the case';
and yet the *hypothesis* that I believe this is the case is not used
like the hypothesis that this is the case.

So it *looks* as if the assertion 'I believe' were not the assertion
of what is supposed in the hypothesis 'I believe'!

Similarly: the statement 'I believe it's going to rain' has a
meaning like, that is to say a use like, 'It's going to rain', but the
meaning of 'I believed then that it was going to rain', is not like
that of 'It did rain then'.

'But surely "I believed" must tell of just the same thing in the
past as "I believe" in the present!' – Surely $\sqrt{-1}$ must mean
just the same in relation to $-1$, as $\sqrt{1}$ means in relation to $1$!
This means nothing at all.

'At bottom, when I say "I believe ... " I am describing my
own state of mind – but this description is indirectly an assertion
of the fact believed.' – As in certain circumstances I describe a
photograph in order to describe the thing it is a photograph of.

But then I must also be able to say that the photograph is a
good one. So here too: 'I believe it's raining and my belief is
reliable, so I have confidence in it.' – In that case my belief
would be a kind of sense-impression.

One can mistrust one's own senses, but not one's own belief.

If there were a verb meaning 'to believe falsely', it would not
have any significant first person present indicative.

Don't look at it as a matter of course, but as a most
remarkable thing, that the verbs 'believe', 'wish', 'will' display
all the inflexions possessed by 'cut', 'chew', 'run'.

The language-game of reporting can be given such a turn that a report is not meant to inform the hearer about its subject matter but about the person making the report.

It is so when, for instance, a teacher examines a pupil. (You can measure to test the ruler.)

Suppose I were to introduce some expression – 'I believe', for instance – in this way: it is to be prefixed to reports when they serve to give information about the reporter. (So the expression need not carry with it any suggestion of uncertainty. Remember that the uncertainty of an assertion can be expressed impersonally:'He might come today.') – 'I believe . . ., and it isn't so' would be a contradiction.

'I believe . . .' throws light on my state. Conclusions about my conduct can be drawn from this expression. So there is a *similarity* here to expressions of emotion, of mood, etc.

If, however, 'I believe it is so' throws light on my state, then so does the assertion 'It is so'. For the sign 'I believe' can't do it, can at the most hint at it.

Imagine a language in which 'I believe it is so' is expressed only by means of the tone of the assertion 'It is so'. In this language they say, not 'He believes' but 'He is inclined to say . . .' and there exists also the hypothetical (subjunctive) 'Suppose I were inclined etc.', but not the expression 'I am inclined to say'.

Moore's paradox would not exist in this language; instead of it, however, there would be a verb lacking one inflexion.

But this ought not to surprise us. Think of the fact that one can predict one's *own* future action by an expression of intention.

I say of someone else 'He seems to believe . . .' and other people say it of me. Now, why do I never say it of myself, not even when others *rightly* say it of me? – Do I myself not see and hear myself, then? – That can be said.

'One feels conviction within oneself, one doesn't infer it from one's own words or their tone.' – What is true here is: one does not infer one's own conviction from one's own words; nor yet the actions which arise from that conviction.

'Here it *looks* as if the assertion "I believe" were not the assertion of what is supposed in the hypothesis.' – So I am tempted to look for a different development of the verb in the first person present indicative.

This is how I think of it: Believing is a state of mind. It has duration; and that independently of the duration of its expression in a sentence, for example. So it is a kind of disposition of the believing person. This is shewn me in the case of someone else by his behaviour; and by his words. And under this head, by the expression 'I believe . . .' as well as by the simple assertion. – What about my own case: how do I myself recognize my own disposition? – Here it will have been necessary for me to take notice of myself as others do, to listen to myself talking, to be able to draw conclusions from what I say!

My own relation to my words is wholly different from other people's.

That different development of the verb would have been possible, if only I could say 'I seem to believe'.

If I listened to the words of my mouth, I might say that someone else was speaking out of my mouth.

'Judging from what I say, *this* is what I believe.' Now, it is possible to think out circumstances in which these words would make sense.

And then it would also be possible for someone to say 'It is raining and I don't believe it', or 'It seems to me that my ego believes this, but it isn't true.' One would have to fill out the picture with behaviour indicating that two people were speaking through my mouth.

Even in the *hypothesis* the pattern is not what you think.

When you say 'Suppose I believe . . .' you are presupposing the whole grammar of the word 'to believe', the ordinary use, of which you are master. – You are not supposing some state of affairs which, so to speak, a picture presents unambiguously to you, so that you can tack on to this hypothetical use some assertive use other than the ordinary one. – You would not know at all what you were supposing here (i.e. what, for example, would follow from such a supposition), if you were not already familiar with the use of 'believe'.

Think of the expression 'I say . . .' for example in 'I say it will rain today', which simply comes to the same thing as the assertion 'It will . . .'. 'He says it will . . .' means approximately 'He believes it will . . .'. 'Suppose I say . . .' does *not* mean: Suppose it rains today.

Different concepts touch here and coincide over a stretch. But you need not think that all lines are *circles*.

Consider the misbegotten sentence 'It may be raining, but it isn't'.

And here one should be on one's guard against saying that 'It may be raining' really means 'I think it'll be raining'. For why not the other way round, why should not the latter mean the former?

Don't regard a hesitant assertion as an assertion of hesitancy.

GILBERT RYLE

# A Puzzling Element in the Notion of Thinking

Usually when we philosophers discuss questions about thinking, we concentrate, for very good reasons, upon what people do or might think; that is, on the opinions that they form, the beliefs that they have, the theories that they construct, the conclusions that they reach and the premisses from which they reach them. In a word, our usual questions are questions about the truths or falsehoods that people do or might accept. Their thoughts, of which we discuss the structures, the implications and the evidential backings, are the results in which their former ponderings and calculations have terminated. For when a person knows or believes that something is the case, his knowledge or belief is something that he now has or possesses, and the pondering which got him there is now over. While he is still wondering and pondering, he is still short of his destination. When he has settled his problem, his task of trying to settle it is finished.

It should not be forgotten that some of the problems that we have to try to settle are not theoretical problems but practical problems. We have to try to decide what to do, as well as try to decide what is the case. The solution of a problem is not always a truth or a falsehood.

We should not assume, either, that all thinking is trying to settle problems, whether theoretical or practical. This would be too restrictive. A person is certainly thinking when he is going over a poem that he knows perfectly, or dwelling on the incidents of yesterday's football match. He has, or need have, no problems to solve or results to aim at. Not all of our walks are journeys.

Lastly, we should not assume that all or even most of the truths or falsehoods that are ours are the fruits of our own ponderings. Fortunately and unfortunately, a great part of what we believe and know we have taken over from other people. Most of the things that we know we have not discovered for ourselves, but have been taught. Most of the things that we believe we believe simply because we have been told them. As with worldly goods, so with truths and falsehoods, much of what we possess is inherited or donated.

It is a vexatious fact about the English language that we use the verb 'to think' both for the beliefs or opinions that a man has, and for the pondering and reflecting that a man does; and that we use the noun 'thought' both for the truth or falsehood that he accepts, and for the activity of reflecting which, perhaps, preceded his acceptance of it. To think, in the sense of 'believe', is not to think, in the sense of 'ponder'. There is only the verbal appearance of a contradiction in saying that while a person is still thinking, he does not yet know what to think; and that when he does know what to think, he has no more thinking to do.

The problems which I wish to discuss are questions not about the propositions that a person does or might believe, but about his activities of pondering, perpending, musing, reflecting, calculating, meditating, and so on. I shall be talking about the thinking which is the travelling and not the being at one's destination; the winnowing and not the grain; the bargaining and not the goods; the work and not the repose.

A person does not have to be advanced in age or highly schooled in order to be able to give satisfactory answers to ordinary interrogations about his thinking. A child who has never heard a word of psychological or philosophical discourse is not in the least embarrassed at being asked what he had been thinking about while sitting in the swing. Indeed, if asked not very long afterwards, he is likely to be quite ready to give a moderately detailed account of the thoughts that he had had, and even perhaps of the rough sequence in which he had had them. The task does not feel to him hugely different from the task of recounting what he had been doing so quietly or so noisily in the nursery or what he had seen and whom he had met during his afternoon walk.

Nonetheless, familiar though we are with the task of recounting our thoughts, we are embarrassed by a quite different task, set to us by the psychologist or the philosopher, the task, namely, of saying what the having of these thoughts had consisted in. I mean this. If during a certain period I had been, say, singing or mending a gate or writing a testimonial, then when recounting afterwards what I had been doing, I could, if required, mention the concrete ingredients of my activity, namely the noises that I had uttered, the hammer-blows that I had struck, and the ink-marks that I had made on the paper. Of course, a mere catalogue of these concrete happenings would not yet amount to an account of what I had been doing. Singing a song is not just uttering one noise after another; the sequence of noises must be a directed sequence. Still, if no noises are made, no song is sung; and if no ink-marks are produced, no testimonial is written. If I recollect singing or writing a testimonial, then I recollect that I made some noises or some ink-marks.

But when I recollect, however clearly, a stretch, however recent, of my musing or pondering, I do not seem to be, in the same way, automatically primed with answers to questions about the concrete ingredients of the thoughts the having of which I have no difficulty in recounting. I tell you, for example, '. . . and then the idea occurred to me that, since it was Sunday, I might not be able to get petrol at the next village.' If now you ask me to say what concrete shape the occurring of this slightly complex idea had taken, I may well be stumped for an answer, so stumped, even, as half to resent the putting of the question.

You might press your irksome question in this way. You say, 'Well, you have just recounted to us in a dozen or more English words the idea that had occurred to you. Did the idea itself occur to you in English words? Does your recollection of the idea occurring to you incorporate the recollection of your saying something to yourself in a dozen or more English words, whether in your head or *sotto voce*? Or, having recently returned from France, did you perhaps say something to the same effect to yourself in a dozen or more French words?' To this very specific question my answer might be, 'Yes; I do now recall saying something to myself in my head, in English words, to the effect that as it was Sunday there might be no petrol available in the next village.' But my answer might be, 'No; I don't recall saying anything to myself at all.' Or my answer might be, 'Well, I'm not absolutely sure that I did not just say "Sunday" in my head, but I'm sure that I did not say anything more.'

Your pertinacity is irritating, since I want to say that it does not really matter whether I said anything to myself or not. Having the idea in question did not require my saying anything to myself, in the way in which singing does require uttering noises and repairing a gate does require *either* hammering *or* wire-tying *or* bolt-tightening *or* something of the same concrete sort.

Ignoring my irritation you now press me with another batch of specific queries. You say, 'If when you had that idea you did not say anything to yourself in your head or *sotto voce*, then was it that instead you saw some things in your mind's eye? Was it that you had mental pictures blurred or sharp, well coloured or ill coloured, maybe of villagers entering a village church, and of a garage with its doors closed; so that it was in this concrete shape, or something like it, that the idea came to you that since it was Sunday you might not be able to get petrol?' Again I might answer, 'Yes, I did visualize scenes like this.' But I might answer, 'No, I am sure that I did not visualize anything.' Or I might answer, 'Well, I do remember seeing in my mind's eye the duck-pond of the village in question: I usually do when I think of that village. But this had nothing to do with the special idea that the garage there might be closed for Sunday.' Once again I might be irked at the question being pressed at all. Why should my thinking the thought have gone with either the saying of something to myself or with the seeing of something in my mind's eye or with any other proprietary happenings?

There are, however, certain special thinking-activities which certainly do seem to require our saying things in our heads or *sotto voce* or aloud, and we need to examine what there is about these special activities which requires the inward or outward production of words and phrases.

(a) If I have been trying to compose a poem or an after-dinner speech, then I must indeed have been producing to myself words and phrases, examining them, cancelling or improving them, assembling them and rehearsing assemblages of them. That is, if my thinking happens to be a piece of thinking what to say and how to say it, then it must incorporate the tentative, exploratory, and critical saying of things to myself; and then, if asked to recount in retrospect whether I had been saying things to myself in English or in French, I should answer without hesitation. There is here no question of my first thinking out my poem or my speech, and only then, in reply to posthumous interrogations, putting my composition into words. The thinking was itself a piece of word-hunting, phrase-concocting, and sentence-mending. It was thinking *up* words, phrases and sentences.

(b) If I have been doing a slightly complex piece of computation, whether in my head or on paper, like multiplying £13 12s. 4d. by 7, then not only must my answer, if I obtain one, be a numerical or worded formula, £95 6s. 4d., perhaps, but also the results of the interim multiplying-operations, dividing-operations, and adding-operations will be numbers. What I say to myself in my head, if I do the sum in my head, will parallel the things that I should write down one after another if I worked the sum out on paper, and these will be numbers of pounds, shillings, or pence. If asked afterwards whether I had, at a certain stage, said to myself 'Seven twelves are eighty-four, plus two, makes eighty-six' or whether I had in my mind's eye seen the corresponding numerals, or both together, I might recollect just which I had done; and I should not feel irked at the suggestion that I must have done one or the other. Certainly, multiplying does not consist merely in saying numbers aloud or in our heads; but we are ready to allow that it requires this, or some alternative, in the same sort of way as singing a song requires, though it does not reduce to, the uttering of noises. Trying to get the correct answer, unlike just making a guess at it, involves trying to establish checkable intermediate steps, in order to make the correct moves from those steps to the right answer; and these steps, to be checkable, must be formulated.

(c) Some kinds of problems, like those of advocates, debaters, and philosophers, have something in common with the task of composition and something in common with the task of computation. The thinker has, all the time, both to be trying to find out what to say and how to say it, and also to be trying to establish as true what he says. He wants his hearers – including himself – not only to understand what he says but also to accept it, and to accept it perforce. As his task is, in two dimensions, a forensic task, his thinking involves him in producing and canvassing, in however sketchy a manner, words, phrases, and sentences, conclusions, reasons, and rebuttals of objections.

Now if, improvidently, we pick on one of these three special varieties of thinking as our universal model, we shall be tempted to say, as Plato said, that 'in thinking the soul is conversing [or perhaps 'debating'] with herself', and so postulate that any piece of meditating or pondering whatsoever has got, so to speak, to run on the wheels of words, phrases, and sentences.

Or, if forced by our own reminiscences to allow that sometimes we have thoughts when no wording of these thoughts takes place, we may then be tempted simply to give to the model one extension and postulate that in thinking the soul is *either* conversing with itself *or else* performing some one specific alternative to conversing, such as visualizing things. In either case we are presupposing that thinking, of whatever sort, must, so to speak, employ a concrete apparatus of some specifiable kind or other, linguistic or pictorial or something else. This general presupposition is sometimes formulated in the following way. Just as an Englishman who has become perfectly familiar with the French language may say that he can now think in French, so, and in the same sense of 'in', he must always think either 'in' his native English or else 'in' some alternative apparatus, like French or visual imagery or algebraical symbols or gestures or something else that he can produce, on demand, from his own resources. The generic term 'symbol' is sometimes used to cover all the postulated vehicles of thinking. It is a psychological necessity, or perhaps even a part of the very concept of thinking, that when thinking occurs, there occur, internally or externally, things or symbols that the thinker thinks in.

It is if we make this presupposition that we are especially embarrassed at being required to tell in retrospect in what symbols (in this awkwardly distended use of the word) we had, for example, the idea that as it was Sunday there might be no petrol available at the next village. For often we cannot recollect any such vehicles being present on the occasion when, as we clearly do recollect, we had that thought.

I want to attack this presupposition. I want to deny that it even makes sense to ask, in the general case, what special sort or sorts of things we think *in*. The very collocation of 'think' with 'in so and so' seems to me factitious, save in our very special case of the Englishman who describes himself as now being able to think in French. So let us clear his case out of the way.

The primary thing that he means when he says that he now thinks in French is that when he has to talk to Frenchmen, he does not any longer have to think out how to say in French what he wants to say. He no longer, for example, has first to say to himself in English what he wants to say, and then to struggle to translate from English into French for the benefit of his French audience. The composition of French remarks is no longer any more difficult for him than the composition of English remarks, that is, it is not difficult at all. But to say that he no longer has to think out how to say things in French has not the slightest tendency to show that all or most of the thoughts that he thinks are now accompanied or 'carried' by the production of French words. It is only to say that *when he is conversing with Frenchmen* he does not have to think about the vehicles of this conversing. When he does have to compose in French he does not have to think *up* French words. But most of the things he thinks about are not matters of French composition, just as most of the things we think about are not matters of English composition. Roughly, he thinks in French when he says what he wants to say in French without any groping or fumbling.

Secondarily, when he says that he now thinks in French, he may also mean that *when* he debates matters with himself he conducts these debates in French without wondering how to put his points in French; and, more generally, that *when* he converses with himself in internal monologue he does this in French without having to consider how to say in French what he wants to say. Even so, to describe him as thinking in French, because what he says to himself he says effortlessly in French, is to put a new strain on the phrase 'thinking in', under which it did not labour in our primary use of the phrase 'to think in French'. One never does ask it, but *could* one ask a friend who has been deliberating what to do whether he had been deliberating in English? If we did ask him this, I suspect that he would reply that while he had said or half-said a lot of things to himself in English, this had not been any part of his deliberating. He had not deliberated *by means* of saying things to himself, any more than the proof-corrector searches for misprints *by means of* putting marks in the margins of the galley-proof.

But anyhow, what is true of his debatings and conversings, whether with Frenchmen or with himself, need not be true of his thinkings which are done when no debating or conversing is done. The phrases 'in French' and 'in English' do attach natively to verbs of saying; it does not follow that they attach to verbs of thinking, unless the thinking happens to be thinking what to say or how to say it.

Strained though it may be, save in the one special context, to speak of a person thinking in French or in English, it is worse than strained to speak of him as thinking in, say, mental pictures. Certainly it is true, not of all people, but of many, when thinking about certain sorts of matters, though not of all, that they see things in their mind's eyes, and even that their ability to solve some of their problems is tied up, somehow, with their ability to visualize clearly. Doubtless, some chess-players can think out chess problems in their heads, if and only if they can visualize chess situations clearly and steadily.

Consider this case of the would-be solver of a chess problem. First let us provide him with a chess-board and the requisite chess-men. He disposes the pieces in their proper places and then, with his eyes fixed on the board and his fingers moving piece after piece, he tries to think out the solution to his problem. Are we to say that the thinking that he is doing is done 'in' pieces of ivory or 'in' the experimental moves that he makes with these pieces of ivory? Clearly, there is no place for the word 'in' here. He is thinking *about* the pieces; he is thinking out what they could and could not do or suffer if he moved elsewhere or if kept where they are.

But now suppose that we refuse to provide him with a chess-board, so that he has to tackle his task entirely in his head. The chess problem itself that he has to solve is exactly the same as before; but he is now confronted with an extra set of tasks which he had not had to cope with before. He has, among other things, to remember, at each given moment, exactly where each of the pieces is, whereas previously he just looked and saw where it was. He is like the hostess who can see which of her guests is sitting next to which until the light fails; then she has to remember their positions. This remembering may be preceded by the labour of trying to remember; or she may not have to try. She may just remember. Now if the chess-player has to struggle to remember the positions of his pieces, this struggling could obviously not be described as involving the employment of mental pictures of their positions. He struggles because he cannot yet remember and therefore cannot yet see in his mind's eye how the pieces had been disposed. If in the course of this struggling alternative possible dispositions are pictured, still these, if wrong, have to be scrapped. They are not the vehicles but the boss-shots of the thinking. Conversely, when, after struggling to remember the positions of the pieces, the chess-player does remember, then his seeing them in his mind's eye, if he does do this, is not something by means of which he gets himself to remember. It is the goal, not a vehicle of his struggle to remember. *A fortiori*, if he remembers without having to try to remember, then his mental picture of the positions of the pieces is not something that he thought *in* or *with* or *on*, since he did not have to think at all.

Certainly this chess-player has to *use his memory* in trying to solve the chess problem in his head, where he had not had to use his memory when he had had the board in front of him. But this is not at all the same thing as to say that he *uses his memory images* in trying to solve the problem in his head. If we hanker still to reserve some special sense for the phrase 'using images', this will be very different from the sense of the verb in which we speak of someone using such and such French words when speaking to Frenchmen. That we cannot talk French without using French words is a dull truism; that some people cannot solve chess problems in their heads without, in some sense, using mental pictures may be true, but it is not a logicians' truism.

So now we seem to be farther off than ever from achieving what we thought that we wanted, namely to nominate some reasonably concrete stuff to be the peculiar apparatus of all of our thinkings.

No singing without noises, no testimonial-writing without ink-marks, no thinking without . . ., but we can nominate no proprietary things or sets of things to fill this gap. Indeed, we have, I hope, become suspicious of the very attempt to assimilate in this way thinking with these other special activities, which do possess their own proprietary implements or materials.

We may be tempted to postpone the evil day by suggesting that thinking differs from singing and testimonial-writing just because its proprietary stuff is a very peculiar stuff, more transparent and more shapeless than jelly-fishes, more scentless than the most scentless gases, and more uncapturable than rainbows. Perhaps its stuff is the stuff that dreams are made of, mental or spiritual stuff, and that is why it slips through our retrospective sieves. But we are soon brought to our senses if we remind ourselves that our own neighbours' very ordinary children, Tommy and Clara, make no more bones about recounting the thoughts that they have had than in recounting the games that they have played or the incidents that they have witnessed. They seem to need no esoteric instructions in order to be able to tell us of the ideas that have come to them or the thinking that they have done. In a way these are the most domestic and everyday sorts of things that there could be. The seeming mysteriousness of thinking derives from some sophisticated theoretical presuppositions, presuppositions which induce us, though only when theorizing, to try to squeeze out of our reminiscences or our introspections some evasive but pervasive drop of something, some psychic trace-element the presence of which, in bafflingly minute doses, is required if thinking is to occur. Yet Tommy and Clara, who were never told of any such psychic trace-element, describe their thinkings in ways which we understand perfectly; nor, when we tell them of the thoughts that crossed Cinderella's mind as she sat among the ashes, do we employ a strange para-chemical vocabulary.

Now let us drop, for the time being, the attempt to find a filling or a set of alternative fillings for the gap in the slogan 'No thinking without such and such' and consider a different, though connected, problem.

When a person who has been for a short or a long time musing or pondering is asked what he had been thinking about, he can usually, though not quite always, give a seemingly complete and definite answer. All sorts of answers are allowable; for example, that he had been thinking about his father, or about the next General Election, or about the possibility of getting his annual holiday early, or about yesterday's football match, or how to answer a letter. What he has been thinking about may or may not be, or contain, a problem. We can ask him whether he had decided how to answer the letter and if so what his decision was. But his thoughts about yesterday's football match may have been entirely uninterrogative. He was thinking it over, but not trying to think anything out. His thinking terminated in no results; it aimed at none. Now though, normally, the thinker can give a seemingly complete and definite answer to the question, What had he been thinking about?, he can very often be brought to acknowledge that he had had in mind things which, at the start, it had not occurred to him to mention. To take a simple instance. A rowing enthusiast says that he had been thinking about the Oxford University crew; and if asked bluntly, would deny that he had at that moment been thinking about the Cambridge crew. Yet it might transpire that his thought about the Oxford crew was, or included, the thought that, though it was progressing, it was not progressing fast enough. 'Not fast enough for what?' we ask. 'Not fast enough to beat Cambridge next Saturday.' So he had been thinking about the Cambridge crew, only thinking about it in a sort of threshold way. Or I ask a tired visitor from London what he has been thinking about. He says, 'Just about the extraordinary peacefulness of your garden.' If asked, 'Than what do you find it so much more peaceful?' he replies, 'Oh, London, of course.' So in a way he was thinking not only of my garden but of London, though he would not, without special prompting, have said for himself that he had had London in mind at all. Or my visitor says, 'How lovely your roses are,' and then sighs. Why does he sigh? May he not, in a marginal way, be thinking of his dead wife who had been particularly fond of roses? – though he himself would have said, if asked, that he was only thinking about my roses. He does not say to me or to himself, 'Roses – her favourite flower.' But roses are, for him, her favourite flower. The thought of them is an incipient thought of her.

Take one more case. I ask the schoolboy what he is thinking about, and he says that he had been trying to think what $8 \times 17$ makes. On further questioning it turns out that his total task is to multiply £9 17s. 4d. by 8, and that at that particular moment he had got to the 17s. So I ask him whether he had forgotten the 2s. 8d. that he had got when multiplying the 4d. by 8; and now he says that he had not forgotten this; indeed he was keeping the 2s. in mind ready to add to his shillings column. So, in a way, his thought was not totally filled by the problem of multiplying $17 \times 8$. The thought of the total multiplication task was, in a controlling though background way, built into his interim but foreground task of multiplying $17 \times 8$. For it was not just 17, but the seventeen shillings of the £9 17s. 4d. that he was then engaged in multiplying by 8. He would have gone on from the shillings to the pounds if I had not interrupted.

It was not that my widowed visitor just *forgot* and had to be reminded that he had been thinking about his wife as well as about the roses, but that his task of telling just what he had had in mind was in some important ways totally unlike the task of trying to recall, say, just how many telephone calls he had made during the morning. The difference between merely thinking how fine these roses are and thinking how she would have admired them is not like the difference between having made eleven and having made twelve telephone calls, namely a difference in the number of happenings to be recorded. Recounting one's thoughts is not like turning back to an earlier page and trying to give an exhaustive inventory of the items one rediscovers there. The question whether or not the Cambridge crew had been in the rowing-enthusiast's mind was not one that he could settle by racking his brains to recollect a bygone fleeting something. In our example it was settled in quite a different way, namely by asking him what the rate of progress of the Oxford crew had seemed to him inadequate for. When he acknowledges that he had been, in a threshold way, thinking of the Cambridge crew, one thing that he does not say is, 'Ah yes, your question *reminds* me that the Cambridge crew was in my thoughts after all.' He had not been reminded of a forgotten item but shown how his account of his thought had been an incomplete account. He had failed to indicate part of its internal tenor.

Reporting one's thoughts is not a matter of merely chronicling the items of a procession of quick-fading internal phenomena. If we can pick out any such phenomena and record them, our record of them is not yet a statement of the drift or content of a piece of thinking. The way in which the widower's thinking of the roses was, in a way, thinking about his wife is not that during the time that he was thinking about the roses there occurred one or two very fleeting wafts of recollections of his wife. Such wafts do occur, but it was not them that he was acknowledging when he acknowledged that in thinking of the roses he had been incipiently thinking of his wife. Rather, he had thought of the roses *as* her favourite flower; in the way in which the rowing-enthusiast had thought of the progress of the Oxford crew *as* insufficient to beat Cambridge; or in the way in which the schoolboy had thought of the 17 that he was multiplying by 8 *as* the 17s. to be dealt with after the 4d. and before the £9.

What, then, is the virtue of this 'as', which makes a young

man's thought of next Thursday *as* his 21st birthday different from his mother's thought of next Thursday *as* early-closing day for Oxford shops?

We can approach at least a part of the answer in this way. Sometimes we deliberately advise people to think of something *as* so and so. For instance, when giving a child his very first explanation of what a map is, we might tell him to think of the map of Berkshire *as* a photograph taken from an aeroplane very high up over the middle of Berkshire. This may already lead him to expect to find big things showing on the map, like towns, rivers, highroads, and railways, but not very small things like people, motor-cars, or bushes. A little later he enquires, in perplexity, what the contour-lines are which wriggle so conspicuously along and around the Berkshire Downs. We tell him to think of them *as* high-water marks left by the sea, which had risen to drown even the highest parts of the county. This flood, he is to suppose, subsided exactly fifty feet every night, leaving a high-water mark each time. So a person walking along one high-water mark would remain all the time at the same height above the normal level of the sea; and he would all the time be 100 feet higher than somone else who was following the next high-water mark but one below him. Quite likely the child could now work out for himself why the contour-lines are closely packed on the side of a steep hill and widely separated on a gradual incline.

Getting him to think of the map as a photograph taken from very high up, and of the contour-lines as high-water marks makes it natural or at least quite easy for him to think further thoughts for himself. It is to implant the germs of these further thoughts into his initially sterile thoughts about the map. If there was no follow-up, however embryonic and whether in the desired direction or any other, then he had not thought of the map as a photograph or of the contours as high-water marks. To describe someone as thinking of something as so and so is to say of him, at least *inter alia*, that it would be natural or easy for him to follow up this thought in some particular direction. His thinking had those prospects, that trend in it. It should be noticed that what thinking of something as so and so leads naturally or easily into may be subsequent thinkings, but it may equally well be subsequent doings. The golf professional who tells me to think of my driver not as a sledgehammer but as a rope with a weight on the end expects me to cease to bang at the ball and to begin to sweep smoothly through the ball. The parent who gets his child to think of policemen not as enemies but as friends gets him not only to think certain consequential thoughts but also to go to policemen for help when lost.

A person who thinks of something as something is, *ipso facto*, primed to think and do some particular further things; and this particular possible future that his thinking paves the way for needs to be mentioned in the description of the particular content of that thinking – somewhat as the mention of where the canal goes to has to be incorporated in our account of what this adjacent canal-stretch is. Roughly, a thought comprises what it is incipiently, namely what it is the natural vanguard of. Its burthen embodies its natural or easy sequel.

There are other things as well which are, in partly similar ways, constitutionally inceptive. To lather one's chin is to prepare to wield one's razor. Here the vanguard act is an intentional or even deliberate preparation for the future act. We had to learn thus to pave the way for shaving. To brace oneself is to get ready to jump or resist at the next moment; but this inceptive movement is not normally intentional or the result of training; it is instinctive. The tenors that our thoughts possess are similarly sometimes the products of training; but often not. In all cases alike, however, the description of an inceptive act requires the prospective specification of its due or natural sequel. Notice that its due or natural sequel may not actually come about. Having lathered my chin, I may be called to the telephone; and the dog, having braced himself, may be reassured or shot. We must employ the future tense in our description of the inceptive act, but we must hedge this future tense with some 'unlesses'.

At first sight we may suspect the presence of a circularity in the description of something as essentially the foreshadowing of its own succession. But this feature, without any air of circularity, belongs also to our descriptions of promises, precautions, threats and betrothals, and even of nightfalls, thaws and germinations. There could be no complete description of such things which was not proleptic. However, our special case seems to be in a worse plight since I am saying that a piece of thinking of something as something is natively inceptive of, *inter alia*, subsequent thinkings in a way in which a thaw is not the inception of another thaw, or a nightfall the beginning of another nightfall.

So here we are reminded, if not of circles, at least of the verse:

> Big fleas have little fleas upon their backs to bite 'em,
> Little fleas have lesser fleas and so *ad infinitum*.

But is this reminder disconcerting? Were we not already aware in our bones of just such a feature of thinking, namely that any attempt to catch a particular thought tends to develop into an attempt to catch up with something further? Our story of a particular piece of thinking seems in the nature of the case to terminate in nothing stronger than a semi-colon. It is not incidental to thoughts that they belong to trains of thought.

Now maybe we can begin to see the shape of the answers to both of our two dominant questions. We can begin to see why it is that the narrative of a piece of my thinking cannot be merely the chronicling of actual, monitored happenings 'in my head'. For the content of the thinking comprised its tenor and to describe its particular tenor is prospectively to mention its natural or easy sequels.

But also we can begin to see why we cannot, and do not in our heart of hearts wish to reserve for our thinkings any peculiar concrete stuff, apparatus, or medium, X, such that we can say, 'As no singing without noises, so no thinking without X.' For adverting to anything whatsoever can be what puts a person, at a particular moment, in mind of something or other. The motorist in the last village but one before home may think of the petrol-station alongside of him *as* being possibly the last place for buying petrol on a Sunday. The widower thinks of my roses that he is gazing at as being of the sort of which she was so fond. The schoolboy thinks of the number 17 that his eye is on as the 17s. in the total of £9 17s. 4d. that he has to multiply by eight. The poet thinks of the word 'annihilating' that crops up in a conversation as a candidate for the gap in his half-composed couplet. The housewife thinks of next Thursday as the day when she will not be able to shop in Oxford after lunch, while her son thinks of it as the day when he comes of age. We could stretch our slogan, if we hanker for a slogan, to read 'No thinking without adverting to something or other, no matter what', but then it would be as empty as the slogans 'no eating without food', 'no building without materials' and 'no purchases without commodities'.

However, the very vacuousness of our new slogan 'no thinking without adverting to something or other, no matter what' has a certain tension-relieving effect. From the start we felt, I hope, a gnawing uneasiness at the very programme of treating thinking as a special, indeed a very special activity, special in the way in which singing is one special activity and gardening is a battery of other special activities. For while there certainly are lots of special kinds or brands of thinking, such as computing, sonnet-composing, anagram-solving, philosophizing, and translating, still thinking is not an activity in which we are engaged only when we are *not* singing, writing testimonials, gardening and so on. Thinking is not a rival occupation to these special occupations, in the sense that our time has to be parcelled out between them and thinking, in the way in which our time does have to be parcelled out between golf and gardening, between testimonial-writing and lecturing, between anagram-solving and chess-playing, and so on. For we have to be thinking if we are to be singing well, writing a just testimonial, or gardening efficiently. Certainly, we had better not be doing sums or anagrams in our heads while singing or lecturing; but this is because we had better be thinking how to perform our present task of singing or lecturing. We had unwittingly sold the central fort from the start, when we asked ourselves, in effect, 'Given that noise-making, of a certain sort, is what goes to make singing the proprietary occupation that it is, what is it that, analogously, makes thinking the proprietary occupation that it is?' The verbal noun 'thinking' does not, as we knew in our bones all along, denote a special or proprietary activity in the way in which 'singing' does. Thinking is not one department in a department-store, such that we can ask, What line of goods does it provide, and what lines of goods does it, *ex officio, not* provide? Its proper place is in all the departments – that is, there is no particular place which is its proper place, and there are no particular places which are not its proper place.

If we had worded our original programme by asking 'What department and what proprietary apparatus are reserved for *the using of our wits*?' we should have seen through this question straightaway. We do not, notoriously, use our wits wherever and whenever we should use them, but there is no field or department of human activity or experience of which we can say, 'Here people can use their fingers, their noses, their vocal chords or their golf-clubs, but not their wits.' Or if we had worded our early question by asking 'In what special medium or with what special instruments is our use of our wits conducted?', we should have seen through this question too. We swim in water, we sing in noises, we hammer with hammers, but using our wits is not a co-ordinate special operation with its own counterpart medium, material, or implements. For one can use one's wits in swimming, singing, hammering, or in anything else whatsoever. I do not suggest that the idiom of *using one's wits* is a pure substitute for the idiom of *thinking*. There is an element of congratulation in our description of someone as having used his wits, an element which would be out of place, for example, in talking of my widower's thinking of roses as his wife's favourite flower. None the less, if we realize why it would be absurd to try to isolate out a proprietary activity of using one's wits and a reserved field for it, we realize why it actually was absurd to try to isolate out a proprietary activity of thinking and a reserved field for it.

Why do we not require our schools to give separate lessons in thinking, as they do give separate lessons in computing, translating, swimming, and cricket? The answer is obvious. It is because all the lessons that they give are lessons in thinking. Yet they are not lessons in two subjects at the same time.

U. T. PLACE

# Is Consciousness a Brain Process?

The thesis that consciousness is a process in the brain is put
forward as a reasonable scientific hypothesis, not to be dismissed
on logical grounds alone. The conditions under which two sets
of observations are treated as observations of the same process,
rather than as observations of two independent correlated
processes, are discussed. It is suggested that we can identify
consciousness with a given pattern of brain activity, if we can
explain the subject's introspective observations by reference to
the brain processes with which they are correlated. It is argued
that the problem of providing a physiological explanation of
introspective observations is made to seem more difficult than it
really is by the 'phenomenological fallacy', the mistaken idea
that descriptions of the appearances of things are descriptions
of the actual state of affairs in a mysterious internal
environment.

## I. Introduction

The view that there exists a separate class of events, mental
events, which cannot be described in terms of the concepts
employed by the physical sciences no longer commands the
universal and unquestioning acceptance among philosophers
and psychologists which it once did. Modern physicalism,
however, unlike the materialism of the seventeenth and eight-
eenth centuries, is behavioristic. Consciousness on this view is
either a special type of behavior, 'sampling' or 'running-back-
and-forth' behavior as Tolman has it,[1] or a disposition to behave
in a certain way, an itch for example being a temporary
propensity to scratch. In the case of cognitive concepts like
'knowing', 'believing', 'understanding', 'remembering', and volitional concepts like 'wanting' and 'intending', there can be little
doubt, I think, that an analysis in terms of dispositions to behave
is fundamentally sound.[2] On the other hand, there would seem

to be an intractable residue of concepts clustering around the notions of consciousness, experience, sensation, and mental imagery, where some sort of inner process story is unavoidable.[3] It is possible, of course, that a satisfactory behavioristic account of this conceptual residuum will ultimately be found. For our present purposes, however, I shall assume that this cannot be done and that statements about pains and twinges, about how things look, sound, and feel, about things dreamed of or pictured in the mind's eye, are statements referring to events and processes which are in some sense private or internal to the individual of whom they are predicated. The question I wish to raise is whether in making this assumption we are inevitably committed to a dualist position in which sensations and mental images form a separate category of processes over and above the physical and physiological processes with which they are known to be correlated. I shall argue that an acceptance of inner processes does not entail dualism and that the thesis that consciousness is a process in the brain cannot be dismissed on logical grounds.

## II. The 'Is' of Definition and the 'Is' of Composition

I want to stress from the outset that in defending the thesis that consciousness is a process in the brain, I am not trying to argue that when we describe our dreams, fantasies, and sensations we are talking about processes in our brains. That is, I am not claiming that statements about sensations and mental images are reducible to or analyzable into statements about brain processes, in the way in which 'cognition statements' are analyzable into statements about behavior. To say that statements about consciousness are statements about brain processes is manifestly false. This is shown (a) by the fact that you can describe your sensations and mental imagery without knowing anything about your brain processes or even that such things exist, (b) by the fact that statements about one's consciousness and statements about one's brain processes are verified in entirely different ways, and (c) by the fact that there is nothing self-contradictory about the statement 'X has a pain but there is nothing going on in his brain.' What I do want to assert, however, is that the statement 'Consciousness is a process in the brain,' although not necessarily true, is not necessarily false.

'Consciousness is a process in the brain,' in my view is neither
self-contradictory nor self-evident; it is a reasonable scientific
hypothesis, in the way that the statement 'Lightning is a motion
of electric charges' is a reasonable scientific hypothesis.

The all but universally accepted view that an assertion of
identity between consciousness and brain processes can be ruled
out on logical grounds alone, derives, I suspect, from a failure
to distinguish between what we may call the 'is' of definition
and the 'is' of composition. The distinction I have in mind here
is the difference between the function of the word 'is' in
statements like 'A square is an equilateral rectangle', 'Red is a
color', 'To understand an instruction is to be able to act
appropriately under the appropriate circumstances', and its
function in statements like 'His table is an old packing case',
'Her hat is a bundle of straw tied together with string', 'A cloud
is a mass of water droplets or other particles in suspension'.
These two types of 'is' statements have one thing in common. In
both cases it makes sense to add the qualification 'and nothing
else'. In this they differ from those statements in which the 'is' is
an 'is' of predication; the statements 'Toby is 80 years old and
nothing else', 'Her hat is red and nothing else' or 'Giraffes are
tall and nothing else', for example, are nonsense. This logical
feature may be described by saying that in both cases both the
grammatical   subject   and   the   grammatical   predicate   are
expressions which provide an adequate characterization of the
state of affairs to which they both refer.

In another respect, however, the two groups of statements are
strikingly different. Statements like 'A square is an equilateral
rectangle' are necessary statements which are true by definition.
Statements like 'His table is an old packing case,' on the other
hand, are contingent statements which have to be verified by
observation. In the case of statements like 'A square is an
equilateral rectangle' or 'Red is a color', there is a relationship
between the meaning of the expression forming the grammatical
predicate and the meaning of the expression forming the grammatical subject, such that whenever the subject expression is
applicable the predicate must also be applicable. If you can
describe something as red then you must also be able to describe
it as colored. In the case of statements like 'His table is an old
packing case,' on the other hand, there is no such relationship
between the meanings of the expressions 'his table' and 'old

packing case'; it merely so happens that in this case both expressions are applicable to and at the same time provide an adequate characterization of the same object. Those who contend that the statement 'Consciousness is a brain process' is logically untenable base their claim, I suspect, on the mistaken assumption that if the meanings of two statements or expressions are quite unconnected, they cannot both provide an adequate characterization of the same object or state of affairs: if something is a state of consciousness, it cannot be a brain process, since there is nothing self-contradictory in supposing that someone feels a pain when there is nothing happening inside his skull. By the same token we might be led to conclude that a table cannot be an old packing case, since there is nothing self-contradictory in supposing that someone has a table, but is not in possession of an old packing case.

## III. The Logical Independence of Expressions and the Ontological Independence of Entities

There is, of course, an important difference between the table/packing case case and the consciousness/brain process case in that the statement 'His table is an old packing case' is a particular proposition which refers only to one particular case, whereas the statement 'Consciousness is a process in the brain' is a general or universal proposition applying to all states of consciousness whatever. It is fairly clear, I think, that if we lived in a world in which all tables without exception were packing cases, the concepts of 'table' and 'packing case' in our language would not have their present logically independent status. In such a world a table would be a species of packing case in much the same way that red is a species of color. It seems to be a rule of language that whenever a given variety of object or state of affairs has two characteristics or sets of characteristics, one of which is unique to the variety of object or state of affairs in question, the expression used to refer to the characteristic or set of characteristics which defines the variety of object or state of affairs in question will always entail the expression used to refer to the other characteristic or set of characteristics. If this rule admitted of no exception it would follow that any expression which is logically independent of another expression which uniquely characterizes a given variety of object or state of affairs, must refer to a characteristic or set of characteristics which is not normally or necessarily associated with the object or state of affairs in question. It is because this rule applies almost universally, I suggest, that we are normally justified in arguing from the logical independence of two expressions to the ontological independence of the states of affairs to which they refer. This would explain both the undoubted force of the argument that consciousness and brain processes must be independent entities because the expressions used to refer to them are logically independent and, in general, the curious phenomenon whereby questions about the furniture of the universe are often fought and not infrequently decided merely on a point of logic.

The argument from the logical independence of two expressions to the ontological independence of the entities to which they refer breaks down in the case of brain processes and consciousness, I believe, because this is one of a relatively small number of cases where the rule stated above does not apply. These exceptions are to be found, I suggest, in those cases where the operations which have to be performed in order to verify the presence of the two sets of characteristics inhering in the object or state of affairs in question can seldom if ever be performed simultaneously. A good example here is the case of the cloud and the mass of droplets or other particles in suspension. A cloud is a large semi-transparent mass with a fleecy texture suspended in the atmosphere whose shape is subject to continual and kaleidoscopic change. When observed at close quarters, however, it is found to consist of a mass of tiny particles, usually water droplets, in continuous motion. On the basis of this second observation we conclude that a cloud is a mass of tiny particles and nothing else. But there is no logical connection in our language between a cloud and a mass of tiny particles; there is nothing self-contradictory in talking about a cloud which is not composed of tiny particles in suspension. There is no contradiction involved in supposing that clouds consist of a dense mass of fibrous tissue; indeed, such a consistency seems to be implied by many of the functions performed by clouds in fairy stories and mythology. It is clear from this that the terms 'cloud' and 'mass of tiny particles in suspension' mean quite different things. Yet we do not conclude from this that there must be two things, the mass of particles in suspension and the cloud. The reason for this, I suggest, is that although the characteristics of being a cloud and being a mass of tiny particles in suspension are invariably associated, we never make the observations necessary to verify the statement 'That is a cloud' and those necessary to verify the statement 'This is a mass of tiny particles in suspension' at one and the same time. We can observe the microstructure of a cloud only when we are enveloped by it, a condition which effectively prevents us from observing those characteristics which from a distance lead us to describe it as a cloud. Indeed, so disparate are these two experiences that we use different words to describe them. That which is a cloud when we observe it from a distance becomes a fog or mist when we are enveloped by it.

## IV. When are Two Sets of Observations Observations of the Same Event?

The example of the cloud and the mass of tiny particles in suspension was chosen because it is one of the few cases of a general proposition involving what I have called the 'is' of composition which does not involve us in scientific technicalities. It is useful because it brings out the connection between the ordinary everyday cases of the 'is' of composition like the table/ packing case example and the more technical cases like 'Lightning is a motion of electric charges' where the analogy with the consciousness/brain process case is most marked. The limitation of the cloud/tiny particles in suspension case is that it does not bring out sufficiently clearly the crucial problem of how the identity of the states of affairs referred to by the two expressions is established. In the cloud case the fact that something is a cloud and the fact that something is a mass of tiny particles in suspension are both verified by the normal processes of visual observation. It is arguable, moreover, that the identity of the entities referred to by the two expressions is established by the continuity between the two sets of observations as the observer moves towards or away from the cloud. In the case of brain processes and consciousness there is no such continuity between the two sets of observations involved. A closer introspective scrutiny will never reveal the passage of nerve impulses over a thousand synapses in the way that a closer scrutiny of a cloud will reveal a mass of tiny particles in suspension. The operations

required to verify statements about consciousness and statements about brain processes are fundamentally different.

To find a parallel for this feature we must examine other cases
where an identity is asserted between something whose occurrence is verified by the ordinary processes of observation and
something whose occurrence is established by special scientific
procedures. For this purpose I have chosen the case where we
say that lightning is a motion of electric charges. As in the case
of consciousness, however closely we scrutinize the lightning we
shall never be able to observe the electric charges, and just as
the operations for determining the nature of one's state of
consciousness are radically different from those involved in
determining the nature of one's brain processes, so the operations for determining the occurrence of lightning are radically
different from those involved in determining the occurrence of a
motion of electric charges. What is it, therefore, that leads us to
say that the two sets of observations are observations of the
same event? It cannot be merely the fact that the two sets of
observations are systematically correlated such that whenever
there is lightning there is always a motion of electric charges.
There are innumerable cases of such correlations where we have
no temptation to say that the two sets of observations are
observations of the same event. There is a systematic correlation,
for example, between the movement of the tides and the stages
of the moon, but this does not lead us to say that records of
tidal levels are records of the moon's stages or vice versa. We
speak rather of a causal connection between two independent
events or processes.

The answer here seems to be that we treat the two sets of
observations as observations of the same event in those cases
where the technical scientific observations set in the context of
the appropriate body of scientific theory provide an immediate
explanation of the observations made by the man in the street.
Thus we conclude that lightning is nothing more than a motion
of electric charges, because we know that a motion of electric
charges through the atmosphere, such as occurs when lightning
is reported, gives rise to the type of visual stimulation which
would lead an observer to report a flash of lightning. In the
moon/tide case, on the other hand, there is no such direct causal
connection between the stages of the moon and the observations
made by the man who measures the height of the tide. The

causal connection is between the moon and the tides, not between the moon and the measurement of the tides.

## V. *The Physiological Explanation of Introspection and the Phenomenological Fallacy*

If this account is correct, it should follow that in order to establish the identity of consciousness and certain processes in the brain, it would be necessary to show that the introspective observations reported by the subject can be accounted for in terms of processes which are known to have occurred in his brain. In the light of this suggestion it is extremely interesting to find that when a physiologist as distinct from a philosopher finds it difficult to see how consciousness could be a process in the brain, what worries him is not any supposed self-contradiction involved in such an assumption, but the apparent impossibility of accounting for the reports given by the subject of his conscious processes in terms of the known properties of the central nervous system. Sir Charles Sherrington has posed the problem as follows:

> The chain of events stretching from the sun's radiation entering the eye to, on the one hand, the contraction of the pupillary muscles, and on the other, to the electrical disturbances in the brain-cortex are all straightforward steps in a sequence of physical 'causation', such as, thanks to science, are intelligible. But in the second serial chain there follows on, or attends, the stage of brain-cortex reaction an event or set of events quite inexplicable to us, which both as to themselves and as to the causal tie between them and what preceded them science does not help us; a set of events seemingly incommensurable with any of the events leading up to it. The self 'sees' the sun; it senses a two-dimensional disc of brightness, located in the 'sky', this last a field of lesser brightness, and overhead shaped as a rather flattened dome, coping the self and a hundred other visual things as well. Of hint that this is within the head there is none. Vision is saturated with this strange property called 'projection', the unargued inference that what it sees is at a 'distance' from the seeing 'self'. Enough has been said to stress that in the sequence of events a step is reached where a physical situation in the brain leads to a psychical, which however contains no hint of the brain or any other bodily part ... The supposition has to be, it would seem, two continuous series of

events, one physicochemical, the other psychical, and at times interaction between them.[4]

Just as the physiologist is not likely to be impressed by the philosopher's contention that there is some self-contradiction involved in supposing consciousness to be a brain process, so the philosopher is unlikely to be impressed by the considerations which lead Sherrington to conclude that there are two sets of events, one physicochemical, the other psychical. Sherrington's argument for all its emotional appeal depends on a fairly simple logical mistake, which is unfortunately all too frequently made by psychologists and physiologists and not infrequently in the past by the philosophers themselves. This logical mistake, which I shall refer to as the 'phenomenological fallacy', is the mistake of supposing that when the subject describes his experience, when he describes how things look, sound, smell, taste, or feel to him, he is describing the literal properties of objects and events on a peculiar sort of internal cinema or television screen, usually referred to in the modern psychological literature as the 'phenomenal field'. If we assume, for example, that when a subject reports a green after-image he is asserting the occurrence inside himself of an object which is literally green, it is clear that we have on our hands an entity for which there is no place in the world of physics. In the case of the green after-image there is no green object in the subject's environment corresponding to the description that he gives. Nor is there anything green in his brain; certainly there is nothing which could have emerged when he reported the appearance of the green after-image. Brain processes are not the sort of things to which color concepts can be properly applied.

The phenomenological fallacy on which this argument is based depends on the mistaken assumption that because our ability to describe things in our environment depends on our consciousness of them, our descriptions of things are primarily descriptions of our conscious experience and only secondarily, indirectly, and inferentially descriptions of the objects and events in our environments. It is assumed that because we recognize things in our environment by their look, sound, smell, taste, and feel, we begin by describing their phenomenal properties, i.e., the properties of the looks, sounds, smells, tastes, and feels which they produce in us, and infer their real properties from their phenomenal properties. In fact, the reverse is the case. We begin by learning to recognize the real properties of things in our environment. We learn to recognize them, of course, by their look, sound, smell, taste, and feel; but this does not mean that we have to learn to describe the look, sound, smell, taste, and feel of things before we can describe the things themselves. Indeed, it is only after we have learned to describe the things in our environment that we can learn to describe our consciousness of them. We describe our conscious experience not in terms of the mythological 'phenomenal properties' which are supposed to inhere in the mythological 'objects' in the mythological 'phenomenal field', but by reference to the actual physical properties of the concrete physical objects, events, and processes which normally, though not perhaps in the present instance, give rise to the sort of conscious experience which we are trying to describe. In other words when we describe the after-image as green, we are not saying that there is something, the after-image, which is green; we are saying that we are having the sort of experience which we normally have when, and which we have learned to describe as, looking at a green patch of light.

Once we rid ourselves of the phenomenological fallacy we realize that the problem of explaining introspective observations in terms of brain processes is far from insuperable. We realize that there is nothing that the introspecting subject says about his conscious experiences which is inconsistent with anything the physiologist might want to say about the brain processes which cause him to describe the environment and his consciousness of that environment in the way he does. When the subject describes his experience by saying that a light which is in fact stationary, appears to move, all the physiologist or physiological psychologist has to do in order to explain the subject's introspective observations, is to show that the brain process which is causing the subject to describe his experience in this way, is the sort of process which normally occurs when he is observing an actual moving object and which therefore normally causes him to report the movement of an object in his environment. Once the mechanism whereby the individual describes what is going on in his environment has been worked out, all that is required to explain the individual's capacity to make introspective observations is an explanation of his ability to discriminate between those cases where his normal habits of verbal description are

appropriate to the stimulus situation and those cases where they
are not and an explanation of how and why, in those cases
where the appropriateness of his normal descriptive habits is in
doubt, he learns to issue his ordinary descriptive protocols
preceded by a qualificatory phrase like 'it appears', 'seems',
'looks', 'feels', etc.[5]

## References

1 E. C. Tolman, *Purposive Behavior in Animals and Men* (Berkeley:
University of California Press, 1932).

2 L. Wittgenstein, *Philosophical Investigations* (Oxford: Blackwell,
1953); G. Ryle, *The Concept of Mind* (London: Hutchinsons's University Library, 1949).

3 U. T. Place, 'The Concept of Heed,' *British Journal of Psychology*,
XLV (1954), 243–55.

4 Sir Charles Sherrington, *The Integrative Action of the Nervous
System* (Cambridge: Cambridge University Press, 1947) pp. xx–xxi.

5 I am greatly indebted to my fellow-participants in a series of informal
discussions on this topic which took place in the Department of
Philosophy, University of Adelaide, in particular to Mr C. B. Martin
for his persistent and searching criticism of my earlier attempts to
defend the thesis that consciousness is a brain process, to Prof. D. A. T.
Gasking, of the University of Melbourne, for clarifying many of the
logical issues involved, and to Prof. J. J. C. Smart for moral support
and encouragement in what often seemed a lost cause.

# J. J. C. SMART

# Sensations and Brain Processes

This paper[1] takes its departure from arguments to be found in U. T. Place's 'Is Consciousness a Brain Process?'[2] I have had the benefit of discussing Place's thesis in a good many universities in the United States and Australia, and I hope that the present paper answers objections to his thesis which Place has not considered and that it presents his thesis in a more nearly unobjectionable form. This paper is meant also to supplement the paper 'The "Mental" and the "Physical"' by H. Feigl,[3] which in part argues for a similar thesis to Place's.

Suppose that I report that I have at this moment a roundish, blurry-edged after-image which is yellowish towards its edge and is orange towards its center. What is it that I am reporting? One answer to this question might be that I am not reporting anything, that when I say that it looks to me as though there is a roundish yellowy-orange patch of light on the wall I am expressing some sort of *temptation*, the temptation to say that there *is* a roundish yellowy-orange patch on the wall (though I may know that there is not such a patch on the wall). This is perhaps Wittgenstein's view in the *Philosophical Investigations* (see §§367, 370). Similarly, when I 'report' a pain, I am not really reporting anything (or, if you like, I am reporting in a queer sense of 'reporting'), but am doing a sophisticated sort of wince. (see §244: 'The verbal expression of pain replaces crying and does not describe it.' Nor does it describe anything else?)[4] I prefer most of the time to discuss an after-image rather than a pain, because the word 'pain' brings in something which is irrelevant to my purpose: the notion of 'distress'. I think that 'he is in pain' entails 'he is in distress', that is, that he is in a certain agitation-condition.[5] Similarly, to say 'I am in pain' may be to do more than 'replace pain behavior': it may be partly to report something, though this something is quite nonmysterious, being an agitation-condition, and so susceptible of behavioristic analysis. The suggestion I wish if possible to avoid is a different one, namely that 'I am in pain' is a genuine report, and that what it reports is an irreducibly psychical something. And similarly the suggestion I wish to resist is also that to say 'I have a yellowish-orange after-image' is to report something irreducibly psychical.

Why do I wish to resist this suggestion? Mainly because of Occam's razor. It seems to me that science is increasingly giving us a viewpoint whereby organisms are able to be seen as physicochemical mechanisms:[6] it seems that even the behavior of man himself will one day be explicable in mechanistic terms. There does seem to be, so far as science is concerned, nothing in the world but increasingly complex arrangements of physical constituents. All except for one place: in consciousness. That is, for a full description of what is going on in a man you would have to mention not only the physical processes in his tissues, glands, nervous system, and so forth, but also his states of consciousness: his visual, auditory, and tactual sensations, his aches and pains. That these should be *correlated* with brain processes does not help, for to say that they are *correlated* is to say that they are something 'over and above'. You cannot correlate something with itself. You correlate footprints with burglars, but not Bill Sikes the burglar with Bill Sikes the burglar. So sensations, states of consciousness, do seem to be the one sort of thing left outside the physicalist picture, and for various reasons I just cannot believe that this can be so. That everything should be explicable in terms of physics (together of course with descriptions of the ways in which the parts are put together – roughly, biology is to physics as radio-engineering is to electromagnetism) except the occurrence of sensations seems to me to be frankly unbelievable. Such sensations would be 'nomological danglers', to use Feigl's expression.[7] It is not often realized how odd would be the laws whereby these nomological danglers would dangle. It is sometimes asked, 'Why can't there be psychophysical laws which are of a novel sort, just as the laws of electricity and magnetism were novelties from the standpoint of Newtonian mechanics?' Certainly we are pretty sure in the future to come across new ultimate laws of a novel type, but I expect them to relate simple constituents: for example, whatever ultimate particles are then in vogue. I cannot believe that ultimate laws of nature could relate simple constituents to configurations consisting of perhaps billions of neurons (and goodness knows how many billion billions of ultimate particles) all put together for all the world as though their main purpose in life was to be a negative feedback mechanism of a complicated sort. Such ultimate laws would be like nothing so far known in science. They have a queer 'smell' to them. I am just unable to believe in the nomological danglers themselves, or in the laws whereby they would dangle. If any philosophical arguments seemed to compel us to believe in such things, I would suspect a catch in the argument. In any case it is the object of this paper to show that there are no philosophical arguments which compel us to be dualists.

The above is largely a confession of faith, but it explains why I find Wittgenstein's position (as I construe it) so congenial. For on this view there are, in a sense, no sensations. A man is a vast arrangement of physical particles, but there are not, over and above this, sensations or states of consciousness. There are just behavioral facts about this vast mechanism, such as that it expresses a temptation (behavior disposition) to say 'there is a yellowish-red patch on the wall' or that it goes through a sophisticated sort of wince, that is, says 'I am in pain.' Admittedly Wittgenstein says that though the sensation 'is not a something', it is nevertheless 'not a nothing either' (§304), but this need only mean that the word 'ache' has a use. An ache is a thing, but only in the innocuous sense in which the plain man, in the first paragraph of Frege's *Foundations of Arithmetic*, answers the question 'What is the number one?' by 'a thing'. It should be noted that when I assert that to say 'I have a yellowish-orange after-image' is to express a temptation to assert the physical-object statement 'There is a yellowish-orange patch on the wall,' I mean that saying 'I have a yellowish-orange after-image' is (partly) the exercise of the disposition[8] which is the temptation. It is not to *report* that I have the temptation, any more than is 'I love you' normally a report that I love someone. Saying 'I love you' is just part of the behavior which is the exercise of the disposition of loving someone.

Though for the reasons given above, I am very receptive to the above 'expressive' account of sensation statements, I do not feel that it will quite do the trick. Maybe this is because I have not thought it out sufficiently, but it does seem to me as though, when a person says 'I have an after-image,' he *is* making a genuine report, and that when he says 'I have a pain,' he *is* doing more than 'replace pain-behavior', and that 'this more' is not just to say that he is in distress. I am not so sure, however, that to admit this is to admit that there are nonphysical correlates of brain processes. Why should not sensations just be brain processes of a certain sort? There are, of course, well-known (as well as lesser-known) philosophical objections to the view that reports of sensations are reports of brain-processes, but I shall try to argue that these arguments are by no means as cogent as is commonly thought to be the case.

Let me first try to state more accurately the thesis that sensations are brain-processes. It is not the thesis that, for example, 'after-image' or 'ache' means the same as 'brain process of sort X' (where 'X' is replaced by a description of a certain sort of brain process). It is that, in so far as 'after-image' or 'ache' is a report of a process, it is a report of a process that *happens to be* a brain process. It follows that the thesis does not claim that sensation statements can be *translated* into statements about brain processes.[9] Nor does it claim that the logic of a sensation statement is the same as that of a brain-process statement. All it claims is that in so far as a sensation statement is a report of something, that something is in fact a brain process. Sensations are nothing over and above brain processes. Nations are nothing 'over and above' citizens, but this does not prevent the logic of nation statements being very different from the logic of citizen statements, nor does it insure the translatability of nation statements into citizen statements. (I do not, however, wish to assert that the relation of sensation statements to brain-process statements is very like that of nation statements to citizen statements. Nations do not just *happen to be* nothing over and above citizens, for example. I bring in the 'nations' example merely to make a negative point: that the fact that the logic of A-statements is different from that of B-statements does not insure that A's are anything over and above B's.)

## Remarks on Identity

When I say that a sensation is a brain process or that lightning is an electric discharge, I am using 'is' in the sense of strict identity. (Just as in the – in this case necessary – proposition '7 is identical with the smallest prime number greater than 5.') When I say that a sensation is a brain process or that lightning is an electric discharge I do not mean just that the sensation is somehow spatially or temporally continuous with the brain process or that the lightning is just spatially or temporally continuous with the discharge. When on the other hand I say that the successful general is the same person as the small boy who stole the apples I mean only that the successful general I see before me is a time slice[10] of the same four-dimensional object of which the small boy stealing apples is an earlier time slice. However, the four-dimensional object which has the general-I-see-before-me for its late time slice is identical in the strict sense with the four-dimensional object which has the small-boy-stealing-apples for an early time slice. I distinguish these two senses of 'is identical with' because I wish to make it clear that the brain-process doctrine asserts identity in the *strict* sense.

I shall now discuss various possible objections to the view that the processes reported in sensation statements are in fact processes in the brain. Most of us have met some of these objections in our first year as philosophy students. All the more reason to take a good look at them. Others of the objections will be more recondite and subtle.

*Objection I.*Any illiterate peasant can talk perfectly well about his after-images, or how things look or feel to him, or about his aches and pains, and yet he may know nothing whatever about neurophysiology. A man may, like Aristotle, believe that the brain is an organ for cooling the body without any impairment of his ability to make true statements about his sensations. Hence the things we are talking about when we describe our sensations cannot be processes in the brain.

*Reply.*You might as well say that a nation of slugabeds, who never saw the Morning Star or knew of its existence, or who had never thought of the expression 'the Morning Star', but who used the expression 'the Evening Star' perfectly well, could not use this expression to refer to the same entity as we refer to (and describe as) 'the Morning Star'.[11]

You may object that the Morning Star is in a sense not the very same thing as the Evening Star, but only something spatiotemporally continuous with it. That is, you may say that the Morning Star is not the Evening Star in the strict sense of 'identity' that I distinguished earlier.

There is, however, a more plausible example. Consider lightning.[12] Modern physical science tells us that lightning is a certain kind of electrical discharge due to ionization of clouds of water vapor in the atmosphere. This, it is now believed, is what the true nature of lightning is. Note that there are not two things: a flash of lightning and an electrical discharge. There is one thing, a flash of lightning, which is described scientifically as an electrical discharge to the earth from a cloud of ionized water molecules. The case is not at all like that of explaining a footprint by reference to a burglar. We say that what lightning really is, what its true nature as revealed by science is, is an electrical discharge. (It is not the true nature of a footprint to be a burglar.)

To forestall irrelevant objections, I should like to make it clear that by 'lightning' I mean the publicly observable physical object, lightning, not a visual sense-datum of lightning. I say that the publicly observable physical object lightning is in fact the electrical discharge, not just a correlate of it. The sense-datum, or rather the having of the sense-datum, the 'look' of lightning, may well in my view be a correlate of the electrical discharge. For in my view it is a brain state *caused* by the lightning. But we should no more confuse sensations of lightning with lightning than we confuse sensations of a table with the table.

In short, the reply to Objection 1 is that there can be contingent statements of the form 'A is identical with B,' and a person may well know that something is an A without knowing that it is a B. An illiterate peasant might well be able to talk about his sensations without knowing about his brain processes, just as he can talk about lightning though he knows nothing of electricity.

*Objection 2.* It is only a contingent fact (if it is a fact) that when we have a certain kind of sensation there is a certain kind of process in our brain. Indeed it is possible, though perhaps in the highest degree unlikely, that our present physiological theories will be as out of date as the ancient theory connecting mental processes with goings on in the heart. It follows that when we report a sensation we are not reporting a brain-process.

*Reply.* The objection certainly proves that when we say 'I have an after-image' we cannot *mean* something of the form 'I have such and such a brain-process.' But this does not show that what we report (having an after-image) is not *in fact* a brain process. 'I see lightning' does not *mean* 'I see an electrical discharge.' Indeed, it is logically possible (though highly unlikely) that the electrical discharge account of lightning might one day be given up. Again, 'I see the Evening Star' does not *mean* the same as 'I see the Morning Star,' and yet 'The Evening Star and the Morning Star are one and the same thing' is a contingent proposition. Possibly Objection 2 derives some of its apparent strength from a 'Fido'-Fido theory of meaning. If the meaning of an expression were what the expression named, then of course it *would* follow from the fact that 'sensation' and 'brain-process' have different meanings that they cannot name one and the same thing.

*Objection 3.*[13] Even if Objections 1 and 2 do not prove that sensations are something over and above brain-processes, they do prove that the qualities of sensations are something over and above the qualities of brain-processes. That is, it may be possible to get out of asserting the existence of irreducibly psychic processes, but not out of asserting the existence of irreducibly psychic *properties*. For suppose we identify the Morning Star with the Evening Star. Then there must be some properties which logically imply that of being the Morning Star, and quite distinct properties which entail that of being the Evening Star. Again, there must be some properties (for example, that of being a yellow flash) which are logically distinct from those in the physicalist story.

Indeed, it might be thought that the objection succeeds at one jump. For consider the property of 'being a yellow flash'. It might seem that this propertly lies inevitably outside the physicalist framework within which I am trying to work (either by 'yellow' being an objective emergent property of physical objects, or else by being a power to produce yellow sense-data, where 'yellow', in this second instantiation of the word, refers to a purely phenomenal or introspectible quality). I must therefore digress for a moment and indicate how I deal with secondary qualities. I shall concentrate on color.

First of all, let me introduce the concept of a normal percipient. One person is more a normal percipient than another if he can make color discriminations that the other cannot. For example, if A can pick a lettuce leaf out of a heap of cabbage leaves, whereas B cannot though he can pick a lettuce leaf out of a heap of beetroot leaves, then A is more normal than B. (I am assuming that A and B are not given time to distinguish the leaves by their slight difference in shape, and so forth.) From the concept of 'more normal than' it is easy to see how we can introduce the concept of 'normal'. Of course, Eskimos may make the finest discriminations at the blue end of the spectrum, Hottentots at the red end. In this case the concept of a normal percipient is a slightly idealized one, rather like that of 'the mean sun' in astronomical chronology. There is no need to go into such subtleties now. I say that 'This is red' means something roughly like 'A normal percipient would not easily pick this out of a clump of geranium petals though he would pick it out of a clump of lettuce leaves.' Of course it does not exactly mean this: a person might know the meaning of 'red' without knowing anything about geraniums, or even about normal percipients. But the point is that a person can be *trained* to say 'This is red' of objects which would not easily be picked out of geranium petals by a normal percipient, and so on. (Note that even a color-blind person can reasonably assert that something is red, though of course he needs to use another human being, not just himself, as his 'color meter'.) This account of secondary qualities explains their unimportance in physics. For obviously the discriminations and lack of discriminations made by a very complex neurophysiological mechanism are hardly likely to correspond to simple and nonarbitrary distinctions in nature.

I therefore elucidate colors as powers, in Locke's sense, to evoke certain sorts of discriminatory responses in human beings. They are also, of course, powers to cause sensations in human beings (an account still nearer Locke's). But these sensations, I am arguing, are identifiable with brain processes.

Now how do I get over the objection that a sensation can be identified with a brain process only if it has some phenomenal property, not possessed by brain processes, whereby one-half of the identification may be, so to speak, pinned down?

*Reply.* My suggestion is as follows. When a person says, 'I see a yellowish-orange after-image,' he is saying something like this:

'*There is something going on which is like what is going on when* I have my eyes open, am awake, and there is an orange illuminated in good light in front of me, that is, when I really see an orange.' (And there is no reason why a person should not say the same thing when he is having a veridical sense-datum, so long as we construe 'like' in the last sentence in such a sense that something can be like itself.) Notice that the italicized words, namely 'there is something going on which is like what is going on when,' are all quasilogical or topic-neutral words. This explains why the ancient Greek peasant's reports about his sensations can be neutral between dualistic metaphysics or my materialistic metaphysics. It explains how sensations can be brain-processes and yet how a man who reports them need know nothing about brain-processes. For he reports them only very abstractly as 'something going on which is like what is going on when . . .' Similarly, a person may say 'someone is in the room,' thus reporting truly that the doctor is in the room, even though he has never heard of doctors. (There are not two people in the room: 'someone' *and* the doctor.) This account of sensation statements also explains the singular elusiveness of 'raw feels' – why no one seems to be able to pin any properties on them.[14] Raw feels, in my view, are colorless for the very same reason that *something* is colorless. This does not mean that sensations do not have plenty of properties, for if they are brain-processes they certainly have lots of neurological properties. It only means that in speaking of them as being like or unlike one another we need not know or mention these properties.

This, then, is how I would reply to Objection 3. The strength of my reply depends on the possibility of our being able to report that one thing is like another without being able to state the respect in which it is like. I do not see why this should not be so. If we think cybernetically about the nervous system we can envisage it as able to respond to certain likenesses of its internal processes without being able to do more. It would be easier to build a machine which would tell us, say on a punched tape, whether or not two objects were similar, than it would be to build a machine which would report wherein the similarities consisted.

*Objection* 4. The after-image is not in physical space. The brain-process is. So the after-image is not a brain-process.

*Reply*. This is an *ignoratio elenchi*. I am not arguing that the after-image is a brain-process, but that the experience of having an after-image is a brain-process. It is the *experience* which is reported in the introspective report. Similarly, if it is objected that the after-image is yellowy-orange, my reply is that it is the experience of seeing yellowy-orange that is being described, and this experience is not a yellowy-orange something. So to say that a brain-process cannot be yellowy-orange is not to say that a brain-process cannot in fact be the experience of having a yellowy-orange after-image. There is, in a sense, no such thing as an after-image or a sense-datum, though there is such a thing as the experience of having an image, and this experience is described indirectly in material object language, not in phenomenal language, for there is no such thing.[15] We describe the experience by saying, in effect, that it is like the experience we have when, for example, we really see a yellowy-orange patch on the wall. Trees and wallpaper can be green, but not the experience of seeing or imagining a tree or wallpaper. (Or if they are described as green or yellow this can only be in a derived sense.)

*Objection 5*. It would make sense to say of a molecular movement in the brain that it is swift or slow, straight or circular, but it makes no sense to say this of the experience of seeing something yellow.

*Reply*. So far we have not given sense to talk of experiences as swift or slow, straight or circular. But I am not claiming that 'experience' and 'brain-process' mean the same or even that they have the same logic. 'Somebody' and 'the doctor' do not have the same logic, but this does not lead us to suppose that talking about somebody telephoning is talking about someone over and above, say, the doctor. The ordinary man when he reports an experience is reporting that something is going on, but he leaves it open as to what sort of thing is going on, whether in a material solid medium or perhaps in some sort of gaseous medium, or even perhaps in some sort of nonspatial medium (if this makes sense). All that I am saying is that 'experience' and 'brain-process' may in fact refer to the same thing, and if so we may easily adopt a convention (which is not a change in our present rules for the use of experience words but an addition to them) whereby it would make sense to talk of an experience in terms appropriate to physical processes.

*Objection 6.* Sensations are private, brain processes are *public*. If I sincerely say, 'I see a yellowish-orange after-image,' and I am not making a verbal mistake, then I cannot be wrong. But I can be wrong about a brain-process. The scientist looking into my brain might be having an illusion. Moreover, it makes sense to say that two or more people are observing the same brain-process but not that two or more people are reporting the same inner experience.

*Reply.* This shows that the language of introspective reports has a different logic from the language of material processes. It is obvious that until the brain-process theory is much improved and widely accepted there will be no *criteria* for saying 'Smith has an experience of such-and-such a sort' *except* Smith's introspective reports. So we have adopted a rule of language that (normally) what Smith says goes.

*Objection 7.* I can imagine myself turned to stone and yet having images, aches, pains, and so on.

*Reply.* I can imagine that the electrical theory of lightning is false, that lightning is some sort of purely optical phenomenon. I can imagine that lightning is not an electrical discharge. I can imagine that the Evening Star is not the Morning Star. But it is. All the objection shows is that 'experience' and 'brain-process' do not have the same meaning. It does not show that an experience is not in fact a brain process.

This objection is perhaps much the same as one which can be summed up by the slogan: 'What can be composed of nothing cannot be composed of anything.'[16] The argument goes as follows: on the brain-process thesis the identity between the brain-process and the experience is a contingent one. So it is logically possible that there should be no brain-process, and no process of any other sort either (no heart process, no kidney process, no liver process). There would be the experience but no 'corresponding' physiological process with which we might be able to identify it empirically.

I suspect that the objector is thinking of the experience as a ghostly entity. So it is composed of something, not of nothing, after all. On his view it is composed of ghost stuff, and on mine it is composed of brain stuff. Perhaps the counter-reply will be[17] that the experience is simple and uncompounded, and so it is not composed of anything after all. This seems to be a quibble, for, if it were taken seriously, the remark 'What can be composed of nothing cannot be composed of anything' could be recast as an a priori argument against Democritus and atomism and for Descartes and infinite divisibility. And it seems odd that a question of this sort could be settled a priori. We must therefore construe the word 'composed' in a very weak sense, which would allow us to say that even an indivisible atom is composed of something (namely, itself). The dualist cannot really say that an experience can be composed of nothing. For he holds that experiences are something over and above material processes, that is, that they are a sort of ghost stuff. (Or perhaps ripples in an underlying ghost stuff.) I say that the dualist's hypothesis is a perfectly intelligible one. But I say that experiences are not to be identified with ghost stuff but with brain stuff. This is another hypothesis, and in my view a very plausible one. The present argument cannot knock it down a priori.

*Objection 8.* The 'beetle in the box' objection (see Wittgenstein, *Philosophical Investigations*, §293). How could descriptions of experiences, if these are genuine reports, get a foothold in language? For any rule of language must have public criteria for its correct application.

*Reply.* The change from describing how things are to describing how we feel is just a change from uninhibitedly saying 'this is so' to saying 'this looks so.' That is, when the naïve person might be tempted to say, 'There is a patch of light on the wall which moves whenever I move my eyes' or 'A pin is being stuck into me,' we have learned how to resist this temptation and say 'It *looks as though* there is a patch of light on the wallpaper' or 'It *feels as though* someone were sticking a pin into me.' The introspective account tells us about the individual's state of consciousness in the same way as does 'I see a patch of light' or 'I feel a pin being stuck into me': it differs from the corresponding perception statement in so far as it withdraws any claim about what is actually going on in the external world. From the point of view of the psychologist, the change from talking about the environment to talking about one's perceptual sensations is simply a matter of disinhibiting certain reactions. These are reactions which one normally suppresses because one has learned that in the prevailing circumstances they are unlikely to provide a good indication of the state of the environment.[18] To say that something looks green to me is simply to say that my experience is like the experience I get when I see something that really is green. In my reply to Objection 3, I pointed out the extreme openness or generality of statements which report experiences. This explains why there is no language of private qualities. (Just as 'someone', unlike 'the doctor', is a colorless word.)[19]

If it is asked what is the difference between those brain processes which, in my view, are experiences and those brain processes which are not, I can only reply that it is at present unknown. I have been tempted to conjecture that the difference may in part be that between perception and reception (in D. M. MacKay's terminology) and that the type of brain process which is an experience might be identifiable with MacKay's active 'matching response'.[20] This, however, cannot be the whole story, because sometimes I can perceive something unconsciously, as when I take a handkerchief out of a drawer without being aware that I am doing so. But at the very least, we can classify the brain processes which are experiences as those brain processes which are, or might have been, causal conditions of those pieces of verbal behavior which we call reports of immediate experience.

I have now considered a number of objections to the brain-process thesis. I wish now to conclude with some remarks on the logical status of the thesis itself. U. T. Place seems to hold that it is a straight-out scientific hypothesis.[21] If so, he is partly right and partly wrong. If the issue is between (say) a brain-process thesis and a heart thesis, or a liver thesis, or a kidney thesis, then the issue is a purely empirical one, and the verdict is overwhelmingly in favor of the brain. The right sorts of things don't go on in the heart, liver, or kidney, nor do these organs possess the right sort of complexity of structure. On the other hand, if the issue is between a brain-or-liver-or-kidney thesis (that is, some form of materialism) on the one hand and epiphenomenalism on the other hand, then the issue is not an empirical one. For there is no conceivable experiment which could decide between materialism and epiphenomenalism. This latter issue is not like the average straight-out empirical issue in science, but like the issue between the nineteenth-century English naturalist Philip Gosse[22] and the orthodox geologists and paleontologists of his day. According to Gosse, the earth was created about 4000 BC exactly as described in *Genesis*, with twisted rock strata, 'evidence' of erosion, and so forth, and all sorts of fossils, all in their appropriate strata, just as if the usual evolutionist story had been true. Clearly this theory is in a sense irrefutable: no evidence can possibly tell against it. Let us ignore the theological setting in which Philip Gosse's hypothesis had been placed, thus ruling out objections of a theological kind, such as 'what a queer God who would go to such elaborate lengths to deceive us.' Let us suppose that it is held that the universe just *began* in 4004 BC with the initial conditions just everywhere as they were in 4004 BC, and in particular that our own planet began with sediment in the rivers, eroded cliffs, fossils in the rocks, and so on. No scientist would ever entertain this as a serious hypothesis, consistent though it is with all possible evidence. The hypothesis offends against the principles of parsimony and simplicity. There would be far too many brute and inexplicable facts. Why are pterodactyl bones just as they are? No explanation in terms of the evolution of pterodactyls from earlier forms of life would any longer be possible. We would have millions of facts about the world as it was in 4004 BC that just have to be *accepted*.

The issue between the brain-process theory and epiphenomenalism seems to be of the above sort. (Assuming that a behavioristic reduction of introspective reports is not possible.) If it be agreed that there are no cogent philosophical arguments which force us into accepting dualism, and if the brain process theory and dualism are equally consistent with the facts, then the principles of parsimony and simplicity seem to me to decide overwhelmingly in favour of the brain-process theory. As I pointed out earlier, dualism involves a large number of irreducible psycho-physical laws (whereby the 'nomological danglers' dangle) of a queer sort, that just have to be taken on trust, and are just as difficult to swallow as the irreducible facts about the paleontology of the earth with which we are faced on Philip Gosse's theory.

# References

1 This is a very slightly revised version of a paper which was first published in the *Philosophical Review*, LXVIII (1959), 141–56. Since that date there have been criticisms of my paper by J. T. Stevenson, *Philosophical Review*, LXIX (1960), 505–10, to which I have replied in *Philosophical Review*, LXX (1961), 406–7, and by G. Pitcher and by W. D. Joske, *Australasian Journal of Philosophy*, XXXVIII (1960), 150–60, to which I have replied in the same volume of that journal, pp. 252–54.

2 *British Journal of Psychology*, XLVII (1956), 44–50; reprinted in this volume, pp. 106–16 above. (Page references are to the reprint in this volume.)

3 *Minnesota Studies in the Philosophy of Science*, Vol. II (Minneapolis: University of Minnesota Press, 1958), pp. 370–497.

4 Some philosophers of my acquaintance, who have the advantage over me in having known Wittgenstein, would say that this interpretation of him is too behavioristic. However, it seems to me a very natural interpretation of his printed words, and whether or not it is Wittgenstein's real view it is certainly an interesting and important one. I wish to consider it here as a possible rival both to the 'brain-process' thesis and to straight-out old-fashioned dualism.

5 See Ryle, *The Concept of Mind* (London: Hutchinson's University Library, 1949), p. 93.

6 On this point see Paul Oppenheim and Hilary Putnam, 'Unity of Science as a Working Hypothesis', in *Minnesota Studies in the Philosophy of Science*, Vol. II (Minneapolis: University of Minnesota Press, 1958), pp. 3–36.

7 Feigl, *op. cit.*, p. 428. Feigl uses the expression 'nomological danglers' for the laws whereby the entities dangle: I have used the expression to refer to the dangling entities themselves.

8 Wittgenstein did not like the word 'disposition'. I am using it to put in a nutshell (and perhaps inaccurately) the view which I am attributing to Wittgenstein. I should like to repeat that I do not wish to claim that my interpretation of Wittgenstein is correct. Some of those who knew him do not interpret him in this way. It is merely a view which I find myself extracting from his printed words and which I think is important and worth discussing for its own sake.

9 See Place, *op. cit.*, p. 107. and Feigl, *op. cit.*, p. 390, near top.

10 See J. H. Woodger, *Theory Construction*, International Encyclope-

dia of Unified Science, II, No. 5 (Chicago: University of Chicago Press, 1939), 38. I here permit myself to speak loosely. For warnings against possible ways of going wrong with this sort of talk, see my note 'Spatialising Time', *Mind*, LXIV (1955), 239–41.

11  Cf. Feigl, *op. cit.*, p. 439.

12  See Place, *op. cit.*, p. 106; also Feigl, *op. cit.*, p. 438.

13  I think this objection was first put to me by Professor Max Black. I think it is the most subtle of any of those I have considered, and the one which I am least confident of having satisfactorily met.

14  See B. A. Farrell, 'Experience', *Mind*, LIX (1950), 170–98.

15  Dr J. R. Smythies claims that a sense-datum language could be taught independently of the material object language ('A Note on the Fallacy of the "Phenomenological Fallacy"', *British Journal of Psychology*, XLVIII [1957], 141–44). I am not so sure of this: there must be some public criteria for a person having got a rule wrong before we can teach him the rule. I suppose someone might *accidentally* learn color words by Dr Smythies' procedure. I am not, of course, denying that we can learn a sense-datum language in the sense that we can learn to report our experience. Nor would Place deny it.

16  I owe this objection to Dr C. B. Martin. I gather that he no longer wishes to maintain this objection, at any rate in its present form.

17  Martin did not make this reply, but one of his students did.

18  I owe this point to Place, in correspondence.

19  The 'beetle in the box' objection is, *if it is sound*, an objection to *any* view, and in particular the Cartesian one, that introspective reports are genuine reports. So it is no objection to a weaker thesis that I would be concerned to uphold, namely, that if introspective reports of 'experiences' are genuinely reports, then the things they are reports of are in fact brain processes.

20  See his article 'Towards an Information-Flow Model of Human Behaviour', *British Journal of Psychology*, XLVII (1956), 30–43.

21  *Op. cit.* For a further discussion of this, in reply to the original version of the present paper, see Place's note 'Materialism as a Scientific Hypothesis', *Philosophical Review*, LXIX (1960), 101–4.

22  See the entertaining account of Gosse's book *Omphalos* by Martin Gardner in *Fads and Fallacies in the Name of Science*, 2nd ed. (New York: Dover, 1957), pp. 124–27.

# Philosophy and Our Mental Life[1]

The question which troubles laymen, and which has long troubled philosophers, even if it is somewhat disguised by today's analytic style of writing philosophy, is this: are we made of matter or soul-stuff? To put it as bluntly as possible, are we just material beings, or are we 'something more'? In this paper, I will argue as strongly as possible that this whole question rests on false assumptions. My purpose is not to dismiss the question, however, so much as to speak to the real concern which is behind the question. The real concern is, I believe, with the autonomy of our mental life.

People are worried that we may be debunked, that our behavior may be exposed as really explained by something mechanical. Not, to be sure, mechanical in the old sense of cogs and pulleys, but in the newer sense of electricity and magnetism and quantum chemistry and so forth. In this paper, part of what I want to do is to argue that this can't happen. Mentality is a real and autonomous feature of our world.

But even more important, at least in my feeling, is the fact that this whole question has nothing to do with our substance. Strange as it may seem to common sense and to sophisticated intuition alike, the question of the autonomy of our mental life does not hinge on and has nothing to do with that all too popular, all too old question about matter or soul-stuff. We could be made of Swiss cheese and it wouldn't matter.

Failure to see this, stubborn insistence on formulating the question as *matter or soul*, utterly prevents progress on these questions. Conversely, once we see that our substance is not the issue, I do not see how we can help but make progress.

The concept which is key to unravelling the mysteries in the philosophy of mind, I think, is the concept of *functional isomorphism*. Two systems are functionally isomorphic if *there is a correspondence between the states of one and the states of the other that preserves functional relations.* To start with computing machine examples, if the functional relations are just sequence relations, e.g. *state* A *is always followed by state* B, then, for F to be a functional isomorphism, it must be the case that state A is followed by state B in system 1 if and only if state F(A) is followed by state F(B) in system 2. If the functional relations are, say, data or print-out relations, e.g. *when print* π *is printed on the tape, system I goes into state A*, these must be preserved. *When print* π *is printed on the tape, system 2 goes into state F(A),* if F is a functional isomorphism between system 1 and system 2. More generally, if T is a correct theory of the functioning of system 1, at the functional or psychological level, then an isomorphism between system 1 and system 2 must map each property and relation defined in system 2 in such a way that T comes out true when all references to system 1 are replaced by references to system 2, and all property and relation symbols in T are reinterpreted according to the mapping.

The difficulty with the notion of functional isomorphism is that it *presupposes the notion of a thing's being a functional or psychological description.* It is for this reason that, in various papers on this subject, I introduced and explained the notion in terms of Turing machines. And I felt constrained, therefore, to defend the thesis that *we* are Turing machines. Turing machines come, so to speak, with a normal form for their functional description, the so-called machine table — a standard style of program. But it does not seem fatally sloppy to me, although it is sloppy, if we apply the notion of functional isomorphism to systems for which we have no detailed idea at present what the normal form description would look like — systems like ourselves. The point is that even if we don't have any idea what a comprehensive psychological theory would look like, I claim that we know enough (and here analogies from computing machines, economic systems, games and so forth are helpful) to point out illuminating differences between any possible psychological theory of a human being, or even a functional description of a computing machine or an economic system, and a physical or chemical description. Indeed, Dennett and Fodor have done a great deal along these lines in recent books.

This brings me back to the question of *copper, cheese, or soul.* One point we can make immediately as soon as we have the basic concept of functional isomorphism is this: two systems can have quite different constitutions and be functionally iso-morphic. For example, a computer made of electrical compo-nents can be isomorphic to one made of cogs and wheels. In other words, for each state in the first computer there is a corresponding state in the other, and, as we said before, the sequential relations are the same – if state $S$ is followed by state $B$ in the case of the electronic computer, state $A$ would be followed by state $B$ in the case of the computer made of cogs and wheels, and it doesn't matter at all that the *physical realizations* of those states are totally different. So a computer made of electrical components can be isomorphic to one made of cogs and wheels or to human clerks using paper and pencil. A computer made of one sort of wire, say copper wire, or one sort of relay, etc. will be in a different physical and chemical state when it computes than a computer made of a different sort of wire and relay. But the functional description may be the same.

We can extend this point still further. Assume that one thesis of materialism (I shall call it the 'first thesis') is correct, and we are, as wholes, just material systems obeying physical laws. Then the second thesis of classical materialism cannot be correct – namely, our mental states, e.g. *thinking about next summer's vacation*, cannot be *identical* with any physical or chemical states. For it is clear from what we already know about computers etc., that whatever the program of the brain may be, it must be physically possible, though not necessarily feasible, to produce something with that same program but quite a different physical and chemical constitution. Then to identify the state in question with its physical or chemical realization would be quite absurd, given that that realization is in a sense quite accidental, from the point of view of psychology, anyway (which is the relevant science).[2] It is as if we met Martians and discovered that they were in all functional respects isomorphic to us, but we refused to admit that they could feel pain because their C fibers were different.

  Now, imagine two possible universes, perhaps 'parallel worlds', in the science fiction sense, in one of which people have good old fashioned souls, operating through pineal glands, perhaps, and in the other of which they have complicated brains. And suppose that the souls in the soul world are functionally isomorphic to the brains in the brain world. Is there any more sense to attaching importance to this difference than to the difference between copper wires and some other wires in the computer? Does it matter that the soul people have, so to speak, immaterial brains, and that the brain people have material souls? What matters is the common structure, the theory $T$ of which we are, alas, in deep ignorance, and not the hardware, be it ever so ethereal.

One may raise various objections to what I have said. I shall try to reply to some of them.

One might, for example, say that if the souls of the soul people are isomorphic to the brains of the brain people, then their souls must be automata-like, and that's not the sort of soul we are interested in. 'All your argument really shows is that there is no need to distinguish between a brain and an automa-ton-like soul.' But what precisely does that objection come to?

I think there are two ways of understanding it. It might come to the claim that the notion of functional organization or functional isomorphism only makes sense for automata. But that is totally false. Sloppy as our notions are at present, we at least know this much, as Jerry Fodor has emphasized: we know that the notion of functional organization applies to anything to which the notion of a psychological theory applies. I explained the most general notion of functional isomorphism by saying that two systems are functionally isomorphic if there is an isomorphism that makes both of them models for the same psychological theory. (That is stronger than just saying that they are both models for the same psychological theory – they are isomorphic realizations of the same abstract structure.) To say that real old fashioned souls would not be in the domain of definition of the concept of functional organization or of the concept of functional isomorphisms would be to take the position that whatever we mean by the soul, it is something for which there can be no theory. That seems pure obscurantism. I will assume, henceforth, that it is not built into the notion of mind or soul or whatever that it is unintelligible or that there couldn't be a theory of it.

Secondly, someone might say more seriously that even if there is a theory of the soul or mind, the soul, at least in the full, rich old fashioned sense, is supposed to have powers that no mechanical system could have. In the latter part of this chapter I shall consider this claim.

If it is built into one's notions of the soul that the soul can do things that violate the laws of physics, then I admit I am stumped. There cannot be a soul which is isomorphic to a brain, if the soul can read the future clairvoyantly, in a way that is not in any way explainable by physical law. On the other hand, if one is interested in more modest forms of magic like telepathy, it seems to me that there is no reason in principle why we couldn't construct a device which would project subvocalized thoughts from one brain to another. As to reincarnation, if we are, as I am urging, a certain kind of functional structure (my identity is, as it were, my functional structure), there seems to be in principle no reason why that could not be reproduced after a thousand years or a million years or a billion years. Resurrection: as you know, Christians believe in resurrection in the flesh, which completely bypasses the need for an immaterial vehicle. So even if one is interested in those questions (and they are not my concern in this paper, although I am concerned to speak to people who have those concerns), even then one doesn't need an immaterial brain or soul-stuff.

So if I am right, and the question of matter or soul-stuff is really irrelevant to any question of philosophical or religious significance, why so much attention to it, why so much heat? The crux of the matter seems to be that both the Diderots of this world and the Descartes of this world have agreed that if we are matter, then there is a physical explanation for how we behave, disappointing or exciting. I think the traditional dualist says '*wouldn't it be terrible if we turned out to be just matter, for then there is a physical explanation for everything we do.*' And the traditional materialist says '*if we are just matter, then there is a physical explanation for everything we do. Isn't that exciting!*' (It is like the distinction between the optimist and the pessimist: an optimist is a person who says 'this is the best of all possible worlds'; and a pessimist is a person who says 'you're right'.)[3]

I think they are both wrong. I think Diderot and Descartes were both wrong in assuming that if we are matter, or our souls are material, then there is a physical explanation for our behavior.

Let me try to illustrate what I mean by a very simple analogy. Suppose we have a very simple physical system – a board in which there are two holes, a circle one inch in diameter and a square one inch high, and a cubical peg one-sixteenth of an inch less than one inch high. We have the following very simple fact to explain: *the peg passes through the square hole, and it does not pass through the round hole.*

In explanation of this, one might attempt the following. One might say that the peg is, after all, a cloud or, better, a rigid lattice of atoms. One might even attempt to give a description of that lattice, compute its electrical potential energy, worry about why it does not collapse, produce some quantum mechanics to explain why it is stable, etc. The board is also a lattice of atoms. I will call the peg 'system $A$', and the holes 'region 1' and 'region 2'. One could compute all possible trajectories of system $A$ (there are, by the way, very serious questions about these computations, their effectiveness, feasibility, and so on, but let us assume this), and perhaps one could deduce from just the laws of particle mechanics or quantum electrodynamics that system $A$ never passes through region 1, but that there is at least one trajectory which enables it to pass through region 2. Is this an explanation of the fact that the peg passes through the square hole and not the round hole?

Very often we are told that if something is made of matter, its behavior must have a physical explanation. And the argument is that if it is made of matter (and we make a lot of assumptions), then there should be a deduction of its behavior from its material structure. *What makes you call this deduction an explanation?*

On the other hand, if you are not 'hipped' on the idea that *the* explanation must be at the level of the ultimate constituents, and that in fact the explanation might have the property that *the ultimate constituents don't matter*, that *only the higher level structure matters*, then there is a very simple explanation here. The explanation is that the board is rigid, the peg is rigid, and as a matter of geometrical fact, the round hole is smaller than the peg, the square hole is bigger than the cross-section of the peg. The peg passes through the hole that is large enough to take its cross-section, and does not pass through the hole that is too small to take its cross-section. That is a correct explanation whether the peg consists of molecules, or continuous rigid substance, or whatever. (If one wanted to amplify the explanation, one might point out the geometrical fact that a square one inch high is bigger than a circle one inch across.)

Now, one can say that in this explanation certain *relevant structural features of the situation* are brought out. The geometrical features are brought out. It is *relevant* that a square one inch high is bigger than a circle one inch around. And the relationship between the size and shape of the peg and the size and shape of the holes is *relevant*. It is *relevant* that both the board and the peg are *rigid* under transportation. And nothing else is relevant. The same explanation will go in any world (whatever the microstructure) in which those *higher level structural features* are present. In that sense *this explanation is autonomous*.

People have argued that I am wrong to say that the microstructural deduction is not an explanation. I think that in terms of the *purposes for which we use the notion of explanation*, it is not an explanation. If you want to, let us say that the deduction *is* an explanation, it is just a terrible explanation, and why look for terrible explanations when good ones are available?

Goodness is not a subjective matter. Even if one agrees with the positivists who saddled us with the notion of explanation as deduction from laws, one of the things we do in science is to look for laws. Explanation is superior not just subjectively, but *methodologically*, in terms of facilitating the aims of scientific inquiry, if it brings out relevant laws. An explanantion is superior if it is more general.

Just taking those two features, and there are many many more one could think of, compare the explanation at the higher level of this phenomenon with the atomic explanation. The explanation at the higher level brings out the relevant geometrical relationships. The lower level explanation conceals those laws. Also notice that the higher level explanation applies to a much more interesting class of systems (of course that has to do with what we are interested in).

The fact is that we are much more interested in generalizing to other structures which are rigid and have various geometrical relations, than we are in generalizing to *the next peg that has exactly this molecular structure*, for the very good reason that there is not going to *be* a next peg that has exactly this molecular structure. So in terms of real life disciplines, real life ways of slicing up scientific problems, the higher level explanation is far more general, which is why it is *explanatory*.

We were only able to deduce a statement which is lawful at the *higher* level, that the peg goes through the hole which is larger than the cross-section of the peg. When we try to deduce the possible trajectories of 'system *A*' from statements about the individual atoms, we use premises which are totally accidental – this atom is here, this carbon atom is there, and so forth. And that is one reason that it is very misleading to talk about a reduction of a science like economics to the level of the elementary particles making up the players of the economic game. In fact, their motions – buying this, selling that, arriving at an equilibrium price – these motions cannot be deduced from just the equations of motion. Otherwise they would be *physically necessitated*, not *economically necessitated*, to arrive at an equilibrium price. They play that game because they are particular systems with particular boundary conditions which are totally accidental from the point of view of physics. This means that the derivation of the laws of economics from *just* the laws of physics is *in principle* impossible. The derivation of the laws of economics from the laws of physics and *accidental statements about which particles were where when* by a Laplacian supermind might be in principle possible, but why want it? A few chapters of, e.g. von Neumann, will tell one far more about regularities at the level of economic structure than such a deduction ever could.

The conclusion I want to draw from this is that we do have the kind of autonomy that we are looking for in the mental realm. Whatever our mental functioning may be, there seems to be no serious reason to believe that it is *explainable* by our physics and chemistry. And what we are interested in is not: given that we consist of such and such particles, could someone have predicted that we would have this mental functioning? because such a prediction is not *explanatory*, however great a feat it may be. What we are interested in is: can we say at this autonomous level that since we have this sort of structure, this sort of program, it follows that we will be able to learn this, we will tend to like that, and so on? These are the problems of mental life – the description of this autonomous level of mental functioning – and that is what is to be discovered.

*

In previous papers, I have argued for the hypothesis that (1) a whole human being is a Turing machine, and (2) that psychological states of a human being are Turing machine states or disjunctions of Turing machine states. In this section I want to argue that this point of view was essentially wrong, and that I was too much in the grip of the reductionist outlook.

Let me begin with a technical difficulty. A *state* of a Turing machine is described in such a way that a Turing machine can be in exactly one state at a time. Moreover, memory and learning are not represented in the Turing machine model as acquisition of new states, but as acquisition of new information printed on the machine's tape. Thus, if human beings have any states at all which resemble Turing machine states, those states must (1) be states the human can be in at any time, independently of learning and memory; and (2) be *total* instantaneous states of the human being – states which determine, together with learning and memory, what the next state will be, as well as totally specifying the present condition of the human being ('totally' from the standpoint of psychological theory, that means).

These characteristics establish that *no* psychological state in any customary sense can be a Turing machine state. Take a particular kind of pain to be a 'psychological state'. If I *am* a Turing machine, then my present 'state' must determine not only whether or not I am having that particular kind of pain, but also whether or not I am about to say 'three', whether or not I am hearing a shrill whine, etc. So the psychological state in question (the pain) is not the same as my 'state' in the sense of *machine state*, although it is possible (so far) that my machine state *determines* my psychological state. Moreover, *no* psychological theory would pretend that having a pain of a particular kind, being about to say 'three', or hearing a shrill whine, etc., all belong to *one* psychological state, although there could well be a machine state characterized by the fact that I was in it only when simultaneously having that pain, being about to say 'three', hearing a shrill whine, etc. So, even if I am a Turing machine, my machine states are *not* the same as my psychological states. My description *qua* Turing machine (machine table) and my description *qua* human being (*via* a psychological theory) are descriptions at two totally different levels of organization.

So far it is still possible that a psychological state is a large disjunction (practically speaking, an almost infinite disjunction) of machine states, although no *single* machine state is a psychological state. But this is very unlikely when we move away from states like 'pain' (which are almost *biological*) to states like 'jealousy' or 'love' or 'competitiveness'. Being jealous is certainly not an *instantaneous* state, and it depends on a great deal of information and on many learned facts and habits. But Turing machine states are instantaneous and are independent of learning and memory. That is, learning and memory may cause a Turing machine to go into a state, but the identity of the state does not depend on learning and memory, whereas, no matter what state I am in, identifying that state as 'being jealous of $X$'s regard for $Y$' involves specifying that I have learned that $X$ and $Y$ are persons and a good deal about social relations among persons. Thus jealousy can neither be a machine state nor a disjunction of machine states.

One might attempt to modify the theory by saying that being jealous = either being in State $A$ and having tape $c_1$ *or* being in State $A$ and having tape $c_2$ *or* ... being in State $B$ and having tape $d_1$ *or* being in State $B$ and having tape $d_2$ ... being in State $Z$ and having tape $y_1$ ... or being in State $Z$ and having tape $y_n$ – i.e. define a psychological state as disjunction, the individual disjuncts being not Turing machine states, as before, but conjunctions of a machine state and a tape (i.e. a total description of the content of the memory bank). Besides the fact that such a description would be literally infinite, the theory is now without content, for the original purpose was to use the machine table as a model of a psychological theory, whereas it is now clear that the machine table description, although different from the description at the elementary particle level, is as removed from the description *via* a psychological theory as the physico-chemical description is.

What is the importance of machines in the philosophy of mind? I think that machines have both a positive and a negative importance. The positive importance of machines was that it was in connection with machines, computing machines in particular, that the notion of functional organization first appeared. Machines forced us to distinguish between an abstract structure and its concrete realization. Not that that distinction came into the world for the first time with machines. But in the case of computing machines, we could not avoid rubbing our noses against the fact that what we had to count as to all intents and purposes the same structure could be realized in a bewildering variety of different ways; that the important properties were not physical-chemical. That the machines made us catch on to the idea of functional organization is extremely important. The negative importance of machines, however, is that they tempt us to oversimplification. The notion of functional organization became clear to us through systems with a very restricted, very specific functional organization. So the temptation is present to assume that we must have that restricted and specific kind of functional organization.

Now I want to consider an example – an example which may seem remote from what we have been talking about, but which may help. This is not an example from the philosophy of mind at all. Consider the following fact. The earth does not go around the sun in a circle, as was once believed, it goes around the sun in an ellipse, with the sun at one of the foci, not in the center of the ellipse. Yet one statement which would hold true if the orbit was a circle and the sun was at the centre still holds true, surprisingly. That is the following statement: the radius vector from the sun to the earth sweeps out equal areas in equal times. If the orbit were a circle, and the earth were moving with a constant velocity, that would be trivial. But the orbit is not a circle. Also the velocity is not constant – when the earth is farthest away from the sun, it is going most slowly, when it is closest to the sun, it is going fastest. The earth is speeding up and slowing down. But the earth's radius vector sweeps out equal areas in equal times.[4] Newton deduced that law in his *Principia*, and his deduction shows that the only thing on which that law depends is that the force acting on the earth is in the direction of the sun. That is absolutely the only fact one needs to deduce that law. Mathematically it is equivalent to that law.[5] That is all well and good when the gravitational law is that every body attracts every other body according to an inverse square law, because then there is always a force on the earth in the direction of the sun. If we assume that we can neglect all the other bodies, that their influence is slight, then that is all we need, and we can use Newton's proof, or a more modern, simpler proof.

But today we have very complicated laws of gravitation. First of all, we say what is really going [on] is that the world lines of freely falling bodies in space-time are geodesics. And the geometry is determined by the mass-energy tensor, and the ankle bone is connected to the leg bone, etc. So, one might ask, how would a modern relativity theorist explain Kepler's law? He would explain it very simply. *Kepler's laws are true because Newton's laws are approximately true.* And, in fact, an attempt to replace that argument by a deduction of Kepler's laws from the field equations would be regarded as almost as ridiculous (but not quite) as trying to deduce that the peg will go through one hole and not the other from the positions and velocities of the individual atoms.

I want to draw the philosophical conclusion that Newton's laws *have a kind of reality in our world* even though they are not *true*. The point is that it will be necessary to appeal to Newton's laws in order to explain Kepler's laws. Methodologically, I can make that claim at least plausible. One remark – due to Alan Garfinkel – is that *a good explanation is invariant under small perturbations of the assumptions.* One problem with deducing Kepler's laws from the gravitational field equations is that if we do it, tomorrow the gravitational field equations are likely to be different. Whereas the explanation which consists in showing that whichever equation we have implies Newton's equation to a first approximation is invariant under even moderate perturbations, quite big perturbations, of the assumptions. One might say that every explanation of Kepler's laws 'passes through' Newton's laws.

Let me come back to the philosophy of mind, now. If we assume a thorough atomic structure of matter, quantization and so forth, then, at first blush, it looks as if *continuities* cannot be relevant to our brain functioning. Mustn't it all be discrete? Physics says that the deepest level is discrete.

There are two problems with this argument. One is that there are continuities even in quantum mechanics, as well as discontinuities. But ignore that, suppose quantum mechanics were a thoroughly discrete theory.

The other problem is that if that were a good argument, it would be an argument against the utilizability of the model of air as a continuous liquid, which is the model on which aeroplane wings are constructed, at least if they are to fly at anything less than supersonic speeds. There are two points: one is that a discontinuous structure, a discrete structure, can approximate a continuous structure. The discontinuities may be irrelevant, just as in the case of the peg and the board. The fact that the peg and the board are not continuous solids is irrelevant. One can say that the peg and the board only approximate perfectly rigid continuous solids. But if the error in the approximation is irrelevant to the level of description, so what? It is not just that discrete systems can approximate continuous systems; the fact is that the system may behave in the way it does *because* a continuous system would behave in such and such a way, and the system approximates a continuous system.

This is not a Newtonian world. Tough. Kepler's law comes out true because the sun-earth system approximates a Newtonian system. And the error in the approximation is quite irrelevant at that level.

This analogy is not perfect because physicists are interested in laws to which the error in the approximation is relevant. It seems to me that in the psychological case the analogy is even better, that continuous models (for example, Hull's model for rote learning which used a continuous potential) could perfectly well be correct, whatever the ultimate structure of the brain is. We cannot deduce that a digital model has to be the correct model from the fact that ultimately there are neurons. The brain may work the way it does because it approximates some system whose laws are best conceptualized in terms of continuous mathematics. What is more, the errors in that approximation may be irrelevant at the level of psychology.

What I have said about *continuity* goes as well for many other things. Let us come back to the question of the soul people and the brain people, and the isomorphism between the souls in one world and the brains in the other. One objection was, if there is a functional isomorphism between souls and brains, wouldn't the souls have to be rather simple? The answer is no. Because brains can be essentially infinitely complex. A system with as many degrees of freedom as the brain can imitate to within the accuracy relevant to psychological theory any structure one can hope to describe. It might be, so to speak, that the ultimate physics of the soul will be quite different from the ultimate physics of the brain, but that at the level we are interested in, the level of functional organization, the same description might go for both. And also that that description might be formally incompatible with the actual physics of the brain, in the way that the description of the air flowing around an aeroplane wing as a continuous incompressible liquid is *formally incompatible with the actual structure of the air.*

Let me close by saying that these examples support the idea that our substance, what we are made of, places almost no first order restrictions on our form. And that what we are really interested in, as Aristotle saw,[6] is form and not matter. *What is our intellectual form?* is the question, not what the matter is. And whatever our substance may be, soul-stuff, or matter or Swiss cheese, it is not going to place any interesting first order restrictions on the answer to this question. It may, of course, place interesting higher order restrictions. Small effects may have to be explained in terms of the actual physics of the brain. But when we are not even at the level of an *idealized* description of the functional organization of the brain, to talk about the importance of small perturbations seems decidedly premature. My conclusion is that we have what we always wanted – an autonomous mental life. And we need no mysteries, no ghostly agents, no *élan vital* to have it.

## References

1 This paper was presented as a part of a Foerster symposium on 'Computers and the Mind' at the University of California (Berkeley) in October, 1973. I am indebted to Alan Garfinkel for comments on earlier versions of this paper.

2 Even if it were not physically possible to realize human psychology in a creature made of anything but the usual protoplasm, DNA etc., it would still not be correct to say that psychological states are identical with their physical realizations. For, as will be argued below, such an identification has no *explanatory* value *in psychology*. On this point, compare Fodor, *Psychological Explanation*, Random House, 1968.

3 Joke Credit: Joseph Weizenbaum.

4 This is one of Kepler's Laws.

5 Provided that the two bodies – the sun and the earth – are the whole

universe. If there are other forces, then, of course, Kepler's law cannot be *exactly* correct.

6 E.g. Aristotle says '... we can wholly dismiss as unnecessary the question whether the soul and the body are one: it is as meaningless to ask whether the wax and the shape given to it by the stamp are one, or generally the matter of a thing and that of which it is the matter.' (See *De Anima*, 412 a6–b9.)

DONALD DAVIDSON

# Psychology as Philosophy

Not all human motion is behavior. Each of us in this room is
moving eastward at about 700 miles an hour, carried by the
diurnal rotation of the earth, but this is not a fact about our
behavior. When I cross my legs, the raised foot bobs gently with
the beat of my heart, but I do not move my foot. Behavior
consists in things we do, whether by intention or not, but where
there is behavior, intention is relevant. In the case of actions, the
relevance may be expressed this way: an event is an action if
and only if it can be described in a way that makes it intentional.
For example, a man may stamp on a hat, believing it is the hat
of his rival when it is really his own. Then stamping on his own
hat is an act of his, and part of his behavior, though he did not
do it intentionally. As observers we often describe the actions of
others in ways that would not occur to them. This does not
mean that the concept of intention has been left behind, however, for happenings cease to be actions or behavior when there
is no way of describing them in terms of intention.

These remarks merely graze a large subject, the relation
between action and behavior on the one hand, and intention on
the other. I suggest that even though intentional action, at least
from the point of view of description, is by no means all the
behavior there is, intention is conceptually central; the rest is
understood and defined in terms of intention. If this is true, then
what can be said to show that the intentional has traits that
segregate it conceptually from other families of concepts (particularly physical concepts) can be applied *mutatis mutandis* to
behavior generally. If the claim is mistaken, then the following
considerations apply to psychology only to the extent that
psychology employs the concepts of intention, belief, desire,
hope, and other attitudes directed (as one says) upon
propositions.

Can intentional human behavior be explained and predicted
in the same way other phenomena are? On the one hand, human

acts are clearly part of the order of nature, causing and being caused by events outside ourselves. On the other hand, there are good arguments against the view that thought, desire and voluntary action can be brought under deterministic laws, as physical phenomena can. An adequate theory of behavior must do justice to both these insights and show how, contrary to appearance, they can be reconciled. By evaluating the arguments against the possibility of deterministic laws of behavior, we can test the claims of psychology to be a science like others (some others).

When the world impinges on a person, or he moves to modify his environment, the interactions can be recorded and codified in ways that have been refined by the social sciences and common sense. But what emerge are not the strict quantitative laws embedded in sophisticated theory that we confidently expect in physics, but irreducibly statistical correlations that resist, and resist in principle, improvement without limit. What lies behind our inability to discover deterministic psycho-physical laws is this. When we attribute a belief, a desire, a goal, an intention or a meaning to an agent, we necessarily operate within a system of concepts in part determined by the structure of beliefs and desires of the agent himself. Short of changing the subject, we cannot escape this feature of the psychological; but this feature has no counterpart in the world of physics.

The nomological irreducibility of the psychological means, if I am right, that the social sciences cannot be expected to develop in ways exactly parallel to the physical sciences, nor can we expect ever to be able to explain and predict human behavior with the kind of precision that is possible in principle for physical phenomena. This does not mean there are any events that are in themselves undetermined or unpredictable; it is only events as described in the vocabulary of thought and action that resist incorporation into a closed deterministic system. These same events, described in appropriate physical terms, may be as amenable to prediction and explanation as any.

I shall not argue here for this version of monism, but it may be worth indicating how the parts of the thesis support one another. Take as a first premise that psychological events such as perceivings, rememberings, the acquisition and loss of knowledge, and intentionai actions are directly or indirectly caused by, and the causes of, physical events. The second premise is that when events are related as cause and effect, then there exists a closed and deterministic system of laws into which these events, when appropriately described, fit. (I ignore as irrelevant the possibility that micro-physics may be irreducibly probabilistic.) The third premise, for which I shall be giving reasons, is that there are no precise psycho-physical laws. The three premises, taken together, imply monism. For psychological events clearly cannot constitute a closed system; much happens that is not psychological, and affects the psychological. But if psychological events are causally related to physical events, there must, by premise two, be laws that cover them. By premise three, the laws are not psycho-physical, so they must be purely physical laws. This means that the psychological events are describable, taken one by one, in physical terms, that is, they are physical events. Perhaps it will be agreed that this position deserves to be called *anomalous monism*: monism, because it holds that psychological events are physical events; anomalous, because it insists that events do not fall under strict laws when described in psychological terms.

My general strategy for trying to show that there are no strict psycho-physical laws depends, first, on emphasizing the holistic character of the cognitive field. Any effort at increasing the accuracy and power of a theory of behavior forces us to bring more and more of the whole system of the agent's beliefs and motives directly into account. But in inferring this system from the evidence, we necessarily impose conditions of coherence, rationality, and consistency. These conditions have no echo in physical theory, which is why we can look for no more than rough correlations between psychological and physical phenomena.

Consider our common-sense scheme for describing and explaining actions. The part of this scheme that I have in mind depends on the fact that we can explain why someone acted as he did by mentioning a desire, value, purpose, goal or aim the person had, and a belief connecting the desire with the action to be explained. So, for example, we may explain why Achilles returned to the battle by saying he wished to avenge the death of Patroclus. (Given this much, we do not need to mention that he believed that by returning to the battle he could avenge the death of Patroclus.) This style of explanation has many variants. We may adumbrate explanation simply by expanding the description of the action: 'He is returning to battle with the intention of avenging the death of Patroclus.' Or we may more simply redescribe: 'Why is he putting on his armour?' 'He is getting ready to avenge Patroclus' death.' Even the answer 'He just wanted to' falls into the pattern. If given in explanation of why Sam played the piano at midnight, it implies that he wanted to make true a certain proposition, that Sam plays the piano at midnight, and he believed that by acting as he did, he would make it true.

A desire and a belief of the right sort may explain an action, but not necessarily. A man might have good reasons for killing his father, and he might do it, and yet the reasons not be his reasons in doing it (think of Oedipus). So when we offer the fact of the desire and belief in explanation, we imply not only that the agent had the desire and belief, but that they were *efficacious* in producing the action. Here we must say, I think, that causality is involved, i.e., that the desire and belief were causal conditions of the action. Even this is not sufficient, however. For suppose, contrary to the legend, that Oedipus, for some dark oedipal reason, was hurrying along the road intent on killing his father, and, finding a surly old man blocking his way, killed him so he could (as he thought) get on with the main job. Then not only did Oedipus want to kill his father, and actually kill him, but his desire caused him to kill his father. Yet we could not say that in killing the old man he intentionally killed his father, nor that his reason in killing the old man was to kill his father.

Can we somehow give conditions that are not only necessary, but also sufficient, for an action to be intentional, using only such concepts as those of belief, desire, and cause? I think not. The reason, very sketchily stated, is this. For a desire and a belief to explain an action in the right way, they must cause it in the right way, perhaps through a chain or process of reasoning that meets standards of rationality. I do not see how the right sort of causal process can be distinguished without, among other things, giving an account of how a decision is reached in the light of conflicting evidence and conflicting desires. I doubt whether it is possible to provide such an account at all, but certainly it cannot be done without using notions like evidence, or good reasons for believing, and these notions outrun those with which we began.

What prevents us from giving necessary and sufficient conditions for acting on a reason, also prevents us from giving serious laws connecting reasons and actions. To see this, suppose we had the sufficient conditions. Then we could say: whenever a man has such-and-such beliefs and desires, and such-and-such further conditions are satisfied, he will act in such-and-such a way. There are no serious laws of this kind. By a serious law, I mean more than a statistical generalization (the statistical laws of physics are serious because they give sharply fixed probabilities, which spring from the nature of the theory); it must be a law that, while it may have provisos limiting its application, allows us to determine in advance whether or not the conditions of application are satisfied. It is an error to compare a truism like 'If a man wants to eat an acorn omelette, then he generally will if the opportunity exists and no other desire overrides' with a law that says how fast a body will fall in a vacuum. It is an error, because in the latter case, but not the former, we can tell in advance whether the condition holds, and we know what allowance to make if it doesn't. What is needed in the case of action, if we are to predict on the basis of desires and beliefs, is a quantitative calculus that brings all relevant beliefs and desires into the picture. There is no hope of refining the simple pattern of explanation on the basis of reasons into such a calculus.

Two ideas are built into the concept of acting on a reason (and hence, the concept of behavior generally): the idea of cause and the idea of rationality. A reason is a rational cause. One way rationality is built in is transparent: the cause must be a belief and a desire in the light of which the action is reasonable. But rationality also enters more subtly, since the way desire and belief work to cause the action must meet further, and unspecified, conditions. The advantage of this mode of explanation is clear: we can explain behavior without having to know too much about how it was caused. And the cost is appropriate: we cannot turn this mode of explanation into something more like science.

Explanation by reasons avoids coping with the complexity of causal factors by singling out one, something it is able to do by omitting to provide, within the theory, a clear test of when the antecedent conditions hold. The simplest way of trying to improve matters is to substitute for desires and beliefs more directly observable events that may be assumed to cause them, such as flashing lights, punishments and rewards, deprivations, or spoken commands and instructions. But perhaps it is now obvious to almost everyone that a theory of action inspired by this idea has no chance of explaining complex behavior unless it succeeds in inferring or constructing the pattern of thoughts and emotions of the agent.

The best, though by no means the only, evidence for desires and beliefs is action, and this suggests the possibility of a theory that deals directly with the relations between actions, and treats wants and thoughts as theoretical constructs. A sophisticated theory along these lines was proposed by Frank Ramsey (1960). (This theory, in a less interesting form, was later, and independently, rediscovered by von Neumann and Morgenstern, and is sometimes called a theory of decision under uncertainty, or simply decision theory, by economists and psychologists.) Ramsey was primarily interested in providing a foundation in behavior for the idea that a person accords one or another degree of credence to a proposition. Ramsey was able to show that if the pattern of an individual's preferences or choices among an unlimited set of alternatives meets certain conditions, then that individual can be taken to be acting so as to maximize expected utility, that is, he acts as if he assigns values to the outcomes on an interval scale, judges the plausibility of the truth of propositions on a ratio scale, and chooses the alternative with the highest computed expected yield.

Ramsey's theory suggests an experimental procedure for disengaging the roles of subjective probability (or degree of belief) and subjective value in choice behavior. Clearly, if it may be assumed that an agent judges probabilities in accord with frequencies or so-called objective probabilities, it is easy to compute from his choices among gambles what his values are; and similarly one can compute his degree of belief in various propositions if one can assume that his values are, say, linear in money. But neither assumption seems justified in advance of evidence, and since choices are the resultant of both factors, how can either factor be derived from choices until the other is known? Here, in effect, is Ramsey's solution: we can tell that a man judges an event as likely to happen as not if he doesn't care whether an attractive or an unattractive outcome is tied to it, if he is indifferent, say, between these two options:

|                      | Option 1 | Option 2 |
|----------------------|----------|----------|
| If it rains you get: | $1,000   | a kick   |
| It it doesn't rain:  | a kick   | $1,000   |

Using this event with a subjective probability of one half, it is possible to scale values generally and using these values, to scale probabilities.

In many ways, this theory takes a long step towards scientific respectability. It gives up trying to explain actions one at a time by appeal to something more basic, and instead postulates a pattern in behavior from which beliefs and attitudes can be inferred. This simultaneously removes the need for establishing the existence of beliefs and attitudes apart from behavior, and takes into systematic account (as a construct) the whole relevant network of cognitive and motivational factors. The theory assigns numbers to measure degrees of belief and desire, as is essential if it is to be adequate to prediction, and yet it does this on the basis of purely qualitative evidence (preferences or choices between pairs of alternatives). Can we accept such a theory of decision as a scientific theory of behavior on a par with a physical theory?

Well, first we must notice that a theory like Ramsey's has no predictive power at all unless it is assumed that beliefs and values do not change over time. The theory merely puts restrictions on a temporal cross-section of an agent's dispositions to choose. If we try experimentally to test the theory, we run into the difficulty that the testing procedure disturbs the pattern we wish to examine. After spending several years testing variants of Ramsey's theory on human subjects, I tried the following experiment (with Merrill Carlsmith). Subjects made all possible pairwise choices within a small field of alternatives, and in a series of subsequent sessions, were offered the same set of options over and over. The alternatives were complex enough to mask the fact of repetition, so that subjects could not remember their previous choices, and pay-offs were deferred to the end of the experiment so that there was no normal learning or conditioning. The choices for each session and each subject were then examined for inconsistencies — cases where someone had chosen $a$ over $b$, $b$ over $c$, and $c$ over $a$. It was found that as time went on, people became steadily more consistent; intransitivities were gradually eliminated; after six sessions, all subjects were close to being perfectly consistent. This was enough to show that a static theory like Ramsey's could not, even under the most carefully controlled conditions, yield accurate predictions: merely making choices (with no reward or feedback) alters future choices. There was also an entirely unexpected result. If the choices of an individual over all trials were combined, on the assumption that his 'real' preference was for the alternative of a pair he chose most often, then there were almost no inconsistencies at all. Apparently, from the start there were underlying and consistent values which were better and better realised in choice. I found it impossible to construct a theory that could explain this, and gave up my career as an experimental psychologist.

Before drawing a moral from this experiment, let me return to Ramsey's ingenious method for abstracting subjective values and probabilities simultaneously from choice behavior. Application of the theory depends, it will be remembered, on finding a proposition with a certain property: it must be such that the subject does not care whether its truth or its falsity is tied to the more attractive of two outcomes. In the context of theory, it is clear that this means, *any* two outcomes. So, if the theory is to operate at all, if it is to be used to measure degrees of belief and the relative force of desire, it is first necessary that there be a proposition of the required sort. Apparently, this is an empirical question; yet the claim that the theory is true is then a very sweeping empirical claim. If it is ever correct, according to the theory, to say that for a given person a certain event has some specific subjective probability, it must be the case that a detailed and powerful theory is true concerning the pattern of that person's choice behavior. And if it is ever reasonable to assert, for example, that one event has a higher subjective probability than another for a given person, then there must be good reason to believe that a very strong theory is true rather than false.

From a formal point of view, the situation is analogous to fundamental measurement in physics, say of length, temperature, or mass. The assignment of numbers to measure any of these assumes that a very tight set of conditions holds. And I think that we can treat the cases as parallel in the following respect. Just as the satisfaction of the conditions for measuring length or mass may be viewed as constitutive of the range of application of the sciences that employ these measures, so the satisfaction of conditions of consistency and rational coherence may be viewed as constitutive of the range of application of such concepts as those of belief, desire, intention and action. It is not easy to describe in convincing detail an experiment that would persuade us that the transitivity of the relation of *heavier than* had failed. Though the case is not as extreme, I do not think we can clearly say what should convince us that a man at a given time (or without change of mind) preferred *a* to *b*, *b* to *c*, and *c* to *a*. The reason for our difficulty is that we cannot make good sense of an attribution of preference except against a background of coherent attitudes.

The significance of the experiment I described a page or so back is that it demonstrates how easy it is to interpret choice behavior so as to give it a consistent and rational pattern. When we learn that apparent inconsistency fades with repetition but no learning, we are apt to count the inconsistency as merely apparent. When we learn that frequency of choices may be taken as evidence for an underlying consistent disposition, we may decide to write off what seem to be inconsistent choices as failures of perception or execution. My point is not merely that the data are open to more than one interpretation, though this is obviously true. My point is that if we are intelligibly to attribute attitudes and beliefs, or usefully to describe motions as behavior, then we are committed to finding, in the pattern of behavior, belief, and desire, a large degree of rationality and consistency.

A final consideration may help to reinforce this claim. In the experiments I have been describing, it is common to offer the subject choices verbally, and for him to respond by saying what he chooses. We assume that the subject is choosing between the alternatives described by the experimenter, i.e. that the words used by subject and experimenter have the same interpretation. A more satisfying theory would drop the assumption by incorporating in decision theory a theory of communication. This is not a peripheral issue, because except in the case of the most primitive beliefs and desires, establishing the correctness of an attribution of belief or desire involves much the same problems as showing that we have understood the words of another. Suppose I offer a person an apple and a pear. He points to the apple, and I record that he has chosen the apple. By describing his action in this way, I imply that he intended to point to the apple, and that by pointing he intended to indicate his choice. I also imply that he believed he was choosing an apple. In attributing beliefs we can make very fine distinctions, as fine as our own language provides. Not only is there a difference between his believing he is choosing an apple and his believing he is choosing a pear. There is even a difference between his believing he is choosing the best apple in the box and his believing he is choosing the largest apple, and this can happen when the largest is the best.

All the distinctions available in our language are used in the attribution of belief (and desire and intention); this is perhaps obvious from the fact that we can attribute a belief by putting any declarative sentence after the words 'He believes that'. There is every reason to hold, then, that establishing the correctness of an attribution of belief is no easier than interpreting a man's speech. But I think we can go further, and say that the problems are identical. Beliefs cannot be ascertained in general without command of a man's language; and we cannot master a man's language without knowing much of what he believes. Unless someone could talk with him, it would not be possible to know that a man believed Fermat's last theorem was true, or that he believed Napoleon had all the qualities of a great general.

The reason we cannot understand what a man means by what he says without knowing a good deal about his beliefs is this. In order to interpret verbal behavior, we must be able to tell when a speaker holds a sentence he speaks to be true. But sentences are held to be true partly because of what is believed, and partly because of what the speaker means by his words. The problem of interpretation therefore is the problem of abstracting simultaneously the roles of belief and meaning from the pattern of sentences to which a speaker subscribes over time. The situation is like that in decision theory: just as we cannot infer beliefs from choices without also inferring desires, so we cannot decide what a man means by what he says without at the same time constructing a theory about what he believes.

In the case of language, the basic strategy must be to assume that by and large a speaker we do not yet understand is consistent and correct in his beliefs – according to our own standards, of course. Following this strategy makes it possible to pair up sentences the speaker utters with sentences of our own that we hold true under like circumstances. When this is done systematically, the result is a method of translation. Once the project is under way, it is possible, and indeed necessary, to allow some slack for error or difference of opinion. But we cannot make sense of error until we have established a base of agreement.

The interpretation of verbal behavior thus shows the salient features of the explanation of behavior generally: we cannot profitably take the parts one by one (the words and sentences), for it is only in the context of the system (language) that their role can be specified. When we turn to the task of interpreting the pattern, we notice the need to find it in accord, within limits, with standards of rationality. In the case of language, this is apparent, because understanding it is *translating* it into our own system of concepts. But in fact the case is no different with beliefs, desires, and actions.

The constitutive force in the realm of behavior derives from the need to view others, nearly enough, as like ourselves. As long as it is behavior and not something else we want to explain and describe, we must warp the evidence to fit this frame. Physical concepts have different constitutive elements. Standing ready, as we must, to adjust psychological terms to one set of standards and physical terms to another, we know that we cannot insist on a sharp and law-like connection between them. Since psychological phenomena do not constitute a closed system, this amounts to saying they are not, even in theory, amenable to precise prediction or subsumption under determin- istic laws. The limit thus placed on the social sciences is set not by nature, but by us when we decide to view men as rational agents with goals and purposes, and as subject to moral evaluation.

# THOMAS NAGEL

# What Is It Like to Be a Bat?

Consciousness is what makes the mind-body problem really intractable. Perhaps that is why current discussions of the problem give it little attention or get it obviously wrong. The recent wave of reductionist euphoria has produced several analyses of mental phenomena and mental concepts designed to explain the possibility of some variety of materialism, psycho-physical identification, or reduction.[1] But the problems dealt with are those common to this type of reduction and other types, and what makes the mind-body problem unique, and unlike the water-$H_2O$ problem or the Turing machine-IBM machine problem or the lightning-electrical discharge problem or the gene-DNA problem or the oak tree-hydrocarbon problem, is ignored.

Every reductionist has his favorite analogy from modern science. It is most unlikely that any of these unrelated examples of successful reduction will shed light on the relation of mind to brain. But philosophers share the general human weakness for explanations of what is incomprehensible in terms suited for what is familiar and well understood, though entirely different. This has led to the acceptance of implausible accounts of the mental largely because they would permit familiar kinds of reduction. I shall try to explain why the usual examples do not help us to understand the relation between mind and body – why, indeed, we have at present no conception of what an explanation of the physical nature of a mental phenomenon would be. Without consciousness the mind-body problem would be much less interesting. With consciousness it seems hopeless. The most important and characteristic feature of conscious mental phenomena is very poorly understood. Most reductionist theories do not even try to explain it. And careful examination will show that no currently available concept of reduction is applicable to it. Perhaps a new theoretical form can be devised for the purpose, but such a solution, if it exists, lies in the distant intellectual future.

Conscious experience is a widespread phenomenon. It occurs at many levels of animal life, though we cannot be sure of its presence in the simpler organisms, and it is very difficult to say in general what provides evidence of it. (Some extremists have been prepared to deny it even of mammals other than man.) No doubt it occurs in countless forms totally unimaginable to us, on other planets in other solar systems throughout the universe. But no matter how the form may vary, the fact that an organism has conscious experience *at all* means, basically, that there is something it is like to *be* that organism. There may be further implications about the form of the experience; there may even (though I doubt it) be implications about the behavior of the organism. But fundamentally an organism has conscious mental states if and only if there is something that it is like to *be* that organism – something it is like *for* the organism.

We may call this the subjective character of experience. It is not captured by any of the familiar, recently devised reductive analyses of the mental, for all of them are logically compatible with its absence. It is not analyzable in terms of any explanatory system of functional states, or intentional states, since these could be ascribed to robots or automata that behaved like people though they experienced nothing.[2] It is not analyzable in terms of the causal role of experiences in relation to typical human behavior – for similar reasons.[3] I do not deny that conscious mental states and events cause behavior, nor that they may be given functional characterizations. I deny only that this kind of thing exhausts their analysis. Any reductionist program has to to be based on an analysis of what is to be reduced. If the analysis leaves something out, the problem will be falsely posed. It is useless to base the defense of materialism on any analysis of mental phenomena that fails to deal explicitly with their subjective character. For there is no reason to suppose that a reduction which seems plausible when no attempt is made to account for consciousness can be extended to include consciousness. Without some idea, therefore, of what the subjective character of experience is, we cannot know what is required of a physicalist theory.

While an account of the physical basis of mind must explain many things, this appears to be the most difficult. It is impossible to exclude the phenomenological features of experience from a reduction in the same way that one excludes the phenomenal features of an ordinary substance from a physical or chemical reduction of it – namely, by explaining them as effects on the minds of human observers.[4] If physicalism is to be defended, the phenomenological features must themselves be given a physical account. But when we examine their subjective character it seems that such a result is impossible. The reason is that every subjective phenomenon is essentially connected with a single point of view, and it seems inevitable that an objective, physical theory will abandon that point of view.

Let me first try to state the issue somewhat more fully than by referring to the relation between the subjective and the objective, or between the *pour-soi* and the *en-soi*. This is far from easy. Facts about what it is like to be an X are very peculiar, so peculiar that some may be inclined to doubt their reality, or the significance of claims about them. To illustrate the connection between subjectivity and a point of view, and to make evident the importance of subjective features, it will help to explore the matter in relation to an example that brings out clearly the divergence between the two types of conception, subjective and objective.

I assume we all believe that bats have experience. After all, they are mammals, and there is no more doubt that they have experience than that mice or pigeons or whales have experience. I have chosen bats instead of wasps or flounders because if one travels too far down the phylogenetic tree, people gradually shed their faith that there is experience there at all. Bats, although more closely related to us than those other species, nevertheless present a range of activity and a sensory apparatus so different from ours that the problem I want to pose is exceptionally vivid (though it certainly could be raised with other species). Even without the benefit of philosophical reflection, anyone who has spent some time in an enclosed space with an excited bat knows what it is to encounter a fundamentally *alien* form of life.

I have said that the essence of the belief that bats have experience is that there is something that it is like to be a bat. Now we know that most bats (the microchiroptera, to be precise) perceive the external world primarily by sonar, or echolocation, detecting the reflections, from objects within range, of their own rapid, subtly modulated, high-frequency shrieks. Their brains are designed to correlate the outgoing impulses with the subsequent echoes, and the information thus acquired enables bats to make precise discriminations of distance, size, shape, motion, and texture comparable to those we make by vision. But bat sonar, though clearly a form of perception, is not similar in its operation to any sense that we possess, and there is no reason to suppose that it is subjectively like anything we can experience or imagine. This appears to create difficulties for the notion of what it is like to be a bat. We must consider whether any method will permit us to extrapolate to the inner life of the bat from our own case,[5] and if not, what alternative methods there may be for understanding the notion.

Our own experience provides the basic material for our imagination, whose range is therefore limited. It will not help to try to imagine that one has webbing on one's arms, which enables one to fly around at dusk and dawn catching insects in one's mouth; that one has very poor vision, and perceives the surrounding world by a system of reflected high-frequency sound signals; and that one spends the day hanging upside down by one's feet in an attic. In so far as I can imagine this (which is not very far), it tells me only what it would be like for *me* to behave as a bat behaves. But that is not the question. I want to know what it is like for a *bat* to be a bat. Yet if I try to imagine this, I am restricted to the resources of my own mind, and those resources are inadequate to the task. I cannot perform it either by imagining additions to my present experience, or by imagining segments gradually subtracted from it, or by imagining some combination of additions, subtractions, and modifications.

To the extent that I could look and behave like a wasp or a bat without changing my fundamental structure, my experiences would not be anything like the experiences of those animals. On the other hand, it is doubtful that any meaning can be attached to the supposition that I should possess the internal neurophysiological constitution of a bat. Even if I could by gradual degrees be transformed into a bat, nothing in my present constitution enables me to imagine what the experiences of such a future stage of myself thus metamorphosed would be like. The best evidence would come from the experiences of bats, if we only knew what they were like.

So if extrapolation from our own case is involved in the idea of what it is like to be a bat, the extrapolation must be incompletable. We cannot form more than a schematic conception of what it *is* like. For example, we may ascribe general *types* of experience on the basis of the animal's structure and behavior. Thus we describe bat sonar as a form of three-dimensional forward perception; we believe that bats feel some versions of pain, fear, hunger, and lust, and that they have other, more familiar types of perception besides sonar. But we believe that these experiences also have in each case a specific subjective character, which it is beyond our ability to conceive. And if there is conscious life elsewhere in the universe, it is likely that some of it will not be describable even in the most general experiential terms available to us.[6] (The problem is not confined to exotic cases, however, for it exists between one person and another. The subjective character of the experience of a person deaf and blind from birth is not accessible to me, for example, nor presumably is mine to him. This does not prevent us each from believing that the other's experience has such a subjective character.)

If anyone is inclined to deny that we can believe in the existence of facts like this whose exact nature we cannot possibly conceive, he should reflect that in contemplating the bats we are in much the same position that intelligent bats or Martians[7] would occupy if they tried to form a conception of what it was like to be us. The structure of their own minds might make it impossible for them to succeed, but we know they would be wrong to conclude that there is not anything precise that it is like to be us: that only certain general types of mental state could be ascribed to us (perhaps perception and appetite would be concepts common to us both; perhaps not). We know they would be wrong to draw such a skeptical conclusion because we know what it is like to be us. And we know that while it includes an enormous amount of variation and complexity, and while we do not possess the vocabulary to describe it adequately, its subjective character is highly specific, and in some respects describable in terms that can be understood only by creatures like us. The fact that we cannot expect ever to accommodate in our language a detailed description of Martian or bat phenomenology should not lead us to dismiss as meaningless the claim that bats and Martians have experiences fully comparable in richness of detail to our own. It would be fine if someone were to develop concepts and a theory that enabled us to think about those things; but such an understanding may be permanently denied to us by the limits of our nature. And to deny the reality or logical significance of what we can never describe or understand is the crudest form of cognitive dissonance.

This brings us to the edge of a topic that requires much more discussion that I can give it here: namely, the relation between facts on the one hand and conceptual schemes or systems of representation on the other. My realism about the subjective domain in all its forms implies a belief in the existence of facts beyond the reach of human concepts. Certainly it is possible for a human being to believe that there are facts which humans never *will* possess the requisite concepts to represent or comprehend. Indeed, it would be foolish to doubt this, given the finiteness of humanity's expectations. After all, there would have been transfinite numbers even if everyone had been wiped out by the Black Death before Cantor discovered them. But one might also believe that there are facts which *could* not ever be represented or comprehended by human beings, even if the species lasted forever – simply because our structure does not permit us to operate with concepts of the requisite type. This impossibility might even be observed by other beings, but it is not clear that the existence of such beings, or the possibility of their existence, is a precondition of the significance of the hypothesis that there are humanly inaccessible facts. (After all, the nature of beings with access to humanly inaccessible facts is presumably itself a humanly inaccessible fact.) Reflection on what it is like to be a bat seems to lead us, therefore, to the conclusion that there are facts that do not consist in the truth of propositions expressible in a human language. We can be compelled to recognize the existence of such facts without being able to state or comprehend them.

I shall not pursue this subject, however. Its bearing on the topic before us (namely, the mind-body problem) is that it enables us to make a general observation about the subjective character of experience. Whatever may be the status of facts about what it is like to be a human being, or a bat, or a Martian, these appear to be facts that embody a particular point of view.

I am not adverting here to the alleged privacy of experience to its possessor. The point of view in question is not one accessible only to a single individual. Rather it is a *type*. It is often possible to take up a point of view other than one's own, so the comprehension of such facts is not limited to one's own case. There is a sense in which phenomenological facts are perfectly objective: one person can know or say of another what the quality of the other's experience is. They are subjective, however, in the sense that even this objective ascription of experience is possible only for someone sufficiently similar to the object of ascription to be able to adopt his point of view – to understand the ascription in the first person as well as in the third, so to speak. The more different from oneself the other experiencer is, the less success one can expect with this enterprise. In our own case we occupy the relevant point of view, but we will have as much difficulty understanding our own experience properly if we approach it from another point of view as we would if we tried to understand the experience of another species without taking up *its* point of view.[8]

This bears directly on the mind-body problem. For if the facts of experience – facts about what it is like *for* the experiencing organism – are accessible only from one point of view, then it is a mystery how the true character of experiences could be revealed in the physical operation of that organism. The latter is a domain of objective facts *par excellence* – the kind that can be observed and understood from many points of view and by individuals with differing perceptual systems. There are no comparable imaginative obstacles to the acquisiton of knowledge about bat neurophysiology by human scientists, and intelligent bats or Martians might learn more about the human brain than we ever will.

This is not by itself an argument against reduction. A Martian scientist with no understanding of visual perception could understand the rainbow, or lightning, or clouds as physical phenomena, though he would never be able to understand the human concepts of rainbow, lightning, or cloud, or the place these things occupy in our phenomenal world. The objective nature of the things picked out by these concepts could be apprehended by him because, although the concepts themselves are connected with a particular point of view and a particular visual phenomenology, the things apprehended from that point of view are not: they are observable from the point of view but external to it; hence they can be comprehended from other points of view also, either by the same organisms or by others.

Lightning has an objective character that is not exhausted by its visual appearance, and this can be investigated by a Martian without vision. To be precise, it has a *more* objective character than is revealed in its visual appearance. In speaking of the move from subjective to objective characterization, I wish to remain noncommittal about the existence of an end point, the completely objective intrinsic nature of the thing, which one might or might not be able to reach. It may be more accurate to think of objectivity as a direction in which the understanding can travel. And in understanding a phenomenon like lightning, it is legitimate to go as far away as one can from a strictly human viewpoint.[9]

In the case of experience, on the other hand, the connection with a particular point of view seems much closer. It is difficult to understand what could be meant by the *objective* character of an experience, apart from the particular point of view from which its subject apprehends it. After all, what would be left of what it was like to be a bat if one removed the viewpoint of the bat? But if experience does not have, in addition to its subjective character, an objective nature that can be apprehended from many different points of view, then how can it be supposed that a Martian investigating my brain might be observing physical processes which were my mental processes (as he might observe physical processes which were bolts of lightning), only from a different point of view? How, for that matter, could a human physiologist observe them from another point of view?[10]

We appear to be faced with a general difficulty about psychophysical reduction. In other areas the process of reduction is a move in the direction of greater objectivity, toward a more accurate view of the real nature of things. This is accomplished by reducing our dependence on individual or species-specific points of view toward the object of investigation. We describe it not in terms of the impressions it makes on our senses, but in terms of its more general effects and of properties detectable by means other than the human senses. The less it depends on a specifically human viewpoint, the more objective is our description. It is possible to follow this path because although the concepts and ideas we employ in thinking about the external world are initially applied from a point of view that involves our perceptual apparatus, they are used by us to refer to things beyond themselves — toward which we *have* the phenomenal point of view. Therefore we can abandon it in favor of another, and still be thinking about the same things.

Experience itself, however, does not seem to fit the pattern. The idea of moving from appearance to reality seems to make no sense here. What is the analogue in this case to pursuing a more objective understanding of the same phenomena by abandoning the initial subjective viewpoint toward them in favor of another that is more objective but concerns the same thing? Certainly it *appears* unlikely that we will get closer to the real nature of human experience by leaving behind the particularity of our human point of view and striving for a description in terms accessible to beings that could not imagine what it was like to be us. If the subjective character of experience is fully comprehensible only from one point of view, then any shift to greater objectivity – that is, less attachment to a specific viewpoint – does not take us nearer to the real nature of the phenomenon: it takes us farther away from it.

In a sense, the seeds of this objection to the reducibility of experience are already detectable in successful cases of reduction; for in discovering sound to be, in reality, a wave phenomenon in air or other media, we leave behind one viewpoint to take up another, and the auditory, human or animal viewpoint that we leave behind remains unreduced. Members of radically different species may both understand the same physical events in objective terms, and this does not require that they understand the phenomenal forms in which those events appear to the senses of members of the other species. Thus it is a condition of their referring to a common reality that their more particular viewpoints are not part of the common reality that they both apprehend. The reduction can succeed only if the species-specific viewpoint is omitted from what is to be reduced.

But while we are right to leave this point of view aside in seeking a fuller understanding of the external world, we cannot ignore it permanently, since it is the essence of the internal world, and not merely a point of view on it. Most of the neobehaviorism of recent philosophical psychology results from the effort to substitute an objective concept of mind for the real thing, in order to have nothing left over which cannot be reduced. If we acknowledge that a physical theory of mind must account for the subjective character of experience, we must admit that no presently available conception gives us a clue how this could be done. The problem is unique. If mental processes are indeed physical processes, then there is something it is like, intrinsically,[11] to undergo certain physical processes. What it is for such a thing to be the case remains a mystery.

What moral should be drawn from these reflections, and what should be done next? It would be a mistake to conclude that physicalism must be false. Nothing is proved by the inadequacy of physicalist hypotheses that assume a faulty objective analysis of mind. It would be truer to say that physicalism is a position we cannot understand because we do not at present have any conception of how it might be true. Perhaps it will be thought unreasonable to require such a conception as a condition of understanding. After all, it might be said, the meaning of physicalism is clear enough: mental states are states of the body; mental events are physical events. We do not know *which* physical states and events they are, but that should not prevent us from understanding the hypothesis. What could be clearer than the words 'is' and 'are'?

But I believe it is precisely this apparent clarity of the word 'is' that is deceptive. Usually, when we are told that X is Y we know *how* it is supposed to be true, but that depends on a conceptual or theoretical background and is not conveyed by the 'is' alone. We know how both 'X' and 'Y' refer, and the kinds of things to which they refer, and we have a rough idea how the two referential paths might converge on a single thing, be it an object, a person, a process, an event, or whatever. But when the two terms of the identification are very disparate it may not be so clear how it could be true. We may not have even a rough idea of how the two referential paths could converge, or what kind of things they might converge on, and a theoretical framework may have to be supplied to enable us to understand this. Without the framework, an air of mysticism surrounds the identification.

This explains the magical flavor of popular presentations of fundamental scientific discoveries, given out as propositions to which one must subscribe without really understanding them. For example, people are now told at an early age that all matter is really energy. But despite the fact that they know what 'is' means, most of them never form a conception of what makes this claim true, because they lack the theoretical background.

At the present time the status of physicalism is similar to that which the hypothesis that matter is energy would have had if uttered by a pre-Socratic philosopher. We do not have the beginnings of a conception of how it might be true. In order to understand the hypothesis that a mental event is a physical event, we require more than an understanding of the word 'is'. The idea of how a mental and a physical term might refer to the same thing is lacking, and the usual analogies with theoretical identification in other fields fail to supply it. They fail because if we construe the reference of mental terms to physical events on the usual model, we either get a reappearance of separate subjective events as the effects through which mental reference to physical events is secured, or else we get a false account of how mental terms refer (for example, a causal behaviorist one).

Strangely enough, we may have evidence for the truth of something we cannot really understand. Suppose a caterpillar is locked in a sterile safe by someone unfamiliar with insect metamorphosis, and weeks later the safe is reopened, revealing a butterfly. If the person knows that the safe has been shut the whole time, he has reason to believe that the butterfly is or was once the caterpillar, without having any idea in what sense this might be so. (One possibility is that the caterpillar contained a tiny winged parasite that devoured it and grew into the butterfly.)

It is conceivable that we are in such a position with regard to physicalism. Donald Davidson has argued that if mental events have physical causes and effects, they must have physical descriptions. He holds that we have reason to believe this even though we do not – and in fact *could* not – have a general psychophysical theory.[12] His argument applies to intentional mental events, but I think we also have some reason to believe that sensations are physical processes, without being in a position to understand how. Davidson's position is that certain physical events have irreducibly mental properties, and perhaps some view describable in this way is correct. But nothing of which we can now form a conception corresponds to it; nor have we any idea what a theory would be like that enabled us to conceive of it.[13]

Very little work has been done on the basic question (from which mention of the brain can be entirely omitted) whether any sense can be made of experiences' having an objective character at all. Does it make sense, in other words, to ask what my experiences are *really* like, as opposed to how they appear to me? We cannot genuinely understand the hypothesis that their nature is captured in a physical description unless we understand the more fundamental idea that they *have* an objective nature (or that objective processes can have a subjective nature).[14]

I should like to close with a speculative proposal. It may be possible to approach the gap between subjective and objective from another direction. Setting aside temporarily the relation between the mind and the brain, we can pursue a more objective understanding of the mental in its own right. At present we are completely unequipped to think about the subjective character of experience without relying on the imagination — without taking up the point of view of the experiential subject. This should be regarded as a challenge to form new concepts and devise a new method — an objective phenomenology not dependent on empathy or the imagination. Though presumably it would not capture everything, its goal would be to describe, at least in part, the subjective character of experiences in a form comprehensible to beings incapable of having those experiences.

We would have to develop such a phenomenology to describe the sonar experiences of bats; but it would also be possible to begin with humans. One might try, for example, to develop concepts that could be used to explain to a person blind from birth what it was like to see. One would reach a blank wall eventually, but it should be possible to devise a method of expressing in objective terms much more than we can at present, and with much greater precision. The loose intermodal analogies — for example, 'Red is like the sound of a trumpet' — which crop up in discussions of this subject are of little use. That should be clear to anyone who has both heard a trumpet and seen red. But structural features of perception might be more accessible to objective description, even though something would be left out. And concepts alternative to those we learn in the first person may enable us to arrive at a kind of understanding even of our own experience which is denied us by the very ease of description and lack of distance that subjective concepts afford.

Apart from its own interest, a phenomenology that is in this sense objective may permit questions about the physical[15] basis of experience to assume a more intelligible form. Aspects of subjective experience that admitted this kind of objective description might be better candidates for objective explanations of a more familiar sort. But whether or not this guess is correct, it seems unlikely that any physical theory of mind can be contemplated until more thought has been given to the general problem of subjective and objective. Otherwise we cannot even pose the mind-body problem without sidestepping it.

## References

1 Examples are J. J. C. Smart, *Philosophy and Scientific Realism* (London, 1963); David K. Lewis, 'An Argument for the Identity Theory', *Journal of Philosophy*, 63 (1966), reprinted with addenda in David M. Rosenthal, *Materialism and the Mind-Body Problem* (Englewood Cliffs, N.J., 1971); Hilary Putnam, 'Psychological Predicates' in Capitan and Merrill, *Art, Mind, and Religion* (Pittsburgh, 1967), reprinted in Rosenthal, *op. cit.*, as 'The Nature of Mental States'; D. M. Armstrong, *A Materialist Theory of the Mind* (London, 1968); D. C. Dennett, *Content and Consciousness* (London, 1969). I have expressed earlier doubts in 'Armstrong on the Mind', *Philosophical Review*, 79 (1970), 394–403; 'Brain Bisection and the Unity of Consciousness', *Synthese*, 22 (1971); and a review of Dennett, *Journal of Philosophy*, 69 (1972). See also Saul Kripke, 'Naming and Necessity' in Davidson and Harman, *Semantics of Natural Language* (Dordrecht, 1972), esp. pp. 334–342; and M. T. Thornton, 'Ostensive Terms and Materialism', *The Monist*, 56 (1972).

2 Perhaps there could not actually be such robots. Perhaps anything complex enough to behave like a person would have experiences. But that, if true, is a fact which cannot be discovered merely by analyzing the concept of experience.

3 It is not equivalent to that about which we are incorrigible, both because we are not incorrigible about experience and because experience is present in animals lacking language and thought, who have no beliefs at all about their experiences.

4 Cf. Richard Rorty, 'Mind-Body Identity, Privacy, and Categories', *The Review of Metaphysics*, 19 (1965), esp. 37–38.

5 By 'our own case' I do not mean just 'my own case', but rather the mentalistic ideas that we apply unproblematically to ourselves and other human beings.

6 Therefore the analogical form of the English expression 'what it is *like*' is misleading. It does not mean 'what (in our experience) it *resembles*', but rather 'how it is for the subject himself.'

7 Any intelligent extraterrestrial beings totally different from us.

8 It may be easier than I suppose to transcend inter-species barriers with the aid of the imagination. For example, blind people are able to detect objects near them by a form of sonar, using vocal clicks or taps of a cane. Perhaps if one knew what that was like, one could by extension imagine roughly what it was like to possess the much more refined sonar of a bat. The distance between oneself and other persons and other species can fall anywhere on a continuum. Even for other persons the understanding of what it is like to be them is only partial, and when one moves to species very different from oneself, a lesser degree of partial understanding may still be available. The imagination is remarkably flexible. My point, however, is not that we cannot *know* what it is like to be a bat. I am not raising that epistemological problem. My point is rather that even to form a *conception* of what it is like to be a bat (and a fortiori to know what it is like to be a bat) one must take up the bat's point of view. If one can take it up roughly, or partially, then one's conception will also be rough or partial. Or so it seems in our present state of understanding.

9 The problem I am going to raise can therefore be posed even if the distinction between more subjective and more objective descriptions or viewpoints can itself be made only within a larger human point of view. I do not accept this kind of conceptual relativism, but it need not be refuted to make the point that psychophysical reduction cannot be accommodated by the subjective-to-objective model familiar from other cases.

10 The problem is not just that when I look at the 'Mona Lisa', my visual experience has a certain quality, no trace of which is to be found by someone looking into my brain. For even if he did observe there a tiny image of the 'Mona Lisa', he would have no reason to identify it with the experience.

11 The relation would therefore not be a contingent one, like that of a cause and its distinct effect. It would be necessarily true that a certain physical state felt a certain way. Saul Kripke (*op. cit.*, argues that causal behaviorist and related analyses of the mental fail because they construe, e.g., 'pain' as a merely contingent name of pains. The subjective character of an experience ('its immediate phenomenological quality' Kripke calls it [p. 340]) is the essential property left out by such analyses, and the one in virtue of which it is, necessarily, the experience it is. My view is closely related to his. Like Kripke, I find the hypothesis that a certain brain state should *necessarily* have a certain subjective character incomprehensible without further explanation. No such explanation emerges from theories which view the mind-brain relation

as contingent, but perhaps there are other alternatives, not yet discovered.

A theory that explained how the mind-brain relation was necessary would still leave us with Kripke's problem of explaining why it nevertheless appears contingent. That difficulty seems to me surmountable, in the following way. We may imagine something by representing it to ourselves either perceptually, sympathetically, or symbolically. I shall not try to say how symbolic imagination works, but part of what happens in the other two cases is this. To imagine something perceptually, we put ourselves in a conscious state resembling the state we would be in if we perceived it. To imagine something sympathetically, we put ourselves in a conscious state resembling the thing itself. (This method can be used only to imagine mental events and states – our own or another's.) When we try to imagine a mental state occurring without its associated brain state, we first sympathetically imagine the occurrence of the mental state: that is, we put ourselves into a state that resembles it mentally. At the same time, we attempt to perceptually imagine the non-occurrence of the associated physical state, by putting ourselves into another state unconnected with the first: one resembling that which we would be in if we perceived the non-occurrence of the physical state. Where the imagination of physical features is perceptual and the imagination of mental features is sympathetic, it appears to us that we can imagine any experience occurring without its associated brain state, and vice versa. The relation between them will appear contingent even if it is necessary, because of the independence of the disparate types of imagination.

(Solipsism, incidentally, results if one misinterprets sympathetic imagination as if it worked like perceptual imagination: it then seems impossible to imagine any experience that is not one's own.)

12 See 'Mental Events' in Foster and Swanson, *Experience and Theory* (Amherst, 1970); though I don't understand the argument against psychophysical laws.

13 Similar remarks apply to my paper 'Physicalism', *Philosophical Review* 74 (1965), 339–356, reprinted with postscript in John O'Connor, *Modern Materialism* (New York, 1969).

14 This question also lies at the heart of the problem of other minds, whose close connection with the mind-body problem is often overlooked. If one understood how subjective experience could have an objective nature, one would understand the existence of subjects other than oneself.

15 I have not defined the term 'physical'. Obviously it does not apply just to what can be described by the concepts of contemporary physics, since we expect further developments. Some may think there is nothing

to prevent mental phenomena from eventually being recognized as physical in their own right. But whatever else may be said of the physical, it has to be objective. So if our idea of the physical ever expands to include mental phenomena, it will have to assign them an objective character – whether or not this is done by analyzing them in terms of other phenomena already regarded as physical. It seems to me more likely, however, that mental-physical relations will eventually be expressed in a theory whose fundamental terms cannot be placed clearly in either category.

# DAVID ARMSTRONG

# The Causal Theory of the Mind

## Is philosophy just conceptual analysis?

What can philosophy contribute to solving the problem of the relation to mind to body? Twenty years ago, many English-speaking philosophers would have answered: 'Nothing beyond an analysis of the various mental *concepts*.' If we seek knowledge of things, they thought, it is to science that we must turn. Philosophy can only cast light upon our concepts of those things.

This retreat from things to concepts was not undertaken lightly. Ever since the seventeenth century, the great intellectual fact of our culture has been the incredible expansion of knowledge both in the natural and in the rational sciences (mathematics, logic). Everyday life presents us with certain simple verities. But, it seems, through science and only through science can we build upon these verities, and with astonishing results.

The success of science created a crisis in philosophy. What was there for philosophy to do? Hume had already perceived the problem in some degree, and so surely did Kant, but it was not until the twentieth century, with the Vienna Circle and with Wittgenstein, that the difficulty began to weigh heavily. Wittgenstein took the view that philosophy could do no more than strive to undo the intellectual knots it itself had tied, so achieving intellectual release, and even a certain illumination, but no knowledge. A little later, and more optimistically, Ryle saw a positive, if reduced, role for philosophy in mapping the 'logical geography' of our concepts: how they stood to each other and how they were to be analyzed.

On the whole, Ryle's view proved more popular than Wittgenstein's. After all, it retained a special, if much reduced, realm for philosophy where she might still be queen. There was better hope of continued employment for members of the profession!

Since that time, however, philosophers in the 'analytic' tra-

dition have swung back from Wittgensteinian and even Rylean
pessimism to a more traditional conception of the proper role
and tasks of philosophy. Many analytic philosophers now would
accept the view that the central task of philosophy is to give an
account, or at least play a part in giving an account, of the most
general nature of things and of man. (I would include myself
among that many.)

Why has this swing back occurred? Has the old urge of the
philosopher to determine the nature of things by *a priori*
reasoning proved too strong? To use Freudian terms, are we
simply witnessing a return of what philosophers had repressed?
I think not. One consideration that has had great influence was
the realization that those who thought that they were abandoning ontological and other substantive questions for a mere
investigation of concepts were in fact smuggling in views on the
substantive questions. They did not acknowledge that they held
these views, but the views were there; and far worse from their
standpoint, the views imposed a form upon their answers to the
conceptual questions.

For instance, in *The Concept of Mind* (1949), Gilbert Ryle,
although he denied that he was a Behaviorist, seemed to be
upholding an account of man and his mind that was extremely
close to Behaviorism. Furthermore, it seemed in many cases that
it was this view of the mind-body problem that led him to his
particular analyses of particular mental concepts, rather than
the other way around. Faced with examples like this, it began to
appear that, since philosophers could not help holding views on
substantive matters, and the views could not help affecting their
analyses of concepts, the views had better be held and discussed
explicitly instead of appearing in a distorted, because unacknow-
ledged, form.

The swing back by analytic philosophers to first-order questions was also due to the growth of a more sophisticated
understanding of the nature of scientific investigation. For a
philosophical tradition that is oriented towards science, as, on
the whole, Western philosophy is, the consideration of the
*methods* of science must be an important topic. It was gradually
realized that in the past scientific investigation had regularly
been conceived in far too positivistic, sensationalistic and obser-
vationalistic a spirit. (The influence of Karl Popper has been of
the greatest importance in this realization.) As the central role

of speculation, theory and reasoning in scientific investigation began to be appreciated by more and more philosophers, the border-line between science and philosophy began to seem at least more fluid, and the hope arose again that philosophy might have something to contribute to first-order questions.

The philosopher has certain special skills. These include the stating and assessing of the worth of arguments, including the bringing to light and making explicit suppressed premisses of arguments, the detection of ambiguities and inconsistencies, and, perhaps especially, the analysis of concepts. But, I contend, these special skills do not entail that the *objective* of philosophy is to do these things. They are rather the special *means* by which philosophy attempts to achieve further objectives. Ryle was wrong in taking the analysis of concepts to be the end of philosophy. Rather, the analysis of concepts is a means by which the philosopher makes his contribution to great general questions, not about concepts, but about things.

In the particular case of the mind-body problem, the propositions the philosopher arrives at need not be of a special nature. They perhaps might have been arrived at by the psychologist, the neuro-physiologist, the biochemist or others, and, indeed, may be suggested to the philosopher by the results achieved or programs proposed by those disciplines. But the way that the argument is marshalled by a philosopher will be a special way. Whether this special way has or has not any particular value in the search for truth is a matter to be decided in particular cases. There is no *a priori* reason for thinking that the special methods of philosophy will be able to make a contribution to the mind-body problem. But neither is there an *a priori* reason for assuming that the philosopher's contribution will be valueless.

## The concept of a mental state

The philosophy of philosophy is perhaps a somewhat joyless and unrewarding subject for reflection. Let us now turn to the mind-body problem itself, hoping that what is to be said about this particular topic will confirm the general remarks about philosophy that have just been made.

If we consider the mind-body problem today, then it seems that we ought to take account of the following consideration.

The present state of scientific knowledge makes it probable that we can give a purely physico-chemical account of man's body. It seems increasingly likely that the body and the brain of man are constituted and work according to exactly the same principles as those physical principles that govern other, non-organic, matter. The differences between a stone and a human body appear to lie solely in the extremely complex material set-up that is to be found in the living body and which is absent in the stone. Furthermore, there is rather strong evidence that it is the state of our brain that completely determines the state of our consciousness and our mental state generally.

All this is not beyond the realm of controversy, and it is easy to imagine evidence that would upset the picture. In particular, I think that it is just possible that evidence from psychical research might be forthcoming that a physico-chemical view of man's brain could not accommodate. But suppose that the physico-chemical view of the working of the brain is correct, as I take it to be. It will be very natural to conclude that mental states are not simply *determined* by corresponding states of the brain, but that they are actually *identical* with these brain-states, brain-states that involve nothing but physical properties.

The argument just outlined is quite a simple one, and it hardly demands philosophical skill to develop it or to appreciate its force! But although many contemporary thinkers would accept its conclusion, there are others, including many philosophers, who would not. To a great many thinkers it has seemed obvious *a priori* that mental states could not be physical states of the brain. Nobody would identify a number with a piece of rock: it is sufficiently obvious that the two entities fall under different categories. In the same way, it has been thought, a perception or a feeling of sorrow must be a different category of thing from an electro-chemical discharge in the central nervous system.

Here, it seems to me, is a question to which philosophers can expect to make a useful contribution. It is a question about mental concepts. Is our concept of a mental state such that it is an intelligible hypothesis that mental states are physical states of the brain? If the philosopher can show that it is an *intelligible* proposition (that is, a non-self-contradictory proposition) that mental states are physical states of the brain, then the scientific argument just given above can be taken at its face value as a strong reason for accepting the truth of the proposition.

My view is that the identification of mental states with physical states of the brain is a perfectly intelligible one, and that this becomes clear once we achieve a correct view of the analysis of the mental concepts. I admit that my analysis of the mental concepts was itself adopted because it permitted this identification, but such a procedure is commonplace in the construction of theories, and perfectly legitimate. In any case, whatever the motive for proposing the analysis, it is there to speak for itself, to be measured against competitors, and to be assessed as plausible or implausible independently of the identification it makes possible.

The problem of the identification may be put in a Kantian way: 'How is it possible that mental states should be physical states of the brain?' The solution will take the form of proposing an *independently plausible* analysis of the concept of a mental state that will permit this identification. In this way, the philosopher makes the way smooth for a first-order doctrine, which, true or false, is a doctrine of the first importance: a purely physicalist view of man.

The analysis proposed may be called the Causal analysis of the mental concepts. According to this view, the concept of a mental state essentially involves, and is exhausted by, the concept of a state that is *apt to be the cause of certain effects or apt to be the effect of certain causes*.

An example of a causal concept is the concept of poison. The concept of poison is the concept of something that when introduced into an organism causes that organism to sicken and/or die. This is but a rough analysis of the concept the structure of which is in fact somewhat more complex and subtle than this. If A pours molten lead down B's throat, then he may cause B to die[1] as a result, but he can hardly be said to have poisoned him. For a thing to be called a poison, it is necessary that it act in a certain *sort* of way: roughly, in a biological as opposed to a purely physical way. Again, a poison can be introduced into the system of an organism and that organism fail to die or even to sicken. This might occur if an antidote were administered promptly. Yet again, the poison may be present in insufficient quantities to do any damage. Other qualifications could be made.

But the essential point about the concept of poison is that it is the concept of *that, whatever it is, which produces certain effects*. This leaves open the possibility of the *scientific identifi-*

*cation* of poisons, of discovering that a certain sort of substance, such as cyanide, is a poison, and discovering further what it is about the substance that makes it poisonous.

Poisons are accounted poisons in virtue of their active powers, but many sorts of thing are accounted the sorts of thing they are by virtue of their *passive* powers. Thus brittle objects are accounted brittle because of the disposition they have to break and shatter when sharply struck. This leaves open the possibility of discovering empirically what sorts of thing are brittle and what it is about them that makes them brittle.

Now *if* the concepts of the various sorts of mental state are concepts of that which is, in various sorts of way, apt for causing certain effects and apt for being the effect of certain causes, then it would be a quite unpuzzling thing if mental states should turn out to be physical states of the brain.

The concept of a mental state is the concept of something that is, characteristically, the cause of certain effects and the effect of certain causes. What sort of effects and what sort of causes? The effects caused by the mental state will be certain patterns of behavior of the person in that state. For instance, the desire for food is a state of a person or animal that characteristically brings about food-seeking and food-consuming behavior by that person or animal. The causes of mental states will be objects and events in the person's environment. For instance, a sensation of green is the characteristic effect in a person of the action upon his eyes of a nearby green surface.

The general pattern of analysis is at its most obvious and plausible in the case of *purposes*. If a man's purpose is to go to the kitchen to get something to eat, it is completely natural to conceive of this purpose as a cause within him that brings about, or tends to bring about, that particular line of conduct. It is, furthermore, notorious that we are unable to characterize purposes *except* in terms of that which they tend to bring about. How can we distinguish the purpose to go to the kitchen to get something to eat from another purpose to go to the bedroom to lie down? Only by the different outcomes that the two purposes tend to bring about. This fact was an encouragement to Behaviorism. It is still more plausibly explained by saying that the concept of purpose is a causal concept. The further hypothesis that the two purposes are, in their own nature, different physical patterns in, or physical states of, the central nervous system is then a natural (although, of course, not logically inevitable) supplement to the causal analysis.

Simple models have great value in trying to grasp complex conceptions, but they are ladders that may need to be kicked away after we have mounted up by their means. It is vital to realize that the mental concepts have a far more complex logical structure than simple causal notions such as the concept of poison. The fact should occasion no surprise. In the case of poisons, the effect of which they are the cause is a gross and obvious phenomenon and the level of causal explanation involved in simply calling a substance 'a poison' is crude and simple. But in the case of mental states, their effects are all those complexities of behavior that mark off men and higher animals from the rest of the objects in the world. Furthermore, differences in such behavior are elaborately correlated with differences in the mental causes operating. So it is only to be expected that the causal patterns invoked by the mental concepts should be extremely complex and sophisticated.

In the case of the notion of a purpose, for instance, it is plausible to assert that it is the notion of a cause within which drives, or tends to drive, the man or animal through a series of actions to a certain end-state. But this is not the whole story. A purpose is only a purpose if it works to bring about behavioral effects *in a certain sort of way*. We may sum up this sort of way by saying that purposes are *information-sensitive causes*. By this is meant that purposes direct behavior by utilizing *perceptions* and *beliefs*, perceptions and beliefs about the agent's current situation and the way it develops, and beliefs about the way the world works. For instance, it is part of what it is to be a purpose to achieve X that this cause will cease to operate, will be 'switched off', if the agent perceives or otherwise comes to believe that X has been achieved.

At this point, we observe that an account is being given of that special species of cause that is a purpose in terms of *further* mental items: perceptions and beliefs. This means that if we are to give a purely causal analysis even of the concept of a purpose we also will have to give a purely causal analysis of perceptions and beliefs. We may think of man's behavior as brought about by the joint operation of two sets of causes: first, his purposes and, second, his perceptions of and/or his beliefs about the world. But since perceptions and beliefs are quite different sorts of thing from purposes, a Causal analysis must assign quite different causal *roles* to these different things in the bringing about of behavior.

I believe that this can be done by giving an account of perceptions and beliefs as *mappings* of the world. They are structures within us that model the world beyond the structure. This model is created in us by the world. Purposes may then be thought of as driving causes that utilize such mappings.

This is a mere thumb-nail, which requires much further development as well as qualification. One point that becomes clear when that development is given is that just as the concept of purpose cannot be elucidated without appealing to the concepts of perception and belief, so the latter cannot be elucidated without appealing to the concept of purpose. (This comes out, for instance, when we raise Hume's problem: what marks off beliefs from the mere entertaining of the same proposition? It seems that we can only mark off beliefs as those mappings in the light of which we are prepared to *act*, that is, which are potential servants of our purposes.) The logical dependence of purpose on perception and belief, and of perception and belief upon purpose, is not circularity in definition. What it shows is that the corresponding concepts *must be introduced together or not at all*. In itself, there is nothing very surprising in this. Correlative or mutually implicated concepts are common enough: for instance, the concepts of husband and wife or the concepts of soldier and army. No husbands without wives or wives without husbands. No soldiers without an army, no army without soldiers. But if the concepts of purpose, perception and belief are (i) correlative concepts and (ii) different species of purely causal concepts, then it is clear that they are far more complex in structure than a simple causal concept like poison. What falls under the mental concepts will be a complex and interlocking set of causal factors, which together are responsible for the 'minded' behavior of men and the higher animals.

The working out of the Causal theory of the mental concepts thus turns out to be an extremely complex business. Indeed when it is merely baldly stated, the Causal theory is, to use the phrase of Imre Lakatos, a *research program* in conceptual analysis rather than a developed theory. I have tried to show that it is a hopeful program by attempting, at least in outline, a Causal analysis of all the main mental concepts in *A Materialist*

*Theory of the Mind* (1968); and I have supplemented the rather thin account given there of the concepts of belief, knowledge and inferring in *Belief, Truth and Knowledge* (1973).

Two examples of mental concepts where an especially complex and sophisticated type of Causal analysis is required are the notions of introspective awareness (one sense of the word 'consciousness') and the having of mental imagery. Introspective awareness is analyzable as a mental state that is a 'perception' of mental states. It is a mapping of the causal factors themselves. The having of mental imagery is a sort of mental state that cannot be elucidated in *directly* causal terms, but only by resemblance to the corresponding perceptions, which *are* explicated in terms of their causal role.

Two advantages of the Causal theory may now be mentioned. First, it has often been remarked by philosophers and others that the realm of mind is a shadowy one, and that the nature of mental states is singularly elusive and hard to grasp. This has given aid and comfort to Dualist or Cartesian theories of mind, according to which minds are quite different sorts of thing from material objects. But if the Causal analysis is correct, the facts admit of another explanation. What Dualist philosophers have grasped in a confused way is that our direct acquaintance with mind, which occurs in introspective awareness, is an acquaintance with something that we are aware of only as something that is causally linked, directly or indirectly, with behavior. In the case of our purposes and desires, for instance, we are often (though not invariably) introspectively aware of them. What we are aware of is the presence of factors within us that drive in a certain direction. We are not aware of the intrinsic nature of the factors. This emptiness or gap in our awareness is then interpreted by Dualists as immateriality. In fact, however, if the Causal analysis is correct, there is no warrant for this interpretation and, if the Physicalist identification of the nature of the causes is correct, the interpretation is actually false.

Second, the Causal analysis yields a still more spectacular verification. It shows promise of explaining a philosophically notorious feature of all or almost all mental states: their *intentionality*. This was the feature of mental states to which Brentano in particular drew attention, the fact that they may point towards certain objects or states of affairs, but that these objects and states of affairs need not exist. When a man strives, his striving has an objective, but that objective may never be achieved. When he believes, there is something he believes, but what he believes may not be the case. This capacity of mental states to 'point' to what does not exist can seem very special. Brentano held that intentionality set the mind completely apart from matter.

Suppose, however, that we consider a concept like the concept of poison. Does it not provide us with a miniature and unsophisticated model for the intentionality of mental states? Poisons are substances apt to make organisms sicken and die when the poison is administered. So it may be said that this is what poisons 'point' to. Nevertheless, poisons may fail of their effect. A poison does not fail to be a poison because an antidote neutralizes the customary effect of the poison.

May not the intentionality of mental states, therefore, be in principle a no more mysterious affair, although indefinitely more complex, than the death that lurks in the poison? As an intermediate case between poisons and mental states, consider the mechanisms involved in a homing rocket. Given a certain setting of its mechanism, the rocket may 'point' towards a certain target in a way that is a simulacrum of the way in which purposes point towards their objectives. The mechanism will only bring the rocket to the target in 'standard' circumstances: many factors can be conceived that would 'defeat' the mechanism. For the mechanism to operate successfully, some device will be required by which the developing situation is 'mapped' in the mechanism (i.e. what course the rocket is currently on, etc.). This mapping is an elementary analogue of perception, and so the course that is 'mapped' in the mechanism may be thought of as a simulacrum of the perceptual intentional object. Through one circumstance or another (e.g. malfunction of the gyroscope) this mapping may be 'incorrect'.

It is no objection to this analogy that homing rockets are built by men with purposes, who deliberately stamp a crude model of their own purposes into the rocket. Homing rockets might have been natural products, and non-minded objects that operate in a similar but far more complex way are found in nature. The living cell is a case in point.

So the Causal analyses of the mental concepts show promise of explaining both the transparency and the intentionality of mental states. One problem quite frequently raised in connection with these analyses, however, is in what sense they can be called 'analyses'. The welter of complications in which the so-called analyses are involved make it sufficiently obvious that they do not consist of *synonymous translations* of statements in which mental terms figure. But, it has been objected, if synonymous translations of mental statements are unavailable, what precisely can be meant by speaking of 'analyses of concepts'?

I am far from clear what should be said in reply to this objection. Clearly, however, it does depend upon taking all conceptual analyses as claims about the synonymy of sentences, and that seems to be too simple a view. Going back to the case of poison: it is surely not an empirical fact, to be learnt by experience, that poisons kill. It is at the center of our notion of what poisons are that they have the power to bring about this effect. If they did not do that, they would not be properly called 'poisons'. But although this seems obvious enough, it is extremely difficult to give exact translations of sentences containing the word 'poison' into other sentences that do not contain the word or any synonym. Even in this simple case, it is not at all clear that the task can actually be accomplished.

For this reason, I think that sentence translation (with synonymy) is too strict a demand to make upon a purported conceptual analysis. What more relaxed demand can we make and still have a conceptual analysis? I do not know. One thing that we clearly need further light upon here is the concept of a concept, and how concepts are tied to language. I incline to the view that the connection between concepts and language is much less close than many philosophers have assumed. Concepts are linked primarily with belief and thought, and belief and thought, I think, have a great degree of logical independence of language, however close the empirical connection may be in many cases. If this is so, then an analysis of concepts, although of course conducted *in* words, may not be an investigation *into* words. (A compromise proposal: analysis of concepts might be an investigation into some sort of 'deep structure' – to use the currently hallowed phrase – which underlies the use of certain words and sentences.) I wish I were able to take the topic further.

## The problem of the secondary qualities

No discussion of the Causal theory of the mental concepts is complete that does not say something about the *secondary qualities.* If we consider such mental states as purposes and intentions, their 'transparency' is a rather conspicuous feature. It is notorious that introspection cannot differentiate such states except in terms of their different objects. It is not so immediately obvious, however, that *perception* has this transparent character. Perception involves the experience of color and of visual extension, touch of the whole obscure range of tactual properties, including tactual extension, hearing, taste and smell the experience of sounds, tastes and smells. These phenomenal qualities, it may be argued, endow different perceptions with different qualities. The lack of transparency is even more obvious in the case of bodily sensations. Pains, itches, tickles and tingles are mental states, even if mental states of no very high-grade sort, and they each seem to involve their own peculiar qualities. Again, associated with different emotions it is quite plausible to claim to discern special emotion qualities. If perception, bodily sensation and emotions involve qualities, then this seems to falsify a purely Causal analysis of these mental states. They are not mere 'that whiches' known only by their causal role.

However, it is not at all clear how strong is the line of argument sketched in the previous paragraph. We distinguish between the intention and what is intended, and in just the same way we must distinguish between the perception and what is perceived. The intention is a mental state and so is the perception, but what is intended is not in general something mental and nor is what is perceived. What is intended may not come to pass, it is a merely intentional object, and the same may be said of what is perceived. Now in the case of the phenomenal qualities, it seems plausible to say that they are qualities not of the perception but rather of what is perceived. 'Visual extension' is the shape, size, etc. that some object of visual perception is perceived to have (an object that need not exist). Color seems to be a quality of that object. And similarly for the other phenomenal qualities. Even in the case of the bodily sensations, the qualities associated with the sensations do not *appear* to be qualities of mental states but instead to be qualities of portions of our bodies: more or less fleeting qualities that qualify the place where the sensation is located. Only in the case of the emotions does it seem natural to place the quality on the mental rather than the object side: but then it is not so clear whether there really *are* peculiar qualities associated with the emotions. The different patterns of bodily sensations associated with the different emotions may be sufficient to do phenomenological justice to the emotions.

For these reasons, it is not certain whether the phenomenal qualities pose any threat to the Causal analysis of the mental concepts. But what a subset of these qualities quite certainly does pose a threat to, is the doctrine that the Causal analysis of the mental concepts is a step towards: Materialism or Physicalism.

The qualities of color, sound, heat and cold, taste and smell together with the qualities that appear to be involved in bodily sensations and those that may be involved in the case of the emotions, are an embarrassment to the modern Materialist. He seeks to give an account of the world and of man purely in terms of *physical* properties, that is to say in terms of the properties that the physicist appeals to in his explanations of phenomena. The Materialist is not committed to the *current* set of properties to which the physicist appeals, but he is committed to whatever set of properties the physicist in the end will appeal to. It is clear that such properties as color, sound, taste and smell – the so-called 'secondary qualities' – will never be properties to which the physicist will appeal.

It is, however, a plausible thesis that associated with different secondary qualities are properties that are respectable from a physicist's point of view. Physical surfaces *appear* to have color. They not merely appear to, but undoubtedly do, emit light-waves, and the different mixtures of lengths of wave emitted are linked with differences in color. In the same way, different sorts of sound are linked with different sorts of sound-wave and differences in heat with differences in the mean kinetic energy of the molecules composing the hot things. The Materialist's problem therefore would be very simply solved if the secondary qualities could be identified with these physically respectable properties. (The qualities associated with bodily sensations would be identified with different sorts of stimulation of bodily receptors. If there are unique qualities associated with the emotions, they would presumably be identified with some of the physical states of the brain linked with particular emotions.)

But now the Materialist philosopher faces a problem. Previously he asked: 'How is it possible that mental states could be physical states of the brain?' This question was answered by the Causal theory of the mental concepts. Now he must ask: 'How is it possible that secondary qualities could be purely physical properties of the objects they are qualities of?' A Causal analysis does not seem to be of any avail. To try to give an analysis of, say, the quality of being red in Causal terms would lead us to produce such analyses as 'those properties of a physical surface, whatever they are, that characteristically produce *red sensations* in us'. But this analysis simply shifts the problem unhelpfully from property of surface to property of sensation. Either the red sensations involve nothing but physically respectable properties or they involve something more. If they involve something more, Materialism fails. But if they are simply physical states of the brain, having nothing but physical properties, then the Materialist faces the problem: 'How is it possible that red sensations should be physical states of the brain?' This question is no easier to answer than the original question about the redness of physical surfaces. (To give a Causal analysis of red sensations as the characteristic effects of the action of red surfaces is, of course, to move round in a circle.)

The great problem presented by the secondary qualities, such as redness, is that they are *unanalyzable*. They have certain relations of resemblance and so on to each other, so they cannot be said to be completely simple. But they are simple in the sense that they resist any analysis. You cannot give any complete account of the concept of redness without involving the notion of redness itself. This has seemed to be, and still seems to many philosophers to be, an absolute bar to identifying redness with, say, certain patterns of emission of light-waves.

But I am not so sure. I think it can be maintained that although the secondary qualities *appear* to be simple, they are not in fact simple. Perhaps their simplicity is *epistemological* only, not ontological, a matter of our awareness of them rather than the way they are. The best model I can give for the situation is the sort of phenomena made familiar to us by the *Gestalt* psychologists. It is possible to grasp that certain things or situations have a certain special property, but be unable to analyze that property. For instance, it may be possible to perceive that certain people are all alike in some way without being able to make it clear to oneself what the likeness is. We are aware that all these people have a certain likeness to each other, but are unable to define or specify that likeness. Later psychological research may achieve a specification of the likeness, a specification that may come as a complete surprise to us. Perhaps, therefore, the secondary qualities are in fact complex, and perhaps they are complex characteristics of a sort demanded by Materialism, but we are unable to grasp their complexity in perception.

There are two divergences between the model just suggested and the case of the secondary qualities. First, in the case of grasping the indefinable likeness of people, we are under no temptation to think that the likeness is a likeness in some simple quality. The likeness is indefinable, but we are vaguely aware that it is complex. Second, once research has determined the concrete nature of the likeness, our attention can be drawn to, and we can observe individually, the features that determine the likeness.

But although the model suggested and the case of the secondary qualities undoubtedly exhibit these differences, I do not think that they show that the secondary qualities cannot be identified with respectable physical characteristics of objects. Why should not a complex property appear to be simple? There would seem to be no contradiction in adding such a condition to the model. It has the consequence that perception of the secondary qualities involves an element of illusion, but the consequence involves no contradiction. It is true also that in the case of the secondary qualities the illusion cannot be overcome within perception: it is impossible to see a colored surface as a surface emitting certain light-waves. (Though one sometimes seems to *hear* a sound as a vibration of the air.) But while this means that the identification of color and light-waves is a purely *theoretical* one, it still seems to be a possible one. And if the identification is a possible one, we have general scientific reasons to think it a *plausible* one.

The doctrine of mental states and of the secondary qualities briefly presented in this paper seems to me to show promise of meeting many of the traditional philosophical objections to a Materialist or Physicalist account of the world. As I have emphasized, the philosopher is not professionally competent to

argue the positive case for Materialism. There he must rely upon
the evidence presented by the scientist, particularly the physicist.
But at least he may neutralize the objections to Materialism
advanced by his fellow philosophers.

## References

1 'Any substance which, when introduced into or absorbed by a living
organism, destroys life or injures health.' (*Shorter Oxford Dictionary*,
3rd edn., rev., 1978.)

# Intentional Systems[1]

I wish to examine the concept of a system whose behavior can be – at least sometimes – explained and predicted by relying on ascriptions to the system of beliefs and desires (and hopes, fears, intentions, hunches . . .). I will call such systems *intentional systems*, and such explanations and predictions intentional explanations and predictions, in virtue of the intentionality of the idioms of belief and desire (and hope, fear, intention, hunch, . . .).

I used to insist on capitalizing 'intentional' wherever I meant to be using Brentano's notion of *intentionality*, in order to distinguish this technical term from its cousin, e.g., 'an intentional shove', but the technical term is now in much greater currency, and since almost everyone else who uses the term seems content to risk this confusion, I have decided, with some trepidation, to abandon my typographical eccentricity. But let the uninitiated reader beware: 'intentional' as it occurs here is *not* the familiar term of layman's English.[2] For me, as for many recent authors, intentionality is primarily a feature of linguistic entities – idioms, contexts – and for my purposes here we can be satisfied that an idiom is intentional if substitution of codesignative terms do not preserve truth or if the 'objects' of the idiom are not capturable in the usual way by quantifiers. I discuss this in more detail in *Content and Consciousness*.[3]

## I

The first point to make about intentional systems[4] as I have just defined them is that a particular thing is an intentional system only in relation to the strategies of someone who is trying to explain and predict its behavior. What this amounts to can best be brought out by example. Consider the case of a chess-playing computer, and the different strategies or stances one might adopt as its opponent in trying to predict its moves. There are three different stances of interest to us. First there is the *design stance*. If one knows exactly how the computer is designed (including the impermanent part of its design: its program) one can predict its designed response to any move one makes by following the computation instructions of the program. One's prediction will come true provided only that the computer performs as designed – that is, without breakdown. Different varieties of design-stance predictions can be discerned, but all of them are alike in relying on the notion of *function*, which is purpose-relative or teleological. That is, a design of a system breaks it up into larger or smaller functional parts, and design-stance predictions are generated by assuming that each functional part will function properly. For instance, the radio engineer's schematic wiring diagrams have symbols for each resistor, capacitor, transistor, etc. – *each with its task to perform* – and he can give a design-stance prediction of the behavior of a circuit by assuming that each element performs its task. Thus one can make design-stance predictions of the computer's response at several different levels of abstraction, depending on whether one's design treats as smallest functional elements strategy-generators and consequence-testers, multipliers and dividers, or transistors and switches. (It should be noted that not all diagrams or pictures are designs in this sense, for a diagram may carry no information about the functions – intended or observed – of the elements it depicts.)

We generally adopt the design stance when making predictions about the behavior of mechanical objects, e.g., 'As the typewriter carriage approaches the margin, a bell will ring (provided the machine is in working order),' and more simply, 'Strike the match and it will light.' We also often adopt this stance in predictions involving natural objects: 'Heavy pruning will stimulate denser foliage and stronger limbs.' The essential feature of the design stance is that we make predictions solely from knowledge or assumptions about the system's functional design, irrespective of the physical constitution or condition of the innards of the particular object.

Second, there is what we may call the *physical stance*. From this stance our predictions are based on the actual physical state of the particular object, and are worked out by applying whatever knowledge we have of the laws of nature. It is from this stance alone that we can predict the malfunction of systems (unless, as sometimes happens these days, a system is *designed* to malfunction after a certain time, in which case malfunctioning in one sense becomes a part of its proper functioning). Instances of predictions from the physical stance are common enough: 'If you turn on the switch you'll get a nasty shock,' and, 'When the snows come that branch will break right off.' One seldom adopts the physical stance in dealing with a computer just because the number of critical variables in the physical constitution of a computer would overwhelm the most prodigious calculator. Significantly, the physical stance is generally reserved for instances of breakdown, where the condition preventing normal operation is generalized and easily locatable, e.g., 'Nothing will happen when you type in your questions, because it isn't plugged in,' or 'It won't work with all that flood water in it.' Attempting to give a physical account or prediction of the chess-playing computer would be a pointless and herculean labor, but it would work in principle. One could predict the response it would make in a chess game by tracing out the effects of the input energies all the way through the computer until once more type was pressed against paper and a response was printed. (Because of the digital nature of computers, quantum-level indeterminacies, if such there be, will cancel out rather than accumulate, unless of course a radium 'randomizer' or other amplifier of quantum effects is built into the computer.)

The best chess-playing computers these days are practically inaccessible to prediction from either the design stance or the physical stance; they have become too complex for even their own designers to view from the design stance. A man's best hope of defeating such a machine in a chess match is to predict its responses by figuring out as best he can what the best or most rational move would be, given the rules and goals of chess. That is, one assumes not only (1) that the machine will function as designed, but (2) that the design is optimal as well, that the computer will 'choose' the most rational move. Predictions made on these assumptions may well fail if either assumption proves unwarranted in the particular case, but still this *means* of prediction may impress us as the most fruitful one to adopt in dealing with a particular system. Put another way, when one can no longer hope to beat the machine by utilizing one's knowledge of physics or programming to anticipate its responses, one may still be able to avoid defeat by treating the machine rather like an intelligent human opponent.

We must look more closely at this strategy. A prediction relying on the assumption of the system's rationality is relative to a number of things. First, rationality here so far means nothing more than optimal design relative to a goal or optimally weighted hierarchy of goals (checkmate, winning pieces, defense, etc., in the case of chess) and a set of constraints (the rules and starting position). Prediction itself is, moreover, relative to the nature and extent of the information the system has at the time about the field of endeavor. The question one asks in framing a prediction of this sort is: What is the most rational thing for the computer to do, given goals $x,y,z, \ldots$, constraints $a,b,c, \ldots$ and information (including misinformation, if any) about the present state of affairs $p,q,r, \ldots$? In predicting the computer's response to my chess move, my assessment of the computer's most rational move may depend, for instance, not only on my assumption that the computer has information about the present disposition of all the pieces, but also on whether I believe the computer has information about my inability to see four moves ahead, the relative powers of knights and bishops, and my weakness for knight-bishop exchanges. In the end I may not be able to frame a very good prediction, if I am unable to determine with any accuracy what information and goals the computer has, or if the information and goals I take to be given do not dictate any one best move, or if I simply am not so good as the computer is at generating an optimal move from this given. Such predictions then are very precarious; not only are they relative to a set of postulates about goals, constraints, and information, and not only do they hinge on determining an optimal response in situations where we may have no clear criteria for what is optimal, but also they are vulnerable to short-circuit falsifications that are in principle unpredictable from this stance. Just as design-stance predictions are vulnerable to malfunctions (by depending on the assumption of no malfunction), so these predictions are vulnerable to design weaknesses and lapses (by depending on the assumption of optimal design). It is a measure of the success of contemporary program designers that these precarious predictions turn out to be true with enough regularity to make the method useful.

The dénouement of this extended example should now be

obvious: this third stance, with its assumption of rationality, is the *intentional stance*; the predictions one makes from it are intentional predictions; one is viewing the computer as an intentional system. One predicts behavior in such a case by ascribing to the system *the possession of certain information* and supposing it to be *directed by certain goals*, and then by working out the most reasonable or appropriate action on the basis of these ascriptions and suppositions. It is a small step to calling the information possessed the computer's *beliefs*, its goals and subgoals its *desires*. What I mean by saying that this is a small step, is that the notion of possession of information or misinformation is just as intentional a notion as that of belief. The 'possession' at issue is hardly the bland and innocent notion of storage one might suppose; it is, and must be, 'epistemic possession' – an analogue of belief. Consider: the Frenchman who possesses the *Encyclopedia Britannica* but knows no English might be said to 'possess' the information in it, but if there is such a sense of possession, it is not strong enough to serve as the sort of possession the computer must be supposed to enjoy, relative to the information it *uses* in 'choosing' a chess move. In a similar way, the goals of a goal-directed computer must be specified intentionally, just like desires.

Lingering doubts about whether the chess-playing computer *really* has beliefs and desires are misplaced; for the definition of intentional systems I have given does not say that intentional systems *really* have beliefs and desires, but that one can explain and predict their behavior by *ascribing* beliefs and desires to them, and whether one calls what one ascribes to the computer beliefs or belief-analogues or information complexes or intentional whatnots makes no difference to the nature of the calculation one makes on the basis of the ascriptions. One will arrive at the same predictions whether one forthrightly thinks in terms of the computer's beliefs and desires, or in terms of the computer's information-store and goal-specifications. The inescapable and interesting fact is that for the best chess-playing computers of today, intentional explanation and prediction of their behavior is not only common, but works when no other sort of prediction of their behavior is manageable. We do quite successfully treat these computers as intentional systems, and we do this independently of any considerations about what substance they are composed of, their origin, their position or lack of position in the community of moral agents, their consciousness or self-consciousness, or the determinacy or indeterminacy of their operations. The decision to adopt the strategy is pragmatic, and is not intrinsically right or wrong. One can always refuse to adopt the intentional stance toward the computer, and accept its checkmates. One can switch stances at will without involving oneself in any inconsistencies or inhumanities, adopting the intentional stance in one's role as opponent, the design stance in one's role as redesigner, and the physical stance in one's role as repairman.

This celebration of our chess-playing computer is not intended to imply that it is a completely adequate model or simulation of Mind, or intelligent human or animal activity; nor am I saying that the attitude we adopt toward this computer is precisely the same that we adopt toward a creature we deem to be conscious and rational. All that has been claimed is that on occasion, a purely physical system can be so complex, and yet so organized, that we find it convenient, explanatory, pragmatically necessary for prediction, to treat it as if it had beliefs and desires and was rational. The chess-playing computer is just that, a machine for playing chess, which no man or animal is; and hence its 'rationality' is pinched and artificial.

Perhaps we could straightforwardly expand the chess-playing computer into a more faithful model of human rationality, and perhaps not. I prefer to pursue a more fundamental line of enquiry first.

When should we expect the tactic of adopting the intentional stance to pay off? Whenever we have reason to suppose the assumption of optimal design is warranted, and doubt the practicality of prediction from the design or physical stance. Suppose we travel to a distant planet and find it inhabited by things moving about its surface, multiplying, decaying, apparently reacting to events in the environment, but otherwise as unlike human beings as you please. Can we make intentional predictions and explanations of their behavior? If we have reason to suppose that a process of natural selection has been in effect, then we can be assured that the populations we observe have been selected in virtue of their design: they will respond to at least some of the more common event-types in this environment in ways that are normally appropriate – that is, conducive to propagation of the species.[5] Once we have tentatively identified the perils and succors of the environment (relative to the constitution of the inhabitants, not ours), we shall be able to estimate which goals and which weighting of goals will be optimal relative to the creatures' *needs* (for survival and propagation), which sorts of information about the environment will be *useful* in guiding goal-directed activity, and which activities will be appropriate given the environmental circumstances. Having doped out these conditions (which will always be subject to revision) we can proceed at once to ascribe beliefs and desires to the creatures. Their behavior will 'manifest' their beliefs by being seen as the actions which, given the creatures' desires, would be appropriate to such beliefs as would be appropriate to the environmental stimulation. Desires, in turn, will be 'manifested' in behavior as those appropriate desires (given the needs of the creature) to which the actions of the creature would be appropriate, given the creature's beliefs. The circularity of these interlocking specifications is no accident. Ascriptions of beliefs and desires must be interdependent, and the only points of anchorage are the demonstrable needs for survival, the regularities of behavior, and the assumption, grounded in faith in natural selection, of optimal design. Once one has ascribed beliefs and desires, however, one can at once set about predicting behavior on their basis, and if evolution has done its job – as it must over the long run – our predictions will be reliable enough to be useful.

It might at first seem that this tactic unjustifiably imposes human categories and attributes (belief, desire, and so forth) on these alien entities. It is a sort of anthropomorphizing, to be sure, but it is conceptually innocent anthropomorphizing. We do not have to suppose these creatures share with us any peculiarly human inclinations, attitudes, hopes, foibles, pleasures, or outlooks; their actions may not include running, jumping, hiding, eating, sleeping, listening, or copulating. All we transport from our world to theirs are the categories of rationality, perception (information input by some 'sense' modality or modalities – perhaps radar or cosmic radiation), and action. The question of whether we can expect them to share any of our beliefs or desires is tricky, but there are a few points that can be made at this time; in virtue of their rationality they can be supposed to share our belief in logical truths,[6] and

we cannot suppose that they normally desire their own destruc-
tion, for instance.

## II

When one deals with a system – be it man, machine, or alien
creature – by explaining and predicting its behavior by citing its
beliefs and desires, one has what might be called a 'theory of
behavior' for the system. Let us see how such intentional theories
of behavior relate to other putative theories of behavior.

One fact so obvious that it is easily overlooked is that our
'common-sense' explanations and predictions of the behavior of
both men and animals are intentional. We start by assuming
rationality. We do not *expect* new acquaintances to react
irrationally to particular topics or eventualities, but when they
do we learn to adjust our strategies accordingly, just as, with a
chess-playing computer, one sets out with a high regard for its
rationality and adjusts one's estimate downward wherever performance reveals flaws. The presumption of rationality is so
strongly entrenched in our inference habits that when our
predictions prove false, we at first cast about for adjustments in
the information-possession conditions (he must not have heard,
he must not know English, he must not have seen $x$, been aware
that $y$, etc.) or goal weightings, before questioning the rationality
of the system as a whole. In extreme cases personalities may
prove to be so unpredictable from the intentional stance that we
abandon it, and if we have accumulated a lot of evidence in the
meanwhile about the nature of response patterns in the individual, we may find that a species of design stance can be effectively
adopted. This is the fundamentally different attitude we
occasionally adopt toward the insane. To watch an asylum
attendant manipulate an obsessively countersuggestive patient,
for instance, is to watch something radically unlike normal
interpersonal relations.

Our prediction of animal behavior by 'common sense' is also
intentional. Whether or not sentimental folk go overboard when
they talk to their dogs or fill their cats' heads with schemes and
worries, even the most hardboiled among us predict animals'
behavior intentionally. If we observe a mouse in a situation
where it can see a cat waiting at one mousehole and cheese at
another, we know which way the mouse will go, providing it is

not deranged; our prediction is not based on our familiarity with maze-experiments or any assumptions about the sort of special training the mouse has been through. We suppose the mouse can see the cat and the cheese, and hence has beliefs (belief-analogues, intentional whatnots) to the effect that there is a cat to the left, cheese to the right, and we ascribe to the mouse also the desire to eat the cheese and the desire to avoid the cat (subsumed, appropriately enough, under the more general desires to eat and to avoid peril); so we predict that the mouse will do what is appropriate to such beliefs and desires, namely, go to the right in order to get the cheese and avoid the cat. Whatever academic allegiances or theoretical predilections we may have, we would be astonished if, in the general run, mice and other animals falsified such intentional predictions of their behavior. Indeed, experimental psychologists of every school would have a hard time devising experimental situations to support their various theories without the help of their intentional expectations of how the test animals will respond to circumstances.

Earlier I alleged that even creatures from another planet would share with us our beliefs in logical truths; light can be shed on this claim by asking whether mice and other animals, in virtue of being intentional systems, also believe the truths of logic. There is something bizarre in the picture of a dog or mouse cogitating a list of tautologies, but we can avoid that picture. The assumption that something is an intentional system is the assumption that it is rational; that is, one gets nowhere with the assumption that entity $x$ has beliefs $p,q,r, \ldots$ unless one also supposes that $x$ believes what follows from $p,q,r, \ldots$; otherwise there is no way of ruling out the prediction that $x$ will, in the face of its beliefs $p,q,r, \ldots$ do something utterly stupid, and, if we cannot rule out *that* prediction, we will have acquired no predictive power at all. So whether or not the animal is said to *believe* the *truths* of logic, it must be supposed to *follow the rules* of logic. Surely our mouse follows or believes in *modus ponens*, for we ascribed to it the beliefs; (a) *there is a cat to the left*, and (b) *if there is a cat to the left, I had better not go left*, and our prediction relied on the mouse's ability to get to the conclusion. In general there is a trade-off between rules and truths; we can suppose $x$ to have an inference rule taking $A$ to $B$ or we can give $x$ the belief in the 'theorem': *if A then B*. As far as our predictions are concerned, we are free to ascribe to the mouse either a few inference rules and belief in many logical propositions, or many inference rules and few if any logical beliefs.[7] We can even take a patently nonlogical belief like (b) and recast it as an inference rule taking (a) to the desired conclusion.

Will all logical truths appear among the beliefs of any intentional system? If the system were ideally or perfectly rational, all logical truths would appear, but any actual intentional system will be imperfect, and so not all logical truths must be ascribed as beliefs to any system. Moreover, not all the inference rules of an actual intentional system may be valid; not all its inference-licensing beliefs may be truths of logic. Experience may indicate where the shortcomings lie in any particular system. If we found an imperfectly rational creature whose allegiance to *modus ponens*, say, varied with the subject matter, we could characterize that by excluding *modus ponens* as a rule and ascribing in its stead a set of nonlogical inference rules covering the *modus ponens* step for each subject matter where the rule was followed. Not surprisingly, as we discover more and more imperfections (as we banish more and more logical truths from the creature's beliefs), our efforts at intentional prediction become more and more cumbersome and undecidable, for we can no longer count on the beliefs, desires, and actions going together that *ought* to go together. Eventually we end up, following this process, by predicting from the design stance; we end up, that is, dropping the assumption of rationality.[8]

This migration from common-sense intentional explanations and predictions to more reliable design-stance explanations and predictions that is forced on us when we discover that our subjects are imperfectly rational is, independently of any such discovery, the proper direction for theory builders to take whenever possible. In the end, we want to be able to explain the intelligence of man, or beast, in terms of his design, and this in turn in terms of the natural selection of this design; so whenever we stop in our explanations at the intentional level we have left over an unexplained instance of intelligence or rationality. This comes out vividly if we look at theory building from the vantage point of economics.

Any time a theory builder proposes to call any event, state, structure, etc., in any system (say the brain of an organism) a *signal* or *message* or *command* or otherwise endows it with content, he *takes out a loan* of intelligence. He implicitly posits along with his signals, messages, or commands, something that can serve as a signal-*reader*, message-*understander*, or com-*mander*, else his 'signals' will be for naught, will decay unreceived, uncomprehended. This loan must be repaid eventually by finding and analyzing away these readers or comprehenders; for, failing this, the theory wil have among its elements unanalyzed man-analogues endowed with enough intelligence to read the signals, etc., and thus the theory will *postpone* answering the major question: what makes for intelligence? The intentionality of all such talk of signals and commands reminds us that rationality is being taken for granted, and in this way shows us where a theory is incomplete. It is this feature that, to my mind, puts a premium on the yet unfinished task of devising a rigorous definition of intentionality, for if we can lay claim to a purely formal criterion of intentional discourse, we will have what amounts to a medium of exchange for assessing theories of behavior. Intentionality *abstracts* from the inessential details of the various forms intelligence-loans can take (e.g., signal-readers, volition-emitters, librarians in the corridors of memory, egos and superegos) and serves as a reliable means of detecting exactly where a theory is *in the red* relative to the task of explaining intelligence; wherever a theory relies on a formulation bearing the logical marks of intentionality, there a little man is concealed.

This insufficiency of intentional explanation from the point of view of psychology has been widely felt and as widely misconceived. The most influential misgivings, expressed in the behaviorism of Skinner and Quine, can be succinctly characterized in terms of our economic metaphor. Skinner's and Quine's adamant prohibitions of intentional idioms at all levels of theory is the analogue of rock-ribbed New England conservatism: no deficit spending when building a theory! In Quine's case, the abhorrence of loans is due mainly to his fear that they can never be repaid, whereas Skinner stresses rather that what is borrowed is worthless to begin with. Skinner's suspicion is that intentionally couched claims are empirically vacuous, in the sense that they are altogether too easy to accommodate to the data, like the *virtus dormitiva* Molière's doctor ascribes to the sleeping powder. Questions can be begged on a temporary basis, however, permitting a mode of prediction and explanation not totally vacuous. Consider the following intentional prediction: if I were to ask a thousand American mathematicians how much seven times five is, more than nine hundred would respond by saying that it was thirty-five. (I have allowed for a few to mishear my question, a few others to be obstreperous, a few to make slips of the tongue.) If you doubt the prediction, you can test it; I would bet good money on it. It seems to have empirical content because it can, in a fashion, be tested, and yet it is unsatisfactory as a prediction of an empirical theory of psychology. It works, of course, because of the contingent, empirical – but evolution-guaranteed – fact that men in general are well enough designed both to get the answer right and want to get it right. It will hold with as few exceptions for any group of Martians with whom we are able to converse, for it is not a prediction just of *human* psychology, but of the 'psychology' of intentional systems generally.

Deciding on the basis of available empirical evidence that something is a piece of copper or a lichen permits one to make predictions based on the empirical theories dealing with copper and lichens, but deciding on the basis of available evidence that something is (may be treated as) an intentional system permits predictions having a normative or logical basis rather than an empirical one, and hence the success of an intentional prediction, based as it is on no particular picture of the system's design, cannot be construed to confirm or disconfirm any particular pictures of the system's design.

Skinner's reaction to this has been to try to frame predictions purely in non-intentional language, by predicting bodily responses to physical stimuli, but to date this has not provided him with the alternative mode of prediction and explanation he has sought, as perhaps an extremely cursory review can indicate. To provide a setting for non-intentional prediction of behavior, he invented the Skinner box, in which the rewarded behavior of the occupant – say, a rat – is a highly restricted and stereotypic bodily motion – usually pressing a bar with the front paws.

The claim that is then made is that once the animal has been trained, a law-like relationship is discovered to hold between non-intentionally characterized events: controlling stimuli and bar-pressing responses. A regularity is discovered to hold, to be sure, but the fact that it is between non-intentionally defined events is due to a property of the Skinner box and not of the occupant. For let us turn our prediction about mathematicians into a Skinnerian prediction: strap a mathematician in a Skinner box so he can move only his head; display in front of him a card on which appear the marks: 'How much is seven times five?'; move into the range of his head-motions two buttons, over one of which is the mark '35' and over the other '34'; place electrodes on the soles of his feet and give him a few quick shocks; the controlling stimulus is then to be the sound: 'Answer now!' I predict that in a statistically significant number of cases, even *before* training trials to condition the man to press button '35' with his forehead, he will do this when given the controlling stimulus. Is this a satisfactory scientific prediction just because it eschews the intentional vocabulary? No, it is an intentional prediction disguised by so restricting the environment that only one bodily motion is available to fulfill the intentional *action* that anyone would prescribe as appropriate to the circumstances of perception, belief, desire. That it is action, not merely motion, that is predicted can also be seen in the case of subjects less intelligent than mathematicians. Suppose a mouse were trained, in a Skinner box with a food reward, to take exactly four steps forward and press a bar with its nose; if Skinner's laws truly held between stimuli and responses defined in terms of bodily motion, were we to move the bar an inch farther away, so four steps did not reach it, Skinner would have to predict that the mouse would jab its nose into the empty air rather than take a fifth step.

A variation of Skinnerian theory designed to meet this objection acknowledges that the trained response one predicts is not truly captured in a description of skeletal motion alone, but rather in a description of an environmental effect achieved: the bar going down, the '35' button being depressed. This will also not do. Suppose we could in fact train a man or animal to achieve an environmental effect, as this theory proposes. Suppose, for instance, we train a man to push a button under the longer of two displays, such as drawings or simple designs, that is, we reward him when he pushes the button under the longer of two pictures of pencils, or cigars, etc. The miraculous consequence of this theory, were it correct, would be that if, after training him on simple views, we were to present him with the Müller-Lyer arrow-head illusion, he would be immune to it, for *ex hypothesi* he has been trained to achieve an *actual* environmental effect (choosing the display that *is* longer), not a *perceived* or *believed* environmental effect (choosing the display that *seems* longer). The reliable prediction, again, is the intentional one.[9]

Skinner's experimental design is supposed to eliminate the intentional, but it merely masks it. Skinner's non-intentional predictions work to the extent they do, not because Skinner has truly found non-intentional behavioral laws, but because the highly reliable intentional predictions underlying his experimental situations (the rat desires food and believes it will get food by pressing the bar – something for which it has been given good evidence – so it will press the bar) are disguised by leaving virtually no room in the environment for more than one bodily motion to be the appropriate action and by leaving virtually no room in the environment for discrepancy to arise between the subject's beliefs and the reality.

Where, then, should we look for a satisfactory theory of behavior? Intentional theory is vacuous as psychology because it presupposes and does not explain rationality or intelligence. The apparent successes of Skinnerian behaviorism, however, rely on hidden intentional predictions. Skinner is right in recognizing that intentionality can be no *foundation* for psychology, and right also to look for purely mechanistic regularities in the activities of his subjects, but there is little reason to suppose they will lie on the surface in gross behavior – except, as we have seen, when we put an artificial straitjacket on an intentional regularity. Rather, we will find whatever mechanistic regularities there are in the functioning of internal systems whose design approaches the optimal (relative to some ends). In seeking knowledge of internal design our most promising tactic is to take out intelligence-loans, endow peripheral and internal events with contents, and then look for mechanisms that will function appropriately with such 'messages' so that we can pay back the loans. This tactic is hardly untried. Research in artificial intelligence, which has produced, among other things, the chess-playing computer, proceeds by working from an intentionally characterized problem (how to get the computer to consider the right sorts of information, make the right decisions) to a design-stance solution – an approximation of optimal design. Psychophysicists and neurophysiologists who routinely describe events in terms of the transmission of information within the nervous system are similarly borrowing intentional capital – even if they are often inclined to ignore or disavow their debts.

Finally, it should not be supposed that, just because intentional theory is vacuous as psychology, in virtue of its assumption of rationality, it is vacuous from all points of view. Game theory, for example, is inescapably intentional,[10] but as a formal normative theory and not a psychology this is nothing amiss. Game-theoretical predictions applied to human subjects achieve their accuracy in virtue of the evolutionary guarantee that man is well designed as a game player, a special case of rationality. Similarly, economics, the social science of greatest predictive power today, is not a psychological theory and presupposes what psychology must explain. Economic explanation and prediction is intentional (although some is disguised) and succeeds to the extent that it does because individual men are in general good approximations of the optimal operator in the marketplace.

## III

The concept of an intentional system is a relatively uncluttered and unmetaphysical notion, abstracted as it is from questions of the composition, constitution, consciousness, morality, or divinity of the entities falling under it. Thus, for example, it is much easier to decide whether a machine can be an intentional system than it is to decide whether a machine can *really* think, or be conscious, or morally responsible. This simplicity makes it ideal as a source of order and organization in philosophical analyses of 'mental' concepts. Whatever else a person might be – embodied mind or soul, self-conscious moral agent, 'emergent' form of intelligence – he is an intentional system, and whatever follows just from being an intentional system is thus true of a person. It is interesting to see just how much of what we hold to be the case about persons or their minds follows directly from their being intentional systems. To revert for a moment to the economic metaphor, the guiding or challenging question that defines work in the philosophy of mind is this: are there mental treasures that cannot be purchased with intentional coin? If not, a considerable unification of science can be foreseen in outline.

Of special importance for such an examination is the subclass of intentional systems that have language, that can communicate; for these provide a framework for a theory of consciousness. In *Content and Consciousness*, part II, and in parts III and IV of [*Brainstorms*] I have attempted to elaborate such a theory; here I would like to consider its implications for the analysis of the concept of belief. What will be true of human believers just in virtue of their being intentional systems with the capacity to communicate?

Just as not all intentional systems currently known to us can fly or swim, so not all intentional systems can talk, but those which can do this raise special problems and opportunities when we come to ascribe beliefs and desires to them. That is a massive understatement; without the talking intentional systems, of course, there would be no ascribing beliefs, no theorizing, no assuming rationality, no predicting. The capacity for language is without doubt the crowning achievement of evolution, an achievement that feeds on itself to produce ever more versatile and subtle rational systems, but still it can be looked at as an adaptation which is subject to the same conditions of environmental utility as any other behavioral talent. When it is looked at in this way several striking facts emerge. One of the most pervasive features of evolutionary histories is the interdependence of distinct organs and capacities in a species. Advanced eyes and other distance receptors are of no utility to an organism unless it develops advanced means of locomotion; the talents of a predator will not accrue to a species that does not evolve a carnivore's digestive system. The capacities of belief and communication have prerequisites of their own. We have already seen that there is no point in ascribing beliefs to a system unless the beliefs ascribed are in general appropriate to the environment, and the system responds appropriately to the beliefs. An eccentric expression of this would be: the capacity to believe would have no survival value unless it were a capacity to believe truths. What is eccentric and potentially misleading about this is that it hints at the picture of a species 'trying on' a faculty giving rise to beliefs most of which were false, having its inutility demonstrated, and abandoning it. A species might 'experiment' by mutation in any number of inefficacious systems, but none of these systems would deserve to be called belief systems precisely because of their defects, their nonrationality, and hence a false belief system is a conceptual impossibility. To borrow an example from a short story by MacDonald Harris, a soluble fish is an evolutionary impossibility, but a system for false beliefs cannot even be given a coherent description. The same evolutionary bias in favor of truth prunes the capacity to communicate as it develops; a capacity for false communication would not be a capacity for communication at all, but just an emission proclivity of no systematic value to the species. The faculty of communication would not gain ground in evolution unless it was by and large the faculty of transmitting true beliefs, which means only: the faculty of altering other members of the species in the direction of more optimal design.

This provides a foundation for explaining a feature of belief that philosophers have recently been at some pains to account for.[11] The concept of belief seems to have a normative cast to it that is most difficult to capture. One way of putting it might be that an avowal like 'I believe that $p$' seems to imply in some fashion: 'One ought to believe that $p$.' This way of putting it has flaws, however, for we must then account for the fact that 'I believe that $p$' seems to have normative force that 'He believes that $p$', said of me, does not. Moreover, saying that one ought to believe this or that suggests that belief is voluntary, a view with notorious difficulties.[12] So long as one tries to capture the normative element by expressing it in the form of moral or pragmatic injunctions to believers, such as 'one ought to believe the truth' and 'one ought to act in accordance with one's beliefs', dilemmas arise. How, for instance, is one to follow the advice to believe the truth? Could one abandon one's sloppy habit of believing falsehoods? If the advice is taken to mean: believe only what you have convincing evidence for, it is the vacuous advice: believe only what you believe to be true. If alternatively it is taken to mean: believe only what is in fact the truth, it is an injunction we are powerless to obey.

The normative element of belief finds its home not in such injunctions but in the preconditions for the ascription of belief, what Phillips Griffiths calls 'the general conditions for the possibility of application of the concept'. For the concept of belief to find application, two conditions, we have seen, must be met: (1) In general, normally, more often than not, if $x$ believes $p$, $p$ is true. (2) In general, normally, more often than not, if $x$ avows that $p$, he believes $p$ [and, by (1), $p$ is true]. Were these conditions not met, we would not have rational, communicating systems; we would not have believers or belief-avowers. The norm for belief is evidential well-foundedness (assuring truth in the long run), and the norm for avowal of belief is accuracy (which includes sincerity). These two norms determine pragmatic implications of our utterances. If I assert that $p$ (or that I believe that $p$ – it makes no difference), I assume the burden of defending my assertion on two fronts: I can be asked for evidence for the truth of $p$, and I can be asked for behavioral evidence that I do in fact believe $p$.[13] I do not need to examine my own behavior in order to be in a position to avow my belief that $p$, but if my sincerity or self-knowledge is challenged, this is where I must turn to defend my assertion. But again, challenges on either point must be the exception rather than the rule if belief is to have a place among our concepts.

Another way of looking at the importance of this predominance of the normal is to consider the well-known circle of implications between beliefs and desires (or intentions) that prevent non-intentional behavioral definitions of intentional terms. A man's standing under a tree is a behavioral indicator of his belief that it is raining, but only on the assumption that he desires to stay dry, and if we then look for evidence that he wants to stay dry, his standing under the tree will do, but only on the assumption that he believes the tree will shelter him; if we ask him if he believes the tree will shelter him, his positive response is confirming evidence only on the assumption that he desires to tell us the truth, and so forth *ad infinitum*. It is this apparently vicious circle that turned Quine against the intentional (and foiled Tolman's efforts at operational definition of intentional terms), but if it is true that in any particular case a man's saying that $p$ is evidence of his belief only conditionally, we can be assured that in the long run and in general the circle is broken; a man's assertions are, unconditionally, indicative of his beliefs, as are his actions in general. We get around the 'privacy' of beliefs and desires by recognizing that in general anyone's beliefs and desires must be those he 'ought to have' given the circumstances.

These two interdependent norms of belief, one favoring the truth and rationality of belief, the other favoring accuracy of avowal, normally complement each other, but on occasion can give rise to conflict. This is the 'problem of incorrigibility'. If rationality is the mother of intention, we still must wean intentional systems from the criteria that give them life, and set them up on their own. Less figuratively, if we are to make use of the concept of an intentional system in particular instances, at some point we must cease *testing* the assumption of the system's rationality, adopt the intentional stance, and grant without further ado that the system is qualified for beliefs and desires. For mute animals – and chess-playing computers – this manifests itself in a tolerance for less than optimal performance. We continue to ascribe beliefs to the mouse, and explain its actions in terms of them, after we have tricked it into some stupid belief. This tolerance has its limits of course, and the less felicitous the behavior – especially the less adaptable the behavior – the more hedged are our ascriptions. For instance, we are inclined to say of the duckling that 'imprints' on the first moving thing it sees upon emerging from its shell that it 'believes' the thing is its mother, whom it follows around, but we emphasize the scare-quotes around 'believes'. For intentional systems that can communicate – persons for instance – the tolerance takes the form of the convention that a man is incorrigible or a special authority about his own beliefs. This convention is 'justified' by the fact that evolution does guarantee that our second norm is followed. What better source could there be of a system's beliefs than its avowals? Conflict arises, however, whenever a person falls short of perfect rationality, and avows beliefs that either are strongly disconfirmed by the available empirical evidence or are self-contradictory or contradict other avowals he has made. If we lean on the myth that a man is perfectly rational, we must find his avowals less than authoritative: 'You *can't* mean – understand – what you're saying!'; if we lean on his 'right' as a speaking intentional system to have his word accepted, we grant him an irrational set of beliefs. Neither position provides a stable resting place; for, as we saw earlier, intentional explanation and prediction cannot be accommodated either to breakdown or to less than optimal design, so there is no coherent intentional description of such an impasse.[14]

Can any other considerations be brought to bear in such an instance to provide us with justification for one ascription of beliefs rather than another? Where should one look for such considerations? The Phenomenologist will be inclined to suppose that individual introspection will provide us a sort of data

not available to the outsider adopting the intentional stance; but
how would such data get used? Let the introspector amass as
much inside information as you please; he must then communicate it to us, and what are we to make of his communications?
We can suppose that they are incorrigible (barring corrigible
verbal errors, slips of the tongue, and so forth), but we do not
need Phenomenology to give us that option, for it amounts to
the decision to lean on the accuracy-of-avowal norm at the
expense of the rationality norm. If, alternatively, we demand
certain standards of consistency and rationality of his utterances
before we accept them as authoritative, what standards will we
adopt? If we demand perfect rationality, we have simply flown
to the other norm at the expense of the norm of accuracy of
avowal. If we try to fix minimum standards at something less
than perfection, what will guide our choice? Not Phenomenological data, for the choice we make will determine what is to
count as Phenomenological data. Not neurophysiological data
either, for whether we interpret a bit of neural structure to be
endowed with a particular belief content hinges on our having
granted that the neural system under examination has met the
standards of rationality for being an intentional system, an
assumption jeopardized by the impasse we are trying to resolve.
That is, one might have a theory about an individual's neurology
that permitted one to 'read off' or predict the propositions to
which he would assent, but whether one's theory had uncovered
his *beliefs*, or merely a set of assent-inducers, would depend on
how consistent, reasonable, true we found the set of
propositions.

John Vickers has suggested to me a way of looking at this
question. Consider a set $T$ of transformations that take beliefs
into beliefs. The problem is to determine the set $T_s$ for each
intentional system $S$, so that if we know that $S$ believes $p$, we
will be able to determine other things that $S$ believes by seeing
what the transformations of $p$ are for $T_s$. If $S$ were ideally
rational, every valid transformation would be in $T_s$; $S$ would
believe every logical consequence of every belief (and, ideally, $S$
would have no false beliefs). Now we know that no actual
intentional system will be ideally rational; so we must suppose
any actual system will have a $T$ with less in it. But we also know
that, to qualify as an intentional system at all, $S$ must have a $T$
with some integrity; $T$ cannot be empty. What rationale could

we have, however, for fixing some set between the extremes and calling it *the* set for belief (for *S*, for earthlings, or for ten-year-old girls)? This is another way of asking whether we could replace Hintikka's normative theory of belief with an empirical theory of belief, and, if so, what evidence we would use. 'Actually,' one is tempted to say, 'people do believe contradictions on occasion, as their utterances demonstrate; so any adequate logic of belief or analysis of the concept of belief must accommodate this fact.' But any attempt to *legitimize* human fallibility in a theory of belief by fixing a permissible level of error would be like adding one more rule to chess: an Official Tolerance Rule to the effect that any game of chess containing no more than *k* moves that are illegal relative to the other rules of the game is a legal game of chess. Suppose we discovered that, in a particular large population of poor chess-players, each game on average contained three illegal moves undetected by either opponent. Would we claim that these people *actually* play a different game from ours, a game with an Official Tolerance Rule with *k* fixed at 3? This would be to confuse the norm they follow with what gets by in their world. We could claim in a similar vein that people *actually* believe, say, all synonymous or intentionally isomorphic consequences of their beliefs, but not all their logical consequences, but of course the occasions when a man resists assenting to a logical consequence of some avowal of his are unstable cases; he comes in for criticism and cannot appeal in his own defense to any canon absolving him from believing nonsynonymous consequences. If one wants to get away from norms and predict and explain the 'actual, empirical' behavior of the poor chess-players, one stops talking of their *chess moves* and starts talking of their proclivities to move pieces of wood or ivory about on checkered boards; if one wants to predict and explain the 'actual, empirical' behavior of believers, one must similarly cease talking of belief, and descend to the design stance or physical stance for one's account.

The concept of an intentional system explicated in these pages is made to bear a heavy load. It has been used here to form a bridge connecting the intentional domain (which includes our 'common-sense' world of persons and actions, game theory, and the 'neural signals' of the biologist) to the non-intentional domain of the physical sciences. That is a lot to expect of one concept, but nothing less than Brentano himself expected when, in a day of less fragmented science, he proposed intentionality as the mark that sunders the universe in the most fundamental way: dividing the mental from the physical.

## References

1 I am indebted to Peter Woodruff for making extensive improvements in this chapter prior to its initial publication. Since it appeared, I have found anticipations and developments of similar or supporting themes in a variety of writers, most notably Carl Hempel, 'Rational Action', *Proceedings and Addresses of the American Philosophical Association*, XXXV (1962), reprinted in N. S. Care and C. Landesman, eds., *Readings in the Theory of Action* (Bloomington, Indiana: University Press, 1968); L. Jonathan Cohen, 'Teleological Explanation', *Proceedings of the Aristotelian Society* (1950–51), and 'Can there be Artificial Minds?', *Analysis* (1954–55); B. A. O. Williams, 'Deciding to Believe', in H. E. Kiefer and M. K. Munitz, eds., *Language, Belief, and Metaphysics* (Albany: SUNY Press, 1970), and David Lewis, 'Radical Interpretation', *Synthese*, III, IV (1974): 331–44.

2 For a lucid introduction to the concept and its history, see the entry on 'intentionality' by Roderick Chisholm in P. Edwards, ed., *The Encyclopedia of Philosophy* (New York: MacMillan, 1967).

3 *Content and Consciousness* (London: Routledge & Kegan Paul, 1969).

4 The term 'intentional system' occurs in Charles Taylor's *The Explanation of Behaviour* (London: Routledge & Kegan Paul, 1964): p. 62, where its use suggests it is co-extensive with the term as I use it, but Taylor does not develop the notion in depth. See, however, his p. 58ff. For an introduction to the concept of an intentional system with fewer philosophical presuppositions, see the first sections of Chapters 12 and 14 of *Brainstorms*.

5 Note that what is *directly* selected, the gene, is a diagram and not a design; it is selected, however, because it happens to ensure that its bearer has a certain (functional) design. This was pointed out to me by Woodruff.

6 Cf. Quine's argument about the necessity of 'discovering' our logical connectives in any language we can translate in *Word and Object* (Cambridge, Mass.: MIT, 1960), Section 13. More will be said in defense of this below.

7 Accepting the argument of Lewis Carroll, in 'What the Tortoise Said to Achilles', *Mind* (1895), reprinted in I. M. Copi and J. A. Gould,

*Readings on Logic* (New York: MacMillan, 1964) we cannot allow all the rules for a system to be replaced by beliefs, for this would generate an infinite and unproductive nesting of distinct beliefs about what can be inferred from what.

8 This paragraph owes much to discussion with John Vickers, whose paper 'Judgment and Belief', in K. Lambert, *The Logical Way of Doing Things* (New Haven, Conn.: Yale, 1969), goes beyond the remarks here by considering the problems of the relative strength or weighting of beliefs and desires.

9 R. L. Gregory, *Eye and Brain* (London: World University Library, 1966): p. 137, reports that pigeons and fish given just this training are, not surprisingly, susceptible to visual illusions of length.

10 Hintikka notes in passing that game theory is like his epistemic logic in assuming rationality, in *Knowledge and Belief* (Ithaca, N.Y.: Cornell, 1962), p. 38.

11 I have in mind especially A. Phillips Griffiths' penetrating discussion 'On Belief', *Proceedings of the Aristotelian Society*, LXIII (1962/3): 167–86; and Bernard Mayo's 'Belief and Constraint', *ibid.*, LXIV (1964): 139–56, both reprinted in Phillips Griffiths, ed., *Knowledge and Belief* (New York: Oxford, 1967).

12 See, e.g., H. H. Price, 'Belief and Will', *Proceedings of the Aristotelian Society*, suppl. vol. XXVIII (1954), reprinted in S. Hampshire, ed., *Philosophy of Mind* (New York: Harper & Row, 1966).

13 Cf. A. W. Collins, 'Unconscious Belief', *Journal of Philosophy*, LXVI, 20 (Oct. 16, 1969): 667–80.

14 Hintikka takes this bull by the horns. His epistemic logic is acknowledged to hold only for the ideally rational believer; were we to apply this logic to persons in the actual world in other than a normative way, thus making its implications *authoritative* about actual belief, the authority of persons would have go by the board. Thus his rule A.CBB* (*Knowledge and Belief*, pp. 24–26), roughly that if one believes *p* one believes that one believes *p*, cannot be understood, as it is tempting to suppose, as a version of the incorrigibility thesis.

PAUL CHURCHLAND

# Eliminative Materialism and the Propositional Attitudes[1]

Eliminative materialism is the thesis that our common-sense conception of psychological phenomena constitutes a radically false theory, a theory so fundamentally defective that both the principles and the ontology of that theory will eventually be displaced, rather than smoothly reduced, by completed neuroscience. Our mutual understanding and even our introspection may then be reconstituted within the conceptual framework of completed neuroscience, a theory we may expect to be more powerful by far than the common-sense psychology it displaces, and more substantially integrated within physical science generally. My purpose in this paper is to explore these projections, especially as they bear on (1) the principal elements of common-sense psychology: the propositional attitudes (beliefs, desires, etc.), and (2) the conception of rationality in which these elements figure.

This focus represents a change in the fortunes of materialism. Twenty years ago, emotions, qualia, and 'raw feels' were held to be the principal stumbling blocks for the materialist program. With these barriers dissolving,[2] the locus of opposition has shifted. Now it is the realm of the intentional, the realm of the propositional attitude, that is most commonly held up as being both irreducible to and ineliminable in favor of anything from within a materialist framework. Whether and why this is so, we must examine.

Such an examination will make little sense, however, unless it is first appreciated that the relevant network of common-sense concepts does indeed constitute an empirical theory, with all the functions, virtues, *and perils* entailed by that status. I shall therefore begin with a brief sketch of this view and a summary rehearsal of its rationale. The resistance it encounters still surprises me. After all, common sense has yielded up many theories. Recall the view that space has a preferred direction in which all things fall; that weight is an intrinsic feature of a body; that a force-free moving object will promptly return to rest; that the sphere of the heavens turns daily; and so on. These examples are clear, perhaps, but people seem willing to concede a theoretical component within common sense only if (1) the theory and the common sense involved are safely located in antiquity, and (2) the relevant theory is now so clearly false that its speculative nature is inescapable. Theories are indeed easier to discern under these circumstances. But the vision of hindsight is always 20/20. Let us aspire to some foresight for a change.

## Why folk psychology is a theory

Seeing our common-sense conceptual framework for mental phenomena as a theory brings a simple and unifying organiz-ation to most of the major topics in the philosophy of mind, including the explanation and prediction of behavior, the seman-tics of mental predicates, action theory, the other-minds prob-lem, the intentionality of mental states, the nature of introspection, and the mind-body problem. Any view that can pull this lot together deserves careful consideration.

Let us begin with the explanation of human (and animal) behavior. The fact is that the average person is able to explain, and even predict, the behavior of other persons with a facility and success that is remarkable. Such explanations and predic-tions standardly make reference to the desires, beliefs, fears, intentions, perceptions, and so forth, to which the agents are presumed subject. But explanations presuppose laws – rough and ready ones, at least – that connect the explanatory con-ditions with the behavior explained. The same is true for the making of predictions, and for the justification of subjunctive and counterfactual conditionals concerning behavior. Reassur-ingly, a rich network of common-sense laws can indeed be reconstructed from this quotidian commerce of explanation and anticipation; its principles are familiar homilies; and their sundry functions are transparent. Each of us understands others, as well as we do, because we share a tacit command of an integrated body of lore concerning the law-like relations holding among external circumstances, internal states, and overt behavior. Given its nature and functions, this body of lore may quite aptly be called 'folk psychology'.[3]

This approach entails that the semantics of the terms in our familiar mentalistic vocabulary is to be understood in the same manner as the semantics of theoretical terms generally: the meaning of any theoretical term is fixed or constituted by the network of laws in which it figures. (This position is quite distinct from logical behaviorism. We deny that the relevant laws are analytic, and it is the lawlike connections generally that carry the semantic weight, not just the connections with overt behavior. But this view does account for what little plausibility logical behaviorism did enjoy.)

More importantly, the recognition that folk psychology is a theory provides a simple and decisive solution to an old skeptical problem, the problem of other minds. The problematic conviction that another individual is the subject of certain mental states is not inferred deductively from his behavior, nor is it inferred by inductive analogy from the perilously isolated instance of one's own case. Rather, that conviction is a singular *explanatory hypothesis* of a perfectly straightforward kind. Its function, in conjunction with the background laws of folk psychology, is to provide explanations/predictions/understanding of the individual's continuing behavior, and it is credible to the degree that it is successful in this regard over competing hypotheses. In the main, such hypotheses are successful, and so the belief that others enjoy the internal states comprehended by folk psychology is a reasonable belief.

Knowledge of other minds thus has no essential dependence on knowledge of one's own mind. Applying the principles of our folk psychology to our behavior, a Martian could justly ascribe to us the familiar run of mental states, even though his own psychology were very different from ours. He would not, therefore, be 'generalizing from his own case'.

As well, introspective judgments about one's own case turn out not to have any special status or integrity anyway. On the present view, an introspective judgment is just an instance of an acquired habit of conceptual response to one's internal states, and the integrity of any particular response is always contingent on the integrity of the acquired conceptual framework (theory) in which the response is framed. Accordingly, one's *introspective* certainty that one's mind is the seat of beliefs and desires may be as badly misplaced as was the classical man's *visual* certainty that the star-flecked sphere of the heavens turns daily.

Another conundrum is the intentionality of mental states. The 'propositional attitudes', as Russell called them, form the systematic core of folk psychology; and their uniqueness and anomalous logical properties have inspired some to see here a fundamental contrast with anything that mere physical phenomena might conceivably display. The key to this matter lies again in the theoretical nature of folk psychology. The intentionality of mental states here emerges not as a mystery of nature, but as a structural feature of the concepts of folk psychology. Ironically, those same structural features reveal the very close affinity that folk psychology bears to theories in the physical sciences. Let me try to explain.

Consider the large variety of what might be called 'numerical attitudes' appearing in the conceptual framework of physical science: '. . . has a mass$_{kg}$ of $n$', '. . . has a velocity of $n$', '. . . has a temperature$_k$ of $n$', and so forth. These expressions are predicate-forming expressions: when one substitutes a singular term for a number into the place held by '$n$', a determinate predicate results. More interestingly, the relations between the various 'numerical attitudes' that result are precisely the relations between the numbers 'contained' in those attitudes. More interesting still, the argument place that takes the singular terms for numbers is open to quantification. All this permits the expression of generalizations concerning the lawlike relations that hold between the various numerical attitudes in nature. Such laws involve quantification over numbers, and they exploit the mathematical relations holding in that domain. Thus, for example,

(1) $(x)(f)(m)[((x$ has a mass of $m)$ & $(x$ suffers a net force of $f))$
$$\supset (x \text{ accelerates at } f/m)]$$

Consider now the large variety of propositional attitudes: '. . . believes that $p$', '. . . desires that $p$', '. . . fears that $p$', '. . . is happy that $p$', etc. These expressions are predicate-forming expressions also. When one substitutes a singular term for a proposition into the place held by '$p$', a determinate predicate results, e.g., '. . . believes that Tom is tall'. (Sentences do not generally function as singular terms, but it is difficult to escape the idea that when a sentence occurs in the place held by '$p$', it is there functioning as or like a singular term. On this, more below.) More interestingly, the relations between the resulting propositional attitudes are characteristically the relations that hold between the propositions 'contained' in them, relations such as entailment, equivalence, and mutual inconsistency. More interesting still, the argument place that takes the singular terms for propositions is open to quantification. All this permits the expression of generalizations concerning the lawlike relations that hold among propositional attitudes. Such laws involve quantification over propositions, and they exploit various relations holding in that domain. Thus, for example,

(2) $(x)(p)[(x$ fears that $p) \supset (x$ desires that $\sim p)]$
(3) $(x)(p)[(x$ hopes that $p)$ & $(x$ discovers that $p))$
$$\supset (x \text{ is pleased that } p)]$$
(4) $(x)(p)(q)[((x$ believes that $p)$ & $(x$ believes that (if $p$ then $q)))$
$\supset$ (barring confusion, distraction, etc., $x$ believes that $q)]$
(5) $(x)(p)(q)[((x$ desires that $p)$ & $(x$ believes that (if $q$ then $p))$
& $(x$ is able to bring it about that $q))$
$\supset$ (barring conflicting desires or preferred strategies,
$x$ brings it about that $q)]^4$

Not only is folk psychology a theory, it is so *obviously* a theory that it must be held a major mystery why it has taken until the last half of the twentieth century for philosophers to realize it. The structural features of folk psychology parallel perfectly those of mathematical physics; the only difference lies in the respective domain of abstract entities they exploit — numbers in the case of physics, and propositions in the case of psychology.

Finally, the realization that folk psychology is a theory puts a new light on the mind-body problem. The issue becomes a matter of how the ontology of one theory (folk psychology) is, or is not, going to be related to the ontology of another theory (completed neuroscience); and the major philosophical positions on the mind-body problem emerge as so many different anticipations of what future research will reveal about the intertheoretic status and integrity of folk psychology.

The identity theorist optimistically expects that folk psychology will be smoothly *reduced* by completed neuroscience, and its ontology preserved by dint of transtheoretic identities. The dualist expects that it will prove *ir*reducible to completed neuroscience, by dint of being a nonredundant description of an autonomous, nonphysical domain of natural phenomena. The functionalist also expects that it will prove irreducible, but on the quite different grounds that the internal economy character-ized by folk psychology is not, in the last analysis, a law-governed economy of natural states, but an abstract organiz-ation of functional states, an organization instantiable in a variety of quite different material substrates. It is therefore irreducible to the principles peculiar to any of them.

Finally, the eliminative materialist is also pessimistic about the prospects for reduction, but his reason is that folk psychol-ogy is a radically inadequate account of our internal activities, too confused and too defective to win survival through inter-theoretic reduction. On his view it will simply be displaced by a better theory of those activities.

Which of these fates is the real destiny of folk psychology, we shall attempt to divine presently. For now, the point to keep in mind is that we shall be exploring the fate of a theory, a systematic, corrigible, speculative *theory*.

## Why folk psychology might (really) be false

Given that folk psychology is an empirical theory, it is at least an abstract possibility that its principles are radically false and that its ontology is an ilusion. With the exception of eliminative materialism, however, none of the major positions takes this possibility seriously. None of them doubts the basic integrity or truth of folk psychology (hereafter, 'FP'), and all of them anticipate a future in which its laws and categories are con-served. This conservatism is not without some foundation. After all, FP does enjoy a substantial amount of explanatory and predictive success. And what better grounds than this for confidence in the integrity of its categories?

What better grounds indeed? Even so, the presumption in FP's favor is spurious, born of innocence and tunnel vision. A more searching examination reveals a different picture. First, we must reckon not only with FP's success, but with its explanatory failures, and with their extent and seriousness. Second, we must consider the long-term history of FP, its growth, fertility, and current promise of future development. And third, we must consider what sorts of theories are *likely* to be true of the etiology of our behavior, given what else we have learned about ourselves in recent history. That is, we must evaluate FP with regard to its coherence and continuity with fertile and well-established theories in adjacent and overlapping domains – with evolutionary theory, biology, and neuroscience, for example – because active coherence with the rest of what we presume to know is perhaps the final measure of any hypothesis.

A serious inventory of this sort reveals a very troubled situation, one which would evoke open skepticism in the case of any theory less familiar and dear to us. Let me sketch some relevant detail. When one centers one's attention not on what FP can explain, but on what it cannot explain or fails even to address, one discovers that there is a very great deal. As examples of central and important mental phenomena that remain largely or wholly mysterious within the framework of FP, consider the nature and dynamics of mental illness, the faculty of creative imagination, or the ground of intelligence differences between individuals. Consider our utter ignorance of the nature and psychological functions of sleep, that curious state in which a third of one's life is spent. Reflect on the common ability to catch an outfield fly ball on the run, or hit a moving car with a snowball. Consider the internal construction of a 3-D visual image from subtle differences in the 2-D array of stimulations in our respective retinas. Consider the rich variety of perceptual illusions, visual and otherwise. Or consider the miracle of memory, with its lightning capacity for relevant retrieval. On these and many other mental phenomena, FP sheds negligible light.

One particularly outstanding mystery is the nature of the learning process itself, especially where it involves large-scale conceptual change, and especially as it appears in its pre-linguistic or entirely nonlinguistic form (as in infants and animals), which is by far the most common form in nature. FP is faced with special difficulties here, since its conception of learning as the manipulation and storage of propositional atti-tudes founders on the fact that how to formulate, manipulate, and store a rich fabric of propositional attitudes is itself some-thing that is learned, and is only one among many acquired cognitive skills. FP would thus appear constitutionally incapable of even addressing this most basic of mysteries.[5]

Failures on such a large scale do not (yet) show that FP is a false theory, but they do move that prospect well into the range of real possibility, and they do show decisively that FP is *at best* a highly superficial theory, a partial and unpenetrating gloss on a deeper and more complex reality. Having reached this opinion, we may be forgiven for exploring the possibility that FP provides a positively misleading sketch of our internal kinematics and dynamics, one whose success is owed more to selective application and forced interpretation on our part than to genuine theoretical insight on FP's part.

A look at the history of FP does little to allay such fears, once raised. The story is one of retreat, infertility, and decadence. The presumed domain of FP used to be much larger than it is now. In primitive cultures, the behavior of most of the elements of nature were understood in intentional terms. The wind could know anger, the moon jealousy, the river generosity, the sea fury, and so forth. These were not metaphors. Sacrifices were made and auguries undertaken to placate or divine the changing passions of the gods. Despite its sterility, this animistic approach to nature has dominated our history, and it is only in the last two or three thousand years that we have restricted FP's literal application to the domain of the higher animals.

Even in this preferred domain, however, both the content and the success of FP have not advanced sensibly in two or three thousand years. The FP of the Greeks is essentially the FP we use today, and we are negligibly better at explaining human behavior in its terms than was Sophocles. This is a very long period of stagnation and infertility for any theory to display, especially when faced with such an enormous backlog of anomalies and mysteries in its own explanatory domain. Perfect theories, perhaps, have no need to evolve. But FP is profoundly imperfect. Its failure to develop its resources and extend its range of success is therefore darkly curious, and one must query the integrity of its basic categories. To use Imre Lakatos' terms, FP is a stagnant or degenerating research program, and has been for millennia.

Explanatory success to date is of course not the only dimension in which a theory can display virtue or promise. A troubled or stagnant theory may merit patience and solicitude on other grounds; for example, on grounds that it is the only theory or theoretical approach that fits well with other theories about adjacent subject matters, or the only one that promises to reduce to or be explained by some established background theory whose domain encompasses the domain of the theory at issue. In sum, it may rate credence because it holds promise of theoretical integration. How does FP rate in this dimension?

It is just here, perhaps, that FP fares poorest of all. If we approach *homo sapiens* from the perspective of natural history and the physical sciences, we can tell a coherent story of his constitution, development, and behavioral capacities which encompasses particle physics, atomic and molecular theory, organic chemistry, evolutionary theory, biology, physiology, and materialistic neuroscience. That story, though still radically incomplete, is already extremely powerful, outperforming FP at many points even in its own domain. And it is deliberately and self-consciously coherent with the rest of our developing world picture. In short, the greatest theoretical synthesis in the history of the human race is currently in our hands, and parts of it already provide searching descriptions and explanations of human sensory input, neural activity, and motor control.

But FP is no part of this growing synthesis. Its intentional categories stand magnificently alone, without visible prospect of reduction to that larger corpus. A successful reduction cannot be ruled out, in my view, but FP's explanatory impotence and long stagnation inspire little faith that its categories will find themselves neatly reflected in the framework of neuroscience. On the contrary, one is reminded of how alchemy must have looked as elemental chemistry was taking form, how Aristotelean cosmology must have looked as classical mechanics was being articulated or how the vitalist conception of life must have looked as organic chemistry marched forward.

In sketching a fair summary of this situation, we must make a special effort to abstract from the fact that FP is a central part of our current *lebenswelt*, and serves as the principal vehicle of our interpersonal commerce. For these facts provide FP with a conceptual inertia that goes far beyond its purely theoretical virtues. Restricting ourselves to this latter dimension, what we must say is that FP suffers explanatory failures on an epic scale, that it has been stagnant for at least twenty-five centuries, and that its categories appear (so far) to be incommensurable with or orthogonal to the categories of the background physical science whose long-term claim to explain human behavior seems undeniable. Any theory that meets this description must be allowed a serious candidate for outright elimination.

We can of course insist on no stronger conclusion at this stage. Nor is it my concern to do so. We are here exploring a possibility, and the facts demand no more, and no less, than it be taken seriously. The distinguishing feature of the eliminative materialist is that he takes it very seriously indeed.

## Arguments against elimination

Thus the basic rationale of eliminative materialism: FP is a theory, and quite probably a false one; let us attempt, therefore to transcend it.

The rationale is clear and simple, but many find it uncompelling. It will be objected that FP is not, strictly speaking, an *empirical* theory; that it is not false, or at least not refutable by empirical considerations; and that it ought not or cannot be transcended in the fashion of a defunct empirical theory. In what follows we shall examine these objections as they flow from the most popular and best-founded of the competing positions in the philosophy of mind: functionalism.

An antipathy toward eliminative materialism arises from two distinct threads running through contemporary functionalism. The first thread concerns the *normative* character of FP, or at least of that central core of FP which treats of the propositional attitudes. FP, some will say, is a characterization of an ideal, or at least a praiseworthy mode of internal activity. It outlines not only what it is to have and process beliefs and desires, but also (and inevitably) what it is to be rational in their administration. The ideal laid down by FP may be imperfectly achieved by empirical humans, but this does not impugn FP as a normative characterization. Nor need such failures seriously impugn FP even as a descriptive characterization, for it remains true that our activities can be both usefully and accurately understood as rational *except for* the occasional lapse due to noise, interference, or other breakdown, which defects empirical research may eventually unravel. Accordingly, though neuroscience may usefully augment it, FP has no pressing need to be displaced, even as a descriptive theory; nor could it be replaced, qua normative characterization, by any descriptive theory of neural mechanisms, since rationality is defined over propositional attitudes like beliefs and desires. FP, therefore, is here to stay.

Daniel Dennett has defended a view along these lines.[6] And the view just outlined gives voice to a theme of the property dualists as well. Karl Popper and Joseph Margolis both cite the normative nature of mental and linguistic activity as a bar to their penetration or elimination by any descriptive/materialist theory.[7] I hope to deflate the appeal of such moves below.

The second thread concerns the *abstract* nature of FP. The central claim of functionalism is that the principles of FP characterize our internal states in a fashion that makes no reference to their intrinsic nature or physical constitution. Rather, they are characterized in terms of the network of causal relations they bear to one another, and to sensory circumstances and overt behavior. Given its abstract specification, that internal economy may therefore be realized in a nomically heterogeneous variety of physical systems. All of them may differ, even radically, in their physical constitution, and yet at another level, they will all share the same nature. This view, says Fodor, 'is compatible with very strong claims about the ineliminability of mental language from behavioral theories.'[8] Given the real possibility of multiple instantiations in heterogeneous physical substrates, we cannot eliminate the functional characterization in favor of any theory peculiar to one such substrate. That would preclude our being able to describe the (abstract) organization that any one instantiation shares with all the others. A functional characterization of our internal states is therefore here to stay.

This second theme, like the first, assigns a faintly stipulative character to FP, as if the onus were on the empirical systems to instantiate faithfully the organization that FP specifies, instead of the onus being on FP to describe faithfully the internal activities of a naturally distinct class of empirical systems. This impression is enhanced by the standard examples used to illustrate the claims of functionalism – mousetraps, valve-lifters, arithmetical calculators, computers, robots, and the like. These are artifacts, constructed to fill a preconceived bill. In such cases, a failure of fit between the physical system and the relevant functional characterization impugns only the former, not the latter. The functional characterization is thus removed from empirical criticism in a way that is most unlike the case of an

empirical theory. One prominent functionalist – Hilary Putnam
– has argued outright that FP is not a corrigible theory at all.[9]
Plainly, if FP is construed on these models, as regularly it is, the
question of its empirical integrity is unlikely ever to pose itself,
let alone receive a critical answer.

Although fair to some functionalists, the preceding is not
entirely fair to Fodor. On his view the aim of psychology is to
find the *best* functional characterization of ourselves, and what
that is remains an empirical question. As well, his argument for
the ineliminability of mental vocabulary from psychology does
not pick out current FP in particular as ineliminable. It need
claim only that *some* abstract functional characterization must
be retained, some articulation or refinement of FP perhaps.

His estimate of eliminative materialism remains low, however.
First, it is plain that Fodor thinks there is nothing fundamentally
or interestingly wrong with FP. On the contrary, FP's central
conception of cognitive activity – as consisting in the manipulation of propositional attitudes – turns up as the central element
in Fodor's own theory on the nature of thought (*The Language
of Thought, op. cit.*). And second, there remains the point that,
whatever tidying up FP may or may not require, it cannot be
displaced by any naturalistic theory of our physical substrate,
since it is the abstract functional features of his internal states
that make a person, not the chemistry of his substrate.

All of this is appealing. But almost none of it, I think, is right.
Functionalism has too long enjoyed its reputation as a daring
and *avant garde* position. It needs to be revealed for the short-
sighted and reactionary position it is.

## The conservative nature of functionalism

A valuable perspective on functionalism can be gained from the
following story. To begin with, recall the alchemists' theory of
inanimate matter. We have here a long and variegated tradition,
of course, not a single theory, but our purposes will be served
by a gloss.

The alchemists conceived the 'inanimate' as entirely continuous with animated matter, in that the sensible and behavioral
properties of the various substances are owed to the ensoulment
of baser matter by various spirits or essences. These nonmaterial
aspects were held to undergo development, just as we find

growth and development in the various souls of plants, animals, and humans. The alchemist's peculiar skill lay in knowing how to seed, nourish, and bring to maturity the desired spirits enmattered in the appropriate combinations.

On one orthodoxy, the four fundamental spirits (for 'inanimate' matter) were named 'mercury', 'sulphur', 'yellow arsenic', and 'sal ammoniac'. Each of these spirits was held responsible for a rough but characterisitc syndrome of sensible, combinatorial, and causal properties. The spirit mercury, for example, was held responsible for certain features typical of metallic substances – their shininess, liquefiability, and so forth. Sulphur was held responsible for certain residual features typical of metals, and for those displayed by the ores from which running metal could be distilled. Any given metallic substance was a critical orchestration principally of these two spirits. A similar story held for the other two spirits, and among the four of them a certain domain of physical features and transformations was rendered intelligible and controllable.

The degree of control was always limited, of course. Or better, such prediction and control as the alchemists possessed was owed more to the manipulative lore acquired as an apprentice to a master, than to any genuine insight supplied by the theory. The theory followed, more than it dictated, practice. But the theory did supply some rhyme to the practice, and in the absence of a developed alternative it was sufficiently compelling to sustain a long and stubborn tradition.

The tradition had become faded and fragmented by the time the elemental chemistry of Lavoisier and Dalton arose to replace it for good. But let us suppose that it had hung on a little longer – perhaps because the four-spirit orthodoxy had become a thumb-worn part of everyman's common sense – and let us examine the nature of the conflict between the two theories and some possible avenues of resolution.

No doubt the simplest line of resolution, and the one which historically took place, is outright displacement. The dualistic interpretation of the four essences – as immaterial spirits – will appear both feckless and unnecessary given the power of the corpuscularian taxonomy of atomic chemistry. And a reduction of the old taxonomy to the new will appear impossible, given the extent to which the comparatively toothless old theory cross-classifies things relative to the new. Elimination would thus appear the only alternative – *unless* some cunning and determined defender of the alchemical vision has the wit to suggest the following defense.

Being 'ensouled by mercury', or 'sulphur', or either of the other two so-called spirits, is actually a *functional* state. The first, for example, is defined by the disposition to reflect light, to liquefy under heat, to unite with other matter in the same state, and so forth. And each of these four states is related to the others, in that the syndrome for each varies as a function of which of the other three states is also instantiated in the same substrate. Thus the level of description comprehended by the alchemical vocabulary is abstract: various material substances, suitably 'ensouled', can display the features of a metal, for example, or even of gold specifically. For it is the total syndrome of occurrent and causal properties which matters, not the corpuscularian details of the substrate. Alchemy, it is concluded, comprehends a level of organization in reality distinct from and irreducible to the organization found at the level of corpuscularian chemistry.

This view might have had considerable appeal. After all, it spares alchemists the burden of defending immaterial souls that come and go; it frees them from having to meet the very strong demands of a naturalistic reduction; and it spares them the shock and confusion of outright elimination. Alchemical theory emerges as basically all right! Nor need they appear too obviously stubborn or dogmatic in this. Alchemy as it stands, they concede, may need substantial tidying up, and experience must be our guide. But we need not fear its naturalistic displacement, they remind us, since it is the particular orchestration of the syndromes of occurrent and causal properties which makes a piece of matter gold, not the idiosyncratic details of its corpuscularian substrate. A further circumstance would have made this claim even more plausible. For the fact is, the alchemists *did* know how to make gold, in this relevantly weakened sense of 'gold', and they could do so in a variety of ways. Their 'gold' was never as perfect, alas, as the 'gold' nurtured in nature's womb, but what mortal can expect to match the skills of nature herself?

What this story shows is that it is at least possible for the constellation of moves, claims, and defenses characterisitc of functionalism to constitute an outrage against reason and truth, and to do so with a plausibility that is frightening. Alchemy is a terrible theory, well-deserving of its complete elimination, and the defense of it just explored is reactionary, obfuscatory, retrograde and wrong. But in historical context, the defense might have seemed wholly sensible, even to reasonable people.

The alchemical example is a deliberately transparent case of what might well be called 'the functionalist stratagem', and other cases are easy to imagine. A cracking good defense of the phlogiston theory of combustion can also be constructed along these lines. Construe being highly phlogisticated and being dephlogisticated as functional states defined by certain syndromes of causal dispositions; point to the great variety of natural substrates capable of combustion and calxification; claim an irreducible functional integrity for what has proved to lack any natural integrity; and bury the remaining defects under a pledge to contrive improvements. A similar recipe will provide new life for the four humors of medieval medicine, for the vital essence or archeus of pre-modern biology, and so forth.

If its application in these other cases is any guide, the functionalist stratagem is a smokescreen for the preservation of error and confusion. Whence derives our assurance that in contemporary journals the same charade is not being played out on behalf of FP? The parallel with the case of alchemy is in all other respects distressingly complete, right down to the parallel between the search for artificial gold and the search for artificial intelligence!

Let me not be misunderstood on this last point. Both aims are worthy aims: thanks to nuclear physics, artificial (but real) gold is finally within our means, if only in submicroscopic quantities; and artificial (but real) intelligence eventually will be. But just as the careful orchestration of superficial syndromes was the wrong way to produce genuine gold, so may the careful orchestration of superficial syndromes be the wrong way to produce genuine intelligence. Just as with gold, what may be required is that our science penetrate to the underlying *natural* kind that gives rise to the total syndrome directly.

In summary, when confronted with the explanatory impotence, stagnant history, and systematic isolation of the intentional idioms of FP, it is not an adequate or responsive defense to insist that those idioms are abstract, functional, and irreducible in character. For one thing, this same defense could have been mounted with comparable plausibility no matter *what* haywire network of internal states our folklore had ascribed to us. And for another, the defense assumes essentially what is at issue: it assumes that it is the intentional idioms of FP, plus or minus a bit, that express the *important* features shared by all cognitive systems. But they may not. Certainly it is wrong to assume that they do, and then argue against the possibility of a materialistic displacement on grounds that it must describe matters at a level that is different from the important level. This just begs the question in favor of the older framework.

Finally, it is very important to point out that eliminative materialism is strictly *consistent* with the claim that the essence of a cognitive system resides in the abstract functional organization of its internal states. The eliminative materialist is not committed to the idea that the correct account of cognition *must* be a naturalistic account, though he may be forgiven for exploring the possibility. What he does hold is that the correct account of cognition, whether functionalistic or naturalistic, will bear about as much resemblance to FP as modern chemistry bears to four-spirit alchemy.

Let us now try to deal with the argument, against eliminative materialism, from the normative dimension of FP. This can be dealt with rather swiftly, I believe.

First, the fact that the regularities ascribed by the intentional core of FP are predicated on certain logical relations among propositions is not by itself grounds for claiming anything essentially normative about FP. To draw a relevant parallel, the fact that the regularities ascribed by the classical gas law are predicated on arithmetical relations between numbers does not imply anything essentially normative about the classical gas law. And logical relations between propositions are as much an objective matter of abstract fact as are arithmetical relations between numbers. In this respect, the law

(4) $(x)(p)(q)[((x \text{ believes that } p) \& (x \text{ believes that } (\text{if } p \text{ then } q)))$
 l (barring confusion, distraction, etc., $x$ believes that $q$)]

is entirely on par with the classical gas law

(6) $(x)(P)(V)(\mu)[((x \text{ has a pressure } P) \& (x \text{ has a volume } V)$
 $\& (x \text{ has a quantity } \mu))$

⊃ (barring very high pressure or density,

$x$ has a temperature of $PV/\mu R$)]

A normative dimension enters only because we happen to *value* most of the patterns ascribed by FP. But we do not value all of them. Consider

(7) $(x)(p)[(((x$ desires with all his heart that $p)$

& $(x$ learns that $\sim p))$

⊃ (barring unusual strength of character,

$x$ is shattered that $\sim p)]$

Moreover, and as with normative convictions generally, fresh insight may motivate major changes in what we value.

Second, the laws of FP ascribe to us only a very minimal and truncated rationality, not an ideal rationality as some have suggested. The rationality characterized by the set of all FP laws falls well short of an ideal rationality. This is not surprising. We have no clear or finished conception of ideal rationality anyway; certainly the ordinary man does not. Accordingly, it is just not plausible to suppose that the explanatory failures from which FP suffers are owed primarily to human failure to live up to the ideal standard it provides. Quite to the contrary, the conception of rationality it provides appears limping and superficial, especially when compared with the dialectical complexity of our scientific history, or with the ratiocinative virtuosity displayed by any child.

Third, even if our current conception of rationality – and more generally, of cognitive virtue – is largely constituted within the sentential/propositional framework of FP, there is no guarantee that this framework is adequate to the deeper and more accurate account of cognitive virtue which is clearly needed. Even if we concede the categorial integrity of FP, at least as applied to language-using humans, it remains far from clear that the basic parameters of intellectual virtue are to be found at the categorial level comprehended by the propositional attitudes. After all, language use is something that is learned, by a brain already capable of vigorous cognitive activity; language use is acquired as only one among a great variety of learned manipulative skills; and it is mastered by a brain that evolution has shaped for a great many functions, language use being only the very latest and perhaps the least of them. Against the background of these facts, language use appears as an extremely peripheral activity, as a racially idiosyncratic mode of social interaction which is mastered thanks to the versatility and power of a more basic mode of activity. Why accept then, a theory of cognitive activity that models its elements on the elements of human language? And why assume that the fundamental parameters of intellectual virtue are or can be defined over the elements at this superificial level?

A serious advance in our appreciation of cognitive virtue would thus seem to *require* that we go beyond FP, that we transcend the poverty of FP's conception of rationality by transcending its propositional kinematics entirely, by developing a deeper and more general kinematics of cognitive activity, and by distinguishing within this new framework which of the kinematically possible modes of activity are to be valued and encouraged (as more efficient, reliable, productive, or whatever). Eliminative materialism thus does not imply the end of our normative concerns. It implies only that they will have to be reconstituted at a more revealing level of understanding, the level that a matured neuroscience will provide.

What a theoretically informed future might hold in store for us, we shall now turn to explore. Not because we can foresee matters with any special clarity, but because it is important to try to break the grip on our imagination held by the propositional kinematics of FP. As far as the present section is concerned, we may summarize our conclusions as follows. FP is nothing more and nothing less than a culturally entrenched theory of how we and the higher animals work. It has no special features that make it empirically invulnerable, no unique functions that make it irreplaceable, no special status of any kind whatsoever. We shall turn a skeptical ear then, to any special pleading on its behalf.

## Beyond folk psychology

What might the elimination of FP actually involve – not just the comparatively straightforward idioms for sensation, but the entire apparatus of propositional attitudes? That depends heavily on what neuroscience might discover, and on our determination to capitalize on it. Here follow three scenarios in which the operative conception of cognitive activity is progressively divorced from the forms and categories that characterize natural language. If the reader will indulge the lack of actual substance, I shall try to sketch some plausible form.

First suppose that research into the structure and activity of the brain, both fine-grained and global, finally does yield a new kinematics and correlative dynamics for what is now thought of as cognitive activity. The theory is uniform for all terrestrial brains, not just human brains, and it makes suitable conceptual contact with both evolutionary biology and non-equilibrium thermodynamics. It ascribes to us, at any given time, a set or configuration of complex states, which are specified within the theory as figurative 'solids' within a four- or five-dimensional phase space. The laws of the theory govern the interaction, motion, and transformation of these 'solid' states within that space, and also their relations to whatever sensory and motor transducers the system possesses. As with celestial mechanics, the exact specification of the 'solids' involved and the exhaustive accounting of all dynamically relevant adjacent 'solids' is not practically possible, for many reasons, but here also it turns out that the obvious approximations we fall back on yield excellent explanations/predictions of internal change and external behavior, at least in the short term. Regarding long-term activity, the theory provides powerful and unified accounts of the learning process, the nature of mental illness, and variations in character and intelligence across the animal kingdom as well as across individual humans.

Moreover, it provides a straightforward account of 'knowledge', as traditionally conceived. According to the new theory, any declarative sentence to which a speaker would give confident assent is merely a one-dimensional *projection* – through the compound lens of Wernicke's and Broca's areas onto the idiosyncratic surface of the speaker's language – a one-dimensional projection of a four- or five-dimensional 'solid' that is an element in his true kinematical state. (Recall the shadows on the wall of Plato's cave.) Being projections of that inner reality, such sentences do carry significant information regarding it and are thus fit to function as elements in a communication system. On the other hand, being *sub*dimensional projections, they reflect but a narrow part of the reality projected. They are therefore *un*fit to represent the deeper reality in all its kinematically, dynamically, and even normatively relevant respects. That is to say, a system of propositional attitudes, such as FP, must inevitably fail to capture what is going on here, though it may reflect just enough superficial structure to sustain an alchemylike tradition among folk who lack any better theory. From the perspective of the newer theory, however, it is plain that there simply are no law-governed states of the kind FP postulates. The real laws governing our internal activities are defined over different and much more complex kinematical states and configurations, as are the normative criteria for developmental integrity and intellectual virtue.

A theoretical outcome of the kind just described may fairly be counted as a case of elimination of one theoretical ontology in favor of another, but the success here imagined for systematic neuroscience need not have any sensible effect on common practice. Old ways die hard, and in the absence of some practical necessity, they may not die at all. Even so, it is not inconceivable that some segment of the population, or all of it, should become intimately familiar with the vocabulary required to characterize our kinematical states, learn the laws governing their interactions and behavioral projections, acquire a facility in their first-person ascription, and displace the use of FP altogether, even in the marketplace. The demise of FP's ontology would then be complete.

We may now explore a second and rather more radical possibility. Everyone is familiar with Chomsky's thesis that the human mind or brain contains innately and uniquely the abstract structures for learning and using specifically human natural languages. A competing hypothesis is that our brain does indeed contain innate structures, but that those structures have as their original and still primary function the organization of perceptual experience, the administration of linguistic categories being an acquired and additional function for which evolution has only incidentally suited them.[10] This hypothesis has the advantage of not requiring the evolutionary saltation that Chomsky's view would seem to require, and there are other advantages as well. But these matters need not concern us here. Suppose, for our purposes, that this competing view is true, and consider the following story.

Research into the neural structures that fund the organization and processing of perceptual information reveals that they are capable of administering a great variety of complex tasks, some of them showing a complexity far in excess of that shown by natural language. Natural languages, it turns out, exploit only a very elementary portion of the available machinery, the bulk of which serves far more complex activities beyond the ken of the propositional conceptions of FP. The detailed unravelling of what that machinery is and of the capacities it has makes it plain that a form of language far more sophisticated than 'natural' language, though decidedly 'alien' in its syntactic and semantic structures, could also be learned and used by our innate systems. Such a novel system of communication, it is quickly realized, could raise the efficiency of information exchange between brains by an order of magnitude, and would enhance epistemic evaluation by a comparable amount, since it would reflect the underlying structure of our cognitive activities in greater detail than does natural language.

Guided by our new understanding of those internal structures, we manage to construct a new system of verbal communication entirely distinct from natural language, with a new and more powerful combinatorial grammar over novel elements forming novel combinations with exotic properties. The compounded strings of this alternative system – call them 'übersatzen' – are not evaluated as true or false, nor are the relations between them remotely analogous to the relations of entailment, etc., that hold between sentences. They display a different organization and manifest different virtues.

Once constructed, this 'language' proves to be learnable; it has the power projected; and in two generations it has swept the planet. Everyone uses the new system. The syntactic forms and semantic categories of so-called 'natural' language disappear entirely. And with them disappear the propositional attitudes of FP, displaced by a more revealing scheme in which (of course) 'übersatzenal attitudes' play the leading role. FP again suffers elimination.

This second story, note, illustrates a theme with endless variations. There are possible as many different 'folk psychologies' as there are possible differently structured communication systems to serve as models for them.

A third and even stranger possibility can be outlined as follows. We know that there is considerable lateralization of function between the two cerebral hemispheres, and that the two hemispheres make use of the information they get from each other by way of the great cerebral commissure – the corpus callosum – a giant cable of neurons connecting them. Patients whose commissure has been surgically severed display a variety of behavioral deficits that indicate a loss of access by one hemisphere to information it used to get from the other. However, in people with callosal agenesis (a congenital defect in which the connecting cable is simply absent), there is little or no behavioral deficit, suggesting that the two hemispheres have learned to exploit the information carried in other less direct pathways connecting them through the subcortical regions. This suggests that, even in the normal case, a developing hemisphere *learns* to make use of the information the cerebral commissure deposits at its doorstep. What we have then, in the case of a normal human, is two physically distinct cognitive systems (both capable of independent function) responding in a systematic and learned fashion to exchanged information. And what is especially interesting about this case is the sheer amount of information exchanged. The cable of the commissure consists of ≈ 200 million neurons,[11] and even if we assume that each of these fibres is capable of one of only two possible states each second (a most conservative estimate), we are looking at a channel whose information capacity is $> 2 \times 10^8$ binary bits/second. Compare this to the $< 500$ bits/second capacity of spoken English.

Now, if two distinct hemispheres can learn to communicate on so impressive a scale, why shouldn't two distinct brains learn to do it also? This would require an artifical 'commissure' of some kind, but let us suppose that we can fashion a workable transducer for implantation at some site in the brain that research reveals to be suitable, a transducer to convert a symphony of neural activity into (say) microwaves radiated from an aerial in the forehead, and to perform the reverse function of converting received microwaves back into neural activation. Connecting it up need not be an insuperable problem. We simply trick the normal processes of dendretic arborization into growing their own myriad connections with the active microsurface of the transducer.

Once the channel is opened between two or more people, they can learn (*learn*) to exchange information and coordinate their behavior with the same intimacy and virtuosity displayed by your own cerebral hemispheres. Think what this might do for hockey teams, and ballet companies, and research teams! If the entire population were thus fitted out, spoken language of any kind might well disappear completely, a victim of the 'why crawl when you can fly?' principle. Libraries become filled not with books, but with long recordings of exemplary bouts of neural activity. These constitute a growing cultural heritage, an evolving 'Third World', to use Karl Popper's terms. But they do not consist of sentences or arguments.

How will such people understand and conceive of other individuals? To this question I can only answer, 'In roughly the same fashion that your right hemisphere "understands" and "conceives of" your left hemisphere – intimately and efficiently, but not propositionally!'

These speculations, I hope, will evoke the required sense of untapped possibilities, and I shall in any case bring them to a close here. Their function is to make some inroads into the aura of inconceivability that commonly surrounds the idea that we might reject FP. The felt conceptual strain even finds expression in an argument to the effect that the thesis of eliminative materialism is incoherent since it denies the very conditions presupposed by the assumption that it is meaningful. I shall close with a brief discussion of this very popular move.

As I have received it, the reductio proceeds by pointing out that the statement of eliminative materialism is just a meaningless string of marks or noises, unless that string is the expression of a certain *belief*, and a certain *intention* to communicate, and a *knowledge* of the grammar of the language, and so forth. But if the statement of eliminative materialism is true, then there are no such states to express. The statement at issue would then be a meaningless string of marks or noises. It would therefore *not* be true. Therefore it is not true. Q.E.D.

The difficulty with any nonformal reductio is that the conclusion against the initial assumption is always no better than the material assumptions invoked to reach the incoherent conclusion. In this case the additional assumptions involve a certain theory of meaning, one that presupposes the integrity of FP. But formally speaking, one can as well infer, from the incoherent result, that this theory of meaning is what must be rejected. Given the independent critique of FP leveled earlier, this would even seem the preferred option. But in any case, one cannot simply assume that particular theory of meaning without begging the question at issue, namely, the integrity of FP.

The question-begging nature of this move is most graphically illustrated by the following analogue, which I owe to Patricia Churchland.[12] The issue here, placed in the seventeenth century, is whether there exists such a substance as *vital spirit*. At the time, this substance was held, without significant awareness of real alternatives, to be that which distinguished the animate from the inanimate. Given the monopoly enjoyed by this conception, given the degree to which it was integrated with many of our other conceptions, and given the magnitude of the revisions any serious alternative conception would require, the following refutation of any anti-vitalist claim would be found instantly plausible.

> The anti-vitalist says that there is no such thing as vital spirit. But this claim is self-refuting. The speaker can expect to be taken seriously only if his claim cannot. For if the claim is true, then the speaker does not have vital spirit and must be *dead*. But if he is dead, then his statement is a meaningless string of noises, devoid of reason and truth.

The question-begging nature of this argument does not, I assume, require elaboration. To those moved by the earlier argument, I commend the parallel for examination.

The thesis of this paper may be summarized as follows. The propositional attitudes of folk psychology do not constitute an unbreachable barrier to the advancing tide of neuroscience. On the contrary, the principled displacement of folk psychology is not only richly possible, it represents one of the most intriguing theoretical displacements we can currently imagine.

## References

1 An earlier draft of this paper was presented at the University of Ottawa, and to the *Brain, Mind, and Person* colloquium at SUNY/Oswego. My thanks for the suggestions and criticisms that have informed the present version.

2 See Paul Feyerabend, 'Materialism and the Mind-Body Problem', *Review* of *Metaphysics* XVII.1, 65 (September 1963): 49–66; Richard Rorty, 'Mind-Body Identity, Privacy, and Categories', *ibid.*, XIX.1, 73 (September 1965): 24–54; and my *Scientific Realism and the Plasticity of Mind* (New York: Cambridge, 1979).

3 We shall examine a handful of these laws presently. For a more comprehensive sampling of the laws of folk psychology, see my *Scientific Realism and Plasticity of Mind, op. cit.*, ch. 4. For a detailed examination of the folk principles that underwrite action explanations in particular, see my 'The Logical Character of Action Explanations', *Philosophical Review*, LXXIX, (April 1970): 214–236.

4 Staying within an objectual interpretation of the quantifiers, perhaps the simplest way to make systematic sense of expressions like $\diamond x$ believes that $p\diamond$ and closed sentences formed therefrom is just to construe whatever occurs in the nested position held by '$p$' '$q$', etc. as there having the function of a singular term. Accordingly, the standard connectives, as they occur between terms in that nested position, must be construed as there functioning as operators that form compound singular terms from other singular terms, and not as sentence operators. The compound singular terms so formed denote the appropriate compound propositions. Substitutional quantification will of course underwrite a different interpretation, and there are other approaches as well. Especially appealing is the prosentential approach of Dorothy Grover, Joseph Camp, and Nuel Belnap, 'A Prosentential Theory of Truth,' *Philosophical Studies*, XXVII, 2 (February 1975): 73–125. But the resolution of these issues is not vital to the present discussion.

5 A possible response here is to insist that the cognitive activity of animals and infants is linguaformal in its elements, structures, and processing right from birth. J. A. Fodor, in *The Language of Thought* (New York: Crowell 1975), has erected a positive theory of thought on the assumption that the innate forms of cognitive activity have precisely the form here denied. For a critique of Fodor's view, see Patricia Churchland, 'Fodor on Language Learning', *Synthese*, XXXVIII, 1 (May 1978): 149–159.

6 Most explicitly in 'Three Kinds of Intentional Psychology' (in *Reduction, Time and Reality*, cd., R. Healy, Cambridge University Press, 1981), but this theme of Dennett's goes all the way back to his 'Intentional Systems', *Journal of Philosophy*, LXVIII, 4 (Feb. 25, 1971): 87–106; reprinted in his *Brainstorms* (Montgomery, Vt.: Bradford Books, 1978).

7 Popper, *Objective Knowledge* (New York: Oxford, 1972); with J. Eccles, *The Self and Its Brain* (New York: Springer Verlag, 1978). Margolis, *Persons and Minds* (Boston: Reidel, 1978).

8 *Psychological Explanation* (New York: Random House, 1968), p. 116.

9 'Robots: Machines or Artificially Created Life?', *Journal of Philosophy*, LXI, 21 (Nov. 12, 1964): 668–691, pp. 675, 681 ff.

10  Richard Gregory defends such a view in 'The Grammar of Vision', *Listener*, LXXXIII, 2133 (February 1970): 242–246; reprinted in his *Concepts and Mechanisms of Perception* (London: Duckworth, 1975), pp. 622–629.

11  M. S. Gazzaniga and J. E. LeDoux, *The Integrated Mind* (New York: Plenum Press, 1975).

12  'Is Determinism Self-Refuting?', *Mind*, 90, 1981.

JERRY FODOR

# The Persistence of the Attitudes

*A Midsummer Night's Dream*, act 3, scene 2.

Enter Demetrius and Hermia.

*Dem.*   O, why rebuke you him that loves you so?
         Lay breath so bitter on your bitter foe.

*Herm.*  Now I but chide, but I should use thee worse;
         For thou, I fear, hast given me cause to curse.
         If thou hast slain Lysander in his sleep,
         Being o'er shoes in blood, plunge in the deep,
         And kill me too.
         The sun was not so true unto the day
         As he to me: would he have stol'n away
         From sleeping Hermia? I'll believe as soon
         This whole earth may be bor'd; and that the moon
         May through the centre creep, and so displease
         Her brother's noontide with the antipodes.
         It cannot be but thou hast murder'd him;
         So should a murderer look; so dead, so grim.

Very nice. And also very *plausible*; a convincing (though
informal) piece of implicit, nondemonstrative, theoretical
inference.

Here, leaving out a lot of lemmas, is how the inference must
have gone: Hermia has reason to believe herself beloved of
Lysander. (Lysander has told her that he loves her – repeatedly
and in elegant iambics – and inferences from how people say
they feel to how they do feel are reliable, ceteris paribus.) But if
Lysander does indeed love Hermia, then, a fortiori, Lysander
wishes Hermia well. But if Lysander wishes Hermia well, then
Lysander does not voluntarily desert Hermia at night in a
darkling wood. (There may be lions. 'There is not a more fearful
wild-fowl than your lion living.') But Hermia was, in fact, so

deserted by Lysander. Therefore not voluntarily. Therefore *in*voluntarily. Therefore it is plausible that Lysander has come to harm. At whose hands? Plausibly at Demetrius's hands. For Demetrius is Lysander's rival for the love of Hermia, and the presumption is that rivals in love do *not* wish one another well. Specifically, Hermia believes that Demetrius believes that a live Lysander is an impediment to the success of his (Demetrius's) wooing of her (Hermia). Moreover, Hermia believes (correctly) that if $x$ wants that $P$, and $x$ believes that not-$P$ unless $Q$, and $x$ believes that $x$ can bring it about that $Q$, then (ceteris paribus) $x$ tries to bring it about that $Q$. Moreover, Hermia believes (again correctly) that, by and large, people succeed in bringing about what they try to bring about. *So*: Knowing and believing all this, Hermia infers that perhaps Demetrius has killed Lysander. And we, the audience, who know what Hermia knows and believes and who share, more or less, her views about the psychology of lovers and rivals, understand how she has come to draw this inference. We sympathize.

In fact, Hermia has it all wrong. Demetrius is innocent and Lysander lives. The intricate theory that connects beliefs, desires, and actions – the implicit theory that Hermia relies on to make sense of what Lysander did and what Demetrius may have done; and that *we* rely on to make sense of Hermia's inferring what she does; and that Shakespeare relies on to predict and manipulate our sympathies ('*deconstruction' my foot*, by the way) – this theory makes no provision for nocturnal interventions by mischievous fairies. Unbeknownst to Hermia, a peripatetic sprite has sprung the ceteris paribus clause and made her plausible inference go awry. 'Reason and love keep little company together now-a-days: the more the pity that some honest neighbours will not make them friends.'

Granting, however, that the theory fails from time to time – and not just when fairies intervene – I nevertheless want to emphasize *(1) how often it goes right, (2) how deep it is, and (3) how much we do depend upon it*. Commonsense belief/desire psychology has recently come under a lot of philosophical pressure, and it's possible to doubt whether it can be saved in face of the sorts of problems that its critics have raised. There is, however, a prior question: whether it's worth the effort of trying to save it. That's the issue I propose to start with.

## How Often It Works

Hermia got it wrong; her lover was less constant than she had
supposed. Applications of commonsense psychology mediate
our relations with one another, and when its predictions fail
these relations break down. The resulting disarray is likely to
happen in public and to be highly noticeable.

*Herm.*   Since night you lov'd me; yet since night you left me;
          Why, then, you left me, – O, the gods forbid! –
          In earnest, shall I say?

*Lys.*    Ay, by my life,
          And never did desire to see thee more.
          Therefore be out of hope . . .

This sort of thing makes excellent theater; the *successes* of
common-sense psychology, by contrast, are ubiquitous and –
for that very reason – practically invisible.

Commonsense psychology works so well it disappears. It's
like those mythical Rolls Royce cars whose engines are sealed
when they leave the factory; only it's better because it isn't
mythical. Someone I don't know phones me at my office in New
York from – as it might be – Arizona. 'Would you like to lecture
here next Tuesday?' are the words that he utters. 'Yes, thank
you. I'll be at your airport on the 3 p.m. flight' are the words
that I reply. That's *all* that happens, but it's more than enough;
the rest of the burden of predicting behavior – of bridging the
gap between utterances and actions – is routinely taken up by
theory. And the theory works so well that several days later (or
weeks later, or months later, or years later; you can vary the
example to taste) and several thousand miles away, there I am
at the airport, and there he is to meet me. Or if I *don't* turn up,
it's less likely that the theory has failed than that something
went wrong with the airline. It's not possible to say, in quantitative terms, just how successfully commonsense psychology
allows us to coordinate our behaviors. But I have the impression
that we manage pretty well with one another; often rather better
than we cope with less complex machines.

The point – to repeat – is that the theory from which we get
this extraordinary predictive power is just good old common-

sense belief/desire psychology. That's what tells us, for example, how to infer people's intentions from the sounds they make (if someone utters the form of words 'I'll be at your airport on the 3 p.m. flight,' then, ceteris paribus, he intends to be at your airport on the 3 p.m. flight) and how to infer people's behavior from their intentions (if someone intends to be at your airport on the 3 p.m. flight, then, ceteris paribus, he will produce behavior of a sort which will eventuate in his arriving at that place at that time, barring mechanical failures and acts of God). And all this works not just with people whose psychology you know intimately: your closest friends, say, or the spouse of your bosom. It works with *absolute strangers*; people you wouldn't know if you bumped into them. And it works not just in laboratory conditions – where you can control the interacting variables – but also, indeed preeminently, in field conditions where all you know about the sources of variance is what commonsense psychology tells you about them. Remarkable. If we could do that well with predicting the weather, no one would ever get his feet wet; and yet the etiology of the weather must surely be child's play compared with the causes of behavior.

Yes, but what about all those ceteris paribuses? I commence to digress:

Philosophers sometimes argue that the appearance of predictive adequacy that accrues to the generalizations of commonsense psychology is spurious. For, they say, as soon as you try to make these generalizations explicit, you see that they have to be hedged about with ceteris paribus clauses; hedged about in ways that make them *trivially* incapable of disconfirmation. 'False or vacuous' is the charge.

Consider the defeasibility of 'if someone utters the form of words "I'll be at your airport on the 3 p.m. flight," then he intends to be at your airport on the 3 p.m. flight.' This generalization does *not* hold if, for example, the speaker is lying; or if the speaker is using the utterance as an example (of a false sentence, say); or if he is a monolingual speaker of Urdu who happens to have uttered the sentence by accident; or if the speaker is talking in his sleep; or ... whatever. You can, of course, defend the generalization in the usual way; you can say that '*all else being equal*, if someone utters the form of words "I'll be at your airport on the 3 p.m. flight," then he intends to be at your airport on the 3 p.m. flight.' But perhaps this last means nothing more than: 'if someone says that he intends to be there, then he does intend to be there – unless he doesn't.' That, of course, is predictively adequate for sure; nothing that happens will disconfirm it; nothing that happens could.

A lot of philosophers seem to be moved by this sort of argument; yet, even at first blush, it would be surprising if it were any good. After all, we do use commonsense psychological generalizations to predict one another's behavior; and the predictions do – very often – come out true. But how could that be so if the generalizations that we base the predictions on are *empty*?

I'm inclined to think that what is alleged about the implicit reliance of commonsense psychology on uncashed ceteris paribus clauses is in fact a perfectly general property of the *explicit* generalizations in *all* the special sciences; in all empirical explanatory schemes, that is to say, other than basic physics. Consider the following modest truth of geology: A meandering river erodes its outside bank. 'False or vacuous'; so a philosopher might argue. 'Take it straight – as a strictly universal generalization – and it is surely false. Think of the case where the weather changes and the river freezes; or the world comes to an end; or somebody builds a dam; or somebody builds a concrete wall on the outside bank; or the rains stops and the river dries up . . . or whatever. You can, of course, defend the generalization in the usual way – by appending a ceteris paribus clause: '*All else being equal*, a meandering river erodes its outside bank.' But perhaps this last means nothing more than: 'A meandering river erodes its outside bank – unless it doesn't.' That, of course, is predictively adequate for sure. Nothing that happens will disconfirm it; nothing that happens could.

Patently, something has gone wrong. For 'All else being equal, a meandering river erodes its outside bank' is neither false nor vacuous, and it doesn't mean 'A meandering river erodes its outside bank – unless it doesn't.' It is, I expect, a long story how the generalizations of the special sciences manage to be both hedged and informative (or, if you like, how they manage to support counterfactuals even though they have exceptions). Telling that story is part of making clear why we have special sciences at all; why we don't just have basic physics. It is also part of making clear how idealization works in science. For surely 'Ceteris paribus, a meandering river erodes its outside bank' means something like 'A meandering river erodes its outside bank in any nomologically possible world where the operative idealizations of geology are satisfied.' That this is, in general, stronger than '$P$ in any world where not not-$P$' is certain. So if, as it would appear, commonsense psychology relies upon its ceteris paribus clauses, so too does geology.

There is, then, a face similarity between the way implicit generalizations work in commonsense psychology and the way explicit generalizations work in the special sciences. But maybe this similarity is *merely* superficial. Donald Davidson is famous for having argued that the generalizations of real science, unlike those that underlie commonsense belief/desire explanations, are 'perfectible'. In the real, but not the intentional, sciences we can (in principle, anyhow) get rid of the ceteris paribus clauses by actually enumerating the conditions under which the generalizations are supposed to hold.

By this criterion, however, the only real science is basic physics. For it simply isn't true that we can, even in principle, specify the conditions under which – say – geological generalizations hold *so long as we stick to the vocabulary of geology*. Or, to put it less in the formal mode, the causes of exceptions to geological generalizations are, quite typically, not themselves *geological* events. Try it and see: 'A meandering river erodes its outer banks unless, for example, the weather changes and the river dries up.' But 'weather' isn't a term in *geology*; nor are 'the world comes to an end', 'somebody builds a dam', and indefinitely many other descriptors required to specify the sorts of things that can go wrong. All you can say that's any use is: If the generalization failed to hold, then the operative idealizations must somehow have failed to be satisfied. But so, too, in commonsense psychology: If he didn't turn up when he intended to, then something must have gone wrong.

Exceptions to the generalizations of a special science are typically *inexplicable* from the point of view of (that is, in the vocabulary of) that science. That's one of the things that makes it a *special* science. But, of course, it may nevertheless be perfectly possible to explain the exceptions *in the vocabulary of some other science*. In the most familiar case, you go 'down' one or more levels and use the vocabulary of a more 'basic' science. (The current failed to run through the circuit because the terminals were oxidized; he no longer recognizes familiar objects because of a cerebral accident. And so forth.) The availability of this strategy is one of the things that the hierarchical arrangement of our sciences buys for us. Anyhow, to put the point succinctly, the same pattern that holds for the special sciences seems to hold for commonsense psychology as well. On the one hand, its ceteris paribus clauses are ineliminable from the point of view of its proprietary conceptual resources. But, on the other hand, we have – so far at least – no reason to doubt that they can be discharged in the vocabulary of some lower-level science (neurology, say, or biochemistry; at worst, physics).

If the world is describable as a closed causal system at all, it is so only in the vocabulary of our most basic science. From this nothing follows that a psychologist (or a geologist) needs to worry about.

I cease to digress. The moral so far is that the predictive adequacy of commonsense psychology is beyond rational dispute; nor is there any reason to suppose that it's obtained by cheating. If you want to know where my physical body will be next Thursday, mechanics – our best science of middle-sized objects after all, and reputed to be pretty good in its field – is *no use to you at all*. Far the best way to find out (usually, in practice, the *only* way to find out) is: ask me!

## The Depth of the Theory

It's tempting to think of commonsense psychology as merely a budget of such truisms as one learns at Granny's knee: that the burnt child fears the fire, that all the world loves a lover, that money can't buy happiness, that reinforcement affects response rate, and that the way to a man's heart is through his stomach. None of these, I agree, is worth saving. However, as even the simple example sketched above serves to make clear, subsumption under platitudes is *not* the typical form of commonsense psychological explanation. Rather, when such explanations are made explicit, they are frequently seen to exhibit the 'deductive structure' that is so characteristic of explanation in real science. There are two parts to this: the theory's underlying generalizations are defined over unobservables, and they lead to its predictions by iterating and interacting rather than by being directly instantiated.

Hermia, for example, is no fool and no behaviorist; she is

perfectly aware both that Demetrius's behavior is caused by his mental states and that the pattern of such causation is typically intricate. There are, in particular, no plausible and counterfactual-supporting generalizations of the form $(x)(y)(x$ is a rival of $y) \rightarrow (x$ kills $y)$. Nothing like that is remotely true; not even ceteris paribus. Rather, the generalization Hermia takes to be operative – the one that *is* true and counterfactual-supporting – must be something like *If x is y's rival, then x prefers y's discomfiture, all else being equal*. This principle, however, doesn't so much as mention behavior; it leads to behavioral predictions, but only via a lot of further assumptions about how people's preferences may affect their actions in given situations. Or rather, since there probably are no generalizations which connect preferences to actions irrespective of beliefs, what Hermia must be relying on is an implicit theory of how beliefs, preferences, and behaviors interact; an implicit decision theory, no less.

It is a deep fact about the world that the most powerful etiological generalizations hold of unobservable causes. Such facts shape our science (they'd better!). It is thus a test of the depth of a theory that many of its generalizations subsume interactions among unobservables. By this test, our implicit, commonsense *meteorology* is presumably *not* a deep theory, since it consists largely of rule-of-thumb generalizations of the 'red at night, sailor's delight' variety. Correspondingly, the reasoning that mediates applications of commonsense meteorology probably involves not a lot more than instantiation and modus ponens. (All this being so, it is perhaps not surprising that commonsense meteorology doesn't work very well.) Commonsense psychology, by contrast, passes the test. It takes for granted that overt behavior comes at the end of a causal chain whose links are mental events – hence unobservable – and which may be arbitrarily long (and arbitrarily kinky). Like Hermia, we are all – quite literally, I expect – born mentalists and Realists; and we stay that way until common sense is driven out by bad philosophy.

## Its Indispensability

We have, in practice, no alternative to the vocabulary of commonsense psychological explanation; we have no other way of describing our behaviors and their causes if we want our behaviors and their causes to be subsumed by any counterfactual-supporting generalizations that we know about. This is, again, hard to see because it's so close.

For example, a few paragraphs back, I spoke of the commonsense psychological generalization *people generally do what they say that they will do* as bridging the gap between an exchange of utterances ('Will you come and lecture . . .', 'I'll be at your airport on Thursday . . .') and the consequent behaviors of the speakers (my arriving at the airport, his being there to meet me). But this understates the case for the indispensability of commonsense psychology, since without it we can't even describe the utterances as forms of words (to say nothing of describing the ensuing behaviors as kinds of acts). *Word* is a *psychological* category. (It is, indeed, *irreducibly* psychological, so far as anybody knows; there are, for example, no acoustic properties that all and only tokens of the same word type must share. In fact, surprisingly, there are no acoustic properties that all and only *fully intelligible* tokens of the same word type must share. Which is why our best technology is currently unable to build a typewriter that you can dictate to.)

As things now stand – to spell it out – we have *no* vocabulary for specifying event types that meets the following four conditions:

1. My behavior in uttering 'I'll be there on Thursday . . .' counts as an event of type $T_i$.
2. My arriving there on Thursday counts as an event of Type $T_j$.
3. 'Events of type $T_j$ are consequent upon events of type $T_i$' is even roughly true and counterfactual supporting.
4. Categories $T_i$ and $T_j$ are other than irreducibly psychological.

For the only known taxonomies that meet conditions 1–3 acknowledge such event types as uttering the *form of words* 'I'll be there on Thursday', or *saying that* one will be there on Thursday, or *performing the act* of meeting someone at the airport; so they fail condition 4.

Philosophers and psychologists used to dream of an alternative conceptual apparatus, one in which the commonsense inventory of types of *behavior* is replaced by an inventory of

types of *movements*; the counterfactual-supporting generalizations of psychology would then exhibit the contingency of these
movements upon environmental and/or organic variables. That
behavior is indeed contingent upon environmental and organic
variables is, I suppose, not to be denied; yet the generalizations
were not forthcoming. Why? There's a standard answer: It's
because behavior consists of actions, and actions cross-classify
movements. The generalization is that the burnt child avoids the
fire; but what movement constitutes avoidance depends on
where the child is, where the fire is . . . and so, drearily, forth. If
you want to know what generalizations subsume a behavioral
event, you have to know what *action type* it belongs to; knowing
what *motion type* it belongs to usually doesn't buy anything. I
take all that to be Gospel.

Yet is is generally assumed that this situation *must* be reme-
diable, at least in principle. After all, the generalizations of a
completed physics would presumably subsume every motion of
every thing, hence the motions of organisms *inter alia*. So, if we
wait long enough, we will after all have counterfactual-supporting generalizations that subsume the motions of organisms
*under that description*. Presumably, God has them already.

This is, however, a little misleading. For, the (putative)
generalizations of the (putative) completed physics would apply
to the motions of organisms qua motions, but not qua organ-
ismic. Physics presumably has as little use for the categories of
macrobiology as it does for the categories of commonsense
psychology; it dissolves the behav*er* as well as the behav*ior*.
What's left is atoms in the void. The subsumption of motions of
organisms – and of everything else – by the counterfactual-
supporting generalizations of physics does not therefore guarantee that there is any science whose ontology recognizes
organisms and their motions. That is: The subsumption of the
motions of organisms – and of everything else – by the laws of
physics does not guarantee that there are any laws about the
motions of organisms qua motions or organisms. So far as
anybody knows – barring, perhaps, a little bit of the psychology
of classical reflexes – there are no such laws; and there is no
metaphysical reason to expect any.[1]

Anyhow, this is all poppycock. Even if psychology were
dispensable *in principle*, that would be no argument for dispen-
sing with it. (Perhaps geology is dispensable in principle; every

river is a physical object after all. Would that be a reason for supposing that rivers aren't a natural kind? Or that 'meandering rivers erode their outside banks' is untrue?) What's relevant to whether commonsense psychology is worth defending is its dispensability *in fact*. And here the situation is absolutely clear. We have no idea of how to explain ourselves to ourselves except in a vocabulary which is *saturated* with belief/desire psychology. One is tempted to transcendental argument: What Kant said to Hume about physical objects holds, mutatis mutandis, for the propositional attitudes; we can't give them up *because we don't know how to*.[2]

So maybe we had better try to hold onto them. Holding onto the attitudes – vindicating commonsense psychology – means showing how you could have (or, at a minimum, showing *that* you could have) a respectable science whose ontology explicitly acknowledges states that exhibit the sorts of properties that common sense attributes to the attitudes. That is what the rest of this book is about. This undertaking presupposes, however, some consensus about what sorts of properties common sense does attribute to the attitudes. That is what the next bit of this chapter is about.

## The Essence of the Attitudes

How do we tell whether a psychology *is* a belief/desire psychology? How, in general, do we know if propositional attitudes are among the entities that the ontology of a theory acknowledges? These sorts of questions raise familiar and perplexing issues of intertheoretic identification. How do you distinguish elimination from reduction and reconstruction? Is the right story that there's no such thing as dephlogistinated matter, or is 'dephlogistinizing' just a word for oxidizing? Even behaviorists had trouble deciding whether they wanted to deny the existence of the mental or to assert its identity with the behavioral. (Sometimes they did both, in successive sentences. Ah, they really knew about insouciance in those days.)

I propose to stipulate. I will view a psychology as being common-sensical about the attitudes – in fact, as endorsing them – just in case it postulates states (entities, events, whatever) satisfying the following conditions:

    *(i)* They are semantically evaluable.
    *(ii)* They have causal powers.
    *(iii)* The implicit generalizations of commonsense belief/desire
         psychology are largely true of them.

In effect, I'm assuming that *(i)-(iii)* are the essential properties of the attitudes. This seems to me intuitively plausible; if it doesn't seem intuitively plausible to you, so be it. Squabbling about intuitions strikes me as vulgar.
    A word about each of these conditions.

## *(i) Semantic Evaluation*

Beliefs are the kinds of things that are true or false; desires are the kinds of things that get frustrated or fulfilled; hunches are the kinds of things that turn out to be right or wrong; so it goes. I will assume that what makes a belief true (/false) is something about its relation to the nonpsychological world (and not – e.g. – something about its relation to other beliefs; unless it happens to be a belief about beliefs). Hence, to say of a belief that it is true (/false) is to evaluate that belief in terms of its relation to the world. I will call such evaluations 'semantic'. Similarly, mutatis mutandis, with desires, hunches, and so forth.
    It is, as I remarked in the preface, a puzzle about beliefs, desires, and the like that they are semantically evaluable; almost nothing else is. (Trees aren't; numbers aren't; people aren't. Propositions *are* [assuming that there are such things], but that's hardly surprising; propositions exist to be what beliefs and desires are attitudes *toward*.) We will see, later in this book, that it is primarily the semantic evaluability of beliefs and desires that gets them into philosophical trouble – and that a defense of belief/desire psychology needs to be a defense of it.
    Sometimes I'll talk of the *content* of a psychological state rather than its semantic evaluability. These two ideas are intimately interconnected. Consider – for a change of plays – Hamlet's belief that his uncle killed his father. That belief has a certain semantic value; in particular, it's a *true* belief. Why true? Well, because it corresponds to a certain fact. Which fact? Well, the fact that Hamlet's uncle killed Hamlet's father. But why is it *that* fact that determines the semantic evaluation of Hamlet's belief? Why not the fact that two is a prime number, or the fact

that Demetrius didn't kill Lysander? Well, because the *content* of Hamlet's belief is *that* his uncle killed his father. (If you like, the belief 'expresses the proposition' that Hamlet's uncle killed his father.) *If you know what the content of a belief is, then you know what it is about the world that determines the semantic evaluation of the belief*; that, at a minimum, is how the notions of content and semantic evaluation connect.

I propose to say almost nothing more about content at this stage; its time will come. Suffice it just to add that propositional attitudes have their contents essentially: the canonical way of picking out an attitude is to say (a) what sort of attitude it is (a belief, a desire, a hunch, or whatever); and (b) what the content of the attitude is (that Hamlet's uncle killed his father; that 2 is a prime number; that Hermia believes that Demetrius dislikes Lysander; or whatever). In what follows, nothing will count as a propositional-attitude psychology – as a reduction or recon-struction or vindication of commonsense belief/desire expla-nation – that does not acknowledge states that can be individuated in this sort of way.

## (ii) Causal Powers

Commonsense psychological explanation is deeply committed to mental causation of at least three sorts: the causation of behavior by mental states; the causation of mental states by impinging environmental events (by 'proximal stimulation', as psychologists sometimes say); and – in some ways the most interesting commonsense psychological etiologies – the causa-tion of mental states by one another. As an example of the last sort, common sense acknowledges *chains of thought* as species of complex mental events. A chain of thought is presumably a *causal* chain in which one semantically evaluable mental state gives rise to another; a process that often terminates in the fixation of belief. (That, as you will remember, was the sort of thing Sherlock Holmes was supposed to be very good at.)

Every psychology that is Realist about the mental ipso facto acknowledges its causal powers.[3] Philosophers of 'functionalist' persuasion even hold that the causal powers of a mental state determine its identity (that for a mental state to be, as it might be, the state of believing that Demetrius killed Lysander is just for it to have a characteristic galaxy of potential and actual causal relations). This is a position of some interest to us, since if it is true – and if it is also true that propositional attitudes have their contents essentially – it follows that the causal powers of a mental state somehow determine its content. I do not, however, believe that it is true. More of this later.

What's important for now is this: It is characteristic of commonsense belief/desire psychology – and hence of any explicit theory that I'm prepared to view as vindicating commonsense belief/desire psychology – that it attributes contents and causal powers *to the very same mental things that it takes to be semantically evaluable*. It is Hamlet's belief that Claudius killed his father – the very same belief which is true or false in virtue of the facts about his father's death – that causes him to behave in such a beastly way to Gertrude.[4]

In fact, there's a deeper point to make. It's not just that, in a psychology of propositional attitudes, content and causal powers are attributed to the same things. It's also that causal relations among propositional attitudes somehow typically contrive to respect their relations of content, and belief/desire explanations often turn on this. Hamlet believed that somebody had killed his father because he believed that Claudius had killed his father. His having the second belief explains his having the first. How? Well, presumably via some such causal generalization as 'if someone believes *Fa*, then ceteris paribus he believes $Zx(Fx)$'. This generalization specifies a causal relation between two kinds of mental states picked out by reference to (the logical form of) the propositions they express; so we have the usual pattern of a simultaneous attribution of content and causal powers. The present point, however, is that the contents of the mental states that the causal generalization subsumes are themselves semantically related; *Fa entails $Zx(Fx)$*, so, of course, the semantic value of the latter belief is not independent of the semantic value of the former.

Or, compare the pattern of implicit reasoning attributed to Hermia at the beginning of this chapter. I suggested that she must be relying crucially on some such causal generalization as: 'If $x$ wants that $P$, and $x$ believes that not—$P$ unless $Q$, and $x$ believes that it is within his power to bring it about that $Q$, then ceteris paribus $x$ tries to bring it about that $Q$.' Common sense seems pretty clearly to hold that something like that is true and counterfactual supporting; hence that one has explained $x$'s attempt to bring it about that $Q$ if one shows that $x$ had beliefs and desires of the sort that the generalization specifies. What is absolutely typical is (a) the appeal to causal relations among semantically evaluable mental states as part and parcel of the explanation; and (b) the existence of content relations among the mental states thus appealed to.

Witness the recurrent schematic letters; they function precisely to constrain the content relations among the mental states that the generalization subsumes. Thus, unless, in a given case, what $x$ wants is the same as what $x$ believes that he can't have without $Q$, and unless what $x$ believes to be required for $P$ is the same as what he tries to bring about, the generalization isn't satisfied and the explanation fails. It is self-evident that the explanatory principles of commonsense psychology achieve generality by quantifying over agents (the 'practical syllogism' purports to apply, ceteris paribus, to all the $x$'s). But it bears emphasis that they also achieve generality by abstracting over *contents* ('If you want $P$ and you believe not-$P$ unless $Q$ . . . you try to bring it about that $Q$,' whatever the $P$ and $Q$ may be). The latter strategy works only because, very often, the same $P$'s and $Q$'s – the same contents – recur in causally related mental states; viz., only because causal relations very often respect semantic ones.

This parallelism between causal powers and contents engenders what is, surely, one of the most striking facts about the cognitive mind as commonsense belief/desire psychology conceives it: the frequent similarity between trains of thought and *arguments*. Here for example, is Sherlock Holmes doing his thing at the end of 'The Speckled Band':

I instantly reconsidered my position . . . it became clear to me that whatever danger threatened an occupant of the room couldn't come either from the window or the door. My attention was speedily drawn, as I have already remarked to you, to this ventilator, and to the bell-rope which hung down to the bed. The discovery that this was a dummy, and that the bed was clamped to the floor, instantly gave rise to the suspicion that the rope was there as a bridge for something passing through the hole, and coming to the bed. The idea of a snake instantly occurred to me, and when I coupled it with my knowledge that the Doctor was furnished with a supply of the creatures from India I felt that I was probably on the right track.

The passage purports to be a bit of reconstructive psychology: a capsule history of the sequence of mental states which brought Holmes first to suspect, then to believe, that the doctor did it with his pet snake. What is therefore interesting, for our purposes, is that Holmes's story isn't *just* reconstructive psychology. It does double duty, since it also serves to assemble *premises* for a plausible inference to the *conclusion* that the doctor did it with the snake. Because his train of thought is like an argument, Holmes expects Watson to be *convinced* by the considerations which, when they occurred to Holmes, caused his own conviction. What connects the causal-history aspect of Holmes's story with its plausible-inference aspect is the fact that the thoughts that fix the belief that $P$ provide, often enough, reasonable *grounds* for believing that $P$. Were this not the case – were there not this general harmony between the semantical and the causal properties of thoughts, so that, as Holmes puts it in another story, 'one true inference invariably suggests others' – there wouldn't after all, be much profit in thinking.

All this raises a budget of philosophical issues; just *what sorts* of content relations are preserved in the generalizations that subsume typical cases of belief/desire causation? And – in many ways a harder question – how could the mind be so constructed that such generalizations are true of it? What sort of mechanism could have states that are both semantically and causally connected, and such that the causal connections respect the semantic ones? It is the intractability of such questions that causes many philosophers to despair of commonsense psychology. But, of course, the argument cuts both ways: if the parallelism between content and causal relations is, as it seems to be, a deep fact about the cognitive mind, then unless we can save the notion of content, there is a deep fact about the cognitive mind that our psychology is going to miss.

## (iii) Generalizations Preserved

What I've said so far amounts largely to this; An explicit psychology that vindicates commonsense belief/desire explanations must permit the assignment of content to causally efficacious mental state and must recognize behavioral explanations in which covering generalizations refer to (or quantify over) the contents of the mental states that they subsume. I now add that the generalizations that are recognized by vindicating theory mustn't be *crazy* from the point of view of common sense; the causal powers of the attitudes must be, more or less, what common sense supposes that they are. After all, common-sense psychology won't be vindicated unless it turns out to be at least approximately true.

I don't, however, have a shopping list of commonsense generalizations that must be honored by a theory if it wants to be ontologically committed to bona fide propositional attitudes. A lot of what common sense believes about the attitudes must surely be false (a lot of what common sense believes about *anything* must surely be false). Indeed, one rather hopes that there will prove to be many more – and much odder – things in the mind than common sense had dreamed of; or else what's the fun of doing psychology? The indications are, and have been since Freud, that this hope will be abundantly gratified. For example, contrary to common sense, it looks as though much of what's in the mind is unconscious; and, contrary to common sense, it looks as though much of what's in the mind is unlearned. I retain my countenance, I remain self-possessed.

On the other hand, there is a lot of commonsense psychology that we have – so far at least – no reason to doubt, and that friends of the attitudes would hate to abandon. So, it's hard to imagine a psychology of action that is committed to the attitudes but doesn't acknowledge some such causal relations among beliefs, desires, and behavioral intentions (the 'maxims' of acts) as decision theories explicate. Similarly, it's hard to imagine a psycholinguistics (for English) which attributes beliefs, desires, communicative intentions, and such to speaker/hearers but fails to entail an infinity of theorems recognizably similar to these:

- 'Demetrius killed Lysander' is the form of words standardly used to communicate the belief that Demetrius killed Lysander.
- 'The cat is on the mat' is the form of words standardly used to communicate the belief that the cat is on the mat.
- 'Demetrius killed Lysander or the cat is on the mat' is the form of words standardly used to communicate the belief that Demetrius killed Lysander or the cat is on the mat.

And so on indefinitely. Indeed, it's hard to imagine a psycholinguistics that appeals to the propositional attitudes of speakers/

hearers of English to explain their verbal behavior but that doesn't entail that they *know* at least one such theorem for each sentence of their language. So there's an infinite amount of common sense for psychology to vindicate already.

Self-confident essentialism is philosophically fashionable this week. There are people around who have Very Strong Views ('modal intuitions', these views are called) about whether there could be cats in a world in which all the domestic felines are Martian robots, and whether there could be Homer in a world where nobody wrote the *Odyssey* or the *Iliad*. Ducky for them; their epistemic condition is enviable, but I don't myself aspire to it. I just don't know how much commonsense psychology would have to be true for there to be beliefs and desires. Let's say, some of it at a minimum; lots of it by preference. Since I have no doubt at all but that lots of it *is* true, this is an issue about which I do not stay up nights worrying.

## RTM

The main thesis of this book can now be put as follows: *We have no reason to doubt – indeed, we have substantial reason to believe – that it is possible to have a scientific psychology that vindicates commonsense belief/desire explanation*. But though that is my thesis, I don't propose to argue the case in quite so abstract a form. For there is already in the field a (more or less) empirical theory that is, in my view, reasonably construed as ontologically committed to the attitudes and that – again, in my view – is quite probably approximately true. If I'm right about this theory, it *is* a vindication of the attitudes. Since, moreover, it's the only thing of its kind around (it's the *only* proposal for a scientific belief/desire pscychology that's in the field), defending the commonsense assumptions about the attitudes and defending this theory turn out to be much the same enterprise; extensionally, as one might say.

That, in any event, is the strategy that I'll pursue: I'll argue that the sorts of objections philosophers have recently raised against belief/desire explanation are (to put it mildly) not conclusive against the best vindicating theory currently available. The rest of this chapter is therefore devoted to a sketch of how this theory treats the attitudes and why its treatment of the attitudes seems so promising. Since this story is now pretty well

known in both philosophical and psychological circles, I propose
to be quick.

What I'm selling is the Representational Theory of Mind
(hence RTM). At the heart of the theory is the postulation of a
language of thought: an infinite set of 'mental representations'
which function both as the immediate objects of propositional
attitudes and as the domains of mental processes. More precisely, RTM is the conjunction of the following two claims:

> *Claim 1* (the nature of propositional attitudes):
>
> For any organism O, and any attitude A toward the prop-
> osition P, there is a ('computational'/'functional') relation R
> and a mental representation MP such that
>
> MP means that P, and
>
> O has A iff [If and only if] O bears R to MP.

(We'll see presently that the biconditional needs to be watered
down a little; but not in a way that much affects the spirit of the
proposal.)

It's a thin line between clarity and pomposity. A cruder but
more intelligible way of putting claim 1 would be this: To
believe that such and such is to have a mental symbol that
means that such and such tokened in your head in a certain
way; it's to have such a token 'in your belief box', as I'll
sometimes say. Correspondingly, to hope that such and such is
to have a token of that same mental symbol tokened in your
head, but in a rather different way; it's to have it tokened 'in
your hope box'. (The difference between having the token in
one box or the other corresponds to the difference between the
causal roles of beliefs and desires. Talking about belief boxes
and such as a short-hand for representing the attitudes as
*functional* states is an idea due to Steve Schiffer.) And so on for
every attitude that you can bear toward a proposition; and so
on for every proposition toward which you can bear an attitude.

> *Claim 2* (the nature of mental processes):
>
> Mental processes are causal sequences of tokenings of mental
> representations.

A train of thoughts, for example, is a causal sequence of
tokenings of mental representations which express the propositions that are the objects of the thoughts. To a first approxi-

mation, to think 'It's going to rain; so I'll go indoors' is to have a tokening of a mental representation that means *I'll go indoors* caused, in a certain way, by a tokening of a mental representation that means *It's going to rain*.

So much for formulating RTM.

There are, I think, a number of reasons for believing that RTM may be more or less true. The best reason is that some version or other of RTM underlies practically all current psychological research on mentation, and our best science is ipso facto our best estimate of what there is and what it's made of. There are those of my colleagues in philosophy who do not find this sort of argument persuasive. I blush for them. (For a lengthy discussion of how RTM shapes current work on cognition, see Fodor, 1975, especially chapter 1. For a discussion of the connection between RTM and commonsense Intentional Realism – and some arguments that, given the latter, the former is practically mandatory – see the Appendix, Fodor, 1987.)

But we have a reason for suspecting that RTM may be true even aside from the details of its empirical success. I remarked above that there is a striking parallelism between the causal relations among mental states, on the one hand, and the semantic relations that hold among their propositional objects, on the other; and that very deep properties of the mental – as, for example, that trains of thought are largely truth preserving – turn on this symmetry. RTM suggests a plausible mechanism for this relation, and that is something that no previous account of mentation has been able to do. I propose to spell this out a bit; it helps make clear just *why* RTM has such a central place in the way that psychologists now think about the mind.

The trick is to combine the postulation of mental representations with the 'computer metaphor'. Computers show us how to connect semantical with causal properties for *symbols*. So, if having a propositional attitude involves tokening a symbol, then we can get some leverage on connecting semantical properties with causal ones for *thoughts*. In this respect, I think there really has been something like an intellectual breakthrough. Technical details to one side, this is – in my view – the only aspect of contemporary cognitive science that represents a major advance over the versions of mentalism that were its eighteenth- and nineteenth-century predecessors. Exactly what was wrong with Associationism, for example, was that there proved to be no

way to get a *rational* mental life to emerge from the sorts of
causal relations among thoughts that the 'laws of association'
recognized. (See the concluding pages of Joyce's *Ulysses* for a –
presumably inadvertent – parody of the contrary view.)

Here, in barest outline, is how the new story is supposed to
go: You connect the causal properties of a symbol with its
semantic properties *via its syntax*. The syntax of a symbol is one
of its higher-order physical properties. To a metaphorical first
approximation, we can think of the syntactic structure of a
symbol as an abstract feature of its shape.[5] Because, to all intents
and purposes, syntax reduces to shape, and because the shape
of a symbol is a potential determinant of its causal role, it is
fairly easy to see how there could be environments in which the
causal role of a symbol correlates with its syntax. It's easy, that
is to say, to imagine symbol tokens interacting causally *in virtue
of* their syntactic structures. The syntax of a symbol might
determine the causes and effects of its tokenings in much the
way that the geometry of a key determines which locks it will
open.

But, now, we know from modern logic that certain of the
semantic relations among symbols can be, as it were, 'mimicked'
by their syntactic relations; that, when seen from a very great
distance, is what proof-theory is about. So, within certain
famous limits, the semantic relation that holds between two
symbols when the proposition expressed by the one is entailed
by the proposition expressed by the other can be mimicked by
syntactic relations in virtue of which one of the symbols is
derivable from the other. We can therefore build machines
which have, again within famous limits, the following property:

> The operations of the machine consist entirely of transforma-
> tions of symbols;
>
> in the course of performing these operations, the machine is
> sensitive solely to syntactic properties of the symbols;
>
> and the operations that the machine performs on the symbols
> are entirely confined to altering their shapes.

Yet the machine is so devised that it will transform one symbol
into another if and only if the propositions expressed by the
symbols that are so transformed stand in certain *semantic*
relations – e.g., the relation that the premises bear to the

conclusion in a valid argument. Such machines – computers, of course – just *are* environments in which the syntax of a symbol determines its causal role in a way that respects its content. This is, I think, a perfectly terrific idea; not least because it works.

I expect it's clear how this is supposed to connect with RTM and ontological commitment to mental representations. Computers are a solution to the problem of mediating between the causal properties of symbols and their semantic properties. So *if* the mind is a sort of computer, we begin to see how you can have a theory of mental processes that succeeds where – literally – all previous attempts had abjectly failed; a theory which explains how there could be nonarbitrary content relations among causally related thoughts. But, patently, there are going to have to be mental representations if this proposal is going to work. In computer design, causal role is brought into phase with content by exploiting parallelisms between the syntax of a symbol and its semantics. But that idea won't do the theory of *mind* any good unless there are *mental* symbols: mental particulars possessed of both semantical and syntactic properties. There must be mental symbols because, in a nutshell, only symbols have syntax, and our best available theory of mental processes – indeed, the *only* available theory of mental processes that isn't *known* to be false – needs the picture of the mind as a syntax-driven machine.

It is sometimes alleged against commonsense belief/desire psychology, by those who admire it less than I do (see especially Churchland, this volume), that it is a 'sterile' theory; one that arguably hasn't progressed much since Homer and hasn't progressed at all since Jane Austen. There is, no doubt, a sense in which this charge is warranted; commonsense psychology may be implicit science, but it isn't, on anybody's story, implicit *research* science. (What novelists and poets do doesn't count as research by the present austere criteria.) If, in short, you want to evaluate progress, you need to look not at the implicit commonsense theory but at the best candidate for its explicit vindication. And here the progress has been enormous. It's not just that we now know a little about memory and perception (qua means to the fixation of belief), and a little about language (qua means to the communication of belief); see any standard psychology text. The real achievement is that we are (maybe) on the verge of solving a great mystery about the mind: *How could*

*its causal processes be semantically coherent?* Or, if you like
yours with drums and trumpets: *How is rationality mechanically
possible?*[6] Notice that this sort of problem can't even be stated,
let alone solved, unless we suppose – just as commonsense belief/
desire psychology wants us to – that there are mental states with
both semantic contents and causal roles. A good theory is one
that leads you to ask questions that have answers. And vice
versa, ceteris paribus.

Still, RTM won't do in quite the raw form set forth above. I
propose to end this chapter with a little polishing.

According to claim 1, RTM requires both the following:

For each tokening of a propositional attitude, there is a
tokening of a corresponding relation between an organism
and a mental representation;

and

For each tokening of that relation, there is a corresponding
tokening of a propositional attitude.[7]

This is, however, much too strong; the equivalence fails in both
directions.

As, indeed, we should expect it to, given our experience in
other cases where explicit science co-opts the conceptual apparatus of common sense. For example, as everybody points out,
it is simply not true that chemistry identifies each sample of
water with a sample of $H_2O$; not, at least, if the operative notion
of water is the commonsense one according to which what we
drink, sail on, and fill our bathtubs with all qualifies. What
chemistry does is reconstruct the commonsense categories *in
what the theory itself identifies as core cases; chemically pure*
water is $H_2O$. The ecological infrequency of such core cases is,
of course, no argument against the claim that chemical science
vindicates the commonsense taxonomy: Common sense was
right about there being such stuff as water, right about there
being water in the Charles River, and right again that it's the
water in what we drink that quenches our thirst. It never said
that the water in the Charles is chemically pure; 'chemically
pure' isn't a phrase in the commonsense vocabulary.

Exactly similarly, RTM vindicates commonsense psychology
for what RTM identifies as the core cases; in those cases, what
common sense takes to be tokenings of propositional attitudes

are indeed tokenings of a relation between an organism and a mental representation. The other cases – where you get either attitude tokenings without the relation or relation tokenings without the attitudes – the theory treats as derivative. This is all, I repeat, *exactly* what you'd expect from scientific precedent. Nevertheless, philosophers have made an awful fuss about it in discussing the vindication of the attitudes (see the controversy over the 'explicit representation' – or otherwise – of grammars recently conducted by, among others, Stabler, E., 'How are Grammars Represented?' and Demopoulos, N., and Matthews, R., 'On the Hypothesis that Grammars are Mentally Represented', both in *Behavioral and Brain Sciences*, 3, 1983). So let's consider the details awhile. Doing so will lead to a sharpening of claim 1, which is all to the good.

## Case 1. Attitudes without Mental Representations

Here's a case from Dennett:

> In a recent conversation with the designer of a chess-playing program I heard the following criticism of a rival program: 'It thinks it should get its queen out early.' This ascribes a propositional attitude to the program in a very useful and predictive way, for as the designer went on to say, one can usually count on chasing that queen around the board. But for all the many levels of explicit representation to be found in that program, nowhere is anything roughly synonymous with 'I should get my queen out early' explicitly tokened. The level of analysis to which the designer's remark belongs describes features of the program that are, in an entirely innocent way, emergent properties of the computational processes that have 'engineering reality'. I see no reason to believe that the relation between belief/talk and psychological-process talk will be any more direct (Dennett, 1979, p. 107; See also Matthews, R., 'Troubles with Representationalism', *Social Research*, 51(4), 1984).

Notice that the problem Dennett raises isn't just that some of what common sense takes to be one's propositional attitudes are *dispositional*. It's not like the worry that I might now be said to believe some abstruse consequence of number theory – one that I have, commonsensically speaking, never even thought of – because I *would* accept the proof of the theorem *if* I were shown it. It's true, of course, that merely dispositional beliefs couldn't correspond to *occurrent* tokenings of relations to mental representations, and claim 1 must therefore be reformulated. But the problem is superficial, since the relevant revision of claim 1 would be pretty obvious; viz., that for each *occurrent* belief there is a corresponding *occurrent* tokening of a mental representation; and for each *dispositional* belief there is a corresponding *disposition* to token a mental representation.

This would leave open a question that arises independent of one's views about RTM: viz., when are attributions of dispositional beliefs *true*? I suppose that one's dispositional beliefs could reasonably be identified with the closure of one's occurrent beliefs under principles of inference that one explicitly accepts. And, if it's a little vague just what beliefs belong to such a closure, RTM could live with that. *Qua dispositional*, attitudes play no causal role in *actual* mental processes; only occurrent attitudes – for that matter, only occurrent *anythings* – are actual causes. So RTM can afford to be a little operationalist about merely dispositional beliefs (see Lycan, William G., 'Tacit Belief', in Bogdan, R., (ed.) *Belief: Form, Content and Function*, Clarendon Press, 1986) so long as it takes a hard line about occurrent ones.

However, to repeat, the problem raised in Dennett's text is not of this sort. It's not that the program believes 'get your queen out early' *potentially*. Dennett's point is that the program actually operates on this principle; but not in virtue of any tokening of any symbol that expresses it. And chess isn't, of course, the only sort of case. Behavioral commitment to modus ponens, or to the syntactic rule of 'wh'-movement, *might* betoken that these are inscribed in brain writing. But it needn't, since these rules might be – as philosophers sometimes say – complied with but not literally followed.

In Dennett's example, you have an attitude being, as it were, an emergent out of its own implementation. This way of putting it might seem to suggest a way of saving claim 1: The machine doesn't explicitly represent 'get your queen out early', but at least we may suppose that it *does* represent, explicitly, some more detailed rules of play (the ones that Dennett says have 'engineering reality'). For these rules, at least, a strong form of claim 1 would thus be satisfied. But that suggestion won't work either. *None* of the principles in accordance with which a computational system operates need be explicitly represented by a formula tokened in the device; there is no guarantee that the program of a machine will be explicitly represented in the machine whose program it is. (See Cummins, R., 'The Internal Model of Psychological Explanation', *Cognition and Brain Theory*, 5(3), 1982; roughly, the point is that for any machine that computes a function by executing an explicit algorithm, there exists another machine – one that's 'hard-wired' – that computes the same function but *not* by executing an explicit algorithm.) So what, you might wonder, does the 'computer metaphor' buy for RTM after all?

There is even a point of principle here – one that is sometimes read in (or into) Lewis Carroll's dialogue between Achilles and the Tortoise: Not all the rules of inference that a computational system runs on *can* be represented *just* explicitly in the system; some of them have to be, as one says, 'realized in the hardware'. Otherwise the machine won't run at all. A computer in which the principles of operation are *only* explicitly represented is just like a blackboard on which the principles have been written down. It has Hamlet's problem: When you turn the thing on, nothing happens.

Since this is all clearly correct and arguably important, the question arises how to state RTM so that these cases where programs are hardwired don't count as disconfirmations of claim 1. We'll return to this momentarily; first let's consider:

## Case 2. Mental Representations without Attitudes

What RTM borrows from computers is, in the first instance, the recipe for mechanizing rationality: Use a syntactically driven machine to exploit parallelisms between the syntactic and semantic properties of symbols. Some – but not all – versions of RTM borrow more than this; not just a theory of rationality but a theory of intelligence too. According to this story, intelligent behavior typically exploits a 'cognitive architecture' constituted of *hierarchies* of symbol processors. At the top of such a hierarchy might be a quite complex capacity: solving a problem, making a plan, uttering a sentence. At the bottom, however, are only the sorts of unintelligent operations that Turing machines can perform: deleting symbols, storing symbols, copying symbols, and the rest. Filling in the middle levels is tantamount to reducing – analyzing – an intelligent capacity into a complex of dumb ones; hence to a kind of explanation of the former.

Here's a typical example of a kind of representational theory that runs along these lines:

> This is the way we tie our shoes. There is a little man who lives in one's head. The little man keeps a library. When one acts upon the intention to tie one's shoes, the little man fetches down a volume entitled *Tying One's Shoes*. The volume says such things as: 'Take the left free end of the shoelace in the left hand. Cross the left free end of the shoelace over the right free end of the shoelace . . .,'etc. . . . When the little man reads 'take the left free end of the shoelace in the left hand', we imagine him ringing up the shop foreman in charge of grasping shoelaces. The shop foreman goes about supervising that activity in a way that is, in essence, a microcosm of tying one's shoe. Indeed, the shop foreman might be imagined to superintend a detail of wage slaves, whose functions include: searching representations of visual inputs for traces of shoelace, dispatching orders to flex and contract fingers on the left hand, etc. (Fodor, 1981, Chapter 2, pp. 63–4).

At the very top are states which may well correspond to the propositional attitudes that common sense is prepared to acknowledge (knowing how to tie one's shoes, thinking about shoe tying). But at the bottom and middle levels there are bound to be lots of symbol-processing operations that correspond to nothing that *people* – as opposed to their nervous systems – ever do. These are the operations of what Dennett has called 'sub-personal' computational systems; and though they satisfy the present formulation of claim 1 (in that they involve causally efficacious tokenings of mental representations), yet it's unclear that they correspond to anything that common sense would count as the tokening of an attitude. But then how are we to formulate claim 1 so as to avoid disconfirmation by subpersonal information processes?

## Vindication Vindicated

There is a sense in which these sorts of objections to claim 1 strike me as not very serious. As I remarked above, the vindication of belief/desire explanation by RTM does *not* require that every case common sense counts as the tokening of an attitude should correspond to the tokening of a mental representation, or vice versa. All that's required is that such correspondences should obtain in what the vindicating theory itself takes to be the core cases. On the other hand, RTM had better be able to say which cases it does count as core. Chemistry is allowed to hold the Charles River largely irrelevant to the confirmation of 'water is $H_2O$', but only because it provides independent grounds for denying that what's in the Charles is a chemically pure sample. Of anything!

So, what are the core cases for RTM? The answer should be clear from claim 2. According to claim 2, mental processes are causal sequences of transformations of mental representations. It follows that tokenings of attitudes *must* correspond to tokenings of mental representations when they – the attitude tokenings – are episodes in mental processes. If the intentional objects of such causally efficacious attitude tokenings are *not* explicitly represented, then RTM is simply false. I repeat for emphasis: If the occurrence of a thought is an episode in a mental process, then RTM is committed to the explicit representation of its content. The motto is therefore No Intentional Causation without Explicit Representation.

Notice that this way of choosing core cases squares us with the alleged counterexamples. RTM says that the contents of a sequence of attitudes that constitutes a mental process must be expressed by explicit tokenings of mental representations. But the rules that determine the course of the transformation of these representations – modus ponens, 'wh'-movement, 'get the queen out early', or whatever – need not themselves ever be explicit. They can be emergents out of explicitly represented procedures of implementation, or out of hardware structures, or both. Roughly: According to RTM, programs – corresponding to the 'laws of thought' – *may* be explicitly represented; but 'data structures' – corresponding to the contents of thoughts – *have to be*.

Thus, in Dennett's chess case, the rule 'get it out early' may or may not be expressed by a 'mental' (/program language) symbol. That depends on just how the machine works; specifically, on whether *consulting* the rule is a step in the machine's operations. I take it that in the machine that Dennett has in mind, it isn't; *entertaining the thought 'Better get the queen out early' never constitutes an episode in the mental life of that machine*.[8] But then, the intentional content of this thought need *not* be explicitly represented consonant with 'no intentional causation without explicit representation' being true. By contrast, the representations of the board – of actual or possible states of play – over which the machine's computations are defined *must* be explicit, precisely *because* the machine's computations *are* defined over them. These computations constitute the machine's 'mental processes', so either they are causal sequences of explicit representations, or the representational theory of chess playing is simply false of the machine. To put the matter in a nutshell: Restricting one's attention to the status of rules and programs can make it seem that the computer metaphor is neutral with respect to RTM. But when one thinks about the constitution of mental processes, the connection between the idea that they are computational and the idea that there is a language of thought becomes immediately apparent.[9]

What about the subpersonal examples, where you have mental representation tokenings without attitude tokenings? Commonsense belief/desire explanations are vindicated if scientific psychology is ontologically committed to beliefs and desires. But it's *not* also required that the folk-psychological inventory of propositional attitudes should turn out to exhaust a natural kind. It would be astounding if it did; how could common sense know all that? What's important about RTM – what makes RTM a vindication of intuitive belief/desire psychology – isn't that it picks out a kind that is precisely coextensive with the propositional attitudes. It's that RTM shows how intentional states could have causal powers; precisely the aspect of commonsense intentional realism that seemed most perplexing from the metaphysical point of view.

Molecular physics vindicates the intuitive taxonomy of middle-sized objects into liquids and solids. But the nearest kind to the liquids that molecular physics acknowledges includes some of what common sense would not; glass, for example. So what?

So much for RTM; so much for this chapter, too. There is a strong prima facie case for commonsense belief/desire explanation. Common sense would be vindicated if some good theory of the mind proved to be committed to entities which – like the attitudes – are both semantically evaluable and etiologically involved. RTM looks like being a good theory of the mind that is so committed; so if RTM is true, common sense is vindicated. It goes without saying that RTM needs to make an empirical case; we need good accounts, independently confirmed, of mental processes as causal sequences of transformations of mental representations. Modern cognitive psychology is devoted, practically in its entirety, to devising and confirming such accounts. For present purposes, I shall take all that as read. What the rest of this book is about is doubts about RTM that turn on its *semantic* assumptions. This is home ground for philosophers, and increasingly the natives are restless.

## References

1 Perhaps there are laws that relate the *brain states* of organisms to their motions. But then again, perhaps there aren't, since it seems entirely possible that the lawful connections should hold between brain states and *actions* where, as usual, actions cross-classify movements. This is, perhaps, what you would predict upon reflection. Would you really expect the same brain state that causes the utterances of 'dog' in tokens of 'dog' to be the one that causes it in tokens of 'dogmatic'? How about utterances of (the phonetic sequence) [empedokliz lipt] when you're talking English and when you're talking German?

2 The trouble with transcendental arguments being, however, that it's not obvious why a theory couldn't be both indispensable and *false*. I wouldn't want to buy a transcendental deduction of the attitudes if operationalism were the price I had to pay for it.

3 Denying the etiological involvement of mental states was really what behaviorism was about; it's what 'logical' behaviorists and 'eliminativists' had in common. Thus, for example, to hold – as Ryle did, more or less – that mental states are species of dispositions is to refuse to certify as literally causal such psychological explanations as 'He did it with the intention of pleasing her,' or, for that matter, 'His headache made him groan,' to say nothing of 'The mere thought of giving a lecture makes him ill.' (For discussion, see Fodor, 'Something on the State of the Art', Introduction to *Representations*, Cambridge, Massachusetts: MIT Press, 1981.)

4 Some philosophers feel very strongly about enforcing an object/state (or maybe object/event) distinction here, so that what have *causal powers* are tokenings of mental state types (e.g., Hamlet's *believing*

that Claudius killed his father), but what have *semantic values* are *propositions* (e.g., the proposition that Claudius killed Hamlet's father). The point is that it sounds odd to say that Hamlet's *believing* that P is true but all right to say that Hamlet's *belief* that P is.

I'm not convinced that this distinction is one that I will care about in the long run, since sounding odd is the least of my problems and in the long run I expect I want to do without propositions altogether. However, if you are squeamish about ontology, that's all right with me. In that case, the point in the text should be: Belief/desire psychology attributes causal properties to the very same things (viz., tokenings of certain mental state types) to which it attributes propositional objects. It is thus true of Hamlet's believing that Claudius killed his father both that it is implicated in the etiology of his behavior Gertrudeward and that it has as its object a certain belief, viz., the proposition that Claudius killed his father. If we then speak of Hamlet's *state* of believing that Claudius killed his father (or of the event which consists of the tokening of that state) as semantically evaluable, we can take that as an abbreviation for a more precise way of talking. The state S has the semantic value V if S has as its object a proposition whose value is V.

It goes without saying that none of this ontological fooling around makes the slightest progress toward removing the puzzles about intentionality. If (on my way of talking) it's metaphysically worrying that beliefs and desires are semantically evaluable though trees, rocks, and prime numbers aren't, it's equally metaphysically worrying (on the orthodox way of talking) that believings have propositional objects though trees, rocks and prime numbers don't.

5 *Any* nomic property of symbol tokens, however – any property in virtue of the posession of which they satisfy causal laws – would, in principle, do just as well. (So, for example, syntactic structure could be realized by relations among electromagnetic states rather than relations among shapes; as, indeed, it is in real computers.) This is the point of the Functionalist doctrine that, in principle, you can make a mind out of almost anything.

6 Which is not to deny that there are (ahem!) certain residual technical difficulties. (See, for example, part 4 of Fodor, *The Modularity of Mind* [Cambridge, Massachusetts: MIT Press, 1983].) A theory of rationality (i.e., a theory of *our* rationality) has to account not merely for the 'semantic coherence' of thought processes in the abstract but for our ability to pull off the very sorts of rational inferences that we do. (It has to account for our ability to make science, for example.) No such theory will be available by this time next week.

7 Because I don't want to worry about the ontology of mind, I've

avoided stating RTM as an identity thesis. But you could do if you were so inclined.

8 Like Dennett, I'm assuming for purposes of argument that the machine *has* thoughts and mental processes; nothing hangs on this, since we could, of course, have had the same discussion about people.

9 We can now see what to say about the philosophical chestnut about Kepler's Law. The allegation is that intentionalist methodology permits the inference from 'x's behavior complies with rule R' to 'R is a rule that x explicitly represents.' The embarrassment is supposed to be that this allows the inference from 'The movements of the planets comply with Kepler's Law' to some astronomical version of LOT [the Language of Thought Hypothesis].

But in fact no such principle of inference is assumed. What warrants the hypothesis that R is explicitly represented is not mere behavior in compliance with R; it's an etiology according to which R figures as the content of one of the intentional states whose tokenings are causally responsible for x's behavior. And, of course, it's *not* part of the etiological story about the motions of the planets that Kepler's Law occurs to them as they proceed upon their occasions.

COLIN MCGINN

# Can We Solve the Mind–Body Problem?

*How it is that anything so remarkable as a state of consciousness comes about as a result of initiating nerve tissue, is just as unaccountable as the appearance of the Djin, where Aladdin rubbed his lamp in the story . . .*

Julian Huxley

We have been trying for a long time to solve the mind-body problem. It has stubbornly resisted our best efforts. The mystery persists. I think the time has come to admit candidly that we cannot resolve the mystery. But I also think that this very insolubility – or the reason for it – removes the philosophical problem. In this paper I explain why I say these outrageous things.

The specific problem I want to discuss concerns consciousness, the hard nut of the mind-body problem. How is it possible for conscious states to depend upon brain states? How can technicolour phenomenology arise from soggy grey matter? What makes the bodily organ we call the brain so radically different from other bodily organs, say the kidneys – the body parts without a trace of consciousness? How could the aggregation of millions of individually insentient neurons generate subjective awareness? We know that brains are the *de facto* causal basis of consciousness, but we have, it seems, no understanding whatever of how this can be so. It strikes us as miraculous, eerie, even faintly comic. Somehow, we feel, the water of the physical brain is turned into the wine of consciousness, but we draw a total blank on the nature of this conversion. Neural transmissions just seem like the wrong kind of materials with which to bring consciousness into the world, but it appears that in some way they perform this mysterious feat. The mind-body problem is the problem of understanding how the miracle is wrought, thus removing the sense of deep mystery. We want to take the magic out of the link between consciousness and the brain.[1]

Purported solutions to the problem have tended to assume one or two forms. One form, which we may call constructive, attempts to specify some natural property of the brain (or body) which explains how consciousness can be elicited from it. Thus functionalism, for example, suggests a property – namely, causal role – which is held to be satisfied by both brain states and mental states; this property is supposed to explain how conscious states can come from brain states.[2] The other form, which has been historically dominant, frankly admits that nothing merely natural could do the job, and suggests instead that we invoke supernatural entities or divine interventions. Thus we have Cartesian dualism and Leibnizian pre-established harmony. These 'solutions' at least recognize that something pretty remarkable is needed if the mind-body relation is to be made sense of; they are as extreme as the problem. The approach I favour is naturalistic but not constructive: I do not believe we can ever specify what it is about the brain that is responsible for consciousness, but I am sure that whatever it is it is not inherently miraculous. The problem arises, I want to suggest, because we are cut off by our very cognitive constitution from achieving a conception of that natural property of the brain (or of consciousness) that accounts for the psychophysical link. This is a kind of causal nexus that we are precluded from ever understanding, given the way we have to form our concepts and develop our theories. No wonder we find the problem so difficult!

Before I can hope to make this view plausible, I need to sketch the general conception of cognitive competence that underlies my position. Let me introduce the idea of *cognitive closure*. A type of mind $M$ is cognitively closed with respect to a property $P$ (or theory $T$) if and only if the concept-forming procedures at $M$'s disposal cannot extend to a grasp of $P$ (or an understanding of $T$). Conceiving minds come in different kinds, equipped with varying powers and limitations, biases and blindspots, so that properties (or theories) may be accessible to some minds but not to others. What is closed to the mind of a rat may be open to the mind of a monkey, and what is open to us may be closed to the monkey. Representational power is not all or nothing. Minds are biological products like bodies, and like bodies they come in different shapes and sizes, more or less capacious, more or less suited to certain cognitive tasks.[3] This is particularly clear for perceptual faculties, of course: perceptual closure is hardly to be denied. Different species are capable of perceiving different properties of the world, and no species can perceive every property things may instantiate (without artificial instrumentation anyway). But such closure does not reflect adversely on the reality of the properties that lie outside the representational capacities in question; a property is no less real for not being reachable from a certain kind of perceiving and conceiving mind. The invisible parts of the electromagnetic spectrum are just as real as the visible parts, and whether a specific kind of creature can form conceptual representations of these imperceptible parts does not determine whether they exist. Thus cognitive closure with respect to $P$ does not imply irrealism about $P$. That $P$ is (as we might say) *noumenal* for $M$ does not show that $P$ does not occur in some naturalistic scientific theory $T$ – it shows only that $T$ is not cognitively accessible to $M$. Presumably monkey minds and the property of being an electron illustrate this possibility. And the question must arise as to whether human minds are closed with respect to certain true explanatory theories. Nothing, at least, in the concept of reality shows that everything real is open to the human concept-forming faculty – if, that is, we are realists about reality.[4]

Consider a mind constructed according to the principles of classical empiricism, a Humean mind. Hume mistakenly thought that human minds were Humean, but we can at least conceive of such a mind (perhaps dogs and monkeys have Humean minds). A Humean mind is such that perceptual closure determines cognitive closure, since 'ideas' must always be copies of 'impressions', therefore the concept-forming system cannot transcend what can be perceptually presented to the subject. Such a mind will be closed with respect to unobservables; the properties of atoms, say, will not be representable by a mind constructed in this way. This implies that explanatory theories in which these properties are essentially mentioned will not be accessible to a Humean mind.[5] And hence the observable phenomena that are explained by allusion to unobservables will be inexplicable by a mind thus limited. But notice: the incapacity to explain certain phenomena does not carry with it a lack of recognition of the theoretical problems the phenomena pose. You might be able to appreciate a problem without being able to formulate (even in principle) the solution to that problem (I suppose human children are often in this position, at least for a while). A Humean mind cannot solve the problems that our physics solves, yet it might be able to have an inkling of what needs to be explained. We would expect, then, that a moderately intelligent enquiring Humean mind will feel permanently perplexed and mystified by the physical world, since the correct science is forever beyond its cognitive reach. Indeed, something like this was precisely the view of Locke. He thought that our ideas of matter are quite sharply constrained by our perceptions and so concluded that the true science of matter is eternally beyond us – that we could never remove our perplexities about (say) what solidity ultimately is.[6] But it does not follow for Locke that nature is itself inherently mysterious; the felt mystery comes from our own cognitive limitations, not from any objective eeriness in the world. It looks today as if Locke was wrong about our capacity to fathom the nature of the physical world, but we can still learn from his fundamental thought – the insistence that our cognitive faculties may not be up to solving every problem that confronts us. To put the point more generally: the human mind may not conform to empiricist principles, but it must conform to *some* principles – and it is a substantive claim that these principles permit the solution of every problem we can formulate or sense. Total cognitive openness is not guaranteed for human beings and it should not be expected. Yet what is noumenal for us may not be miraculous in itself. We should therefore be alert to the possibility that a problem that strikes us as deeply intractable, as utterly baffling, may arise from an area of cognitive closure in our ways of representing the world.[7] That is what I now want to argue is the case with our sense of the mysterious nature of the connection between consciousness and the brain. We are biased away from arriving at the correct explanatory theory of the psychophysical nexus. And this makes us prone to an illusion of objective mystery. Appreciating this should remove the philosophical problem: consciousness does not, in reality, arise from the brain in the miraculous way in which the Djin arises from the lamp.

I now need to establish three things: (i) there exists some property of the brain that accounts naturalistically for consciousness; (ii) we are cognitively closed with respect to that property; but (iii) there is no philosophical (as opposed to scientific) mind-body problem. Most of the work will go into establishing (ii).

Resolutely shunning the supernatural, I think it is undeniable that it must be in virtue of *some* natural property of the brain that organisms are conscious. There just *has* to be some explanation for how brains subserve minds. If we are not to be eliminativists about consciousness, then some theory must exist which accounts for the psychophysical correlations we observe. It is implausible to take these correlations as ultimate and inexplicable facts, as simply brute. And we do not want to acknowledge radical emergence of the conscious with respect to the cerebral: that is too much like accepting miracles *de re*. Brain states cause conscious states, we know, and this causal nexus must proceed through necessary connections of some kind – the kind that would make the nexus intelligible *if* they were understood.[8] Consciousness is like life in this respect. We know that life evolved from inorganic matter, so we expect there to be some explanation of this process. We cannot plausibly take the arrival of life as a primitive brute fact, nor can we accept that life arose by some form of miraculous emergence. Rather, there must be some natural account of how life comes from matter, whether or not we can know it. Eschewing vitalism and the magic touch of God's finger, we rightly insist that it must be in virtue of some natural property of (organized) matter that parcels of it get to be alive. But consciousness itself is just a further biological development, and so it too must be susceptible of some natural explanation – whether or not human beings are capable of arriving at this explanation. Presumably there exist objective natural laws that somehow account for the upsurge of consciousness. Consciousness, in short, must be a natural phenomenon, naturally arising from certain organizations of matter. Let us then say that there exists some property $P$, instantiated by the brain, in virtue of which the brain is the basis of consciousness. Equivalently there exists some theory $T$, referring to $P$, which fully explains the dependence of conscious states on brain states. If we knew $T$, then we would have a constructive solution to the mind-body problem. The question then is whether we can ever come to know $T$ and grasp the nature of $P$.

Let me first observe that it is surely *possible* that we could never arrive at a grasp of $P$; there is, as I said, no guarantee that our cognitive powers permit the solution of every problem we can recognize. Only a misplaced idealism about the natural world could warrant the dogmatic claim that everything is knowable by the human species at this stage of its evolutionary development (consider the same claim made on behalf of the intellect of cro-Magnon man). It *may* be that every property for which we can form a concept is such that *it* could never solve the mind-body problem. We *could* be like five-year old children trying to understand Relativity Theory. Still, so far this is just a possibility claim: what reason do we have for asserting, positively, that our minds are closed with respect to $P$?

Longstanding historical failure is suggestive, but scarcely conclusive. Maybe, it will be said, the solution is just around the corner, or it has to wait upon the completion of the physical sciences? Perhaps we simply have yet to produce the Einstein-like genius who will restructure the problem in some clever way and then present an astonished world with the solution.[9] However, I think that our deep bafflement about the problem, amounting to a vertiginous sense of ultimate mystery, which resists even articulate formulation, should at least encourage us to explore the idea that there is something terminal about our perplexity. Rather as traditional theologians found themselves conceding cognitive closure with respect to certain of the properties of God, so we should look seriously at the idea that the mind-body problem brings us bang up against the limits of our capacity to understand the world. That is what I shall do now.

There seem to be two possible avenues open to us in our aspiration to identify $P$: we could try to get to $P$ by investigating consciousness directly, or we could look to the study of the brain for $P$. Let us consider these in turn, starting with consciousness. Our acquaintance with consciousness could hardly be more direct; phenomenological description thus comes (relatively) easily. 'Introspection' is the name of the faculty through which we catch consciousness in all its vivid nakedness. By virtue of possessing this cognitive faculty we ascribe concepts of consciousness to ourselves; we thus have 'immediate access' to the properties of consciousness. But does the introspective faculty reveal property $P$? Can we tell just by introspecting what the solution to the mind-body problem is? Clearly not. We have direct cognitive access to one term of the mind-body relation, but we do not have such access to the nature of the link.

Introspection does not present conscious states *as* depending upon the brain in some intelligible way. We cannot therefore introspect $P$. Moreover, it seems impossible that we should ever augment our stock of introspectively ascribed concepts with the concept $P$ – that is, we could not acquire this concept simply on the basis of sustained and careful introspection. Pure phenomenology will never provide the solution to the mind-body problem. Neither does it seem feasible to try to extract $P$ from the concepts of consciousness we now have by some procedure of conceptual analysis – any more than we could solve the life-matter problem simply by reflecting on the concept *life*.[10] $P$ has to lie outside the field of the introspectable, and it is not implicitly contained in the concepts we bring to bear in our first-person ascriptions. Thus the faculty of introspection, as a concept-forming capacity, is cognitively closed with respect to $P$; which is not surprising in view of its highly limited domain of operation (*most* properties of the world are closed to introspection).

But there is a further point to be made about $P$ and consciousness, which concerns our restricted access to the concepts of consciousness themselves. It is a familiar point that the range of concepts of consciousness attainable by a mind $M$ is constrained by the specific forms of consciousness possessed by $M$. Crudely, you cannot form concepts of conscious properties unless you yourself instantiate those properties. The man born blind cannot grasp the concept of a visual experience of red, and human beings cannot conceive of the echolocatory experiences of bats.[11] These are cases of cognitive closure within the class of conscious properties. But now this kind of closure will, it seems, affect our hopes of access to $P$. For suppose that we were cognitively open with respect to $P$; suppose, that is, that we had the solution to the problem of how specific forms of consciousness depend upon different kinds of physiological structure. Then, of course, we would understand how the brain of a bat subserves the subjective experiences of bats. Call this type of experience $B$, and call the explanatory property that links $B$ to the bat's brain $P1$. By grasping $P1$ it would be perfectly intelligible to us how the bat's brain generates $B$-experiences; we would have an explanatory theory of the causal nexus in question. We would be in possession of the same kind of understanding we would have of our own experiences if we had the correct psychophysical theory of them. But then it seems to follow that grasp of the theory that explains B-experiences would *confer* a grasp of the nature of those experiences: for how could we understand that theory without understanding the concept B that occurs in it? How could we grasp the *nature* of B-experiences without grasping the *character* of those experiences? The true psychophysical theory would seem to provide a route to a grasp of the subjective form of the bat's experiences. But now we face a dilemma, a dilemma which threatens to become a reductio: either we *can* grasp this theory, in which case the property B becomes open to us; or we *cannot* grasp the theory, simply because property B is *not* open to us. It seems to me that the looming reductio here is compelling: our concepts of consciousness just *are* inherently constrained by our own form of consciousness, so that any theory the understanding of which required us to transcend these constraints would *ipso facto* be inaccessible to us. Similarly, I think, any theory that required us to transcend the finiteness of our cognitive capacities would *ipso facto* be a theory we could not grasp – and this despite the fact that it might be needed to explain something we can see needs explaining. We cannot simply stipulate that our concept-forming abilities are indefinitely plastic and unlimited just because they would have to be to enable us to grasp the truth about the world. We constitutionally lack the concept-forming capacity to encompass all possible types of conscious state, and this obstructs our path to a general solution to the mind-body problem. Even if we could solve it for our own case, we could not solve it for bats and Martians. P is, as it were, too close to the different forms of subjectivity for it to be accessible to all such forms, given that one's form of subjectivity restricts one's concepts of subjectivity.[12]

I suspect that most optimists about constructively solving the mind-body problem will prefer to place their bets on the brain side of the relation. Neuroscience is the place to look for property P, they will say. My question then is whether there is any conceivable way in which we might come to introduce P in the course of our empirical investigations of the brain. New concepts have been introduced in the effort to understand the workings of the brain, certainly: could not P then occur in conceivable extensions of this manner of introduction? So far, indeed, the theoretical concepts we ascribe to the brain seem as remote from consciousness as any ordinary physical properties are, but perhaps we might reach $P$ by diligent application of essentially the same procedures: so it is tempting to think. I want to suggest, to the contrary, that such procedures are inherently closed with respect to $P$. The fundamental reason for this, I think, is the role of *perception* in shaping our understanding of the brain – the way that our perception of the brain constrains the concepts we can apply to it. A point whose signficance it would be hard to overstress here is this: the property of consciousness itself (or specific conscious states) is not an observable or perceptible property of the brain. You can stare into a living conscious brain, your own or someone else's, and see there a wide variety of instantiated properties – its shape, colour, texture, etc. – but you will not thereby *see* what the subject is experiencing, the conscious state itself. Conscious states are simply not potential objects of perception: they depend upon the brain but they cannot be observed by directing the senses onto the brain. In other words, consciousness is noumenal with respect to perception of the brain.[13] I take it this is obvious. So we know there *are* properties of the brain that are necessarily closed to perception of the brain; the question now is whether $P$ is likewise closed to perception.

My argument will proceed as follows. I shall first argue that $P$ is indeed perceptually closed; then I shall complete the argument to full cognitive closure by insisting that no form of *inference* from what is perceived can lead us to $P$. The argument for perceptual closure starts from the thought that nothing we can imagine perceiving in the brain would ever convince us that we have located the intelligible nexus we seek. No matter what recondite property we could see to be instantiated in the brain we would always be baffled about how it could give rise to consciousness. I hereby invite you to try to conceive of a perceptible property of the brain that might allay the feeling of mystery that attends our contemplation of the brain-mind link: I do not think you will be able to do it. It is trying to conceive of a perceptible property of a rock that would render it perspicuous that the rock was conscious. In fact, I think it is the very impossibility of this that lies at the root of the felt mind-body problem. But why is this? Basically, I think, it is because the senses are geared to representing a spatial world; they essentially present things in space with spatially defined properties. But it is precisely *such* properties that seem inherently incapable of resolving the mind-body problem: we cannot link consciousness to the brain in virtue of spatial properties of the brain. There the brain is, an object of perception, laid out in space, containing spatially distributed processes; but consciousness defies explanation in such terms. Consciousness does not seem made up out of smaller spatial processes; yet perception of the brain seems limited to revealing such processes.[14] The senses are responsive to certain *kinds* of properties – those that are essentially bound up with space – but these properties are of the wrong sort (the wrong *category*) to constitute *P*. Kant was right, the form of outer sensibility is spatial; but if so, then *P* will be noumenal with respect to the senses, since no spatial property will ever deliver a satisfying answer to the mind-body problem. We simply do not understand the idea that conscious states might intelligibly arise from spatial configurations of the kind disclosed by perception of the world.

I take it this claim will not seem terribly controversial. After all, we do not generally expect that every property referred to in our theories should be a potential object of human perception: consider quantum theory and cosmology. Unrestricted perceptual openness is a dogma of empiricism if ever there was one. And there is no compelling reason to suppose that the property needed to explain the mind-brain relation should be in principle perceptible; it might be essentially 'theoretical', an object of thought not sensory experience. Looking harder at nature is not the only (or the best) way of discovering its theoretically significant properties. Perceptual closure does not entail cognitive closure, since we have available the procedure of hypothesis formation, in which *un*observables come to be conceptualized.

I readily agree with these sentiments, but I think there are reasons for believing that no coherent method of concept introduction will ever lead us to *P*. This is because a certain principle of *homogeneity* operates in our introduction of theoretical concepts on the basis of observation. Let me first note that consciousness itself could not be introduced simply on the basis of what we observe about the brain and its physical effects. If our data, arrived at by perception of the brain, do not include anything that brings in conscious states, then the theoretical properties we need to explain these data will not include conscious states either. Inference to the best explanation of purely physical data will never take us outside the realm of the

physical, forcing us to introduce concepts of consciousness.[15]
Everything physical has a purely physical explanation. So the
property of consciousness is cognitively closed with respect to
the introduction of concepts by means of inference to the best
explanation of perceptual data about the brain.

Now the question is whether $P$ could ever be arrived at by
this kind of inference. Here we must be careful to guard against
a form of magical emergentism with respect to concept formation. Suppose we try out a relatively clear theory of how
theoretical concepts are formed: we get them by a sort of
analogical extension of what we observe. Thus, for example, we
arrive at the concept of a molecule by taking our perceptual
representations of macroscopic objects and conceiving of smaller
scale objects of the same general kind. This method seems to
work well enough for unobservable material objects, but it will
not help in arriving at $P$, since analogical extensions of the
entities we observe in the brain are precisely as hopeless as the
original entities were as solutions to the mind-body problem.
We would need a method that left the base of observational
properties behind in a much more radical way. But it seems to
me that even a more unconstrained conception of inference to
the best explanation would still not do what is required: it
would no more serve to introduce $P$ than it serves to introduce
the property of consciousness itself. To explain the observed
physical data we need only such theoretical properties as bear
upon those data, not the property that explains consciousness,
which does not occur in the data. Since we do not need
consciousness to explain those data, we do not need the property
that explains consciousness. We will never get as far away from
the perceptual data in our explanations of those data as we need
to get in order to connect up explanatorily with consciousness.
This is, indeed, why it seems that consciousness is theoretically
epiphenomenal in the task of accounting for physical events. No
concept needed to explain the workings of the physical world
will suffice to explain how the physical world produces consciousness. So if $P$ is perceptually noumenal, then it will be
noumenal with respect to perception-based explanatory inferences. Accordingly, I do not think that $P$ could be arrived at by
empirical studies of the brain alone. Nevertheless, the brain *has*
this property, as it has the property of consciousness. Only a
magical idea of how we come by concepts could lead one to

think that we can reach $P$ by first perceiving the brain and then asking what is needed to explain what we perceive.[16] (The mind-body problem tempts us to magic in more ways than one.)

It will help elucidate the position I am driving towards if I contrast it with another view of the source of the perplexity we feel about the mind-brain nexus. I have argued that we cannot know which property of the brain accounts for consciousness, and so we find the mind-brain link unintelligible. But, it may be said, there is another account of our sense of irremediable mystery, which does not require positing properties our minds cannot represent. This alternative view claims that, even if we *now* had a grasp of $P$, we would *still* feel that there is something mysterious about the link, because of a special epistemological feature of the situation. Namely this: our acquaintance with the brain and our acquaintance with consciousness are necessarily mediated by distinct cognitive faculties, namely perception and introspection. Thus the faculty through which we apprehend one term of the relation is necessarily distinct from the faculty through which we apprehend the other. In consequence, it is not possible for us to use one of these faculties to apprehend the nature of the psychophysical nexus. No single faculty will enable us ever to apprehend the fact that consciousness depends upon the brain in virtue of property $P$. Neither perception alone nor introspection alone will ever enable us to witness the dependence. And this, my objector insists, is the real reason we find the link baffling: we cannot make sense of it in terms of the deliverances of a single cognitive faculty. So, even if we now had concepts for the properties of the brain that explain consciousness, we would still feel a residual sense of unintelligibility; we would still take there to be something mysterious going on. The necessity to shift from one faculty to the other produces in us an illusion of inexplicability. We might in fact have the explanation right now but be under the illusion that we do not. The right diagnosis, then, is that we should recognize the peculiarity of the epistemological situation and stop trying to make sense of the psychophysical nexus in the way we make sense of other sorts of nexus. It only *seems* to us that we can never discover a property that will render the nexus intelligible.

I think this line of thought deserves to be taken seriously, but I doubt that it correctly diagnoses our predicament. It is true enough that the problematic nexus is essentially apprehended by distinct faculties, so that it will never reveal its secrets to a single faculty; but I doubt that our intuitive sense of intelligibility is so rigidly governed by the 'single-faculty condition'. Why *should* facts only seem intelligible to us if we can conceive of apprehending them by one (sort of) cognitive faculty? Why not allow that we can recognize intelligible connections between concepts (or properties) even when those concepts (or properties) are necessarily ascribed using different faculties? Is it not suspiciously empiricist to insist that a causal nexus can only be made sense of by us if we can conceive of its being an object of a single faculty of apprehension? Would we think this of a nexus that called for touch and sight to apprehend each term of the relation? Suppose (*per impossible*) that we were offered P on a plate, as a gift from God: would we still shake our heads and wonder how that could resolve the mystery, being still the victims of the illusion of mystery generated by the epistemological duality in question? No, I think this suggestion is not enough to account for the miraculous appearance of the link: it is better to suppose that we are permanently blocked from forming a concept of what accounts for that link.

How strong is the thesis I am urging? Let me distinguish *absolute* from *relative* claims of cognitive closure. A problem is absolutely cognitively closed if no possible mind could resolve it; a problem is relatively closed if minds of some sorts can in principle solve it while minds of other sorts cannot. Most problems we may safely suppose, are only relatively closed: armadillo minds cannot solve problems of elementary arithmetic but human minds can. Should we say that the mind-body problem is only relatively closed or is the closure absolute? This depends on what we allow as a possible concept-forming mind, which is not an easy question. If we allow for minds that form their concepts of the brain and consciousness in ways that are quite independent of perception and introspection, then there may be room for the idea that there are possible minds for which the mind-body problem is soluble, and easily so. But if we suppose that *all* concept formation is tied to perception and introspection, however loosely, then *no* mind will be capable of understanding how it relates to its own body – the insolubility will be absolute. I think we can just about make sense of the former kind of mind, by exploiting our own faculty of a priori reasoning. Our mathematical concepts (say) do not seem tied either to perception or to introspection, so there does seem to be a mode of concept formation that operates without the constraints I identified earlier. The suggestion might then be that a mind that formed all of its concepts in this way – including its concepts of the brain and consciousness – would be free of the biases that prevent *us* from coming up with the right theory of how the two connect. Such a mind would have to be able to think of the brain and consciousness in ways that utterly prescind from the perceptual and the introspective – in somewhat the way we now (it seems) think about numbers. This mind would conceive of the psychophysical link in totally a priori terms. Perhaps this is how we should think of God's mind, and God's understanding of the mind-body relation. At any rate, something pretty radical is going to be needed if we are to devise a mind that can escape the kinds of closure that make the problem insoluble for us – if I am right in my diagnosis of our difficulty. *If* the problem is only relatively insoluble, then the type of mind that can solve it is going to be very different from ours and the kinds of mind we can readily make sense of (there may, of course, be cognitive closure here too). It certainly seems to me to be at least an open question whether the problem is absolutely insoluble; I would not be surprised if it were.[17]

My position is both pessimistic and optimistic at the same time. It is pessimistic about the prospects for arriving at a constructive solution to the mind-body problem, but it is optimistic about our hopes of removing the philosophical perplexity. The central point here is that I do not think we need to do the former in order to achieve the latter. This depends on a rather special understanding of what the philosophical problem consists in. What I want to suggest is that the nature of the psychophysical connection has a full and non-mysterious explanation in a certain science, but that this science is inaccessible to us as a matter of principle. Call this explanatory scientific theory $T$: $T$ is as natural and prosaic and devoid of miracle as any theory of nature; it describes the link between consciousness and the brain in a way that is no more remarkable (or alarming) than the way we now describe the link between the liver and bile.[18] According to $T$, there is nothing eerie going on in the world when an event in my visual cortex causes me to have an experience of yellow – however much it seems to *us* that there is. In other words, there is no intrinsic conceptual or metaphysical difficulty about how consciousness depends on the brain. It is not that the correct science is compelled to postulate miracles *de re*; it is rather that the correct science lies in the dark part of the world for us. We confuse our own cognitive limitations with objective eeriness. We are like a Humean mind trying to understand the physical world, or a creature without spatial concepts trying to understand the possibility of motion. This removes the philosophical problem because it assures us that the entities *themselves* pose no inherent philosophical difficulty. The case is unlike, for example, the problem of how the abstract world of numbers might be intelligibly related to the world of concrete knowing subjects: here the mystery seems intrinsic to the entities, not a mere artefact of our cognitive limitations or biases in trying to understand the relation.[19] It would not be plausible to suggest that there exists a science, whose theoretical concepts we cannot grasp, which completely resolves any sense of mystery that surrounds the question how the abstract becomes an object of knowledge for us. In this case, then, eliminativism seems a live option. The *philosophical* problem about consciousness and the brain arises from a sense that we are compelled to accept that nature contains miracles – as if the merely metallic lamp of the brain could really spirit into existence the Djin of consciousness. But we do not need to accept this: we can rest secure in the knowledge that some (unknowable) property of the brain makes everything fall into place. What creates the philosophical puzzlement is the assumption that the problem must somehow be scientific but that any science *we* can come up with will represent things as utterly miraculous. And the solution is to recognize that the sense of miracle comes from us and not from the world. There is, in reality, nothing mysterious about how the brain generates consciousness. There is no *metaphysical* problem.[20]

So far that deflationary claim has been justified by a general naturalism and certain considerations about cognitive closure and the illusions it can give rise to. Now I want to marshall some reasons for thinking that consciousness is actually a rather simple natural fact; objectively, consciousness is nothing very special. We should now be comfortable with the idea that our own sense of difficulty is a fallible guide to objective complexity: what is hard for us to grasp may not be very fancy in itself. The grain of our thinking is not a mirror held up to the facts of nature.[21] In particular, it may be that the extent of our understanding of facts about the mind is not commensurate with some objective estimate of their intrinsic complexity: we may be good at understanding the mind in some of its aspects but hopeless with respect to others, in a way that cuts across objective differences in what the aspects involve. Thus we are adept at understanding action in terms of the folk psychology of belief and desire, and we seem not entirely out of our depth when it comes to devising theories of language. But our understanding of how consciousness develops from the organization of matter is non-existent. But now, think of these various aspects of mind from the point of view of evolutionary biology. Surely language and the propositional attitudes are more complex and advanced evolutionary achievements than the mere possession of consciousness by a physical organism. Thus it seems that we are better at understanding some of the more complex aspects of mind than the simpler ones. Consciousness arises early in evolutionary history and is found right across the animal kingdom. In some respects it seems that the biological engineering required for consciousness is less fancy than that needed for certain kinds of complex motor behavior. Yet we can come to understand the latter while drawing a total blank with respect to the former. Conscious states seem biologically quite primitive, comparatively speaking. So the theory $T$ that explains the occurrence of consciousness in a physical world is very probably less objectively complex (by some standard) than a range of other theories that do not defy our intellects. If only we could know the psychophysical mechanism it might surprise us with its simplicity, its utter naturalness. In the manual that God consulted when he made the earth and all the beasts that dwell thereon the chapter about how to engineer consciousness from matter occurs fairly early on, well before the really difficult later chapters on mammalian reproduction and speech. It is not the *size* of the problem but its *type* that makes the mind-body problem so hard for us. This reflection should make us receptive to the idea that it is something about the tracks of our thought that prevents us from achieving a science that relates consciousness to its physical basis: the enemy lies within the gates.[22]

The position I have reached has implications for a tangle of intuitions it is natural to have regarding the mind-body relation. On the one hand, there are intuitions, pressed from Descartes to

Kripke, to the effect that the relation between conscious states
and bodily states is fundamentally contingent.[23] It can easily
seem to us that there is no necessitation involved in the
dependence of the mind on the brain. But, on the other hand, it
looks absurd to try to dissociate the two entirely, to let the mind
float completely free of the body. Disembodiment is a dubious
possibility at best, and some kind of necessary supervenience of
the mental on the physical has seemed undeniable to many. It is
not my aim here to adjudicate this longstanding dispute; I want
simply to offer a diagnosis of what is going on when one finds
oneself assailed with this flurry of conflicting intuitions. The
reason we feel the tug of contingency, pulling consciousness
loose from its physical moorings, may be that we do not and
cannot grasp the nature of the property that intelligibly links
them. The brain has physical properties we can grasp, and
variations in these correlate with changes in consciousness, but
we cannot draw the veil that conceals the manner of their
connection. Not grasping the nature of the connection, it strikes
us as deeply contingent; we cannot make the assertion of a
necessary connection intelligible to ourselves. There *may* then
be a real necessary connection; it is just that it will always strike
us as curiously brute and unperspicuous. We may thus, as
upholders of intrinsic contingency, be the dupes of our own
cognitive blindness. On the other hand, we are scarcely in a
position to assert that there *is* a necessary connection between
the properties of the brain we can grasp and states of consciousness, since we are so ignorant (and irremediably so) about the
character of the connection. For all we know, the connection
may be contingent, as access to $P$ would reveal if we could have
such access. The link between consciousness and property $P$ is
not, to be sure, contingent – virtually by definition – but we are
not in a position to say exactly how $P$ is related to the 'ordinary'
properties of the brain. It may be necessary or it may be
contingent. Thus it is that we tend to vacillate between contingency and necessity; for we lack the conceptual resources to
decide the question – or to understand the answer we are
inclined to give. The indicated conclusion appears to be that we
can never really know whether disembodiment is metaphysically
possible, or whether necessary supervenience is the case, or
whether spectrum inversion could occur. For these all involve
claims about the modal connections between properties of

consciousness and the ordinary properties of the body and brain that we can conceptualize; and the real nature of these connections is not accessible to us. Perhaps $P$ makes the relation between C-fibre firing and pain necessary or perhaps it does not: we are simply not equipped to know. We are like a Humean mind wondering whether the observed link between the temperature of a gas and its pressure (at a constant volume) is necessary or contingent. To know the answer to that you need to grasp atomic (or molecular) theory, and a Humean mind just is not up to attaining the requisite theoretical understanding. Similarly, we are constitutionally ignorant at precisely the spot where the answer exists.

I predict that many readers of this paper will find its main thesis utterly incredible, even ludicrous. Let me remark that I sympathize with such readers: the thesis is not easily digestible. But I would say this: if the thesis *is* actually true, it will still strike us as hard to believe. For the idea of an explanatory property (or set of properties) that is noumenal for us, yet is essential for the (constructive) solution of a problem we face, offends a kind of natural idealism that tends to dominate our thinking. We find it taxing to conceive of the existence of a real property, under our noses as it were, which we are built not to grasp – a property that is responsible for phenomena that we observe in the most direct way possible. This kind of realism, which brings cognitive closure so close to home, is apt to seem both an affront to our intellects and impossible to get our minds around. We try to think of this unthinkable property and understandably fail in the effort; so we rush to infer that the very supposition of such a property is nonsensical. Realism of the kind I am presupposing thus seems difficult to hold in focus, and any philosophical theory that depends upon it will also seem to rest on something systematically elusive.[24] My response to such misgivings, however, is unconcessive: the limits of our minds are just not the limits of reality. It is deplorably anthropocentric to insist that reality be constrained by what the human mind can conceive. We need to cultivate a vision of reality (a metaphysics) that makes it truly independent of our given cognitive powers, a conception that includes these powers as a proper part. It is just that, in the case of the mind-body problem, the bit of reality that systematically eludes our cognitive grasp is an aspect of our own nature. Indeed, it is an aspect that makes it possible for us to have minds at all and to think about how they are related to our bodies. This particular transcendent tract of reality happens to lie within our own heads. A deep fact about our own nature as a form of embodied consciousness is thus necessarily hidden from us. Yet there is nothing inherently eerie or bizarre about this embodiment. We are much more straightforward than we seem. Our weirdness lies in the eyes of the beholder.

The answer to the question that forms my title is therefore 'No and Yes'.[25]

## References

1 One of the peculiarities of the mind-body problem is the difficulty of formulating it in a rigorous way. We have a sense of the problem that outruns our capacity to articulate it clearly. Thus we quickly find ourselves resorting to invitations to look inward, instead of specifying precisely *what* it is about consciousness that makes it inexplicable in terms of ordinary physical properties. And this can make it seem that the problem is spurious. A creature without consciousness would not properly appreciate the problem (assuming such a creature could appreciate other problems). I think an adequate treatment of the mind-body problem should explain why it is so hard to state the problem explicitly. My treatment locates our difficulty in our inadequate conceptions of the nature of the brain and consciousness. In fact, if we knew their natures fully we would already have solved the problem. This should become clear later.

2 I would also classify panpsychism as a constructive solution, since it attempts to explain consciousness in terms of properties of the brain that are as natural as consciousness itself. Attributing specks of proto-consciousness to the constituents of matter is not supernatural in the way postulating immaterial substances or divine interventions is; it is merely extravagant. I shall here be assuming that panpsychism, like all other extant constructive solutions, is inadequate as an answer to the mind-body problem – as (of course) are the supernatural 'solutions'. I am speaking to those who still feel perplexed (almost everyone, I would think, at least in their heart).

3 This kind of view of cognitive capacity is forcefully advocated by Noam Chomsky in *Reflections on Language*, Pantheon Books, 1975, and by Jerry Fodor in *The Modularity of Mind*, Cambridge, Mass., MIT Press, 1983. Chomsky distinguishes between 'problems', which human minds are in principle equipped to solve, and 'mysteries', which systematically elude our understanding; and he envisages a study of our

cognitive systems that would chart these powers and limitations. I am here engaged in such a study, citing the mind-body problem as falling on the side of the mysteries.

4 See Thomas Nagel's discussion of realism in *The View From Nowhere*, Oxford, Oxford University Press, 1986, ch. VI. He argues there for the possibility of properties we can never grasp. Combining Nagel's realism with Chomsky—Fodor cognitive closure gives a position looking very much like Locke's in the *Essay Concerning Human Understanding*: the idea that our God-given faculties do not equip us to fathom the deep truth about reality. In fact, Locke held precisely this about the relation between mind and brain: only divine revelation could enable us to understand how 'perceptions' are produced in our minds by material objects.

5 Hume, of course, argued, in effect, that no theory essentially employing a notion of objective causal necessitation could be grasped by our minds – and likewise for the notion of objective persistence. We might compare the frustrations of the Humean mind to the conceptual travails of the pure sound beings discussed in Ch. II of P. F. Strawson's *Individuals*, London, Methuen, 1959; both are types of mind whose constitution puts various concepts beyond them. We can do a lot better than these truncated minds, but we also have our constitutional limitations.

6 See *An Essay Concerning Human Understanding*, Book II, ch. IV. Locke compares the project of saying what solidity ultimately is to trying to clear up a blind man's vision by talking to him.

7 Some of the more arcane aspects of cosmology and quantum theory might be thought to lie just within the bounds of human intelligibility. Chomsky suggests that the causation of behaviour might be necessarily mysterious to human investigators: see *Reflections on Language*, p. 156. I myself believe that the mind-body problem exhibits a qualitatively different level of mystery from this case (unless it is taken as an aspect of that problem).

8 Cf. Nagel's discussion of emergence in 'Panpsychism', in *Mortal Questions*, Cambridge, Cambridge University Press, 1979. I agree with him that the apparent radical emergence of mind from matter has to be epistemic only, on pain of accepting inexplicable miracles in the world.

9 Despite his reputation for pessimism over the mind-body problem, a careful reading of Nagel reveals an optimistic strain in his thought (by the standards of the present paper): see, in particular, the closing remarks of 'What is it Like to be a Bat?', in *Mortal Questions*. Nagel speculates that we might be able to devise an 'objective phenomenology'

that made conscious states more amenable to physical analysis. Unlike me, he does not regard the problem as inherently beyond us.

10 This is perhaps the most remarkably optimistic view of all – the expectation that reflecting on the ordinary concept of pain (say) will reveal the manner of pain's dependence on the brain. If I am not mistaken, this is in effect the view of common-sense functionalists: they think that $P$ consists in causal role, and that this can be inferred analytically from the concepts of conscious states. This would make it truly amazing that we should ever have felt there to be a mind-body problem at all, since the solution is already contained in our mental concepts. What optimism!

11 See Nagel, 'What is it Like to be a Bat?' Notice that the fugitive character of such properties with respect to our concepts has nothing to do with their 'complexity'; like fugitive colour properties, such experiential properties are 'simple'. Note too that such properties provide counter-examples to the claim that (somehow) rationality is a faculty that, once possessed, can be extended to encompass all concepts, so that if *any* concept can be possessed then *every* concept can.

12 It might be suggested that we borrow Nagel's idea of 'objective phenomenology' in order to get around this problem. Instead of representing experiences under subjective descriptions, we should describe them in entirely objective terms, thus bringing them within our conceptual ken. My problem with this is that, even allowing that there could be such a form of description, it would not permit us to understand how the subjective aspects of experience depend upon the brain – which is really the problem we are trying to solve. In fact, I doubt that the notion of objective phenomenology is any more coherent than the notion of subjective physiology. Both involve trying to bridge the psychophysical gap by a sort of stipulation. The lesson here is that the gap cannot be bridged just by applying concepts drawn from one side to items that belong on the other side; and this is because neither sort of concept could ever do what is needed.

13 We should distinguish two claims about the imperceptibility of consciousness: (i) consciousness is not perceivable by directing the senses onto the brain; (ii) consciousness is not perceivable by directing the senses anywhere, even towards the behaviour that 'expresses' conscious states. I believe both theses, but my present point requires only (i). I am assuming, of course, that perception cannot be unrestrictedly theory-laden; or that if it can, the infusions of theory cannot have been originally derived simply by looking at things or tasting them or touching them or . . .

14 Nagel discusses the difficulty of thinking of conscious processes in

the spatial terms that apply to the brain in *The View From Nowhere*, pp. 50–1, but he does not draw my despairing conclusion. The case is exactly *un*like (say) the dependence of liquidity on the properties of molecules, since here we do think of both terms of the relation as spatial in character; so we can simply employ the idea of spatial composition.

15 Cf. Nagel: 'it will never be legitimate to infer, as a theoretical explanation of physical phenomena alone, a property that includes or implies the consciousness of its subject', 'Panpsychism', p. 183.

16 It is surely a striking fact that the microprocesses that have been discovered in the brain by the usual methods seem no nearer to consciousness than the gross properties of the brain open to casual inspection. Neither do more abstract 'holistic' features of brain function seem to be on the right lines to tell us the nature of consciousness. The deeper science probes into the brain the more remote it seems to get from consciousness. Greater knowledge of the brain thus destroys our illusions about the kinds of properties that might be discovered by travelling along this path. Advanced neurophysiological theory seems only to deepen the miracle.

17 The kind of limitation I have identified is therefore not the kind that could be remedied simply by a large increase in general intelligence. No matter how large the frontal lobes of our biological descendants may become, they will still be stumped by the mind-body problem, so long as they form their (empirical) concepts on the basis of perception and introspection.

18 Or again, no more miraculous than the theory of evolution. Creationism is an understandable response to the theoretical problem posed by the existence of complex organisms; fortunately, we now have a theory that renders this response unnecessary, and so undermines the theism required by the creationist thesis. In the case of consciousness, the appearance of miracle might also tempt us in a 'creationist' direction, with God required to perform the alchemy necessary to transform matter into experience. Thus the mind-body problem might similarly be used to prove the existence of God (no miracle without a miracle-maker). We cannot, I think, refute this argument in the way we can the original creationist argument, namely by actually producing a non-miraculous explanatory theory, but we can refute it by arguing that such a naturalistic theory must *exist*. (It is a condition of adequacy upon any account of the mind-body relation that it avoid assuming theism.)

19 See Paul Benacerraf, 'Mathematical Truth', *Journal of Philosophy*, 1973, for a statement of this problem about abstract entities. Another

problem that seems to me to differ from the mind-body problem is the problem of free will. I do not believe that there is some unknowable property Q which reconciles free will with determinism (or indeterminism); rather, the concept of free will contains internal incoherencies – as the concept of consciousness does not. This is why it is much more reasonable to be an eliminativist about free will than about consciousness.

20 A test of whether a proposed solution to the mind-body problem is adequate is whether it relieves the pressure towards eliminativism. If the data can only be explained by postulating a miracle (i.e. not explained), then we must repudiate the data – this is the principle behind the impulse to deny that conscious states exist. My proposal passes this test because it allows us to resist the postulation of miracles; it interprets the eeriness as merely epistemic, though deeply so. Constructive solutions are not the only way to relieve the pressure.

21 Chomsky suggests that the very faculties of mind that make us good at some cognitive tasks may make us poor at others; see *Reflections on Language*, pp. 155–6. It seems to me possible that what makes us good at the science of the purely physical world is what skews us away from developing a science of consciousness. Our faculties bias us towards understanding matter in motion, but it is precisely this kind of understanding that is inapplicable to the mind-body problem. Perhaps, then, the price of being good at understanding matter is that we cannot understand mind. Certainly our notorious tendency to think of everything in spatial terms does not help us in understanding the mind.

22 I get this phrase from Fodor, *The Modularity of Mind*, p. 121. The intended contrast is with kinds of cognitive closure that stem from exogenous factors – as, say, in astronomy. Our problem with $P$ is not that it is too distant or too small or too large or too complex; rather, the very structure of our concept-forming apparatus points us away from $P$.

23 Saul Kripke, *Naming and Necessity*, Oxford, Blackwell, 1980. Of course, Descartes explicitly argued from (what he took to be) the essential natures of the body and mind to the contingency of their connection. If we abandon the assumption that we know these natures, then agnosticism about the modality of the connection seems the indicated conclusion.

24 This is the kind of realism defended by Nagel in ch. VI of *The View From Nowhere*: to be is not to be conceivable by us. I would say that the mind-body problem provides a demonstration that there *are* such concept-transcending properties – not merely that there *could* be. I

would also say that realism of this kind should be accepted precisely because it helps solve the mind-body problem; it is a metaphysical thesis that pulls its weight in coping with a problem that looks hopeless otherwise. There is thus nothing 'epiphenomenal' about such radical realism: the existence of a reality we cannot know can yet have intellectual significance for us.

25 Discussions with the following people have helped me work out the ideas of this paper: Anita Avramides, Jerry Katz, Ernie Lepore, Michael Levin, Thomas Nagel, Galen Strawson, Peter Unger. My large debt to Nagel's work should be obvious throughout the paper: I would not have tried to face the mind-body problem down had he not first faced up to it.

# SUGGESTIONS FOR FURTHER READING

## Introductory Reading

Carruthers, Peter. *Introducing Persons: Theories and Arguments in the Philosophy of Mind*, Croom Helm, 1986.

Churchland, Paul M. *Matter and Consciousness: A Contemporary Introduction to the Philosophy of Mind*, A Bradford Book: The MIT Press, 1984.

McGinn, Colin. *The Character of Mind*, Oxford University Press, 1982.

Priest, Stephen. *Theories of the Mind*, Penguin, 1991.

Smith, Peter, and Jones, O. R. *The Philosophy of Mind: An Introduction*, Cambridge University Press, 1986.

Teichman, Jenny. *Philosophy and the Mind*, Basil Blackwell, 1988.

## References for the introduction, the selections and Further Reading

Anscombe, G. E. M. *Intention*, Basil Blackwell, 1957.

Armstrong, D. M. *A Materialist Theory of the Mind*, Routledge & Kegan Paul, 1968.

Armstrong, D. M. *The Nature of Mind and Other Essays*, Queensland University Press, 1980.

Armstrong, D. M. *Belief, Truth and Knowledge*, Cambridge University Press, 1973.

Ayer, A. J. (ed.) *Logical Positivism*, Collier Macmillan: The Free Press, 1959.

Ayer, A. J. 'The Vienna Circle', in *The Revolution in Philosophy*, by A. J. Ayer et al., Macmillan, 1956.

Baker, Lynne R. *Saving Belief*, Princeton University Press, 1987.

Bechtel, William. 'Connectionism and the Philosophy of Mind: An Overview', *The Southern Journal of Philosophy* Vol. 26, Supplement, 1987.

Bergson, Henri. *Spiritual Energy* (1919), in Bergson *Oeuvres*, Presses Universitaires de France, 1970.

Blakemore, Colin. *The Mechanics of Mind: BBC Reith Lectures 1976*, Cambridge University Press, 1977.

Blakemore, C. and Greenfield, S. (eds). *Mindwaves*, Basil Blackwell, 1987.

Block, Ned. (ed.) 'Are Absent Qualia Impossible?' *The Philosophical Review*, Vol. 89, 1980.

Block, Ned. (ed.) *Readings in Philosophy of Psychology*, 2 vols., Harvard University Press, 1980–81.

Brentano, Franz. *Psychology from an Empirical Standpoint* (1874), ed. O. Kraus, Engl. ed., Linda L. McAlister, trans., A. C. Rancurello et al., Routledge & Kegan Paul, 1973.

Brentano, Franz. *The True and the Evident* (1930), ed. O. Kraus, Engl. ed. R. M. Chisholm, trans. R. M. Chisholm et al., Routledge & Kegan Paul, 1966.

Broad, C. D. *The Mind and its Place in Nature*, Routledge & Kegan Paul, 1925.

Brown, S. C. (ed.) *Philosophy of Psychology*, The Royal Institute of Philosophy, 1974.

Burge, Tyler. 'Philosophy of Language and Mind: 1950–1990', in *The Philosophical Review*, Centennial issue, Vol. 101, 1992.

Burge, Tyler. 'Individualism and Psychology', *The Philosophical Review*, Vol. 45, 1986.

Burge, Tyler. 'Individualism and the Mental', *Midwest Studies in Philosophy*, Vol. 4, 1979.

Carnap, Rudolf. *The Logical Syntax of Language*, trans. A. Smeaton, Kegan Paul, Trench, Trubner, 1937.

Carnap, Rudolf 'Die physikalische Sprache als Universalsprache de Wissenschaft' (The Language of Physics as the Universal Language of Science), *Erkenntnis*, II, 1931.

Chisholm, R. *Perceiving: A Philosophical Study*, Cornell University Press, 1957.

Chomsky, Noam. *Language and Mind* (2nd ed.), Harcourt Brace Jovanovich, 1972.

Churchland, Patricia. *Neurophilosophy: Toward a Unified Science of the Mind-Brain*, A Bradford Book: The MIT Press, 1986.

Churchland, Paul. *Scientific Realism and the Plasticity of Mind*, Cambridge University Press, 1979.

Davidson, Donald. *Essays on Actions and Events*, Oxford University Press, 1980.

Dennett, Daniel C. *Consciousness Explained*, Little, Brown & Co, 1991.

Dennett, Daniel C. *The Intentional Stance*, A Bradford Book: The MIT Press, 1987.

Dennett, Daniel C. *Brainstorms: Philosophical Essays on Mind and Psychology*, Harvester Press, 1979.

Dennett, Daniel C. *Content and Consciousness*, International Library of Philosophy and Scientific Method, Routledge & Kegan Paul, 1969.

Descartes, René. *Philosophical Letters* (1629–1649), trans. and ed. A. Kenny, Basil Blackwell, 1981.

Descartes, René. *Philosophical Writings* (1619–1648), trans. and ed. E. Anscombe and P. T. Geach, Nelson, 1954.

Dretske, Fred. *Knowledge and the Flow of Information*, A Bradford Book: The MIT Press, 1981.

Ehrenfels, Christian von. 'On Gestalt Qualities' (1890), *The Psychological Review*, Vol. 44, 1937.

Farrell, B. A. 'Experience', *Mind*, Vol. 59, 1950.

Feyerabend, Paul. 'Materialism and the Mind-Body Problem', *The Review of Metaphysics*, Vol. 17, 1963.

Field, Hartry. 'Mental Representation', *Erkenntnis*, Vol. 13, 1978.

Flanagan, Owen. *Consciousness Reconsidered*, A Bradford Book: The MIT Press, 1992.

Fodor, Jerry A. *A Theory of Content and Other Essays*, A Bradford Book: The MIT Press, 1992.

Fodor, Jerry A. *Psychosemantics: The Problem of Meaning in the Philosophy of Mind*, A Bradford Book: The MIT Press, 1987.

Fodor, Jerry A. *The Modularity of Mind: An Essay on Faculty Psychology*, A Bradford Book: The MIT Press, 1983.

Fodor, Jerry A. *Representations: Philosophical Essays on the Foundations of Cognitive Science*, A Bradford Book: The MIT Press, 1981.

Fodor, Jerry A. *The Language of Thought*, 'Language of Thought Series', Thomas Y. Crowell, 1975.

Geach, P. T. *Mental Acts*, Routledge & Kegan Paul, 1957.

Hampshire, Stuart. *Freedom of Mind and Other Essays*, Clarendon Press, 1972.

Harman, G. *Thought*, Princeton University Press, 1973.

Haugeland, John *Artificial Intelligence: The Very Idea*, The MIT Press, 1985.

Hempel, Carl. 'The Logical Analysis of Psychology', *Review de Synthese*, Vol. 10, 1935.

Husserl, Edmund. 'Phenomenology' (1929), trans. C. V. Solomon, in *Realism and the Background of Phenomenology*, ed. R. M. Chisholm, The Free Press, 1960.

Husserl, Edmund. *Ideas: General Introduction to Pure Phenomenology* (1913), trans. W. R. Boyce Gibson, George Allen & Unwin, 1931.

Jackson, Frank. *Perception*, Cambridge University Press, 1977.

James, William. *The Principles of Psychology* (1890), 2 vols., Dover Books, 1950.

James, William. *Psychology: Briefer Course*, Macmillan & Co, 1892; reprinted by Harvard University Press, 1985.

Johnson-Laird, Philip N. *Mental Models: Towards a Cognitive Science of Language, Inference and Consciousness*, Cambridge University Press, 1983.

Kenny, Anthony. *The Legacy of Wittgenstein*, Basil Blackwell, 1984.

Kenny, Anthony. *Action, Emotion, and Will*, Routledge & Kegan Paul, 1963.

Kim, J. 'Causality, Identity, and Supervenience in the Mind-Body Problem', *Midwest Studies in Philosophy*, Vol 4, 1979.

Kim, J. 'Supervenience and Nomological Incommensurables', *American Philosophical Quarterly*, Vol. 15, 1978.

Kim, J. 'On the Psycho-Physical Identity Theory', *The American Philosophical Quarterly*, Vol 3, 1966.

Kripke, S. *Naming and Necessity*, Basil Blackwell, 1980.

Laird, John. *Our Minds and their Bodies*, Oxford University Press, 1925.

Lewis, C. I. 'Some Logical Considerations Concerning the Mental', *The Journal of Philosophy*, Vol 38, 1941.

Lewis, David. 'Psychophysical and Theoretical Identifications', *Australasian Journal of Philosophy*, Vol. 40, 1972.

Lewis, David. 'An Argument for the Identity Theory', in *Materialism and the Mind-Body Problem*, ed. D. Rosenthal, Prentice-Hall, 1971.

Loar, Brian. *Mind and Meaning*, Cambridge University Press, 1981.

Longuet-Higgins, C. *Mental Processes: Studies in Cognitive Science*, A Bradford Book: The MIT Press, 1987.

Lycan, William G. *Consciousness*, A Bradford Book: The MIT Press, 1987.

Lycan, William G. 'Form, Function and Feel', *The Journal of Philosophy*, Vol. 78, 1981.

Lyons, William. *Approaches to Intentionality*, Oxford University Press, 1995.

Lyons, William. *The Disappearance of Introspection*, A Bradford Book: The MIT Press, 1986.

Lyons, William. *Gilbert Ryle: An Introduction to His Philosophy*, Harvester and Humanities Presses, 1980.

Lyons, William. *Emotion*, Cambridge University Press (facsimile reprint 1993 by Gregg Revivals, Surrey), 1980.

Mach, Ernst. *Popular Scientific Lectures*, trans. T. J. McCormack, University of Chicago Press, 1984.

Malcolm, Norman. 'Ludwig Josef Johann Wittgenstein', in *The Encyclopedia of Philosophy*, ed. P. Edwards, Vol. 8, Collier Macmillan: The Free Press, 1967.

Malcolm, Norman. *Ludwig Wittgenstein: A Memoir*, (1958), with a biographical sketch by G. H. von Wright, Oxford University Press, 1966.

Malcolm, Norman. 'Wittgenstein's *Philosophical Investigations*', *Philosophical Review*, Vol. 63, 1954.

McDougall, Wm. *Body and Mind*, Methuen, 1911.

McGinn, Colin. *The Problem of Consciousness*, Basil Blackwell, 1991.

McGinn, Colin. *Mental Content*, Basil Blackwell, 1989.

McGinn, Colin. *The Subjective View: Secondary Qualities and Indexical Thoughts*, Oxford University Press, 1983.

Miller, Jonathan (ed.). *States of Mind: Conversations with Psychological Investigators*, BBC, 1983.

Millikan, Ruth Garrett. *Language, Thought, and other Biological Categories: New Foundations for Realism*, A Bradford Book: The MIT Press, 1984.

Nagel, Thomas. *The View from Nowhere*, Oxford University Press, 1986.

Neisser, Ulric. *Cognition and Reality: Principles and Implications of Cognitive Psychology*, W. H. Freeman, 1976.

Newell, A. 'The Knowledge Level', *Artificial Intelligence*, Vol. 18, 1982.

Parfit, Derek. *Reasons and Persons*, Oxford University Press, 1984.

Peacocke, C. *Sense and Content*, Clarendon Press, 1983.

Peters, R. S. *The Concept of Motivation*, Routledge & Kegan Paul, 1958.

Price, H. H. *Perception*, Methuen, 1932.

Puccetti, Roland. 'Brain Bisection and Personal Identity', *British Journal for the Philosophy of Science*, Vol. 24, 1973.

Putnam, Hilary. *Renewing Philosophy*, Harvard University Press, 1992.

Putnam, Hilary. *Representation and Reality*, A Bradford Book: The MIT Press, 1989.

Putnam, Hilary. *Mind, Language and Reality*, Philosophical Papers, Vol. 2, Cambridge University Press, 1975.

Rorty, Richard. 'Mind-Brain Identity, Privacy, and Categories', *The Review of Metaphysics*, Vol. 19, 1965.

Rumelhart, D., McLelland, J. and the PDP Research Group (eds). *Parallel Distributed Processing*, 2 Vols., The MIT Press, 1986.

Quine, W. V. O. 'Facts of the Matter', in *Essays on the Philosophy of W. V. Quine*, ed. R. W. Shahan and C. Swayer, Harvester Press, 1979.

Quine, W. V. O. 'Mind and Verbal Dispositions', in *Mind and Language*, ed. S. Guttenplan, Clarendon Press, 1975.

Quine, W. V. O. 'Propositional Objects', in Quine *Ontological Relativity and Other Essays*, Columbia University Press, 1969.

Quine, W. V. O. 'On Mental Entities', in Quine *The Ways of Paradox and Other Essays*, Harvard University Press, 1966.

Quine, W. V. O. *Word and Object*, The MIT Press, 1960.

Ramsey, Frank. 'Truth and Probability', in *The Foundations of Mathematics and other Logical Essays*, by R. B. Braithwaite (ed.), Littlefield, Adams & Co., 1960.

Ryle, Gilbert. *On Thinking*, ed. K. Kolenda, Basil Blackwell, 1979.

Ryle, Gilbert. *Dilemmas: The Tarner Lectures (1953)*, Cambridge University Press, 1954.

Ryle, Gilbert. *The Concept of Mind*, Hutchinson, 1949.

Russell, Bertrand. *The Analysis of Mind*, George Allen & Unwin, 1921.

Schlick, Moritz. 'The Turning Point in Philosophy' (1930–31), in *Logical Positivism*, ed. A. J. Ayer, The Free Press 1959.

Searle, John, *The Rediscovery of the Mind*, A Bradford Book: The MIT Press, 1992.

Searle, John. *Intentionality: An Essay in the Philosophy of Mind*, Cambridge University Press, 1983.

Searle, John. *Minds, Brains and Science*, BBC, 1985.

Searle, John. 'Minds, Brains and Programs', *The Behavioral and Brain Sciences*, Vol. 3, 1980.

Sellars, Wilfrid. *Science, Perception and Reality*, Routledge & Kegan Paul, 1963.

Shoemaker, S. *Self-Knowledge and Self-Identity*, Cornell University Press, 1963.

Shoemaker, S. 'Functionalism and Qualia', *Philosophical Studies*, Vol. 27, 1975.

Skinner, B. F. *Science and Human Behaviour* (1953), Collier Macmillan: The Free Press, 1965.

Smart, J. J. C. *Philosophy and Scientific Realism*, Routledge & Kegan Paul, 1963.

Smolensky, Paul. 'On the Proper Treatment of Connectionism', *Journal of the Behavioral and Brain Sciences*, Vol. 11, 1988.

Stalnaker, Robert. 'What's in the Head', *Philosophical Perspectives*, Vol. 8, 1989.

Stalnaker, Robert. *Inquiry*, A Bradford Book: The MIT Press, 1984.

Stalnaker, Robert. 'Propositions', in *Issues in the Philosophy of Language*, ed. A. McKay and D. Merrill, Yale University Press, 1976.

Stich, S. *From Folk Psychology to Cognitive Science: The Case Against Belief*, A Bradford Book: The MIT Press, 1983.

Stout, G. F. *Mind and Matter*, Cambridge University Press, 1931.

Strawson, P. F. *Individuals*, Methuen, 1959.

Taylor, Charles. *The Explanation of Behaviour*, Routledge & Kegan Paul, 1964.

Tienson, John L. 'An Introduction to Connectionism', *The Southern Journal of Philosophy*, Vol. 26, supplement, 1987.

Titchener, E. B. *Experimental Psychology: A Manual of Laboratory Practice*, 2 vols., Macmillan, 1901, 1905.

Turing, Alan. 'Computing Machinery and Intelligence', *Mind*, Vol. 59, 1950.

Vygotsky, Lev. *Thought and Language* (1937), trans and ed. Alex Kozulin, The MIT Press, 1986.

Watson, J. B. *Psychology from the Standpoint of a Behaviourist*, J. B. Lippincott, 1919.

Williams, Bernard. *Problems of the Self: Philosophical Papers (1956–1972)*, Cambridge University Press, 1973.

Wisdom, John *Problems of Mind and Matter*, Cambridge University Press, 1934.

Wittgenstein, Ludwig. *Remarks on the Philosophy of Psychology*, Vol. 1, ed. G. E. M. Anscombe and G. H. von Wright, trans., G. E. M. Anscombe, University of Chicago Press, 1980.

Wittgenstein, Ludwig. *Tractatus Logico-Philosophicus* (1921), trans. D. F. Pears and B. F. McGuinness, Routledge & Kegan Paul, 1961.

Wittgenstein, Ludwig. *The Blue and Brown Books*, edit. R. Rhees, Basil Blackwell, 1958.

Wittgenstein, Ludwig. *Philosophical Investigations* (1953), trans. G. E. M. Anscombe, Basil Blackwell, 1958.

Wundt, Wilhelm. *Lectures on Human and Animal Psychology*, (1894), trans. J. E. Creighton and E. B. Titchener, Swann Sonnenschein, 1896.

# ACKNOWLEDGEMENTS

The editor and publishers wish to thank the following for permission to use copyright material:

*The Psychological Review* for material from John B. Watson, 'Psychology as the Behaviorist Views It', in Volume 20, 1913, pp. 158–77;

Basil Blackwell for material from Ludwig Wittgenstein, *The Brown Book*, 1958 and an extract from *Philosophical Investigations*, Part II, 1953;

The British Academy for material from Gilbert Ryle, 'A Puzzling Element in the Notion of Thinking', in *Proceedings of the British Academy*, vol. XLIV, 1958;

The British Psychological Society for material from U. T. Place, 'Is Consciousness a Brain Process?' in *British Journal of Psychology*, Vol. 47, 1956, pp. 44–50;

Cambridge University Press and Hilary Putnam for material from Hilary Putnam, 'Philosophy and Our Mental Life' in *Mind Language and Reality, Philosophical Papers*, Vol. 2, 1975, pp. 291–303;

Donald Davidson and the Royal Institute of Philosophy for material from Donald Davidson, 'Psychology as Philosophy' in S. C. Brown ed., *Philosophy of Psychology*, The Royal Institute of Philosophy, 1974;

The University of Queensland Press for material from David Armstrong, 'The Causal Theory of Mind', reprinted in *The Nature of Mind and Other Essays*, 1980;

Harvester Wheatsheaf for material from Daniel Dennett, 'Intentional Systems' in *Brainstorms: Philosophical Essays on Mind and Psychology*, 1979;

*The Journal of Philosophy* for material from Paul M. Churchland, 'Eliminative Materialism and the Propositional Attitudes' in *The Journal of Philosophy* LXXVIII, 2, February 1981, pp. 67–90;

The MIT Press for material from Jerry Fodor, 'The Persistence of the Attitudes' in *Psychosemantics: The Problem of Meaning in the Philosophy of Mind*, 1987;

Oxford University Press for material from Colin McGinn, 'Can We Solve the Mind-Body Problem?' in *Mind* Vol XCVIII, No. 391, 1989, pp. 349–66.

Every effort has been made to trace all the copyright holders, but if any have been inadvertently overlooked the publishers will be pleased to make the necessary arrangement at the first opportunity.

I would like to express my special indebtedness to my editors, Hilary Laurie, Phyllis Richardson, Andrea Henry and David Berman. I should also like to record my gratitude for the advice, help or encouragement given to me by a number of colleagues and correspondents: David Bell, Maeve Cooke, Daniel Dennett, Jim Edwards, John Gaskin, John Haldane, Bob Kirk, Hugh Mellor, Gerry Myers, Vasilis Politis, Paul Simpson, Galen Strawson and Steve Yalowitz. I am also most grateful to the authors and copyright holders for permission to reprint the passages which make up this anthology.

Finally, I would like to express my gratitude to Trinity College, Dublin, for awarding me a grant from the Arts and Social Sciences Benefaction Fund to enable me to bring this book to completion .

WL

# INDEX

actions, 148, 203, 238
aesthetics, 21
after-image, 114–25
anger, 46, 54–5
anomolous monism, lvii, 150
anthropomorphising, 197
'applied' psychology, 34
Aristotle, 121, 146, 147(n), 222
Armstrong, D., 171(n)
artificial intelligence, lxii, lxiii, 228
assertion, 85–88, 208

Bechtel, W., lxviii(n)
behavior, lviii, 48, 55, 60–61, 63, 70,
    107, 118–20, 148–58, 160, 180,
    196, 202, 216, 222, 242–3, 248,
    265
behavior
    animal, xlvii, 25, 39, 199
    human, xlviii, 24, 39, 70
    verbal, 61, 129, 157–8
behavioral
    evidence, 208
    laws, 204
behaviorism, xlxix, l–liii, 24–42
    (passim) 60–61, 106, 117,
    131(n), 176, 180, 204, 250
Bekhterev, xlvii
belief, passim
Benacerraf, P., 293(n)
Berkeley, G., 14
biology, 27, 30, 45, 118, 142, 220,
    223, 232, 276, 287
Black, M., 132(n)
brain, liv, lix, lx, lxii, 7, 12–13, 135,
    178, 201, 231, 282, 285

brain
    activity, 106
    cerebral hemispheres of, 234–6
    processes, lxv, lxvi, 106–16, 120
    states, lvii, lxvi, 269(n) 276
Brentano, F., xlvi, xlvii, 183–4, 191,
    211

Carnap, R., l, li, lvi, lxvi, lxvii(n)
Carroll, L., 212(n) 265
Cartesian(ism), xlv–xlviii, lvi, lxiii,
    132 (see also Descartes)
causal
    analysis, 179–90 passim
    connection, 112
    explanation, 181
    inference, 76
    nexus, 278
    power, 252–6
    processes, 262
    properties, 260
    relations, 224, 253
causation, 113, 255
cause, 152, 179, 248
cause and effect, 150, 169, 180
central nervous system, lix, 51, 54,
    67, 75, 113, 125
Central State Materialism, liv
character-traits, 66–70
chemistry, 28, 39, 133, 140, 262
Chomsky, N., 233, 290(n), 294(n)
Churchland, Patricia, lvi
Churchland, Paul, lvi, 238
cognitive closure, 273–90 passim
common-sense psychology, 213,

240–71 (see also *folk psychology*)
computation, 93
computers, lviii, lix, lx, lxii, 135–6, 191–3, 259, 261
computing machine, 132
concepts, 56, 175
conceptual schemes, 165
Connectionism, lxii–lxiii, lxviii(n)
consciousness, xlv–xlviii, lxiii–lxvii, 3–23, 24–40, 57, 74, 106–16, 118–19, 128, 159, 183, 196, 271–90 *passim*
consciousness, stream of, 3–23, 26
conscious
  processes, 30
  states, 272
content, 5, 29, 30, 43, 50, 74, 102, 251, 254, 261, 267–8
convention, 126
conviction, 80–81, 86
Copernicus, 45
correlations, 112, 118, 122
Crick, F., lvi
Cummins, R., 265

Darwin, C., 27, 45
Davidson, D., lvii, lxvi, lxvii(n) 169, 245
death, xlvi
decision theory, 156
Demopoulos, N. 263
Dennett, D., lxi, lxvi, 134, 171(n), 224, 238(n) 263–6, 270
Descartes, xlv, xlvi, liii, lxiv, 126, 137, 287, 294(n)
desires, lvi, lix–lxi, lxiv, 149–58 *passim*, 191, 195, 215
Diderot, 137
disposition, 66–8, 87, 106, 119, 131, 154, 263–4
dualism, lxvi, 107, 119, 125, 128, 131, 137, 183, 218, 273

Einstein, A., 53
Eccles, J., 238(n)
elimination, 22, 250
Eliminative Materialism, lv–lvii, lxvi, 214–39
eliminativism, 276, 286
emotion, 7, 24, 30, 86, 153, 214
environment, 114–15, 129, 149, 180, 204
environment, internal, 106
epiphenomenalism, 129–30, 282
Evening Star/Morning Star, lv, 121–3
evolution, lxvi, 27–28, 220, 222, 230, 287
experience, 74, 81, 82, 107, 111, 115, 126–9, 160, 164, 166–7, 285
experimental psychology, 33–4
explanation, 113, 138–9, 151, 152, 200, 215, 282
expression, 80, 83, 84, 86, 87, 109

feelings, 12, 18, 29–30, 54, 57, 67, 81–2
Feigl, H., 117, 131(n)
Feyerabend, P., 237(n)
Fodor, J., lx–lxii, lxvi, lxviii(n) 134, 146(n) 224–5, 238(n) 290(n) 294(n)
'folk' psychology, xlviii, lvi, lix, 215–39 *passim*, 268, 287 (see also *common-sense psychology*)
Frege, G., xlix, 119
Freud, S., 46, 176
Functionalism, xlviii, lviii–lxii, lxiv, lxvii(n), 219, 223, 224–5, 252, 273
functionalist account of mind, xlv, 30
functional isomorphism, 133–47 *passim*
functional organisation, 136, 143, 146, 229

Garfinkel, A., 144
Gasking, D.A.T., 114(n)
Gazzaniga, M.S., 239(n)

*gestalt*, xlvii, 48, 188
graphology, 66–71
Gregory, R.L., 212(n) 238(n)

Hintikka, J., 211, 212(n)
Hume, D., 11, 14, 175, 182, 250,
    274–5, 286, 289, 291(n)
Husserl, E., xlvi–xlvii

ideas, 3, 6, 8, 11, 91, 98
idealism, 289
identity 108, 111–13, 120, 122, 127,
    135, 168, 178, 270
Identity Theory, liii–lvi, lxvi, 218
imagery, 31, 41
images, 18, 97
imagination, 37, 127
impressions, 6, 58, 62, 68
induction, 47, 74–5
inference, 77, 200, 240–41, 264,
    281–2
innateness, 233
instinct, 26
Intellectualists, 11–12
intelligence, 200
intention, 14, 83, 102, 148–58
    *passim*, 236, 243
intentional
    explanation, 201
    objects, 267
    realm, 214
    stance, 195–212 *passim*
    states, 160
    systems, 191–212
intentionality, 183–4, 201, 217
interaction, 31, 52, 114
introspection, xlv, xlvii, lxvii, 11, 24,
    28–30, 34, 36, 39, 40, 75–7,
    106, 111, 113, 115, 126, 128,
    130, 132, 209, 214, 216, 277,
    283, 285
Introspectionism, xlviii, l, lxvi
introspective
    awareness, 183
    psychology, 71, 74

quality, 123
intuition, 58, 133, 257, 284, 287
intuitive, 49, 50, 54, 62, 65–6, 68–9

James, W., xlvii, liv, lxvii(n) 41(n)
Johnson-Laird, P., lx
Joske, W.D., 131(n)

Kant, I, 175, 179, 250, 281
Kenny, A., xlvii, lxviii(n)
Kepler, 144–5, 146(n) 271(n)
Klages, L., 79(n)
knowledge, lii, 9, 16–17, 54, 57, 60,
    70, 89, 106, 232
Kripke, S., 171(n), 172(n), 288,
    294(n)

Lakatos, I., 182, 221
language, 10, 17, 40(n), 55, 59, 126,
    128, 158, 164, 207, 230, 261,
    287
language-game, xlviii, 85
language
    of physics, 43–79 *passim*
    of thought, lx
learning, 77, 141–2, 154, 220
LeDeux, J.E. 239
Leibniz, 273
Lewis, D., 172(n)
Locke, J., 124, 275
Logical Positivism, xlix, liv, lvi, lxvi
Lycan, W.G., 264
lying, 82

McGinn, C., lxiv–lxv
Mach, E., xlix, 53
Malcolm, N., lxvii(n)
Margolis, J., 224, 238(n)
Martin, C.B., 116(n) 132(n)
Marx, K., 45
materialism, 106, 125, 129–30, 135,
    159–60, 187, 190, 213
matter, 133–47
Matthews, R., 263
meaning, xlviii, 1, 11, 58–9, 74,

80–83, 87, 123, 127, 149, 157, 237
mechanical system, 136–7
memory, 37, 141–2, 220, 261
mental
  acts, 82
  concepts, 159, 176
  events, lviii, lxvi, 106, 107, 169
  imagery, 107, 183
  life, 146
  pictures, 92, 96
  phenomena, 159
  processes, 26, 30, 107, 168, 258, 267
  representations, 257–271
  states, *passim*
metaphysics, 44, 53, 125, 289
mind-body problem, 31, 158, 164–5, 171, 175–6, 272–90
mind's eye, 92, 97, 107
monism, 150
moods, 7, 86
Moore's paradox, 85–6
Morning Star/Evening Star, lv, 121, 123, 127

Nagel, T., lxiii, lxviii(n), 291(n), 293(n), 294(n)
natural law, 77
Neisser, U., lx
neural processes, 15
neurons, 145
neurophysiology, l, liv, lv, lviii, lix, lxi, lxii, 120, 124, 206
neuroscience, 214–22, 231, 279
Newton I., 143–5
Nietzsche, F., 46
'nomological danglers', 118–19, 130

Oppenheim, P., 131(n)
other minds, 216

parallelism, 31, 75, 256
parapsychology, 34
Pavlov, xlvii

perception, 30–31, 48, 50, 58, 60, 128–9, 157, 163, 181–2, 186, 197, 215, 261, 275, 280–2, 285
Phenomenology, xlvi, xlvii, 47, 165, 170, 209–10, 272
phenomenological fallacy, 106, 113–15, 132
phenomenal quality, 123
Phillips Griffiths, A., 207
physical
  process, 169
  sciences, 211, 214, 217
  state, 78, 179, 180, 192
physicalism, 43–4, 54, 106, 161, 168
physics, lix, 28, 38, 39, 59, 78, 114, 124, 141, 144, 147, 155, 222
physiology, 65
Pillsburg, Y. W. B., 31
Pitcher, G., 131(n)
Place, U.T., liii, lxvii(n), 116(n), 117, 131(n)
Plato, xlvi, 93, 232
Poincare, H., 53
Popper, K., 176, 224, 237, 238(n)
positivists, 139
powers, 124, 181
prediction, 243–4, 248
privacy, liii, lv, 107, 127, 164, 208
propositional attitudes, lx, lxi, lxvi, 213–39, 240–71, 287
propositions, 155, 182, 200
pseudo-sentence, 55–6
psyche, 48, 50, 53, 57–8, 71–2, 74, 77–8
psychic processes, 123
psychology, *passim*
Putnam, H., lix, lxvi, lxvii(n) 131(n) 171(n) 225

qualia, 214
qualities, 123, 129
qualities, secondary, 123–4, 185–90
Quine, W.V.O., lvi, lxvi, 201, 208, 212(n)

Ramsay, F., 153
rationality, 152, 194–5, 197–8, 201, 209–10, 224, 230–1
realism, 164, 274, 269
reasoning, 5, 21, 37, 284
reactions, 67
reduction, 141, 159, 166, 167, 218, 250
remembering, lii, 5, 9, 96–7, 106
representational
    power, 273
    system, lxii, 164
    Theory of Mind, 257–71
Rorty, R., 171(n) 236(n)
Russell, B., xlix, 217
Ryle, G., li–lii, lx, lxiii–lxvi, lxvii(n), 131(n), 175, 269

'saying to oneself', 91–2
Schiffer, S., 258
Schlick, M., xlix
Schopenhauer, 22
science, xlix, 1, 44, 56, 59–60, 76, 106, 108, 113, 118–19, 122, 135, 139, 149, 174, 176–7, 244, 285–6
Searle, J., lxiv, lxv
self, 4, 5, 113
    consciousness, xlv, xlvi, 196
    knowledge, 209
semantic
    evaluation, 251–5
    properties, 260
sensation, 3, 5–7, 26, 29–31, 36, 107, 118–22, 125, 186, 188, 231
Sensationalism, 11–12
sense
    data, 122, 125, 126
    experience, xlix
    impressions, 85
senses, 19, 85
sensory apparatus, 161
sentences
    singular, 46
    general, 46–7, 74, 76

Sherrington, Sir Charles, 113, 116(n)
sincerity, 208
Skinner, B. lii, lxvii(n) 201–205
Smart, J.J.C., lv, lxvii(n), 116(n) 171(n)
skepticism, 220
Smythies J.R., 132(n)
soul, xlvi, lv, 64, 93–4, 133, 135, 227
'soul-stuff', 133–47
speech, 12, 41, 43–4, 60, 76–7, 84, 157
Stabler, E., 263
statements, 108, 120
Stevenson, J.T., 131(n)
stimulus, 24–6, 32–3, 35, 40, 48, 51, 62, 67–8, 202–3
Strawson P.F., 291(n)
structures, 89
Structuralists, 30
substance, xlv, 132
supervenience, 288
syntax, 260

Taine, H. 21
telepathy, 57–8, 137
Thorndike, E. L., xlvii, 41(n)
Thornton, M.T., 171(n)
thoughts, 4, 12, 19, 57, 89, 137, 149, 153
thoughts, trains of, 254–5, 258–9
Tienson, J., lxviii(n)
Titchener, E.B., xlvii, 29
Tolman, E.C., 1, 6, 116(n), 208
Turing machine, 134, 141, 265

understanding, lii, 61–2, 106
univeral language, 43, 48

verification, 43, 53, 58, 72, 74–5, 107, 111, 112
*verstehen*, 61
Vickers, J., 210(n)
Vienna Circle, xlix, 175
visualising, 94

visual observation, 111, 113
volition, 30, 104

wanting, lii, lvi, lix, 106
Warren, H.C., 40(n)
Watson, J.B., xlvii, 79(n)

willing, lii, 5, 85
Wittgenstein, L., xlvii–xlix, lvii,
    lxiii–lxvi, 115, 116(n), 119, 128,
    131(n), 175

Zeno, 11
zoology, 27